# ALSO AVAILABLE FROM HANS BEUMER

----------TRAVEL----------

Swiss Camino – Volume II: Central Switzerland

Swiss Camino – Volume III: South-West Switzerland

Kumano Kodo Pilgrimage

Japan's Travel Culture



20'000 km by Train

----------SELF-HELP----------

Success for Everyone

Happiness for Everyone

Travel Guide to Self-actualization

----------INTERNAL AUDIT----------

The Leadership & Managerial Habits of Highly Effective CAEs

The 7 Leadership Habits of Highly Effective CAEs

The 7 Managerial Habits of Highly Effective CAEs

The Internal Audit Handbook

Audit Function Strategy

Audit Engagement Strategy

Audit Risk Management

--------------------

**Visit www.hansbeumer.com**

## Swiss Camino – Volume II: Central Switzerland

<u>EINSIEDELN TO FRIBOURG</u> via Alpine Lakes

| | | |
|---|---|---|
| Stage 5: | Einsiedeln to Ingenbohl | 27 km |
| Stage 6: | Ingenbohl to Stans | 26 km |
| Stage 7: | Stans to Sachseln | 22 km |
| Stage 8: | Sachseln to Brienzwiler | 26 km |
| Stage 9: | Brienzwiler to Interlaken | 27 km |
| Stage 10: | Interlaken to Spiez | 19 km |
| Stage 11: | Spiez to Wattenwil | 26 km |
| Stage 12: | Wattenwil to Schwarzenburg | 24 km |
| Stage 13: | Schwarzenburg to Fribourg | 27 km |

<u>ALTERNATIVE VIA LUZERN/BERN</u>

| | | |
|---|---|---|
| Stage L1: | Ingenbohl to Werthenstein | 24 km |
| Stage L2: | Werthenstein to Huttwil | 31 km |
| Stage L3: | Huttwil to Burgdorf | 25 km |
| Stage L4: | Burgdorf to Bern | 31 km |
| Stage L5: | Bern to Schwarzenburg | 36 km |

<u>Available as</u>

- Hiking edition: ISBN 978-3-906861-35-7
- Luxury edition: ISBN 978-3-906861-36-4
- eBook edition: ISBN 978-3-906861-37-1

---

## Swiss Camino – Volume III: South-West Switzerland

<u>FRIBOURG TO MOUDON</u>

| | | |
|---|---|---|
| | *via Romont* | |
| Stage 14: | Fribourg to Romont | 30 km |
| Stage 15: | Romont to Moudon | 17 km |
| | *via Payerne* | |
| Stage P1: | Fribourg to Payerne | 25 km |
| Stage P2: | Payerne to Moudon | 29 km |

<u>MOUDON TO GENEVA</u>

| | | |
|---|---|---|
| Stage 16: | Moudon to Lausanne | 30 km |
| Stage 17: | Lausanne to Rolle | 33 km |
| Stage 18: | Rolle to Coppet | 32 km |
| Stage 19: | Coppet to Geneva | 19 km |
| Stage 20: | Geneva to French border | 8 km |

<u>Available as</u>

- Hiking edition: ISBN 978-3-906861-38-8
- Luxury edition: ISBN 978-3-906861-39-5
- eBook edition: ISBN 978-3-906861-40-1

# SWISS CAMINO

Volume I: North-East Switzerland

300 Churches
800 km Hiking
1'000 yrs History
on
the Way of St. James
through Switzerland

HANS BEUMER

HB Publications
Unterägeri, Switzerland
www.hansbeumer.com



First edition published in September 2019

This book is available as:
- Hiking edition (B/W): ISBN 978-3-906861-32-6
- Luxury edition (Color): ISBN 978-3-906861-33-3
- eBook edition (EPUB): ISBN 978-3-906861-34-0

Printed and distributed by Lulu Press, Inc.

# CONTENTS

## RORSCHACH TO EINSIEDELN 183



## APPENDICES 301

# Foreword

*Liber Sancti Jacobi Helvetia*

The first Way of St. James Pilgrim's Handbook was handwritten around 1130. The Latin manuscript was called the 'Liber Sancti Jacobi' (also Codex Callixtus – attributed to Pope Callixtus II) and consisted of five parts. Two parts related to stories, miracles, and legends of St. James. The fifth part described four French Ways to the Pyrenees and Santiago de Compostela. These route descriptions included all important churches the pilgrim was to visit along the way.

Nearly 900 years after the Liber Sancti Jacobi for France, my book describes the Way of Saint James for Switzerland in a comparable manner. The 'Swiss Camino' is the definitive guide for the 21st century pilgrim on the Swiss routes. Hence its Latin title: *Liber Sancti Jacobi Helvetia.*

*Three Volumes*

The Swiss Camino pilgrim's guide is split into three volumes:

**Volume I** (this book) consists of two main sections:

1. A general introduction to the 18- to 21-day pilgrimage on the Way of St. James through Switzerland, including:
    - Organizational tips for a successful pilgrimage at a low cost in this high-cost country.
    - Religious context of St. James, Roman catacomb relics, saints, monastic Orders, and the Swiss religious Reformation in the 1520s-30s.
    - Church terminology, designations, architecture, interiors, and monastic Order terminology.
    - Route decisions, route possibilities, stages, and route signaling.
    - Raising expectations of the routes, churches, monasteries, and points of interest.
2. A complete coverage of the pilgrimage routes with details of the trails, churches, saints, catacomb relics, monasteries, castles, cities, and other points of interest in German-speaking North-East Switzerland:
    - From Konstanz to Einsiedeln, via Rapperswil (101 km in 4 stages); and
    - From Rorschach to Einsiedeln, via Rapperswil (101 km in 4 or 5 stages) and via Siebnen (105 km in 4 or 5 stages).

**Volume II** provides a complete coverage of the pilgrimage routes with details of the trails, churches, saints, catacomb relics, monasteries, castles, cities, and other points of interest in German-speaking Central Switzerland:

- From Einsiedeln to Fribourg, via Alpine Lakes (224 km in 9 stages); and
- From Einsiedeln to Fribourg, via Luzern/Bern (200 km in 7 stages).

**Volume III** provides a complete coverage of the pilgrimage routes with details of the trails, churches, saints, catacomb relics, monasteries, castles, chateaus, cities, and other points of interest in French-speaking South-West Switzerland:

- From Fribourg to Moudon, via Romont (47 km in 2 stages) and via Payerne (54 km in 2 stages);
  and onwards
- From Moudon to Geneva, and French border (123 km in 5 stages).

The 54-page General Introduction to the Swiss Way of St. James of Volume I is not copied in the other two volumes. This prevents a repetition of many pages, even though its content equally applies to Volumes II and III.

*Experience and Information*

The Swiss Camino volumes contain two interwoven elements: experience and information.

The experience element guides you from church to church. This is the travel guide element of the book. '*The way is the goal*'. '*Der Weg ist das Ziel*'. '*Le chemin est le but*'. '*El camino es la meta*'. The book includes extensive descriptions of hiking routes, ascents, descents, views, paths, under-footing, trails, and so forth, which are based on my hiking experiences of the nearly 800 km in the summer of 2018. The travel guide element describes the routes between the churches and chapels; how to get from one church/chapel to the next. It describes the hiking segment of the pilgrimage and is a minor element of the content of the three volumes.

Additionally, the book describes what you come across along the nearly 800 km routes of the Swiss Way of St. James. You will visit many churches, chapels, monasteries, castles, ruins, and so forth. Each of them has a specific artistic, religious, and cultural appearance. What do the retables (winged altars) look like? What saints are depicted on the 700-year-old frescos on the walls of the church? What are the elaborately decorated skeleton-relics displayed in glass vitrines? What is the architectural style of the bell tower? These descriptions are a major element of the content of the three volumes and are based on my personal observations.

Each of these artistic, religious, and cultural appearances have their own (his)story to tell. Sometimes their history is available in a brochure or on an information board at the church, chapel, or castle. Very often, however, their history will be kept hidden from you and other passing pilgrims. What are the stories behind the churches, chapels, monasteries, castles, and ruins? Why is a monastery in ruins or abandoned by its monks? Why are some churches Roman-Catholic and others Evangelic-Reformed (protestant)? Why do some Cantons have many churches and chapels, whereas others have only a few? Your visits to the many churches and points of interest will raise more questions than there are answers.

The information element of the book provides such answers. A major part of the content of the three volumes contains historical information on churches, chapels, relics, saints, monasteries, and other landmarks along the routes. These landmarks include castles, ruins, fountains, medieval city fortifications, chateaus, bridges, cities, and so forth. Some information about events, people, and buildings will date as far back as 2'000 years, to the inception of Christianity. The book describes the religious, cultural, and societal development of Switzerland from the time when the first monasteries were established in the 8th century and the first cities were founded in the 10th century.

The historical data in this book was gathered from many sources. This book neither ascertains the historical correctness of such data, nor provides a complete historical account of all topics and events. Rather, the book provides the historical data relevant to the storyline of the Swiss Way of St. James. It not only focuses on the individual churches, chapels, monasteries, castles, and points of interest, but also on their interwoven historical connections to the pilgrimage route from Konstanz and Rorschach to Geneva (and French border). Many of the histories are interconnected with local, regional, or national events during the medieval development of Switzerland and its Cantons.

*Connecting Histories*

The power of the book lies in piecing together the over 500 stories and histories of churches, chapels, monasteries, castles, cities, and points of interest along the nearly 800 km of the Way of St. James through Switzerland. The depth of the individual stories is limited; intentionally, to provide the passing pilgrim a brief summary, without an information overload. After all, the average pilgrim will take in a church and move on to the next one in a relatively short time ('the way is the goal'). Their stories and histories describe the key facts and legends that set a particular church or point of interest apart from all the others. The number of stories, covering all 310 churches and chapels, 48 monasteries, and 118 points of interest along the nearly 800 km, is extraordinary. No other pilgrim's guide for Switzerland has taken inventory of all churches and points of interest along the Way of St. James and combined them into one comprehensive storyline.

*Why are you going on a Pilgrimage?*

There may be many reasons for leaving home and starting on a pilgrimage:

- You may pilgrimage to visit the grave of a saint, to admire holy relics kept at a church, or to see a worshipped statue. You may seek forgiveness of sins, healing of suffering, or may want to make good on a promise.
- You may want to take time out from your job and daily life, to escape the pressures and routines of a life at home.
- You may seek time for reflection, taking stock of your past, present, or future, to find your true self.
- You may follow the trails of meaningful historical memorials and artefacts that shaped the history of a region or country.
- You may look for adventure, exploring a new country and culture, and meeting different people.
- You may enjoy hiking through nature with scenic landscapes.

Whatever motivates you to start a pilgrimage, in the end all pilgrims have two things in common once on the Way of St. James:

- Mentally you are never alone on a pilgrimage, even when physically walking alone. You walk with your joys, sorrows, and questions. You walk with the people you left at home, who cannot or do not want to walk with you.
- Physically you walk in an environment that is the same for every pilgrim on the trail. The mountains, ascents, descents, forests, lakes, churches, monasteries, castles, points of interest, panoramic views, and weather conditions are all shared.

What is your motivation to start a pilgrimage along the Way of St. James through Switzerland? What do you expect to get out of it? Forgiveness? Healing? Reflection? Relaxation? Physical condition? Friends? Alpine scenery? Every reason is good enough when it motivates you to undertake the pilgrimage. Every reason is individual and it is up to you to make the most out of your pilgrimage.

This Swiss Camino book cannot help you with your individual mental or spiritual fulfilment. You must do that yourself. However, the book does help with fulfilling your understanding of the environment you (and all other pilgrims) are in along the Swiss Way of St. James.

*What is this Book that is split in three Volumes?*

This book follows nearly 800 km hiking routes. Is it a hiking book?
This book describes over 300 churches along this way. Is it a religious book?
This book catalogues special features and artefacts of many churches, monasteries, and points of interest. Is it an art book?
This book describes over 1'000 years of history. Is it a history book?

It is a combination of the above. Foremost it is a pilgrim's guide that:

- opens the Swiss Way of St. James to international pilgrims;
- provides comprehensive historical and contemporary information on the routes and the churches, chapels, monasteries, and points of interest along these routes;
- describes the religious, cultural, and societal history and development of Switzerland and its Cantons along these routes.

It is a pilgrim's guide that enables you to successfully organize, plan, and execute your pilgrimage through Switzerland, providing insight on what you encounter along the nearly 800 km trails. That is the purpose of this 21st century Liber Sancti Jacobi Helvetia.

*Thank You*

Thank you to all the sources that provided their copyright permissions and historical information, gave me access to and photos of churches and chapels that are normally closed, and so forth. Without your support it would not have been possible to put together the histories and special features of the many churches, monasteries, and points of interest along the Swiss Way of St. James.

Thank you for using this book as your pilgrim guide on the Swiss Way of St. James.

Bon Camino!
drs. Hans Beumer
September 2019

# GENERAL INTRODUCTION

# TO THE WAY OF ST. JAMES THROUGH SWITZERLAND

# Organizational Tips

*Organizing a low-cost and successful Pilgrimage*

The cost of a 20-day pilgrimage through Switzerland may be your biggest hurdle to overcome (apart from having the time available). You might be wondering about the need for heavy mountaineering shoes and equipment for crossing the Alps. You might be uncertain what and how much clothing to bring and the type of weather to expect. You might wonder which health and safety precautions to take. The following seven tips address these and several more organizational questions and hurdles. Read these tips to resolve your concerns and realize a low-cost and successful pilgrimage along the Swiss Way of St. James:

#1: Keep your costs low
#2: Stay healthy and safe
#3: Keep dry and warm
#4: Travel light
#5: Travel easy
#6: Find your way
#7: Collect pilgrim stamps

## *Tip #1: Keep your costs low*

The cost of living in Switzerland is probably the highest in the world. The cities Geneva and Zurich rank in the top 10. Apart from the cost of travel from your home (country) to Switzerland (and return), the cost of your pilgrimage is mostly influenced by two factors: food and accommodation.

Food at restaurants is of good quality but expensive, and the local cuisine may not be to your liking (in small towns it may be difficult to find international food, though you come across an Italian restaurant in most towns). A simple two-course meal with a non-alcoholic beverage generally costs between CHF 20 and 30. Most locals do not eat out every night, but cook dinner at home. You can keep your costs low by buying your dinner (or meal ingredients) at a supermarket. Most supermarkets offer possibilities to warm up food (though not when deep-frozen) or even sell warm meals. A takeout could be another option (if there is one). Pilgrim inns offer possibilities for self-cooking.

For lunch try planning it low cost and time saving too. A restaurant lunch may be expensive, take long to be prepared (no fast food), and the menu may be limited. Recommendable is buying your lunch at a supermarket/bakery (note that these will be closed on Sundays), or preparing it before you start hiking. You will often be in nature during lunch time; it is simplest to pack snacks and lunch for the day, and find a nice spot in nature to sit down and enjoy your midday food.

Hotel accommodations in Switzerland can be really expensive and will be your biggest budget challenge. In cities such as Bern (political capital) and Geneva (banking capital) a night at a three-star hotel may start at CHF 200 (depending on location and season). The Way of St. James passes through several larger cities, but most of the time accommodations need to be found in small towns. Finding accommodation in the larger towns is easy, but finding a fairly-priced one is not. Finding a place to spend the night in a small town may also be challenging.

Two Swiss organizations of the Way of St. James provide lists with details and price ranges of accommodations: *https://jakobsweg.ch/en/eu/ch/unterkunft-pilger/* and *http://www.viajacobi4.ch/Gites/gites-de.htm.* On these sites you find links to detailed lists of accommodations for all the towns along the route. You can download the PDF's for each of the sections. The information includes details on the type of accommodation, name, address, telephone number, email, website, opening times, as well as the number of beds, price range, and whether breakfast and dinner are available or included. You can keep your accommodation costs low by using these lists to select the pilgrim inns or B&B at private guesthouses.

A night at a pilgrim inn may cost CHF 20 to 35 only. In most pilgrim inns you sleep in a room with bunkbeds and need to bring your own sleeping bag liner or travel bed sheets (they offer blankets). Kitchen, washing machine, toilets, and showers are shared. One condition, though, is that you need to show a pilgrim pass with stamps. Reservations can be made in advance by email or by phone on your day of arrival. Most pilgrim inns are open daily from 16:00, from 1 April until 31 October. Not only do pilgrim inns keep your costs low, they are also a great place to connect with other pilgrims.

Pilgrim inns are available at the following locations along the route:

- North-East Switzerland: Märstetten, Fischingen, St. Gallen, Wattwil, Rapperswil, and Einsiedeln.
- Central Switzerland: Ingenbohl, St. Niklausen, Brienzwiler, Werthenstein, Burgdorf (from May 2020), and Fribourg.
- South-West Switzerland: Romont, Gland, and Geneva.

Several larger cities (Interlaken, Bern, Lausanne, Geneva) that are tourist hot spots also have youth hostels or backpacker inns. At the other locations B&B at private residences can keep your costs low.

If you are a student and under the age of 26, you might be able to get some discounts (e.g. at museums). So, bring your student pass.

Entrance to all the churches along the Swiss Way of St. James is free.

How much would a 20-day thru-hike pilgrimage on the Swiss Way of St. James cost? A low-cost pilgrimage on the route via the Alpine Lakes would be around CHF 1'500 (approx. EUR 1'300, USD 1'500):

| Low-cost Budget | CHF | split in North-East | split in Central | split in South-West |
|---|---|---|---|---|
| - Accommodations | 890 | 125 | 409 | 356 |
| - Food and beverages | 560 | 120 | 250 | 190 |
| - Local transportation | 50 | 0 | 44 | 6 |
| Total CHF | 1'500 | 245 | 703 | 552 |
| Days | 19.5 | 4 | 9 | 6.5 |

The average daily cost (per person) during a 20-day pilgrimage is around CHF 75:

- average CHF 45 per night accommodation cost (based on nine low-cost pilgrim inns). Average cost of accommodation in pilgrim inns is CHF 30, in youth hostels and private B&Bs CHF 50, and in low-cost hotels CHF 80.
- average CHF 30 per day for food and beverages (breakfast, lunch, dinner).

Entrance fees to the most interesting museums along the route accumulates to around CHF 100 (St. Gallen, Einsiedeln, Sachseln, Romont, Nyon, Geneva).

## *Tip #2: Stay healthy and safe*

Switzerland is in the top 10 of the safest countries in the world for tourists and travel. A pilgrim on the Way of St. James through Switzerland does not need to have any concerns about their safety when hiking through the country. No special precautions (other than common sense) are required to ensure your physical safety from other people (such as violence or robbery). There is no safety risk from mountain climbing or paths along dangerous cliffs or abysses. The route is well marked, so there is no risk of getting lost. The pathways follow the beaten track and a significant part of the trails pass through urban areas. In the sections through forests or mountainous terrain, the nearest settlements (farms, villages) or roads are never far away.

Safety is not a risk, but as on any hiking trail, you need to mind your health. The food at restaurants and accommodations, the ready-made food from supermarkets, and the fresh food, for example from bakeries, comply with the world's highest standards for hygiene and food safety.

Water from the tap is the best quality in the world and potable without any concerns. Instead of buying an expensive Evian bottle, you can simply ask for your drinking bottle to be filled at the tap or fill it yourself at your accommodation's, restaurant's, or church's restroom. Most of the fountains in the villages and towns have potable water as well. Some fountains may carry a sign stating the water is potable (or is not potable), but most will not. Should it not, have a closer look at the color of the water (is it clear), the cleanness of the basin, the state of the facet (is it clean), or for any other indications it would be better not to drink it. If all is clear, it is safe to drink. In the rural areas the water basins are often for the cows. In some cases a farmer will have put up a sign that the water is not potable, but most of the time there is no warning. For health reasons you should not take any water from drinking basins or fountains in rural areas. Carry enough water and wait with refilling your bottle until you arrive at a restaurant, farm, church, or a clean fountain in a village or town.

In case you are wondering about restrooms along the Swiss Way of St. James: most parish churches have toilet facilities and so do restaurants, hotels, and shopping malls. These restrooms are neat and clean, consistent with the Swiss standards of hygiene. The tap and sink can also be used to refill your drinking bottle or freshen up.

Occasional health hazards may arise from farm dogs and stinging insects in the rural areas. Most farm dogs will only bark at you, but some may chase you while growling viciously (usually they are not chained). Carry a hiking stick to keep such a dog at a distance if need be. Horseflies can be extremely annoying: they can follow you for 50 meters or more, buzzing around the exposed skin of your legs or arms. Some will even sting through your clothing. They are mostly near farms and cows. Just pay attention when walking through such areas, particularly while resting or standing still to take photos. Their bite will sting, but normally does not cause a health problem (unless you have a particular allergy or sensitivity). Most of the time they are just really annoying, buzzing around your head.

Many hiking stages lead through grasslands, forests, and bushes, which may contain ticks. Some ticks carry infectious diseases and their bites may cause mild to extremely serious diseases requiring hospitalization (TBE, Lyme disease, paralysis). Ticks feed on the blood of cows, deer, and other animals, and will not hesitate to try to feed on the blood of a human. Ticks live in forests, bushes, grasslands, and on animals. They crawl on leaves, tall grass, and low bushes, usually not higher than 150 centimeters (they are unlikely to fall on you from a tall tree). They are very small and their bite does not sting (it may happen unnoticed).

- Risk exposures along the Swiss Way of St. James are:
  - seasonal: mostly limited to the period April to September, when temperatures are moderate to high;
  - high: along the routes in North-East Switzerland (Lake Constance to Einsiedeln);
  - moderate: along the routes in Central Switzerland (Einsiedeln to Fribourg) and in South-West Switzerland (Fribourg to Geneva).
- Your tick-bite prevention may consist of the following measures: spraying tick repellent on your clothing and exposed skin; wearing long pants and sleeves; and walking in the middle of the trails.
- After a day's hike through a risk area (grasslands, forests, bushes) check your clothing and your body for any ticks. Put tick-removal tweezers in your backpack.

Consult your local physician about preventing, detecting, removing, and treating tick bites before you head out to the Swiss Camino. You can consider getting a vaccination against tick-borne diseases prior to your journey. Make sure you are well-informed about what to do to avoid tick-borne infections.

In case you have hay fever or pollen allergies, be aware that in the months March to October many kinds of pollen will be in the air. As soon as the weather is sunny and dry the farmers start mowing their meadows, causing a significant increase in pollen. Many of the trails in rural and agricultural areas are exposed to increased levels of pollen during these months. Bring your hay fever medicine when hiking in this period.

A limited range of large wild animals live in the wilderness of Switzerland. Wolves, brown bears, alpine ibex, lynx, red deer, fox, eagles, and vultures mostly roam the national wild parks, away from the urban areas. Basically, there are no deadly poisonous snakes, scorpions, or other life-endangering animals along the Swiss Way of St. James (see above for ticks). It is highly unlikely that you will come across any of these large animals or snakes on the Swiss Camino hiking routes.

However, you will come in close vicinity of large domesticated animals, i.e. cows. Most of the time cows graze peacefully in the meadows, separated from the hiking trail by barbwire or low-voltage electrified wires. Cows are curious and will notice that you are passing by; they might turn their head to follow you as you walk by their meadow. In quite a few areas the hiking trails cross the meadows. This mostly happens in North-East Switzerland, a few times in the Central Switzerland (Luzern/Bern route), but not at all in South-West Switzerland. When crossing a meadow, cows may be grazing or standing in the middle of your path and turn their head to see what you are doing. Making a wide curve around a cow is usually sufficient to pass by this 'obstacle', as they are generally not aggressive. However, cows may be aggressive when they have suckling calves with them. Swiss newspapers report about hikers with injuries from cow attacks several times a year. In case you are confronted with cows in a meadow, avoid coming close to them.

## *Tip #3: Keep dry and warm*

The climate in Switzerland is influenced by two major factors: the Alps and the Atlantic Ocean. About 70 percent of the weather is determined by high- or low-pressure fronts from the west, bringing humid and mild ocean air to the country (though global warming is increasingly causing air streams to come from the south (north-Africa), bringing dry and warm weather in summer). The Alps divide the country in climate zones and influence the weather in small geographical areas. It could be overcast and raining where you are, while it is beautiful sunny weather 30 km away. This means you need to be prepared for warm and sunny weather (sunscreen, breathable clothing), cool and wet weather (warm clothing, rain protection), and cold wind (wind stopper). You will break a sweat while ascending a steep hill in a weather protecting forest, while on the crest you may be exposed to a cold wind. Dressing in layers is the only solution. Wear clothing that quickly dries (no cotton) from sweat and rain.

Depending on the time of year of your pilgrimage, generally expect temperatures to vary between 5 degrees Celsius (on a spring morning) and 30 degrees Celsius (in high summer) from April to October. In the months April, May, and occasionally in June, there could be one or more days with snowfall down to an altitude of 600 meters. Most of the time this snow melts the next day, though above elevations of 900 meters it may stay when temperatures remain low. This may mean that certain mountainous passages (e.g. Hörnli, Etzel, Haggenegg, Brünig) may become unpassable for an extended number of days. From October early snowfall could block certain mountainous passages. Also expect multiple days with continuous rainfall and low clouds during any of the months from April to October. During the summer months (July, August) you can expect regular thunderstorms with lightning, heavy rain, and strong wind. Usually these do not last longer than an hour, as they blow over relatively quickly (though low clouds and rain in their tail may stay longer).

The weather differs per region (influenced by the Alps) and by month. As part of your planning, it is best to consult online weather forecasts. They will give you the most up to date weather predictions. A good local website (with an English language button) to use is: *https://www.meteoswiss.admin.ch/home.html*.

Two weather phenomena are typical for Switzerland: alpine *föhn* wind and heavy fog (or high fog). The alpine *föhn* wind blows relatively warm and dry air down the slopes into the valleys of the Alps. These *föhn* winds can develop hurricane-like speeds that bring relatively warm air, without precipitation, and clear away clouds and fog. They mostly blow in the areas and valleys close to the higher mountains. Heavy fog arises when the water temperature of the rivers and lakes is still much colder (spring/summer) or warmer (summer/autumn/winter) than the air temperature. This fog is then trapped between the hills and mountains, and can only dissipate when the sun dries the humid air. In summer this fog may stay for several hours in the morning. In case of a cold eastern/northern wind (called *Bise*), this fog may stay for several days (spring) or even weeks (autumn, winter). The fog then stubbornly remains at an altitude of 600-900 meters, above which it is usually beautiful sunny weather (and warmer than below the fog).

## *Tip #4: Travel light*

The Swiss Way of St. James does not go through isolated areas. There is no need to carry camping gear or multiple day-rations of food and water. You are never more than a few hours away from possibilities to eat or drink; a half-day ration is the most you will need. Accommodations (hotels, bed and breakfasts, inns, hostels) are plentiful along the daily routes. The daily trails and distances in this book have been designed in such a manner that you will always end in a town or village with choices of accommodations and transportation. You can leave your heavy camping gear and multi-day food rations at home, and travel light (unless you want to go camping of course).

Most of the routes are on hard surfaces, such as tarmac, concrete, or gravel. A smaller section is on soft underground through meadows (grass) and forests (soil). The routes do not follow high-alpine trails, so you do not need heavy mountaineering shoes. Your shoes do need to have a good grip, as many of the daily hikes incur altitude meters where you go up and down hills or mountains. Some ascents and descents are very steep and on loose gravel, grass, tree roots, or rocks, which require a good grip of the soles of your shoes. Surfaces may be slippery, particularly when wet. Sports shoes with a good profile, trail running shoes, or light hiking shoes (below the ankle) are all you need, as long as they have a good profile and a sturdy (not too flexible) sole. Ideally your hiking shoes should be able to dry quickly when wet. Leave your heavy leather mountaineering shoes at home and come with lightweight hiking shoes to travel light.

The bigger your backpack, the more you will pack to fill it up and the heavier it becomes. You do not need a large backpack of 50+ liters that is used on expeditions. Nor do you need a medium backpack of 35-50 liters for multiday hikes. If you want to travel light, fill up a 30- to 35-liter backpack with the items strictly necessary for your pilgrimage.

## *Tip #5: Travel easy*

Switzerland probably has the world's most extensive public transportation network with the highest reliability. Public transportation (bus, train, boat) will get you everywhere you want, though it is not cheap (but much more available and cheaper than renting a car). When you fly in from abroad and need to go to the starting point of your pilgrimage in Konstanz or Rorschach, take the train from Zurich Airport to get there. When you fly back home from Geneva, take the train from the city to Geneva Airport. In case you have a return flight from Zurich Airport, you can take the train from Geneva to Zurich Airport. Connections are seamless. Public transportation is clean, safe, and reliable, with friendly staff who can communicate in English, German, and French. Use the app or website of the Swiss Federal Railways (*SBB*) to plan your train and bus journeys, and buy the tickets online: *https://www.sbb.ch/en/timetable.html*.

All hiking stages in this book start and end in small towns or large cities near transportation hubs (bus stops or train stations). Public transportation is the easiest way to go to the starting point or away from the ending point, particularly if you are a day-hiker.

Swiss public transportation is relatively expensive. For this reason, most Swiss people buy the SBB Half Fare Travelcard (*Halbtax-Abo/Abonnement demi-tarif*) for an annual fee of CHF 165. This card entitles to 50 percent discount on all train, bus, tram, and boat tickets, and on most mountain railways as well. For international tourists an SBB Swiss Half Fare Card is available for CHF 120 for one month (available as print-at-home version). The ticket prices of public transportation mentioned in this book (Volumes I, II, III) are the full prices. In case you have the SBB Half Fare Travelcard or Swiss Half Fare Card you can divide the stated price in two.

## *Tip #6: Find your way*

The Way of St. James route- and hiking-signaling in Switzerland is really good. Signposts are at key locations for direction changes, while signaling frequently confirms being on the right track (for the details on the signaling see the fourth chapter of this General Introduction).

Still, it may regularly happen that you overlook a signpost, that a signpost points in a wrong direction, or that there is no signpost at a change of direction. You may overlook signposts when: they are difficult to spot in the busy streets of cities; they are covered by branches of overhanging trees and bushes in forests; you are not paying attention to them (you might be lost in thought, in conversation, physically or mentally struggling with the hike, or focusing on the ground in front of you). As a result of erroneous signaling, or vandalism, a few signposts point in a wrong direction. At some locations in forests and on agricultural fields/meadows, signaling at a direction change or a trail split is missing.

Switzerland***Mobility***

Download the SwitzerlandMobility App for your smart phone to overcome these route uncertainties. Use the app to regularly confirm your location or use it to support direction changes. You can download the app for free from *https://www.schweizmobil.ch/en/switzerlandmobility-app-e.html.* The app provides detailed maps of Switzerland (on a scale of 1:10'000) with the full 779-km route of the Swiss Way of St. James pre-drawn (green line with red dots). Through its GPS and compass function, you can always determine where you are and whether you are still on the red-dotted green route. For a small annual fee of CHF 35 you can upgrade to the SwitzerlandMobility Plus subscription. This subscription enables you to download the full 779-km route maps for offline use (you can do this from home, in preparation of your Swiss Camino pilgrimage). This means you neither incur roaming nor need a Swiss SIM card for use of the maps. You can determine your position on the offline maps anywhere, even in the areas where there is poor or no mobile network reception. You will never lose your way or be in doubt whether you are still on the right track.

## *Tip #7: Collect pilgrim stamps*

Approximately 40 percent of the churches and chapels along the Swiss Way of St. James provide pilgrim stamps (around 130 stamps can be obtained in total). You can collect these stamps for three reasons: to reduce your lodging costs, as proof, and as souvenir.

The economic use of the pilgrim stamps should not be underestimated. When you show your pilgrim pass (with stamps of the churches along the route), the pilgrim inn will give you their pilgrim rate. Quite often a pilgrim inn or a private guest house will only accept guests who can present their pilgrim pass with the relevant stamps. Without these, you might be forced to stay at more expensive commercial hotels.

A pilgrim pass full of stamps is a unique souvenir and proof of your pilgrimage. Include the stamp 'hunt' in your daily pilgrimage schedule.

The stamps should be collected in a Swiss pilgrim pass. For the complete 779 km routes you will need two booklets (each pass has space for at least 72 stamps). For a 20-day pilgrimage from Lake Constance to Geneva/French border, one booklet should suffice. You can pre-order the pass (CHF 12) and have it delivered by post to your home address: *https://jakobsweg.ch/en/eu/ch/jakobsweg-shop/pilgerpass/*. Alternatively, you can buy it at the starting point in Rorschach (see stage R1a) or at the first pilgrim inn you spend the night (Märstetten from Konstanz – stage K1 or St. Gallen from Rorschach – stage R1a).

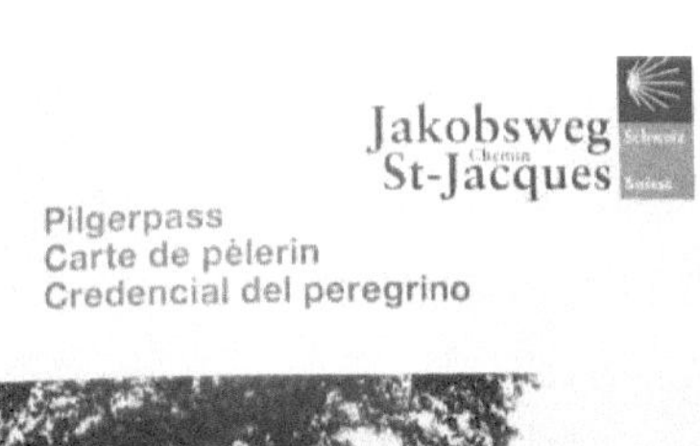

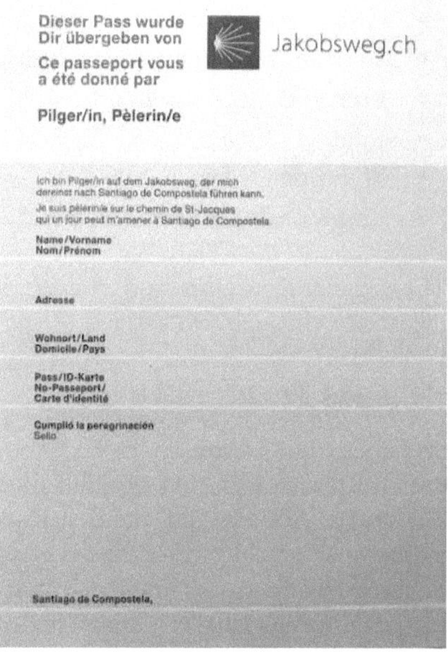

# Religious Context

*Understanding religious historical background*

The seven tips in the first chapter help with the physical preparation of your pilgrimage along the Swiss Way of St. James. Equally important is your spiritual preparation. Do you know who Saint James was and why Santiago de Compostela was Western Europe's third-most-important pilgrimage destination during the middle ages? Why is James called a saint, what is a saint, and how to become one? What is the main event that shaped the religious history of Switzerland?

This chapter answers these and several more questions. The next sections explain the historical background and put key religious themes in context of the Way of St. James through Switzerland:

- Who was St. James?
- History of the Way of St. James
- Swiss regional pilgrimage destinations along the route
- Roman catacomb relics
- Saints
- Monastic Orders
- Religious Reformation in the 1520s-30s

These general insights and context will enable you to optimize your spiritual pilgrimage through Switzerland.

## *Who was St. James?*

St. James (the Greater or the Elder) was one of the Twelve Apostles. He is called the Greater (or Elder) to distinguish from James the Lesser, who was also one of the Twelve Apostles and the first Bishop of Jerusalem. St. James the Greater was either taller or older than the other James. King Herod had James (the Greater) beheaded by the sword in Jerusalem in the year 44; he is considered the first apostle who died for his faith in Christ. He became the patron Saint of Spain and pilgrims.

The legend that the remains of St. James were kept in Spain (Santiago de Compostela) arose around 900. According to this legend, St. James was a missionary in Iberia and after his execution in Jerusalem, his remains were miraculously shipped from Jerusalem to Santiago de Compostela. His remains were allegedly discovered in Spain in the 9$^{th}$ century (although he had died in the 1$^{st}$ century). In the 9$^{th}$ century the Spanish hermit Pelagius was said to have had a revelation of the location of the tomb of St. James. The then bishop of the region identified the tomb, the Spanish King Alfonso II had a church built for the relics in Santiago de Compostela, and Pope Leo XIII officially recognized this legend in 1884. Several versions of the legend were told: some said that St. James was an apostle in Spain before going back to Jerusalem (this version surfaced in the 9th century); others said he was never in Spain. It is, however, likely that his remains were spread over several locations in Europe, amongst others Santiago de Compostela.

On all statues and paintings representing St. James, you will see three medieval pilgrim attributes: walking cane, travel bag, and scallops. Scallops are often depicted on his hat or cape. The **scallop**, found in the sea along the Spanish coast, is considered a sign of a successful pilgrimage to Santiago de Compostela. They were used to decorate a pilgrim's robe after having reached the destination. Practically, the scallops were used to scoop up water for drinking. The scallop symbolizes the pilgrim reaching heaven, not far from the end of the – at that time known – world, Cabo Finisterre (meaning cape at the end of world). This was at the time that a major part of the medieval European population believed that the earth was flat and that you could fall off its edge. Nowadays most pilgrims on the Way of St. James still carry a scallop, usually attached to their backpack, as a sign of being on the way to Santiago de Compostela.

James is the English name of this saint. In the German-speaking part of Switzerland, St. James is referred to as *St. Jakob* and the route is called the *Jakobsweg*. In the French-speaking part of Switzerland, St. James is referred to as *St-Jacques* and the route is called the *Chemin de St-Jacques*. Keep this in mind when you are following signposts and directions in the respective regions. In Spain the route is called *El Camino de Santiago*. Hence the title of this book, derived from 'the Way' in Spanish.

## *History of the Way of St. James*

Pilgrimage started in the 4th century after the Roman persecutions of Christians ceased, when Christianity was officially recognized as a religion by the Roman Emperor Constantine. The first major Christian pilgrimage destination was Jerusalem in the Holy Land, where pilgrims wanted to walk in the footsteps of

Jesus. Rome (Italy) became the second major destination in the following centuries, as pilgrims visited the graves of the apostles St. Peter and Paul. The third European destination for Christian pilgrims became Santiago de Compostela (Spain) from the 9th century, after the legend of the discovery of the remains of St. James.

By the 11th century many pilgrims from all over Europe had created a network of routes that all converged in northern Spain and led to the church in Santiago de Compostela. Monastic Orders established monasteries and hospices along the routes to care for the passing pilgrims, while many commercial pilgrim inns offered low-priced accommodations and meals. Many churches and chapels were built along the routes to provide pilgrims with religious support. The network of routes is called 'the Way of St. James', implying St. James himself walked this route, which is of course not the case. A better name for the European network of routes would be 'the Way to St. James'.

During the 14th and 15th centuries pilgrimages were increasingly criticized, being considered useless for the strengthening of one's Christian belief. In the 16th century the Reformation swept through Europe. Reformers rejected the worship of relics, as a result of which pilgrimages reduced significantly (in the Germanic countries they nearly ceased). In the 17th century the pilgrimage to Santiago de Compostela regained a certain popularity, but reduced again as a result of the European wars and the industrial revolution in the 18th and 19th centuries. From the 1980s it regained its popularity, especially after Santiago de Compostela was listed as a UNESCO World Heritage Site in 1985.

Nowadays more than two million tourists visit Santiago de Compostela every year, while around 300'000 pilgrims get their completion certificate (of the last 100 km) from the Cathedral. During the high-season month of August 50'000 pilgrims arrive in the city (more than 1'600 a day).

## *Swiss regional pilgrimage destinations along the route*

Apart from the three major European pilgrimage destinations (Jerusalem, Rome, Santiago de Compostela), each country and region had its own pilgrimage destinations as well. Medieval pilgrims on their way to Santiago de Compostela would pass by these regional pilgrimage places to pray for a safe journey, rest, be treated when ill, or find other pilgrims and continue in a group.

The major medieval regional pilgrimage destinations along the Swiss Way of St. James are:

- in North-East Switzerland:
    - **Bernrain:** legend of the Holy Cross (from 1388 until today)
    - **Fischingen**: relics (grave) of St. Idda (from 1100 until 1848 – secularization of monastery)
    - **Ufenau**: relics (grave) of St. Adalrich (from 973 until 1959)
    - **St. Gallen**: relics (graves) of St. Gall, St. Magnus, and St. Wiborada (from 700 until 1805 – secularization of monastery)
    - **Einsiedeln**: relics (grave) of St. Meinrad and statue of the Black Madonna (from 900 until today)

- in Central Switzerland:
    - **Werthenstein**: legends of miraculous healings (from 1500 until today)
    - **Flüeli-Ranft/Sachseln**: relics (grave) and hermit cell of St. Nicholas of Flüe (from 1500 until today)
    - **St. Beatus Caves**: relics (grave) of St. Beatus (from 600 until 1530 – Reformation)
    - **Einigen**: relics and legends (from 700 until 1528 – Reformation)
    - **Fribourg**: relics and legends of St. Victor (from 1748 until today)

- in South-West Switzerland:
    - **Posat**: healing spring and Mysteries of the Holy Rosary (from 1700 until today)
    - **Tours**: statue of Virgin Mary (from 1400 until 1536 – Reformation)
    - **Lausanne**: golden Virgin Mary statue (until 1536 – Reformation)
    - **Nyon**: relics of martyrs of the Theban Legion (1300 until 1536 – Reformation)
    - **Geneva**: relics of St. Peter (until 1535 – Reformation)

In addition, many Swiss churches collected relics (bones, skulls, or skeletons of Saints, or particles of the Holy Cross) that attracted regional pilgrims. A significant portion of such relics came from the Roman catacombs, which have a special history.

## *Roman catacomb relics*

In 1578 Roman catacombs were discovered containing 500'000-750'000 skeletons, believed to have been from people who died for their faith after persecution by the Romans during the first three centuries AD. With so many skeletons of possible martyrs available for distribution to catholic churches, the Vatican started selling them within their global network. Officially it was a sin to sell human remains, so the Vatican found another way to be paid for them, by charging high transportation costs. This enabled many catholic churches worldwide to obtain relics from the Roman catacombs, dating from the first few centuries. These bones were marketed as relics of martyrs, who died for their faith. Later archaeological investigations revealed that most skeletons were from ordinary Christians, dating from a later period.

Because the skulls and bones were from unknown martyrs, the Vatican had to designate the remains to a saint of their choice. Though the bones did not belong to the chosen saint, their veneration as such by the Vatican gave the receiving church a significant boost in image with parishioners and pilgrims.

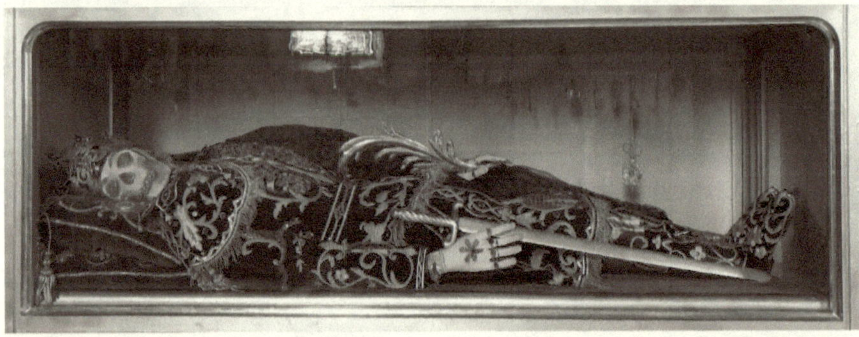

Upon arrival the bones were often given to nuns in nearby convents, who specialized in decorating the skeletons with expensive embroidered robes, crowns, gold, pearls, and precious stones. Because they were venerated as Roman martyrs, they were usually dressed in a red legion tunic and given a crown, a sword, and the palm of martyrdom. The crown (or laurel) symbolized the victory over death. The sword was an indication of how they died, while the palm branch identified them as a martyr. Quite often the nuns had to repair bones or replace missing pieces. This work could take several months to several years, before the decorated relics would be introduced with much publicity in a holy ceremony (called translation) and subsequently exhibited in all its splendor in a vitrine at the local church.

It was a display of wealth and intensified devotion during the 16th to 18th centuries. Particularly in the Germanic countries, the Reformation in the 1520s-30s had caused the destruction and removal of many relics. The possibility to purchase relics of Roman martyrs (designated as saints) gave churches the opportunity to replace the destroyed relics.

Swiss churches made intensive use of the possibility to purchase Roman catacomb relics. During your pilgrimage along the Swiss Way of St. James, you will come across 14 entire skeletons exquisitely decorated and dressed up, in churches in: Tobel, Rorschach, St. Gallen, St. Gallenkappel, Eschenbach, Schmerikon, Schwyz (2), Luzern, Malters, Stans (2), Fribourg, and Romont.

As you will notice, you only come across such relics in the catholic Cantons. In the protestant (reformed) Cantons all similar relics were destroyed or removed at the time of the Reformation in the 1520s-30s, and none such Roman catacomb relics were purchased in the subsequent centuries.

## *Saints*

These relics were designated as saints, who were called upon and prayed to for protection against illnesses (or healing), failing harvests (or good harvests), bad weather (or good weather), and so forth. Medieval events attributed to acts of God (that could not be influenced by a person) were safeguarded by a large number of saints that could positively influence the outcome of such events when prayed to.

Along the Swiss Way of St. James more than 100 different saints are represented in the names of churches, relics, statues, paintings, and frescos. The most popular saints are: St. Mary (also called Virgin Mary or Our Lady), St. Nicholas of Flüe (also called Brother Klaus), St. Peter and Paul, St. Michael, St. James the Greater, St. Mary Magdalene, and St. Anthony of Padua. Each saint has its own religious importance and biography. These are described in **Appendix 2** of each of the three Volumes.

Switzerland has 28 'domestic' Holy Saints. The most well-known are St. Idda (Fischingen), St. Gall (St. Gallen), St. Meinrad (Einsiedeln), St. Nicholas of Flüe

(Flüeli-Ranft/Sachseln), St. Beatus (Beaten mountain), and St. Maurice (Saint-Maurice). St. Nicholas of Flüe and Our Lady of Einsiedeln (Black Madonna) are the official patron Saints of Switzerland.

The process of elevating a religious figure to the status of saint is called canonization.

- The first persons elevated to saint were Christians close to Jesus and Christians who died for their faith during persecutions under Roman Emperors in the 1st-4th centuries (e.g. the catacomb saints). These saints often died a gruesome death after excruciating torture (at least according to their legends). In depicting such saints, they are usually painted with their torture instrument. For example, according to legend, St. Lawrence was executed by being roasted on a metal grating above hot coal. On paintings he is usually depicted with a metal grating and flames. When you have a good look at paintings depicting 1st-4th century saints, you can usually guess how they died (how they were martyred).
- In the subsequent centuries, Catholics who embraced their belief and provided a contribution to the spread of Christianity (missionaries, preachers, heroic deeds in converting pagans) were called saints. Until the mid 12th century local bishops mostly decided on the canonization process, which was informal and inconsistently applied.
- From the 12th century the Popes centralized the authority for canonization at the Vatican. Since then a standardized, diligent, and long process has been maintained. Key in the process is establishing that the person had lived (some saints were proven to be fictional persons), provided an exceptional contribution to Catholicism, and died in a devout way. Additionally, at least two miracles (e.g. healing someone of an illness or disability) had to be attributed to the person and confirmed during their lifetime or after their death. Only deceased can be canonized, based on the presumption that their soul is with God in Heaven.
- There are four levels of designation, of which Saint is the highest: Servant of God, Venerable, Blessed, and Saint. Saints are assigned a feast day, churches may be named after them, and altars may be erected in their honor.

A special characteristic of saints is that they are assigned a specific patronage (guardian). Churches and chapels are often named after a saint, to invoke their protection. Saints have a wide variety of patronages. For the martyrs of the 1st-4th centuries, their patronage is usually linked to the way they were tortured and died. For example, St. Lawrence was roasted on a metal grating above fire: he became the patron Saint of cooks and firefighters. St. Leodegar got his eyes drilled out and his sockets scorched: he is invoked against blindness and eye problems. St. Bartholomew was skinned alive: he became the patron Saint of butchers and leatherworkers.

## *Monastic Orders*

Monastic Orders played a significant role in the religious, cultural, intellectual, and societal development of western countries. For medieval pilgrims they were equally important as they provided shelter, food, treatment in case of illness, and of course religious comfort. They were important stations providing safety along a long and perilous journey through medieval Europe.

The western monastic Orders can be divided into three major groups: founding Orders (before the year 1000); mendicant Orders (founded in the years 1200-50); and Counter-Reformation Orders (founded in the years 1525-50).

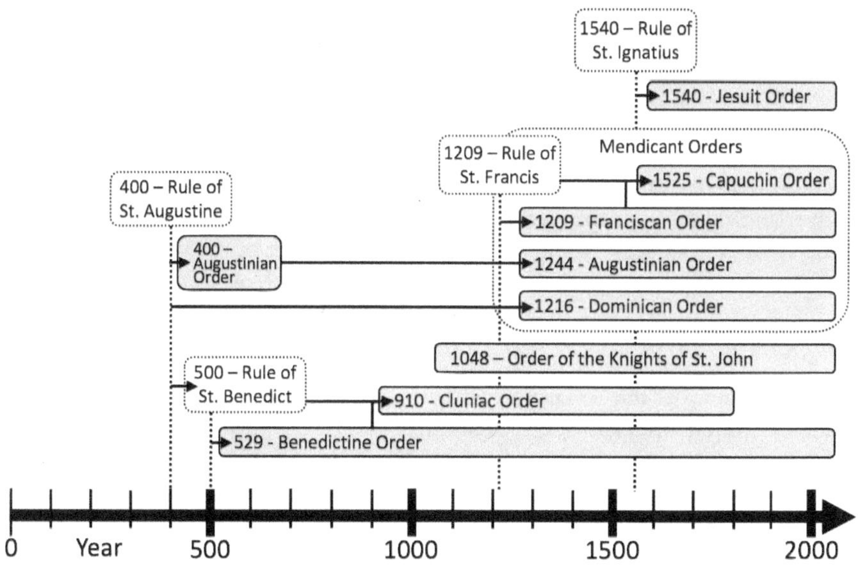


The Benedictine and Cluniac Orders were the first ones to dominate the western monastic landscape. They focused on hard work, manually copying handwritten books, and intellectual development (Latin schooling and libraries) of themselves and nobility. These Orders accumulated significant wealth from their work and donations by Kings and nobility. By the 13th century these Orders were in decline, as they could not adjust to the societal changes caused by people concentrating in newly founded cities. Many of the Benedictine and Cluniac monasteries were at isolated locations, deep in the forests, and failed to connect with the people in the newly developing cities along lakes and rivers. Their way of monastic life became outdated.

New Orders of Franciscans, Dominicans, and Augustinians were founded at the beginning of the 13th century as a counter-force, opposing the complacent and wealthy 'old' Orders. These new Orders were called mendicant, beggar, or barefoot Orders, based on their vows to poverty (no possessions) and austerity. They traveled to the people, begged for food, and lived in the cities, where they were tasked with caring for and preaching to the poor. Their focus and activities were the opposite of the 'old' Orders.

In the early 16th century the Reformation swept through Central Europe and brought many changes and challenges to the religious society that was suddenly divided in two: Catholics and Protestants. The Reformation resulted in the closure and secularization of many monasteries and convents (that were located in the reformed territories). Catholics concentrated in a few large cities and started a Counter-Reformation to protect their catholic way of life and stave off Protestantism. This brought about a third group of Orders such as the Capuchins and Jesuits. Both had yet another focus compared to their two predecessor groups of Orders. This third group concentrated on catholic education as a new way of evangelization and strengthening of Catholicism. The Capuchins and Jesuits settled in catholic cities, where they founded and managed catholic schools (elementary, secondary, and universities) and engaged in intellectual and cultural development.

Each Order has its own religious and societal importance and history in Switzerland. These are explained in the chapters of the 33 hiking stages, where you come across the Orders. Additionally, the general history of the relevant monastic Orders is described in **Appendix 3** of each of the three Volumes.

## *Religious Reformation in the 1520s-30s*

By the beginning of the 16th century there was widespread dissatisfaction with the Catholic Church amongst clergy, politicians, and the population in general. Many churches had become wealthy as a result of their focus on earthly matters. Religious corruption led to profiteering; absolution of sins could be bought with donations. Many clergy maintained loose morality and indulged in luxury, while the common people suffered in their daily existence. The Catholic Church was involved in politics, economics, education, and ran social institutions (schools, hospitals, care for the poor and homeless). They kept much of the wealth and wisdom (libraries) to themselves and only shared with a few selected noblemen, who had paid them for their favors. Bishopric Kingdoms (Lausanne, Geneva) or Abbey Kingdoms (St. Gallen) were earthly and spiritual rulers.

From 1517 the German monk Martin Luther started criticizing the practices of the Catholic Church and clergy in Germany. He promoted a reformation of practices to bring Catholicism closer to laymen and root out the excesses and corruption in the Church. Luther protested the old practices of the Catholic Church and clergy, from which the word Protestant was derived. The Reformation was based on the main doctrines that: The Bible (Scripture) was the source of faith and behavior (not the Church or monasteries); saving by God came from faith alone (not from what the Church or clergy said or did); and every believer had direct access to God through Christ (not via a Pope or Saints). Consequently, Reformers rejected monasteries, churches that were not a parish church, saints, bishops, confessions to a priest, icons of worship, and so forth. The Reformation movement spread from Germany to Switzerland, the Netherlands, Scandinavia, and England and Scotland.

This spark of renewal jumped over to Switzerland and priest Ulrich Zwingli proposed radical reforms in the City of Zurich and the German-speaking part of Switzerland from 1522. Berchtold Haller convinced the City of Bern of the Reformation in 1528. From 1526 Guillaume Farel continued these reform proposals in the French-speaking part of Switzerland. Jean Calvin pursued this Reformation in Geneva from 1535. Acceptance of the Reformation by Zurich, Bern, and Geneva had history-defining consequences for Swiss politics and religion.

The **political impact** was fourfold:

- Division (of Cantons into catholic and protestant). This division had severe consequences for their populations in terms of freedom and education, and for the political representation of the Cantons to the outside world. The Cantons along the Swiss Way of St. James were divided as follows:

| Catholic | Protestant | Confessional Parity/Mix |
|---|---|---|
| Schwyz | Zurich | Thurgau |
| Uri | Appenzell Ausserrhoden | St. Gallen |
| Nidwalden | Bern | |
| Obwalden | Vaud | |
| Luzern | Geneva | |
| Fribourg | | |

- Civil war (between the catholic and protestant Cantons). This civil war frequently ignited military battles between catholic and protestant Cantons throughout a period of 325 years (1523-1848). Frequently, the protestant Cantons tried to force the Reformation onto the catholic Cantons using military power. The biggest military impact was the forceful occupation of the lands of Vaud by troops from Bern in 1536. Their occupation to enforce the Reformation in Vaud lasted 275 years, until Napoleon's armies invaded Switzerland in 1798. The religious civil war finally ended at the inception of the Swiss Confederation in 1848, when the new Federal Constitution declared freedom of religion in all Cantons.

- Persecution (of Catholics in the protestant Cantons, and vice versa). Catholic Cantons forbade protestant worship, exiled such worshippers, and seized their assets. The Protestants did the same with the Catholics in their Cantons. This mutual exclusion lasted from the 1520s-30s until 1848. The only exceptions were the Cantons that allowed confessional parity, i.e. the (peaceful) coexistence of Catholics and Protestants within the Canton.

- Reorganization (of society in the territories of the protestant Cantons). The Church's influence on the State and its politics was eliminated. The Church as a provider of education (schools), knowledge (libraries), hospitals, and social care for the poor, was replaced with new and neutral institutions managed by the Cantons. Social functions had been a responsibility of the Catholic Church for many centuries, with rules that they had determined. The Reformation changed these rules and made the services more and better accessible to the common people. Therefore, many laymen supported the Reformation that eliminated the power of the Church over these social institutions. The new rules denounced the worship of relics; hence pilgrimages were forbidden. Catholic pilgrims who walked through protestant Cantons were frowned upon. The Reformation caused a significant decline in inter-Cantonal pilgrimages (as a result of which local pilgrimages within the catholic Cantons gained importance).

The **religious impact** was fourfold, still clearly noticeable today, as you pilgrimage along the Swiss Way of St. James:

- Destruction (of catholic artefacts in the protestant Cantons). A significant number of catholic religious artefacts and relics that had been accumulated over more than 500 years were destroyed in only a few years. Laymen and clergy demolished or removed statues, altars, paintings, frescos, crucifixes, carpets, relics, paraments, organs, gold and silver chalices, and so forth. All catholic icons that were symbolic of the Church's excesses, corruption, and earthly focus that were rejected by the protestant doctrine, were destroyed. As you hike along the Swiss Way of St. James, this impact is still clearly noticeable. All protestant churches have a similar austere interior. Their interior decorations and furniture are limited to: pulpit, baptismal font, communion table, cross, organ, and parishioners' pews. You will not see any gold decorated marble altars, crucifixes, statues, paintings, frescos, and so forth. This in stark contrast to the catholic churches that were not 'cleaned out' in the 1520s-30s. Many of these still display opulence and wealth in their interior decorations.

- Transformation or demolition (of all churches and chapels not needed as a parish church in the protestant Cantons). Former catholic churches were converted to storage facilities (e.g. for grain or beer barrels), garages for carriages, horse stables, or reconstructed as military barracks or farmhouses. Regional pilgrimage destinations were closed (for example the St. Beatus caves were bricked up). As you hike along the Swiss Way of St. James, this impact is still clearly noticeable. The number of churches and chapels in the protestant Cantons is about three times lower than in the catholic Cantons.

- Secularization (of all monasteries in the protestant Cantons). Monasteries and convents were closed, the monks and nuns expelled, their buildings either demolished or utilized for a different purpose (e.g. as hospital or home for the poor). The protestant Cantons seized their sources of knowledge (schools, libraries) and wealth, which were, among other things, used to finance military assaults on the catholic Cantons. As you hike along the Swiss Way of St. James, this impact is still clearly noticeable. In the protestant Cantons you will pass by only a few monastic buildings from before 1536, which nowadays have a different purpose; none were established after the Reformation. This in stark contrast to the catholic Cantons that still house monastic Orders established before and after the Reformation.

- Counter-Reformation (efforts in the catholic Cantons). This led to a concentration of catholic institutions (monasteries, churches, catholic schools) in their main cities. These efforts intended to strengthen Catholicism in the Canton and stave off any efforts by the reformed Cantons to try to convert the catholic citizens to Protestantism. As you hike along the Swiss Way of St. James, this impact is still clearly noticeable. The cities Schwyz, Luzern, Stans, and especially Fribourg have many of such catholic institutions, most of them dating from after 1530.

In the catholic Cantons you will come across many catholic churches and chapels, and only a few protestant churches that were built after 1848. In the protestant Cantons you will pass by a small number of protestant parish churches and only a few catholic churches that were built after 1848. In the Cantons with confessional parity you will see both catholic and protestant churches, often in close vicinity of each other.

# Church Terminology

*Understanding religious terms*

Along the Swiss Way of St. James, you will visit more than 300 churches and chapels. A wide variety of terminology is used to name churches and describe their features, architecture, and interior decorations. This chapter introduces you to the most common terminology relating to:

- Church designations
- Church architecture
- Church interiors

During your pilgrimage you will encounter nearly 50 monasteries and convents. Similar to churches, the monastic Orders use specific terminology that may be confusing. The last section of this chapter introduces you to the most common terminology relating to monastic Orders.

A good understanding of church and monastic Order terminology increases your awareness and improves your interpretation of what you see.

## *Church designations*

Along the Swiss Way of St. James, you will come across the following church designations:

- **Cathedral**: a church that contains a bishop's seat (administrative headquarters with the seat of power and authority of a bishop). Because a bishop oversees a certain geographical region (called diocese or bishopric), there is usually only one church designated cathedral in a region. It is the mother church of all the other churches within that region and therefore of much larger size than the regular parish churches. You pass by cathedrals in St. Gallen, Bern, Fribourg, Lausanne, and Geneva.

- **Basilica**: a church that received this designation from the Pope. This designation is granted in recognition of special spiritual or historical significance. There are only two basilicas along the route: in Fribourg and Geneva.

- **Parish church**: a church that is the main place of worship for a religious community within the territory of a parish.

- **Collegiate church**: a church that is managed by a community (college) of clergy (multiple priests) called canons (in German *Stift*). The community does not belong to a monastic Order, is relatively independent of the Bishopric (the Holy See needs to approve its formation and dissolution), and functions as a self-governing entity under leadership of a provost. There are only two (active) Collegiate churches along the route: in Luzern and Fribourg.

- **Ecumenical church:** a place of worship that is shared by both Catholics and Protestants in joint ownership and responsibility for the building. Ecumenical churches were the initiative of the World Council of Churches (1948) in promoting unity between western religious streams. There are only three ecumenical churches along the route: in Halden (St. Gallen), Kehrsatz (Bern), and Bossey (Vaud).

- **Chapel**: a small sanctuary or place of worship. This can be a separate building, or inside a church, castle, school, prison, retirement home, and so forth.

- **Farm or Yard Chapel**: The term yard relates to a courtyard that belonged to a farm or stately residence. In the catholic Cantons many farmers and landowners built their private chapels during the middle ages. These chapels served as house chapels and were often built to commemorate certain events, such as recovery from the plague, safe return from a battle, recovery of cattle from diseases, or to make good on a promise. Additionally, a private chapel raised the standing of the family in the local community. These farm chapels are often located in meadows, close to the farmhouse to which they belong. Most of such chapels are still privately owned by the descendants of the original builders or the subsequent landowners. They use it for their weddings and services dedicated to special events in the life of the family.

- **Ossuary** (bone chapel or charnel house): a cemetery chapel that served as storage place for bones and corpses of the deceased.

- **Confessional Parity**: churches that are catholic and allow a protestant parish to use their church, or vice versa.

## *Church architecture*

Churches and chapels are designed in a limited number of **footprints**:

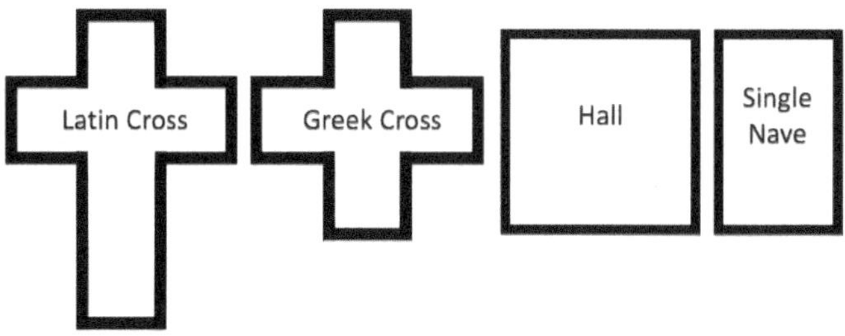

Many of the old churches from before the 12th century have the footprint of a single nave (as architecturally it was still challenging to span a roof over a wide space). Chapels have a single nave footprint as well. Most large churches built from the 12th/13th century (cathedrals, basilicas, and parish churches) have the footprint of a Latin cross. Hall churches were mostly built from the 17th/18th centuries and are typical for protestant church designs of the last centuries. Churches with the footprint of a Latin or Greek cross have their chancel separated from the nave. Most churches are oriented to the east (Jerusalem): the entrance of the parishioners is in the west, while the chancel is aligned to the east.

The most common **architectural designs** of churches relate to their construction periods. Along the Swiss Way of St. James, you will come across the following architecture:

- Romanesque: 900-1200. Romanesque church designs are characterized by massive walls, tiny windows that are high up the walls, decorative Lombard arches, round arches, vaulted ceilings, and low bell towers. Most early Romanesque churches were relatively small with a narrow single nave footprint. Later Romanesque churches were of larger size with the footprint of a Latin cross. Along the Swiss Way of St. James, you will come across typical Romanesque churches in Payerne, Spiez, Einigen, Amsoldingen, and several other places (mostly in Central and South-West Switzerland). Some churches only have a remaining bell tower from the Romanesque period; one of the most beautiful examples can be found in Stans. From the 13th century onwards, most Romanesque churches were reconstructed in Gothic designs (hence only a few Romanesque churches are left nowadays).

- Gothic: 1200-1400. Gothic church designs are characterized by pointed arches, tall stained-glass windows with tracery masonry at their top, buttresses supporting the outer walls, high vaulted ceilings, and elaborate masonry. Many Gothic churches are of large size with the footprint of a Latin cross. The cathedrals in Bern, Fribourg, Lausanne, and Geneva date from this period and demonstrate exquisite 12th/13th century

construction and masonry. During the 17th/18th centuries many Gothic churches were rebuilt or redecorated in a baroque style. Hence, only a few large Gothic churches are left nowadays; these are found in the protestant Cantons, where no remodeling to a baroque style was undertaken – that mostly occurred in the catholic Cantons.

- Renaissance: 1400-1600. Renaissance church designs are a revival of the classical Roman and Greek architecture, characterized by classical shapes such as columns, entablatures, semicircular arches, domes, elaborate frescos, mosaics, and sculptures. Renaissance church architecture came relatively late to Switzerland (after 1550 north of the Alps) and was limitedly applied. At the most you may see some Renaissance-style elements as an add-on to other architectural designs. Most of such style elements, though, were applied long after the Renaissance period had ended: for example, the colonnade at the front facade of the reformed St. Peter Cathedral in Geneva is called neoclassical, being added in 1752-56. The largest neo-Renaissance building along the Swiss Way of St. James is the House of Parliament in Bern (built in 1852-1902).

- Baroque: 1600-1800. Baroque church designs are characterized by an extravagant decorative style with significant focus on details. Many baroque churches have elaborate ceiling and wall frescos and stucco. Their altars are lusciously decorated with statues and carvings in gold on a base of marble. The most exquisite examples of baroque interior decorations are at the abbey churches of St. Gallen, Fischingen, and Einsiedeln, and the Jesuit church in Luzern. Along the Swiss Way of St. James, you will come across many baroque churches in the catholic Cantons in North-East and Central Switzerland – in the protestant Cantons this remodeling never occurred (though a few protestant churches were newly built in a baroque style after 1600).

- neo-Gothic: 1800-1930. Neo-Gothic church designs are a revival of medieval Gothic architecture, characterized by pointed arches and spires, vaulted ceilings, and other imitations. Good examples of neo-Gothic churches are found in Rorschach, Dussnang, and Lungern. Similar to baroque churches, neo-Gothic churches along the Way of St. James are only found in the catholic Cantons. The neo-Gothic architectural church designs fell out of taste with the catholic parishes as rapidly as they appeared. By the end of the 19th/beginning of the 20th century their designs were generally disapproved. Many parishes removed the imitation designs and changed back to baroque or austere interiors.

- Modern: from 1930. Modern churches, particularly those built after 1960, break with the traditional footprints and interiors of church architecture. Churches built in the 1960s-80s are mostly made of concrete and often have an unusual shape, e.g. triangular. Interior decorations are usually limited and in a modern style. Often there are no altars and pews may be replaced by chairs, allowing for a multipurpose use of the space. In many cases the interiors of modern catholic and protestant churches are very similar, dominated by simplicity and austerity. Along the Swiss Way of St. James, you will come across modern churches in Münchwilen, Pfäffikon, Nyon, Bellevue, and several other places.

Understanding and observing the specific features of churches along the Swiss Way of St. James help you identify the construction period (and thus age) of these churches. It gives you a better grasp of what you are seeing along the nearly 800 km of routes.

## *Church interiors*

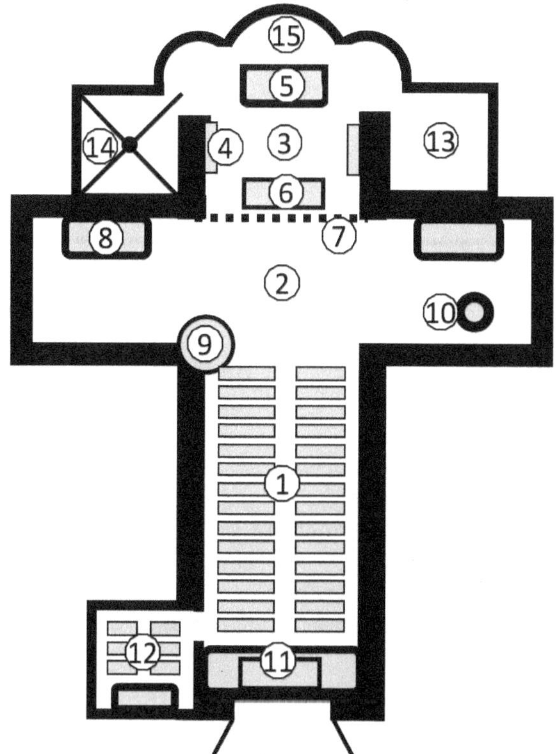


Inside a church, the most common terminology is as follows:

(1) The **nave** is the rectangular bottom/vertical part of the cross, with the pews for the parishioners (also called congregation). Large churches and cathedrals often have additional narrow side-naves, left and right of a broad center aisle.

(2) The **transept** is the horizontal part of the cross, between the nave and the chancel.

(3) The **chancel** is the square, rectangular, or semicircular top part of the cross, restricted to the clergy. Quite often the floor of the chancel is raised in relation to the transept and nave. The chancel consists of two main areas: the quire and the sanctuary.

(4) The **quire** is the area between the transept and the sanctuary, reserved for the group of singers (choir). In medieval times the group of singers consisted of the clergy or monks (laymen did not have access to the chancel). The **choir stalls** (a row of seats) lined the walls and faced the center of the quire area. Most medieval choir stalls were made from walnut wood and had elaborate carvings.

Nowadays the term choir is often used as a synonym of chancel, though this is not correct. The same occurs in German: most of the time *Chor* (choir) is used as a synonym of *Altarraum* (chancel).

(5) The **sanctuary** (also called presbytery) contains the **high-altar** and is the most holy place of the church. The high-altar is the primary altar of the church, often made from marble, with statues and paintings representing Jesus, Mary, saints, or a combination thereof. Quite often the high-altar contains reliquaries with small particles of decorated relics (bones, skull) of saints at its base or front.

The **tabernacle** is the cabinet in which the sacrament or Host is stored (the bread consecrated in the Eucharist). These cabinets are often elaborately decorated pieces of catholic art made from gold or silver. The tabernacle is usually placed on the table of the high-altar.

(6) The **communion table** is usually at the front of the chancel. The priests stand behind this table facing the congregation in the nave, while preaching, preparing the sacrament, reading from The Bible, praying, or chanting.

(7) A **rood screen** is a decorated partitioning between the chancel and the transept/nave. It is usually a tall grating, made of wood, iron, or stone. The partitioning may be decorative or block access to the chancel.

(8) The **side-altars** are secondary altars, usually placed in the left- and right-side transepts. These side-altars are often dedicated to the patron Saints of the church. Most of the time they have the same design, material, and color as the high-altar. Side-altars have a smaller format and like the high-altar, often display statues, paintings, and elaborate decorations. If the church has a skeleton relic of a catacomb saint, it is usually kept in a vitrine at one of these side-altars.

(9) The **pulpit** is an elevated speaker platform, from which the priests deliver their sermons to the parishioners in the nave. The position of the pulpit is usually at the front left of the nave. Pulpits are often elaborately decorated in the same design, material, and style as the altars. Usually they have statues or carvings of the Four Evangelists (Matthew, Mark, Luke, and John).

(10) The **baptismal font** is a free-standing round stone column that holds a receptacle with water used for baptism. It is usually placed in one of the transepts, at the back of the nave, or in a separate side-chapel.

(11) A **gallery** is an elevated balcony (also called loft) that houses an organ and/or provides additional seating. A church may have one or more galleries. In most catholic churches, galleries are located above the entrance and house the organ. In protestant churches these galleries may cover three sides of the nave and are mostly used for additional seating.

The **pipe organ** is usually placed on a gallery above the western entrance of the nave. The tones are produced by air flowing through differently sized pipes. A small organ may have the size of a cupboard with 10 pipes, whereas a large organ may contain more than 7'000 pipes of different sizes. Large churches and cathedrals often have multiple pipe organs.

Additional constructional extensions of the shape of the cross may be:

(12) A **side-chapel** may be either inside the shape of the cross or an extension thereof. A side-chapel usually contains an altar dedicated to a specific saint or the Virgin Mary.

(13) A **sacristy** is an enclosed room next to the chancel used by priests for the preparation of services. The room stores their liturgical clothing and cloths (vestments, paraments), chalices, books, and other items used during services.

(14) A **bell tower** holds the bells of the church that toll the present time (hourly or quarterly) and the start of services to the surrounding community. A bell tower can be a small steeple on the roof (e.g. one meter high), or an attached or free-standing tower of up to 100 meters high. Cathedrals and other large churches often have two tall bell towers.

(15) An **apse** is a semicircular recess extending the outer walls on the eastern side of the chancel. They may be decorative or include a small chapel or altar. The chancel may be the largest apse in the middle.

A **crypt** was originally a burial chamber below the chancel. Nowadays crypts may be of significant size and be used as an underground place of worship.

Decorative elements in the interior of a church may be: wall- and ceiling-frescos (also called murals), paintings, statues of saints, stained-glass windows, crucifixion way stations, and votives:

- The **crucifixion way** tells the story of the Crucifixion of Christ in 14 stations (small paintings), of which the 14th depicts Jesus' resurrection. Usually seven stations are placed on the right wall and seven stations on the left wall of the nave (clockwise from the parishioner's perspective).

- **Votives** are small paintings that are hanging on the walls, particularly at pilgrimage churches/chapels. These votives are often self-made by parishioners in fulfilment of a vow (e.g. after healing of an illness).

Catholic and protestant churches have distinct differences in interior decorations. The above described decorations are found in most catholic churches. Catholic churches that converted to Protestantism during the Reformation in the 1520s-30s had all their catholic religious icons removed. As a consequence, the interior decorations of the reformed churches are usually limited to: communion table, pulpit, and baptismal font (sometimes the baptismal font has a flat cover for the use as communion table).

## *Monastic Order terminology*

Western Christian monastic Orders use specific terminology that can be confusing. The following explanations help navigate the most frequently used terms.

- A **monastic Order** is a group of men or women who live a religious life devoted to a spiritual cause. These communities strictly separate between men and women (separate buildings and communities; no commingling). They often renounce earthly pursuits (possessions, marriage, profession) and live by a specific set of Rules. These **Rules** are often named after the founder of the monastic Order, such as the Rule of St. Augustine or the Rule of St. Francis. The Rules revolve around vows, most commonly vows of poverty, celibacy, and obedience. Most Rules determine a strict schedule of daily routines (silence, prayers, meals, reading, working, sleeping).

- The western Christian monastic Orders are generally divided in two categories: Orders that are internally or externally focused. **Enclosed Orders** concentrate on separation from the earthly world. Their members retreat from the world, live an ascetic life in isolation (hermitage), are self-sufficient, and devote their lives to prayer and contemplation. The Benedictine Order established the basis of such secluded Orders in the 6th century. Medieval female monastic Orders were often enclosed Orders, disallowing any contact with the outside world. From the 12th century externally focused Orders developed, as a reaction to the internally focused ones. They were called **Mendicant Orders** and concentrated on services to the surrounding community (e.g. Franciscans and Capuchins). Their members took care of the poor and needy (spiritually and physically), for which they traveled outside the monastery. The mendicant Orders were dependent on donations; they denounced the principle of possessions and wealth.

- A **monastery** is a building complex that houses a monastic Order. The complex usually consists of a church or chapel, communal areas (e.g. dining room, library, work places), and single cells (rooms) where the monastics read, pray, and sleep. Work places are generally dedicated to two aspects of a monastic Order's life: service to the surrounding community and self-sufficiency. Service areas may comprise a school, hospice, brewery, and so forth. Self-sufficiency may comprise working on an agricultural field or vegetable garden.

- Historically, the male members of a monastic Order are called **monks** (or brothers) and the female members **nuns** (or sisters). The term **friars** is used to name the monks of the mendicant Orders. **Beguines** are religious laywomen that live in a community, without being bound to vows or a specific monastic Rule.

- Nowadays the term monastery is often used to denote the residence of a male monastic Order. Historically, a convent or friary designated the housing of a male mendicant Order. This terminology changed from the 19th century. Nowadays the term convent is often used to indicate a female Order or nunnery. For simplicity reasons this book uses the term **monastery** for the housing of male Orders and **convent** for the housing of female Orders.

- The term **cloister** means covered walkway or corridor. It denotes the walkway around a square courtyard of a monastery. This is different in German; the German term ***Kloster*** means monastery (for men or women). Nowadays cloister is often used as a synonym of monastery or convent, though this is not correct. *Kloster* and cloister do not mean the same and should not be confused with each other.

- An **abbey** is a monastery (or convent) under leadership of an abbot (or abbess). A monastery (or convent) becomes an abbey when a certain number of monks (or nuns) is reached (usually 12); abbeys are large monasteries/convents. The abbot (or abbess) is usually nominated by the monks (or nuns), appointed by a bishop, and answers directly to the Pope. A **priory** is a monastery (or convent) under leadership of a prior (or prioress), with less than 12 monks (or nuns); they are small monasteries/convents. The prior (or prioress) is usually nominated by the monks (or nuns), appointed by the mother abbey, and answers directly to the abbot (or abbess). A large autonomous mother abbey often has small dependent subsidiary priories.

# Hiking Routes

*Finding your way*

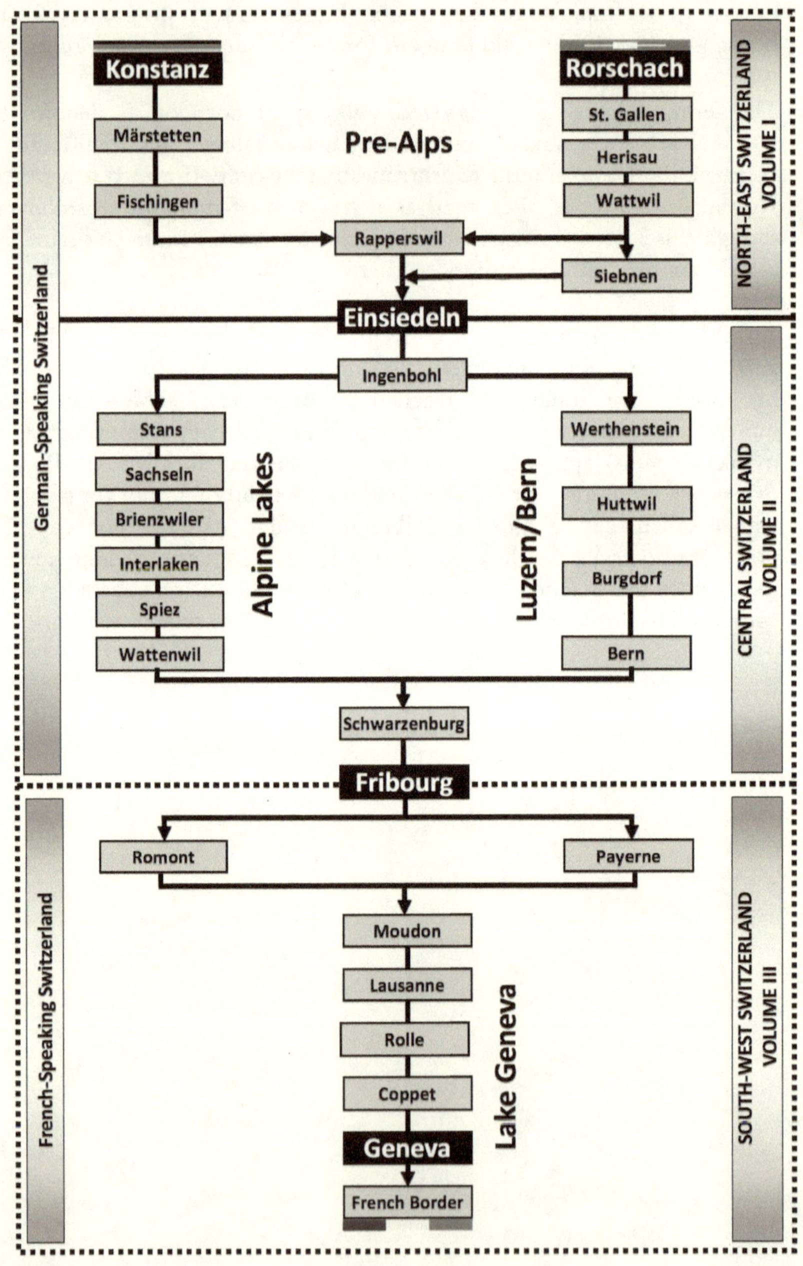

As you can gather from the chart, the Swiss Way of St. James has two alternative starting points: Konstanz and Rorschach. In case you start in Rorschach, you need to decide to hike to Einsiedeln either via Rapperswil or Siebnen. From Ingenbohl you need to decide to hike either the route of the Alpine Lakes (via Interlaken) or the route via Luzern/Bern (agricultural fields). Finally, when you leave Fribourg you need to decide to hike to Moudon either via Romont or Payerne. These four route decisions lead to 12 possible routes.

But which route to take? How to decide on the route alternatives? What are the individual stages you need to hike to get from one overnight location to another? How easy or difficult are these individual stages? How will you find the route? What is the signaling?

This chapter addresses these questions with the following focus:

- 12 route possibilities
- 4 route decisions
- 33 possible stages
- 13 Cantons
- 779 km route signaling

## *12 route possibilities*

The officially signposted route nr. 4 of the Swiss Way of St. James offers 12 route possibilities with varying profiles:

| | Routes from Konstanz | | | | | | | |
|---|---|---|---|---|---|---|---|---|
| | Start | | Via | Via | Days | Km | Alt. m | Churches |
| 1 | Konstanz | | Interlaken | Romont | 20 | 494 | 23'435 | 217 |
| 2 | Konstanz | | Interlaken | Payerne | 20 | 502 | 22'971 | 215 |
| 3 | Konstanz | | Luzern/Bern | Romont | 18 | 472 | 21'486 | 191 |
| 4 | Konstanz | | Luzern/Bern | Payerne | 18 | 480 | 21'022 | 189 |

| | Routes from Rorschach | | | | | | | |
|---|---|---|---|---|---|---|---|---|
| | Start | Via | Via | Via | Days | Km | Alt. m | Churches |
| 5 | Rorschach | Rapperswil | Interlaken | Romont | 21 | 494 | 24'939 | 228 |
| 6 | Rorschach | Rapperswil | Interlaken | Payerne | 21 | 502 | 24'475 | 226 |
| 7 | Rorschach | Rapperswil | Luzern/Bern | Romont | 19 | 472 | 22'990 | 202 |
| 8 | Rorschach | Rapperswil | Luzern/Bern | Payerne | 19 | 479 | 22'526 | 200 |
| 9 | Rorschach | Siebnen | Interlaken | Romont | 21 | 498 | 25'484 | 226 |
| 10 | Rorschach | Siebnen | Interlaken | Payerne | 21 | 506 | 25'020 | 224 |
| 11 | Rorschach | Siebnen | Luzern/Bern | Romont | 19 | 475 | 23'535 | 200 |
| 12 | Rorschach | Siebnen | Luzern/Bern | Payerne | 19 | 483 | 23'071 | 198 |

From this table you can conclude that:

- The route via Luzern/Bern shortens the pilgrimage by 2 days compared to the route via Alpine Lakes (Interlaken), because it has 2 fewer stages. Two days are saved due to a combination of a shorter overall distance and longer individual stages (tougher but two days less to hike).

- The route via Luzern/Bern incurs fewer altitude meters compared to the route via Interlaken. The Interlaken route is longer and closer to the mountainous area of the Alps, whereas the route via Luzern/Bern goes through agricultural fields around the western foothills of the Alps.

- The route via Alpine Lakes (Interlaken) passes by many more churches compared to the route via Luzern/Bern. The Interlaken route is longer and passes through one protestant and three catholic Cantons, whereas the route via Luzern/Bern passes through one protestant and two catholic Cantons.

- 472 km (18 days) is the shortest route: from Konstanz via Einsiedeln, Luzern/Bern, and Romont.

- 506 km (21 days) is the longest route: from Rorschach via Siebnen, Interlaken, and Payerne.

- 21'022 is the lowest number of altitude meters: on the route from Konstanz, via Luzern/Bern, and Payerne (18 days).

- 25'484 is the highest number of altitude meters: on the route from Rorschach, via Siebnen, Interlaken, and Romont (21 days).

How to decide on these 12 alternative routes? Which route to take? These routes are based on four decisions.

## *4 route decisions*

As a pilgrim on the Way of St. James through Switzerland you have four route decisions to make:

1. Start in Konstanz or Rorschach?
2. When starting in Rorschach, take the route from Wattwil to Einsiedeln via Rapperswil or Siebnen?
3. From Ingenbohl, take the route via Interlaken or Luzern/Bern?
4. From Fribourg, take the route via Romont or Payerne?

### 1. Start in Konstanz or Rorschach?

The question whether to start in Konstanz or Rorschach has three possible answers, depending on where you are coming from:

- If you are a pilgrim coming from/through southwestern Germany (Baden-Württemberg, Stuttgart) you will most likely arrive in Konstanz.

- If you are a pilgrim coming from/through southeastern Germany (Bavaria, Munich) you will most likely arrive in Lindau (Germany) and take the ferry across Lake Constance to Rorschach. Alternatively, you could also hike via Bregenz (Austria) around the eastern side of Lake Constance to Rorschach.

- If you are a pilgrim from Switzerland or arrive from a location other than the southern German feeder routes (e.g. by flying to Zurich Airport), you need to decide where to start. Consider the following for your decision:

    - The route via Konstanz to Rapperswil is one day shorter than the route from Rorschach. The number of km is the same (84), but the sightseeing highlights are spread differently. In Konstanz the highlight is the basilica, which is visited before you start hiking. From Rorschach the highlight is the former Benedictine Kingdom-Abbey of St. Gallen, which is visited at the end of day 1. Because there is a lot to see in St. Gallen, day 2 is very short to provide time for this sightseeing (hence the extra day).
    - The difficulty in terms of altitude meters is a lot less on the route from Konstanz. From Konstanz to Rapperswil are 3'268 altitude meters, whereas from Rorschach there are 4'772 (46 percent more).
    - Konstanz has a beautiful basilica (a former cathedral) with a history of more than 1'200 years, worthwhile visiting and sightseeing.
    - The route from Rorschach passes by the former Benedictine Kingdom-Abbey of St. Gallen with a history of more than 1'300 years, worthwhile visiting and sightseeing. The former Kingdom-Abbey is unique for Switzerland and boasts extraordinary treasures in its museum (the famous St. Gallen library and historical artefacts). Two additional 1'000-year-old churches in St. Gallen add to the religious historical significance.
    - Konstanz is a lively international city where there is a lot to do. Rorschach is a small provincial town without much action.
    - Konstanz can be reached by direct train from Zurich Airport in 1hr:4min (ticket CHF 30). St. Gallen can be reached in 51 min (ticket CHF 28) from the airport. From St. Gallen to Rorschach is an additional 18 min (ticket CHF 7.20) by train.

In case you decide to start in Konstanz, you may rightfully ask the question, why Konstanz, which lies in Germany, and not Kreuzlingen, which lies in Switzerland? Historically, Konstanz is an assembly point for pilgrims coming to the south of Germany. Konstanz looks back on a long history as a catholic center; a church was first mentioned in the 7th century and its cathedral was a bishop's seat for 1'200 years. In contrast, Kreuzlingen's pilgrimage history is non-distinctive, overshadowed by the town 1 km north of the Swiss-German border. Konstanz and Kreuzlingen basically form one urban agglomeration (with a political border splitting it in two); for many hundreds of years Kreuzlingen was a suburb of Konstanz, until an official border was established in 1818. As a result, the Swiss Way of St. James does not have a starting point in Kreuzlingen.

**2. When starting in Rorschach, take the route from Wattwil to Einsiedeln via Rapperswil or Siebnen?**

Consider the following for your decision:

- Rapperswil has several historical points of interest, such as a castle, Capuchin monastery, Switzerland's longest wooden footbridge, and a bustling promenade at the lakeside. There are no such comparable interesting scenes in Siebnen.

- Rapperswil is a lively town, with good choices of hotels and restaurants. Rapperswil has a pilgrim inn, Siebnen does not. Siebnen is a small town surrounded by agricultural fields, without the livelihood of Rapperswil.

- The Siebnen route is 3 km longer and has 545 (23 percent) more altitude meters. The route mostly goes through rural areas, whereas the trails via Rapperswil are much more urban walkways.

My recommendation: choose the route via Rapperswil.

**3. From Ingenbohl, take the route via Interlaken or Luzern/Bern?**

Consider the following for your decision:

- The route via Interlaken passes by turquoise alpine lakes with snow-capped Alps in the distance. This is a unique scenery and probably the main reason you came to Switzerland. Such scenery and landscapes are not available on the route via Luzern/Bern. The route via Interlaken goes through alpine and agricultural rural areas, whereas the trails via Luzern/Bern are through agricultural rural areas over rolling foothills.

- The route via Interlaken passes through three catholic Cantons (Nidwalden, Obwalden, and Fribourg) that display many religious artefacts and treasures in their churches and chapels. Above all, this route passes by the birthplace, hermit cell, and grave of Switzerland's patron Saint, Nicholas of Flüe (Brother Klaus). The route via Luzern/Bern passes through two catholic Cantons (Luzern and Fribourg).

- The route via Luzern/Bern passes through two major Swiss tourist cities: Luzern and Bern. Both have a significant number of medieval historical sites that are unique for Switzerland. Luzern was a catholic powerhouse during the Counter-Reformation, while Bern is the capital of Switzerland and had a significant influence on the history of the country. The route via Interlaken does not pass through comparable power-cities; the towns along the route are small.

- The Interlaken route is 23 km longer, has 1'949 (23 percent) more altitude meters, and takes 2 days longer to hike. On average the daily hikes on the route via Interlaken are 5 km shorter than on the route via Luzern/Bern.

My recommendation: choose the route via Interlaken, the Alpine Lakes.

**4. From Fribourg, take the route via Romont or Payerne?**

Consider the following for your decision:

- Romont is a unique small medieval town built on top of a hill, surrounded by agricultural fields. The town has a beautiful 800-year-old church, a medieval castle, and remnants of medieval city fortifications. Unique in Switzerland is the stained-glass museum, where you get insight in the art and craft of making stained-glass church windows (of which you see many hundreds along the Swiss Way of St. James). The town is a historical pilgrimage station on the way to Santiago de Compostela and has a pilgrim inn in a Cistercian convent.

- Payerne is a larger and livelier town in the Broye River valley, which is well-known for its 1'050-year-old former Cluniac Abbey. The Cluniac church is a magnificent example of 10$^{th}$ century Cluniac architecture, but is undergoing a four-year renovation project that will be completed in May 2020. From then the monumental church will be open again. The attached museum provides great insight in the history of the former Cluniac Abbey and its church. Payerne has no pilgrim inn.

- The Payerne route to Moudon is 7 km longer but has 464 (24 percent) fewer altitude meters. This route closely follows the Broye River valley for a large part, which is very relaxed and easy to hike (without any hills).

My recommendation: choose the route via Romont.

Now that you understand the 12 route possibilities and the four route choices you need to make, let us have a closer look at the 33 possible hiking stages.

## *33 possible stages*

Your four route decisions determine which of the 18 to 21, out of the possible 33 stages, you will hike.

| | # | From | To | | Km | Alt. m | Churches |
|---|---|---|---|---|---|---|---|
| 1 | K1 | Konstanz | Märstetten | From Konstanz | 16 | 484 | 3 |
| 2 | K2 | Märstetten | Fischingen | | 35 | 969 | 15 |
| 3 | K3 | Fischingen | Rapperswil | | 33 | 1'815 | 8 |
| 4 | 4 | Rapperswil | Einsiedeln | | 18 | 925 | 13 |
| | | | | or | | | |
| 5 | R1a | Rorschach | St. Gallen | From Rorschach | 18 | 950 | 13 |
| 6 | R1b | St. Gallen | Herisau | | 11 | 443 | 7 |
| 7 | R2 | Herisau | Wattwil | | 26 | 1'978 | 7 |
| 8 | R3 | Wattwil | Rapperswil | Via Rapperswil | 29 | 1'401 | 10 |
| | 4 | Rapperswil | Einsiedeln | | 18 | 925 | 13 |
| 9 | S1 | Wattwil | Siebnen | or, Via Siebnen | 31 | 1'704 | 12 |
| 10 | S2 | Siebnen | Einsiedeln | | 19 | 1'167 | 9 |
| | **North-East Switzerland (w/o overlaps)** | | | | **209** | **10'129** | **82** |

| | # | From | To | | Km | Alt. m | Churches |
|---|---|---|---|---|---|---|---|
| 11 | 5 | Einsiedeln | Ingenbohl | | 27 | 1'884 | 24 |
| 12 | 6 | Ingenbohl | Stans | Via Alpine Lakes | 26 | 1'564 | 25 |
| 13 | 7 | Stans | Sachseln | | 22 | 1'566 | 14 |
| 14 | 8 | Sachseln | Brienzwiler | | 26 | 1'728 | 7 |
| 15 | 9 | Brienzwiler | Interlaken | | 27 | 1'852 | 8 |
| 16 | 10 | Interlaken | Spiez | | 19 | 930 | 7 |
| 17 | 11 | Spiez | Wattenwil | | 26 | 1'310 | 4 |
| 18 | 12 | Wattenwil | Schwarzenburg | | 24 | 1'313 | 5 |
| | | | | or | | | |
| 19 | L1 | Ingenbohl | Werthenstein | Via Luzern/ Bern | 24 | 961 | 16 |
| 20 | L2 | Werthenstein | Huttwil | | 31 | 1'715 | 10 |
| 21 | L3 | Huttwil | Burgdorf | | 25 | 1'615 | 5 |
| 22 | L4 | Burgdorf | Bern | | 31 | 1'968 | 6 |
| 23 | L5 | Bern | Schwarzenburg | | 36 | 2'055 | 7 |
| 24 | 13 | Schwarzenburg | Fribourg | | 27 | 1'549 | 24 |
| | **Central Switzerland (w/o overlaps)** | | | | **356** | **21'243** | **155** |

| | # | From | To | | Km | Alt. m | Churches |
|---|---|---|---|---|---|---|---|
| 25 | 14 | Fribourg | Romont | Via Romont | 30 | 1'224 | 16 |
| 26 | 15 | Romont | Moudon | | 17 | 683 | 6 |
| | | | | or | | | |
| 27 | P1 | Fribourg | Payerne | Via Payerne | 25 | 1'017 | 11 |
| 28 | P2 | Payerne | Moudon | | 29 | 426 | 9 |
| 29 | 16 | Moudon | Lausanne | | 30 | 1'476 | 6 |
| 30 | 17 | Lausanne | Rolle | | 33 | 732 | 10 |
| 31 | 18 | Rolle | Coppet | | 32 | 720 | 9 |
| 32 | 19 | Coppet | Geneva | | 19 | 502 | 9 |
| 33 | 20 | Geneva | French Border | | 8 | 209 | 4 |
| | **South-West Switzerland (w/o overlaps)** | | | | **214** | **6'744** | **73** |

| | Km | Alt. m | Churches |
|---|---|---|---|
| **Total Swiss Way of St. James (w/o overlaps)** | **779** | **38'116** | **310** |

From this table you can conclude that:

- The longest hiking day is stage L5 with 36 km from Bern to Schwarzenburg. This stage from the Luzern/Bern route converges with the route from Wattenwil to Schwarzenburg (Interlaken route).
- The shortest hiking day is stage R1b with 11 km from St. Gallen to Herisau. This stage is short to provide time for sightseeing in St. Gallen and its more than 1'300-year-old former Benedictine Kingdom-Abbey.
- The hiking day with the highest altitude meters is also stage L5 with 2'055 altitude meters from Bern to Schwarzenburg, influenced by the length of the stage.
- The toughest hiking day is probably stage R2 with 1'978 altitude meters over the relatively short distance of 26 km. This route goes over two mountains (1'083 and 989 meters) and follows grassland trails with difficult under-footing.
- The hiking day with the lowest altitude meters is stage P2 with 426 altitude meters from Payerne to Moudon. Despite its length of 29 km, it is a relaxing hiking day because it follows the Broye River valley, without any hills.

## *13 Cantons*

The Swiss Way of St. James passes through 13 Cantons:

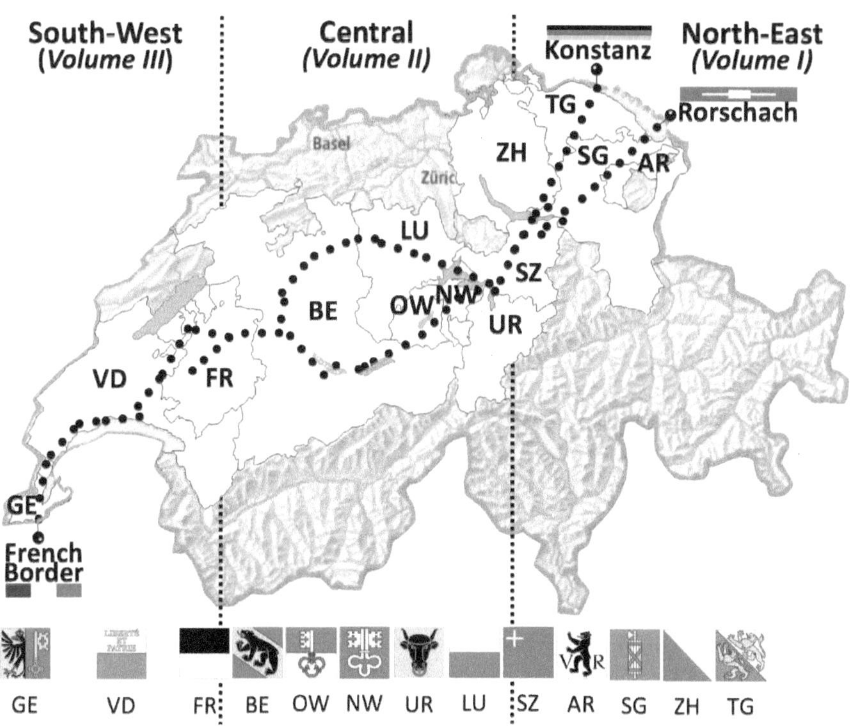

| | Canton | Abbr. | Region | Confession | Km | Alt. m | Churches |
|---|---|---|---|---|---|---|---|
| 1 | Thurgau | TG | NE | Confessional Parity | 56 | 1'851 | 19 |
| 2 | Zurich | ZH | NE | Protestant | 23 | 1'293 | 3 |
| 3 | St. Gallen | SG | NE | Catholic+Protestant | 83 | 4'583 | 37 |
| 4 | Appenzell Ausserrhoden | AR | NE | Protestant | 11 | 692 | 2 |
| 5 | Schwyz | SZ | NE/CE | Catholic | 64 | 3'628 | 48 |
| 6 | Luzern | LU | CE | Catholic | 52 | 2'518 | 21 |
| 7 | Uri | UR | CE | Catholic | 2 | 100 | 1 |
| 8 | Nidwalden | NW | CE | Catholic | 31 | 2'021 | 23 |
| 9 | Obwalden | OW | CE | Catholic | 36 | 2'148 | 18 |
| 10 | Bern | BE | CE | Protestant | 186 | 11'526 | 41 |
| 11 | Fribourg | FR | CE/SW | Catholic | 74 | 3'105 | 45 |
| 12 | Vaud | VD | SW | Protestant | 137 | 4'016 | 39 |
| 13 | Geneva | GE | SW | Protestant | 25 | 635 | 13 |
| | **Total Swiss Way of St. James (w/o overlaps)** | | | | **779** | **38'116** | **310** |

From this table you can conclude that:

- The routes cross through the center of all listed Cantons, except for the Cantons Zurich, Appenzell Ausserrhoden, and Uri. Only a minor distance is passed through the territories of these three Cantons. The route stays far east of the city of Zurich.

- Canton Bern is Switzerland's second-largest Canton in terms of land area and lies in the center of Switzerland. It has a large part of the Swiss Alps on its territory (hence the many altitude meters). It is 85 percent bigger than the second-largest Canton on the above list, Vaud. No wonder that 24 percent of the Swiss Way of St. James passes through Canton Bern. Together, the two protestant Cantons Bern and Vaud cover 41 percent of the total route.

- The catholic Cantons around Lake Lucerne in Central Switzerland (Schwyz, Luzern, Nidwalden, and Obwalden) have by far the highest number of churches and chapels. The routes through these four catholic Cantons cover 183 km (23 percent of the total distance) and 110 churches (35 percent of the total number of churches). The impact of the Swiss religious Reformation of the 1520s-30s is clearly visible in the concentration of churches.

Each Canton is a highly independent province within the Swiss Confederation (comparable to the States in America). The relevant social, cultural, and religious history of the Cantons is explained at the beginning of each Volume (chapter **Overview of Cantons**). The summary of their religious history provides the appropriate context for the churches, monasteries, and points of interest along the route through the respective Cantons.

*779 km route signaling*

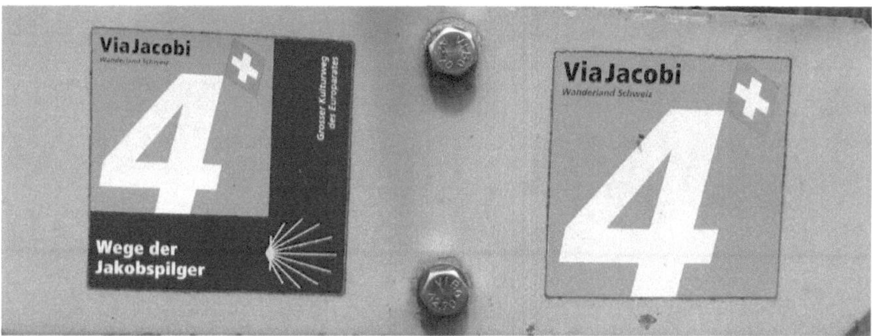


The hiking signaling along the Swiss Way of St. James is easy to recognize. The risk of getting lost or away from the trail is negligible: signs are placed at regular distances and direction changes along the complete 779 km route.

- The route through Switzerland is called the ViaJacobi (Via stands for Way, Jacobi for James), which is represented by the number 4. It is one of seven Swiss national hiking routes.

- The square nr. 4 sign has two versions: green with a blue border and green without a blue border. The nr. 4 signs with the blue border point in the direction of Santiago de Compostela (and during the hike through Switzerland to Geneva and the French border). The nr. 4 signs without the blue border point in the opposite direction (in case you would want to walk the Way of St. James in opposite direction – from Geneva to Konstanz or Rorschach). These two signs are always placed together at a signpost. The nr. 4 signs are mostly at locations with direction changes or where there is a choice between hiking routes (other than the Way of St. James).

- The nr. 4 signs are alternated with hiking signs confirming that you are on the right route. These signs do not have the nr. 4, but may consist of: yellow diamonds (with or without a small Cantonal coat-of-arms), yellow arrows, or yellow signs with a hiking figure. In forests these yellow diamonds and arrows are often painted on tree trunks.

- The square nr. 4 signs are often attached to the general yellow hiking signposts indicating a location name, direction, and duration to reach that location. Note that these signs indicate the time, not the distances. The times are calculated based on an average walking speed of 4.2 km per hour (without breaks) of an untrained adult on horizontal surfaces, with adjustments in speed for altitude meters ascending and descending. In case you are trained you will have a speed of 5 to 6 km/h (also depending on the weight of your backpack) on horizontal surfaces. In case you are well-trained and travel light, you may achieve a speed of 6 to 7 km/h. As a well-trained and lightly packed hiker you can achieve the destinations within 60 to 70 percent of the pre-calculated times on the signposts. Hiking apps such as Runtastic can help you measure your own speed with the simple use of your smart phone.

# Raising Expectations

*Enhancing your spiritual and cultural pilgrimage*

You are undertaking, or planning, your pilgrimage on the Swiss Way of St. James for specific reasons. You may have certain expectations of the routes, hiking, spirituality, sights, or scenery along the nearly 800 km routes through Switzerland. What are your expectations? What do you expect to encounter along the routes? Do you expect a sufficient number of churches to ensure the achievement of your spiritual goals? Do you expect to spend the night at a monastery? Do you expect to be surrounded by the typical Swiss alpine scenery? Do you expect to see medieval cities and castles?

Whatever you are expecting, raise your expectations. The Swiss Way of St. James provides a unique, once in a lifetime experience. The following sections indicate what you can expect to see and discover along your pilgrimage through Switzerland:

- 779 km Way of St. James
- 310 churches and chapels
- 48 monasteries and convents
- 118 points of interest

Let the following sections raise your expectations to optimize your spiritual and cultural pilgrimage through Switzerland.

## *779 km Way of St. James*

Compared to the number of pilgrims arriving in Santiago de Compostela, the Swiss Way of St. James is completely different. You will come across relatively few other pilgrims. Most pilgrims are either alone or in pairs. On occasion (particularly on weekends) you might pass by a small hiking group with a pilgrim guide. In tourist areas (St. Gallen, Rapperswil, Einsiedeln, Luzern, Interlaken, Bern, Fribourg, Lausanne, and Geneva) you will be surrounded by a small to large number of Swiss and International tourists. In other words, you will mostly be alone on the hiking trails through nature, but in the major cities you will be surrounded by many other tourists. If you are looking for time alone while hiking through beautiful landscapes, the Swiss Way of St. James might be something for you.

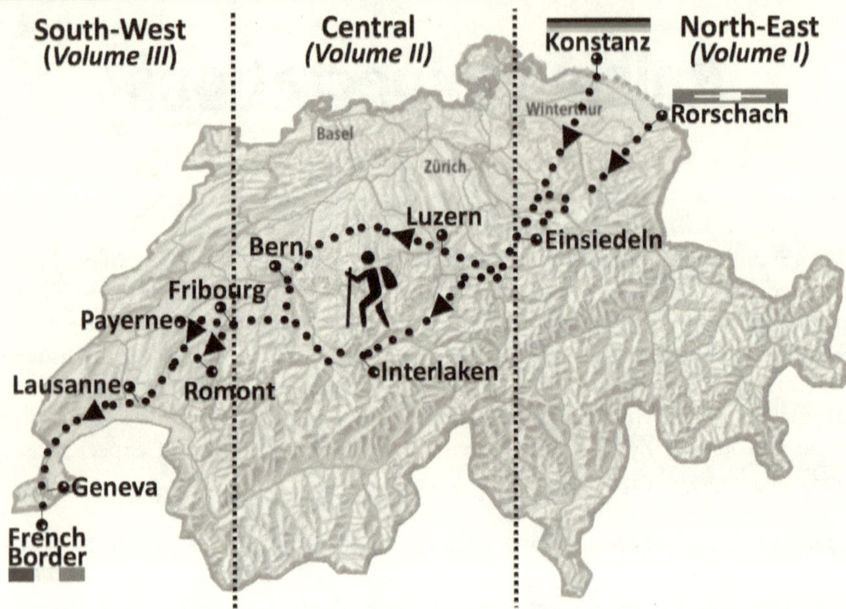

The **North-East routes** of the Swiss Way of St. James (Volume I) start at the Lake Constance basin (Konstanz or Rorschach; you need to decide where to start) and end at the highland plateau of Einsiedeln. The black Madonna at the 1'100-year-old Benedictine Abbey of Einsiedeln is Switzerland's number one pilgrimage destination, attracting nearly a million visitors every year. It is one of the religious and cultural highlights of the Swiss Way of St. James. The southbound routes from Lake Constance to Einsiedeln cross over the northern pre-Alps with a significant number of altitude meters.

The **Central routes** of the Swiss Way of St. James (Volume II) continue south from Einsiedeln and descend to the Lake Lucerne basin. From Lake Lucerne the route splits and you need to decide which route to take from there. One route follows the scenic turquoise Alpine Lakes surrounded by snow-capped Alps (7 days), while the other goes via Luzern and Bern, following agricultural fields in the rolling foothills west of the Alps (5 days). The Alpine Lakes route via Interlaken not only borders lakes such as Lake Lucerne, Lakes Brienz, and Lake Thun, but also provides panoramic views of the alpine peaks of the Eiger, Mönch, and Jungfrau. Both routes have a significant number of altitude meters, before converging near Fribourg. The town Fribourg was a catholic stronghold during the Reformation and the Counter-Reformation in the 16th-19th centuries. Many monastic Orders settled in Fribourg, built their own churches, and set up catholic schools as a deterrent to Protestantism, shaping its history until today. The town has the tomb of a Saint and the highest concentration of churches and monasteries along the Swiss Way of St. James.

The **South-West routes** of the Swiss Way of St. James (Volume III) continue south from Fribourg. Upon leaving Fribourg you need to make a route decision. One route goes via Romont (2 days), while the other goes via Payerne (2 days). Both routes converge shortly before Moudon. From Moudon the route goes over the Jorat highland plateau down to Lausanne at the Lake Geneva basin. The route continues along the western shore of Lake Geneva, with few altitude meters. Two of the three stages from Lausanne to Geneva are long, but the routes are on easy hiking trails, offering the most beautiful views along vineyards, castles, and chateaus over Lake Geneva towards the Savoy Alps with the snow-capped Mont Blanc. The town Geneva was a protestant center during the Swiss religious Reformation in the 1530s, and nowadays is the most international city of Switzerland, with the diplomatic head offices of many international organizations. Finally, a short hike south of Geneva leads you to the Swiss-French border. From Fribourg until Geneva you are in the French-speaking part of Switzerland (Lake Constance until Fribourg is all German-speaking).

You reach the **highest point** of the Swiss Way of St. James on the hike from Einsiedeln to Ingenbohl. Three of the four highest altitudes are reached within the first five days of the pilgrimage from Konstanz or Rorschach. Four stages reach altitudes over 1'000 meters:

- Stage 5 Einsiedeln to Ingenbohl 1'414 m
- Stage K3 Fischingen to Rapperswil 1'132 m
- Stage R2 Herisau to Wattwil 1'083 m
- Stage 8 Sachseln to Brienzwiler 1'083 m

The Swiss Way of St. James passes by many **historical religious monuments** (depending on your route choices) such as: the 1'300-year-old former Benedictine Kingdom-Abbey of St. Gallen with its many treasures; the 900-year-old Benedictine Abbey of Fischingen with the grave of Saint Idda; the 1'100-year-old Benedictine Abbey of Einsiedeln with the Black Madonna; the more than 500-year-old birth place, hermit cell, and grave of Saint Nicholas of Flüe in Flüeli-Ranft/Sachseln; the 1'400-year-old grave of Saint Beatus in a cave high above Lake

Thun; three 1'000-year-old churches at the southern shore of Lake Thun; the more than 400-year-old working place and grave of Saint Canisius in Fribourg; the 1'050-year-old former Cluniac Abbey church in Payerne; and the medieval cathedrals in Bern, Fribourg, Lausanne, and Geneva.

In your planning you should consider that you may need about half a day to visit the churches, cathedrals, and points of interest in certain cities. These locations could be good for scheduling a resting day:

- St. Gallen: because of the former Benedictine Abbey-Kingdom and its cathedral and treasures (half a day for sightseeing is already included in the very short stage R1b).
- Einsiedeln: because of the Benedictine Abbey with the Black Madonna and its treasures (half a day for sightseeing is already included in the short stage 4 and S2).
- Luzern: because of the historical medieval city, churches, and points of interest, and its hotspot during the Swiss Counter-Reformation.
- Bern: because of the historical medieval city, churches, cathedrals, points of interest, and its hotspot during the Swiss Reformation.
- Fribourg: because of the historical medieval city, churches, cathedral, and its hotspot during the Swiss Counter-Reformation.
- Geneva: because of the churches, cathedral, and its hotspot during the Swiss Reformation (half a day for sightseeing is already included in the short stage 19 and 20).

## *310 churches and chapels*

The Swiss Way of St. James nr. 4 signposts direct you on your earthly path. The churches and chapels may help direct you on your spiritual path. And there are plenty of them to do so. In medieval times pilgrims used the churches along the trail for prayers, rest, and safety. Food, beverages, and shelter were obtained either at the monastery or the pilgrim inn in close vicinity of the churches. Modern-day pilgrims on the Way of St. James use the churches for prayer, reflection, admiration of the religious art and decorations, and rest. The Swiss Way of St. James passes by 310 churches and chapels.

Some special churches along the Swiss Way of St. James are:

- Cathedrals: St. Gallen, Bern, Fribourg, Lausanne, Geneva
- Basilicas: Fribourg, Geneva
- Two-story ossuaries: Rapperswil, Schwyz, Stans

Central Switzerland (Volume II) has the highest concentration of churches. The reasons are simple: it encompasses the catholic Cantons (Schwyz, Nidwalden, Obwalden, Luzern, and part of Fribourg) and the covered distance is the longest. These catholic Cantons have a high concentration of churches and chapels, much higher when compared to the confessional parity Cantons in the North-East (Volume I) or the protestant Cantons in the South-West (Volume III). In these catholic Cantons you will pass by a church or chapel every 1.3 km on average; in the protestant Cantons this is every 4.3 km on average. This means that in the catholic Cantons you will be making frequent stops to visit a church or chapel.

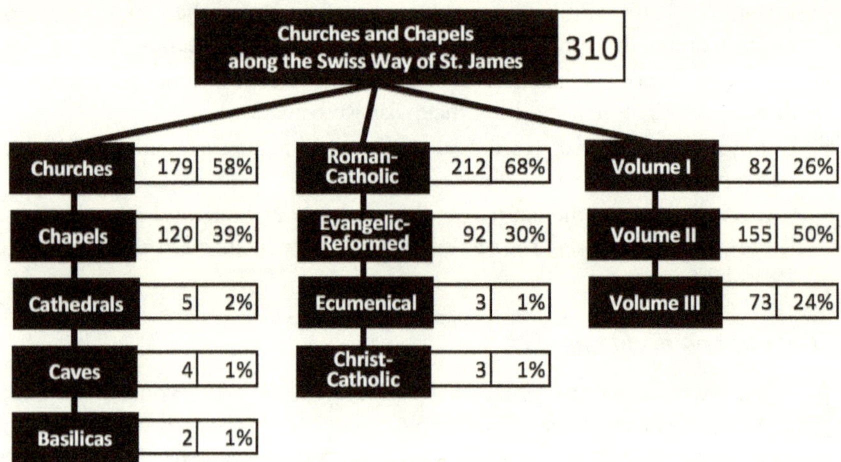


More than two-thirds of the churches and chapels along the Swiss Way of St. James are Roman-Catholic (simply called catholic in the three volumes). Nearly one-third are Evangelic-Reformed (simply called reformed or protestant in the three volumes). Many of the reformed churches are former catholic churches that were converted to Protestantism during the Reformation in the 1520s-30s. In the three volumes the reformed churches are always designated as such. In case there is no designation in the text of either reformed or catholic, the church is catholic. You can usually recognize the latter by the use of names of saints (reformed churches do not use the names of saints, though there are some exceptions – see below) and the interior decorations (altars).

The Evangelic-Reformed Church of Switzerland has neither designated Bishops nor Cathedrals. Still, three Evangelic-Reformed churches are nowadays called Cathedral: the St. Vincent Cathedral in Bern, the Our Lady Cathedral in Lausanne, and the St. Peter Cathedral in Geneva. Technically these designations are incorrect and protestant churches usually do not have the name of a saint. These are reformed churches that were former catholic Cathedrals, until the Reformation in the 1520s-30s. The Saint's name and the name Cathedral have been maintained due to their rich heritage and popularity.

In many areas along the route interesting churches are often in close vicinity (up to 500 meters) left or right of the signposted route nr. 4 (so not directly on the trail). The route descriptions and distances in this book (Volumes I, II, and III) include detours from the signposted route nr. 4 to visit such churches, chapels, monasteries, castles, and other points of interest that are worthwhile a visit. The average detour from the signposted route to visit a church is 10 percent of the distance of a stage.

Each church has its own history and religious and societal importance. These are explained in the chapters of the 33 hiking stages, where you come across the respective church. Additionally, **Appendix 1** of each of the three Volumes contains a complete list of all the churches and chapels passed along the routes.

### *48 monasteries and convents*

The Swiss Way of St. James passes by 48 monasteries and convents. The generic term monastery is used for a male monastic Order (monks or friars), while the generic term convent is used for a female Order (nuns or sisters).

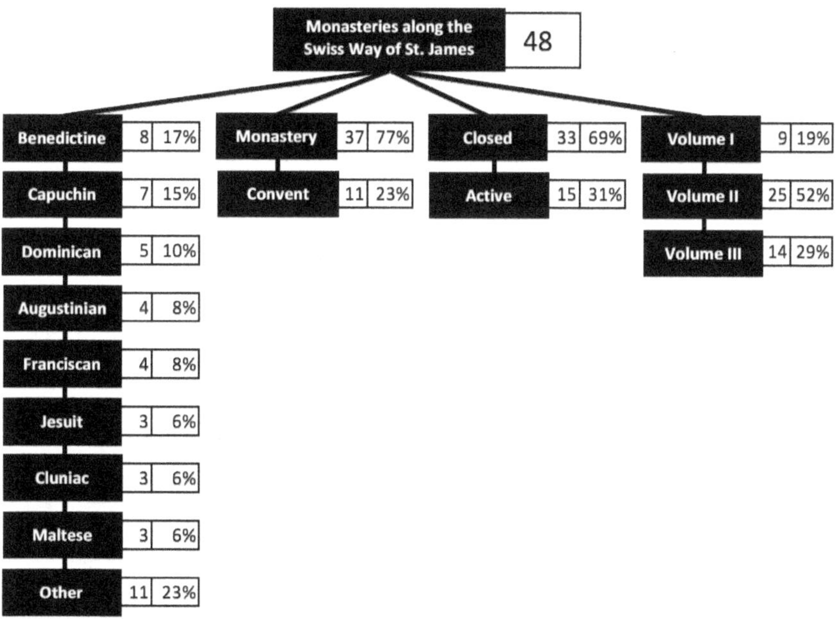


Central Switzerland (Volume II) has the highest concentration of monasteries, for the same reason that it has the highest number of churches. It encompasses the catholic Cantons (Schwyz, Nidwalden, Obwalden, Luzern, and part of Fribourg) and the covered distance is the longest. These catholic Cantons attracted many monastic Orders as part of the Counter-Reformation between 1550 and 1650. In contrast, the confessional parity Cantons in the North-East (Volume I) maintained but did not expand the number of monasteries and convents, whereas the protestant Cantons in the South-West (Volume III) secularized and closed all monasteries and convents during the Reformation in the 1520s-30s.

The high number of closed monasteries/convents compared to the ones that are still active (open) has three causes: the Reformation (1520s-30s), the French occupation (1798), and societal changes in the 20th century. Because of the Reformation, 17 out of 33 monasteries/convents were closed, when they were secularized by the protestant Cantons. The French occupation resulted in the closure of yet an additional number of monasteries/convents in 1798. During the time of the Helvetic Republic, new Cantons were formed, which decided on the closure of several monasteries/convents in 1798-1803. Finally, from the 1960s a number of monasteries/convents were not able to attract novices and over-ageing of a dwindling number of monks/nuns, lack of succession, and the problematic maintenance of their buildings forced the closure of some more.

The only closed monastery that still flourishes today is the former Benedictine Kingdom-Abbey of St. Gallen. This monastery was closed after St. Gallen became a Canton in 1803, but because of its religious and cultural treasures became a major tourist attraction. The most flourishing active monastery is the Benedictine Abbey of Einsiedeln. It mostly owes its present-day success to the Black Madonna, which still makes it a major pilgrimage destination in the 21st century.

Each monastery/convent has its own history, religious and societal importance. These are explained in the chapters of the 33 hiking stages, where you come across the respective monastery/convent. Additionally, the general history of the relevant monastic Orders is described in **Appendix 3** of each of the three Volumes.

## *118 points of interest*

During your pilgrimage along the Swiss Way of St. James you pass by more than 100 locations that are of historical and cultural importance.

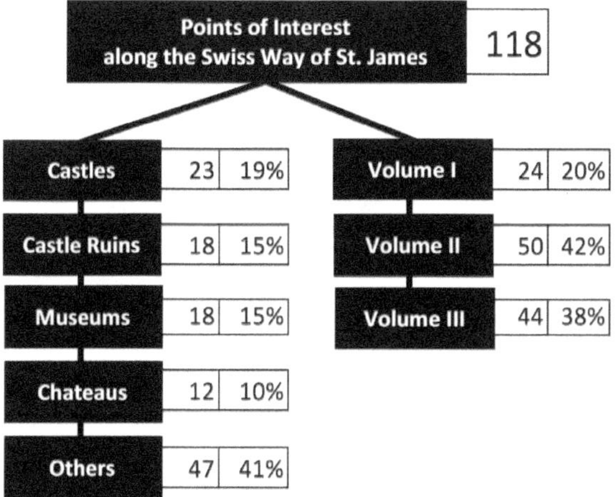

The major points of interest are **Castles** and **Castle Ruins**, both representing the Swiss medieval political and feudal history of the 12th and 13th centuries. These were the times when the first cities and Cantons were formed, and Switzerland began to rise as a central-European power. Regional nobility (Lords, Counts, Knights) drove much of this development, often with support of the Regional Monastic powerhouses (Abbey-Kingdom of St. Gallen, Bishopric Kingdoms of Lausanne and Geneva) and European Royal powerhouses (German Emperors, Austrian Habsburg, Italian Savoy, French Burgundy).

**Chateaus** are large residential mansions that were built by wealthy bankers and industrialists in the 17th to 19th centuries. Ten out of 12 chateaus are located along the vineyards at the southern end of Lake Geneva. Geneva became a refuge for many wealthy French Protestants after the Reformation in the 1530s. They brought money, developed the banking system, and built large mansions along the lake's shore, north of Geneva. This area is considered the Beverly Hills of

Switzerland, with one of the most beautiful hiking routes of the Swiss Way of St. James (vineyards, chateaus, and views over Lake Geneva).

The other **Points of Interest** comprise a large variety of cultural, natural, and historical sightseeing objects. They include fountains, springs, bridges, gallows, waterfalls, caves, medieval cities and their fortifications and clock towers, 2'000-year-old Roman archaeological sites, islands in lakes, and so forth.

The Way of St. James routes in North-East Switzerland have the lowest number of points of interest, because of the 1'000-year dominance of the former Benedictine Abbey-Kingdom of St. Gallen, from the 8th until the 18th century. As earthly and religious rulers of large territories south and north of Lake Constance, they suppressed the development of other rulers and monastic Orders in their region.

Each point of interest has its own history and societal importance. These are explained in the chapters of the 33 hiking stages, where you come across the respective point of interest. Additionally, **Appendix 4** of each of the three Volumes contains a complete list of all the points of interest along the routes.

## *Use of the stage chapters*

Each stage chapter has a standardized structure with five sections:

1. **Stage overview**: statistics, route summary, geographical map, and profile. This provides an overview of the stage, useful for planning the hiking day. This section covers three to four pages of each stage chapter.

   The statistics include estimates of the time needed to hike the distance and visit the churches and chapels of the respective stage. The hiking times are calculated based on approximately 5.2 km/h walking pace (on horizontal surfaces, with adjustments in speed for altitude meters ascending and descending) of a trained person. The time allocated to churches takes into consideration the length of the stage, the number of churches, and their level of appeal. These time estimates are indicative only; they should be used as guidance to plan the stage, not as a fixed time table. Depending on your walking speed and interest in churches, you may need less or more time than these estimates suggest.

2. **Getting to the starting point**: information on how to best get to the start of the stage at the signposted route nr. 4 (for a day-hiker: from the nearest train station). This section is limited to a few paragraphs.

3. **Hiking the route**: a detailed description of the route, including all matters of interest along the route. This section covers the better part of the stage chapter, containing many pages.

4. **From the ending point**: information on where to go from the end of the stage (for a day-hiker, to the nearest train station; for a thru-hiker, the accommodation possibilities). This section is limited to a few paragraphs.

5. **Next stage**: a short introduction of the route of the following stage. This section is limited to one paragraph.

Before you start walking the route, read the summary history of the Canton that you will be in. This provides the religious context, enabling a better understanding of the churches, chapels, and monasteries along the route.

Throughout the hike, consult the information in the section 'Hiking the Route'. This information has two main elements: the route and the interesting points along the route (churches, chapels, monasteries, castles, ruins, and other points of interest).

The churches and monasteries are sequentially numbered and their information is presented in a structured way, supported by icons:

The address; in case you intend to visit the location by car or public transportation.

The monastic Order; look up a short history of the monastic Order in **Appendix 3**.

The saints; look up a short biography of the saints in **Appendix 2**.

The stamp; the location of the pilgrim stamp, often together with a pilgrim guestbook.

The history; a short history of the construction of the building and main events that influenced its present-day appearance.

The features; the special features of the building, particularly the interior religious objects and characteristics, which make it stand out from the other churches, chapels, and monasteries.

The relics; identification of the venerated and decorated skeletons of catacomb saints or bone particles of local saints.

## *First step*

Now that you are aware of how to organize a low-cost pilgrimage in the high-cost country of Switzerland, now that you understand the route choices and what routes to hike, now that you comprehend the religious context in Switzerland, and now that your expectations have been raised, it is time for you to start your pilgrimage and make the first step.

In case you are a thru-hiker, your first step will either be in Konstanz or Rorschach. Continue reading the following chapters in this book (Volume I) for guidance on the Way of St. James route from either Konstanz or Rorschach to the Black Madonna in Einsiedeln.

In case you are a day-hiker, you can of course select any individual hiking stage out of 33 possible stages. The following chapters of this book (Volume I) guide you on 10 out of 33 possible stages.

Whatever type of hiker you are, the remainder of this book (Volume I) will guide you along the routes, churches, monasteries, and points of interest in North-East Switzerland. For similar guidance in Central Switzerland and South-West Switzerland, see Volume II and Volume III respectively.

Bon Camino!

# NORTH-EAST SWITZERLAND

# TO THE BLACK MADONNA OF EINSIEDELN

# Overview of Routes

*The Way of St. James in North-East Switzerland*

## North-East Switzerland routes

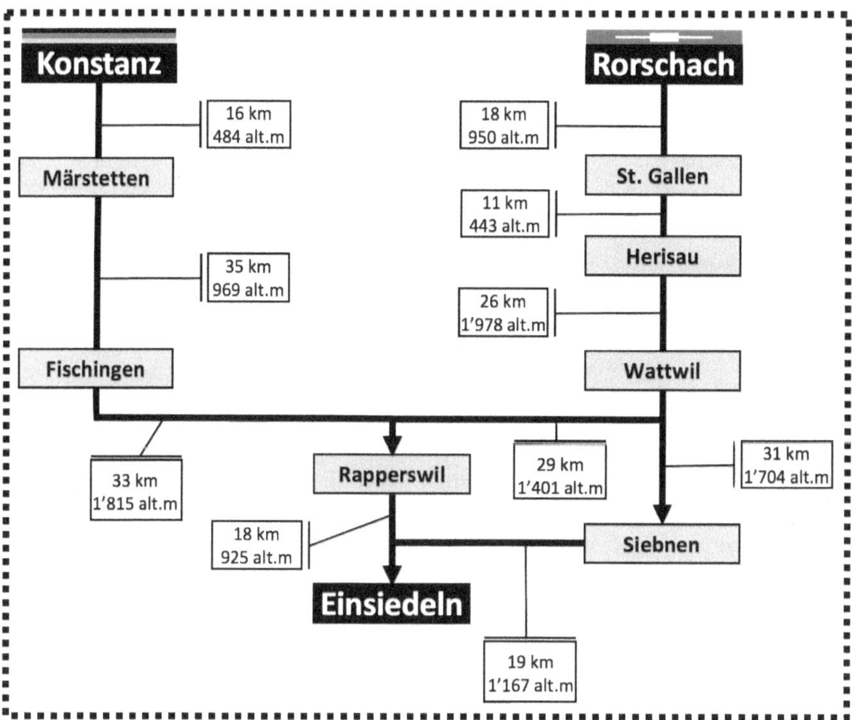


## Route choices

For the choice of the start in either Konstanz or Rorschach, and the route options from Rorschach via Rapperswil or Siebnen, see pages 50-52.

## Route stats

The three possible routes (with overlapping stage 4) compare as follows.

| | # | From | To | Km | Alt. m | Churches |
|---|---|---|---|---|---|---|
| 1 | K1 | Konstanz | Märstetten | 16 | 484 | 3 |
| 2 | K2 | Märstetten | Fischingen | 35 | 969 | 15 |
| 3 | K3 | Fischingen | Rapperswil | 33 | 1'815 | 8 |
| 4 | 4 | Rapperswil | Einsiedeln | 18 | 925 | 13 |
| | **From Konstanz to Einsiedeln** | | | **101** | **4'193** | **39** |
| 1 | R1a | Rorschach | St. Gallen | 18 | 950 | 13 |
| 2 | R1b | St. Gallen | Herisau | 11 | 443 | 7 |
| 3 | R2 | Herisau | Wattwil | 26 | 1'978 | 7 |
| 4 | R3 | Wattwil | Rapperswil | 29 | 1'401 | 10 |
| 5 | 4 | Rapperswil | Einsiedeln | 18 | 925 | 13 |
| | **From Rorschach to Einsiedeln, via Rapperswil** | | | **101** | **5'697** | **50** |
| 1 | R1a | Rorschach | St. Gallen | 18 | 950 | 13 |
| 2 | R1b | St. Gallen | Herisau | 11 | 443 | 7 |
| 3 | R2 | Herisau | Wattwil | 26 | 1'978 | 7 |
| 4 | S1 | Wattwil | Siebnen | 31 | 1'704 | 12 |
| 5 | S2 | Siebnen | Einsiedeln | 19 | 1'167 | 9 |
| | **From Rorschach to Einsiedeln, via Siebnen** | | | **105** | **6'242** | **48** |

## *Route summaries*

From Konstanz to Einsiedeln

**Stage K1** (Konstanz to Märstetten) guides you out of the Lake Constance basin, over the rolling foothills of the pre-Alps, to Märstetten near the Thur River valley. With 16 km this first stage is relatively short. Reason is the late start from Konstanz. The Basilica of Konstanz only opens for sightseeing at 10:00 in the morning. You can easily spend two hours there, so that the day's hike starts around 12:00 (or after lunch). With only the afternoon left for hiking, the 16 km ensure a relaxed warm-up for the tougher hiking days to come. The route is in Canton Thurgau and passes by castle ruins and three catholic churches. There are no monasteries along this short route. Märstetten has a low-cost pilgrim inn.

**Stage K2** (Märstetten to Fischingen) guides you over rolling hills to the foot of the Hörnli mountain. Similar to stage K1, the second stage passes by several towns' outskirts and over rolling pre-Alp hills with agricultural fields and apple orchards. The total of 969 altitude meters is spread over a long distance, without any steep ascents or descents. The closer you get to Fischingen, the narrower the valleys, the more forested, and the higher the elevation becomes. The route is still in Canton Thurgau that allowed confessional parity. Along the way you pass by 15 churches (four protestant and 11 catholic) and a former Commandry of the Knights of St. John. The religious and artistic highlight is the Benedictine Abbey of Fischingen with its baroque church and exquisite St. Idda chapel, which contains the tomb of this female Swiss Saint. The Abbey of Fischingen has a low-cost pilgrim inn.

**Stage K3** (Fischingen to Rapperswil) guides you over the Hörnli mountain (1'132 meters) and across a highland valley and plateau, from where the route descends to the Lake Zurich basin. Stage 3 is one of the toughest hiking sections of the Swiss Way of St. James, because of both the distance (33 km) and the number of altitude meters (1'815). On the Hörnli mountain you are at the second-highest altitude of the Swiss Way of St. James. The route starts in Canton Thurgau (confessional parity), changes to Canton Zurich (protestant), and ends in Canton St. Gallen (catholic part). You pass by eight churches, of which six catholic and two reformed. The highlight is the Castle of Rapperswil with the adjoining church. The stage ends at the St. Anthony cave of the Capuchin monastery of Rapperswil. Rapperswil has a low-cost pilgrim inn.

**Stage 4** (Rapperswil to Einsiedeln) guides you across the Lake Zurich basin, over the Etzel mountain (951 meters), to the highland plateau of Einsiedeln. Stage 4 is relatively short, a hike of maximum half a day, because you will need sufficient time for sightseeing at the Abbey of Einsiedeln. The route enters catholic Canton Schwyz and passes by 13 catholic churches. Ten points of interest, including a castle, are dotted along the 18 km route. The highlight is the visit to the Benedictine Abbey of Einsiedeln with the Black Madonna, at the end of the stage. A guided tour around the Abbey and its historical library starts at 14:00. Without the tour, there is no access to the library and limited insight in one of Switzerland's most important abbeys. Einsiedeln has a low-cost pilgrim inn.

From Rorschach to Einsiedeln, via Rapperswil

**Stage R1a** (Rorschach to St. Gallen) guides you from the Lake Constance basin to the highland plateau and urban agglomerations of St. Gallen. The route goes up the rolling foothills of the pre-Alps in a steady ascent. The final 5.5 km are through the St. Gallen agglomeration and are more or less flat. The route goes through the catholic part of Canton St. Gallen, until reaching the city, which is protestant. The route passes by 10 churches, of which four reformed. Five points of interest include the highlight of the day, the former Kingdom-Abbey of St. Gallen, a UNESCO World Cultural Heritage Site, at the end of the stage. The world-famous Abbey Library and a historical Abbey and City Tour complete one of the cultural highlights of the Swiss Way of St. James. St. Gallen has a low-cost pilgrim inn.

**Stage R1b** (St. Gallen to Herisau) guides you from the highland plateau with the St. Gallen agglomerations to the beginning of the Appenzell hills. The route passes from Canton St. Gallen (protestant part) into Canton Appenzell Ausserrhoden (protestant), and passes by seven churches, of which three reformed. Stages R1a and R1b have to be seen in combination with each other. Stage R1a guides you to the Kingdom-Abbey of St. Gallen. The historic city and Abbey of St. Gallen may require half a day to take in their religious, cultural, and historical significance. Stage R1b intentionally has a short distance of only 11 km to enable a late hiking start on your second day. In case you start early in Rorschach and need limited time to see the sights in St. Gallen, it is also possible to hike stages R1a and R1b in one day. Herisau has no pilgrim-inn.

**Stage R2** (Herisau to Wattwil) guides you over the Appenzell and Toggenburg foothills west of the Alpstein mountain range to the town Wattwil in the Thur River valley. Stage R2 is probably the toughest hiking section of the Swiss Way of St. James. Most of the pathway is through farm grasslands with nearly 2'000 altitude meters. The distance profile is straightforward: 1 km down, 7 km up, 6 km down, 5 km up, and 3 km down. The final 4 km in Wattwil are more or less flat. The trail goes up and down two mountains with peaks of 1'083 meters and 989 meters. The former is the third-highest altitude of the Swiss Way of St. James. In between these two peaks the trail descends to 703 meters, when crossing the Necker River at St. Peterzell. There you pass by three churches and a former Benedictine monastery. In Wattwil the route passes by four more churches to end at the former Capuchin convent. The ruins of the Castle of Iberg guard over Wattwil and have an interesting history. The stage starts in Canton Appenzell Ausserrhoden (protestant) and after 9 km changes back to Canton St. Gallen (confessional parity part). Wattwil has a low-cost pilgrim inn inside the former Capuchin convent, with a unique opportunity to sleep in an original nun's cell.

**Stage R3** (Wattwil to Rapperswil) guides you from Wattwil, in the Thur River valley, in a steep ascent to the Laad Pass and in a long descent to Rapperswil at the Lake Zurich basin. You already reach the highest point of the day (987 meters) at km 4 (Laad Pass). At km 24.5 you reach the outskirts of Jona and for the remaining 4.2 km you hike through the urban environment of the towns Jona and Rapperswil. The last 2 km converge with route K3 coming from Fischingen (Konstanz). Most of the route is through the catholic part of Canton St. Gallen, where you pass by 10 catholic churches. Two of these contain relics of catacomb saints. The highlight is the Castle of Rapperswil and the adjoining church. The stage ends at the St. Anthony cave of the Capuchin monastery of Rapperswil. Rapperswil has a low-cost pilgrim inn.

**Stage 4** from Rapperswil to Einsiedeln is the same as described above.

From Rorschach to Einsiedeln, via Siebnen

For **stages R1a**, **R1b**, and **R2**, see the descriptions above.

**Stage S1** (Wattwil to Siebnen) guides you from Wattwil, in the Thur River valley, in a steep ascent to the Laad Pass and in a long descent to the Linth Plain at the eastern end of the Lake Zurich basin. The first 16 km from Wattwil to Neuhaus are the same as in stage R3. At Neuhaus (km 16) the route splits and stage S1 continues to follow a southern direction. Within 2 km from Neuhaus you ascend the Goldberg (521 meters) and from there the route goes down to the most eastern side of Lake Zurich. You hike through the Linth Plain and partly along the Linth canal (all flat). From Tuggen the route goes over an extension of the Buechberg and descends again to a plain called March. After 22 km through Canton St. Gallen (catholic part), the route enters catholic Canton Schwyz. Out of the 12 churches along the way, only one is protestant. The Castle of Grynau is the only point of interest of the stage. Siebnen has no pilgrim inn.

**Stage S2** (Siebnen to Einsiedeln) guides you from Siebnen in the March Plain, over the Etzel Pass (951 meters), to the highland plateau of Einsiedeln, and the Black Madonna at the Benedictine monastery of Einsiedeln. Stage S2 is intentionally short to enable sufficient time to visit the Benedictine monastery and its treasures in Einsiedeln. The route goes through catholic Canton Schwyz where you pass by nine churches and seven points of interest. The highlight is the visit to the Benedictine Abbey of Einsiedeln with the Black Madonna. A guided tour around the Abbey and its historical library starts at 14:00. Without the tour, there is no access to the library and limited insight in one of Switzerland's most important abbeys. Einsiedeln has a low-cost pilgrim inn.

## *Route Map and Profile*

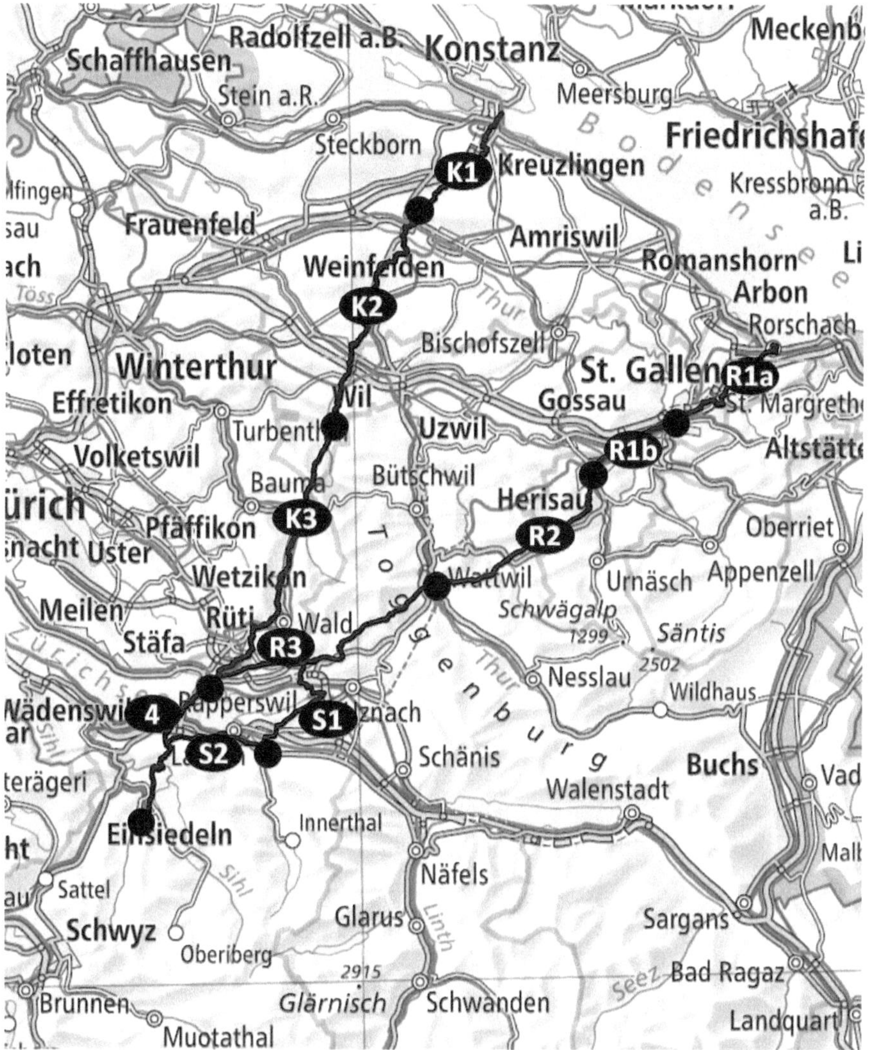

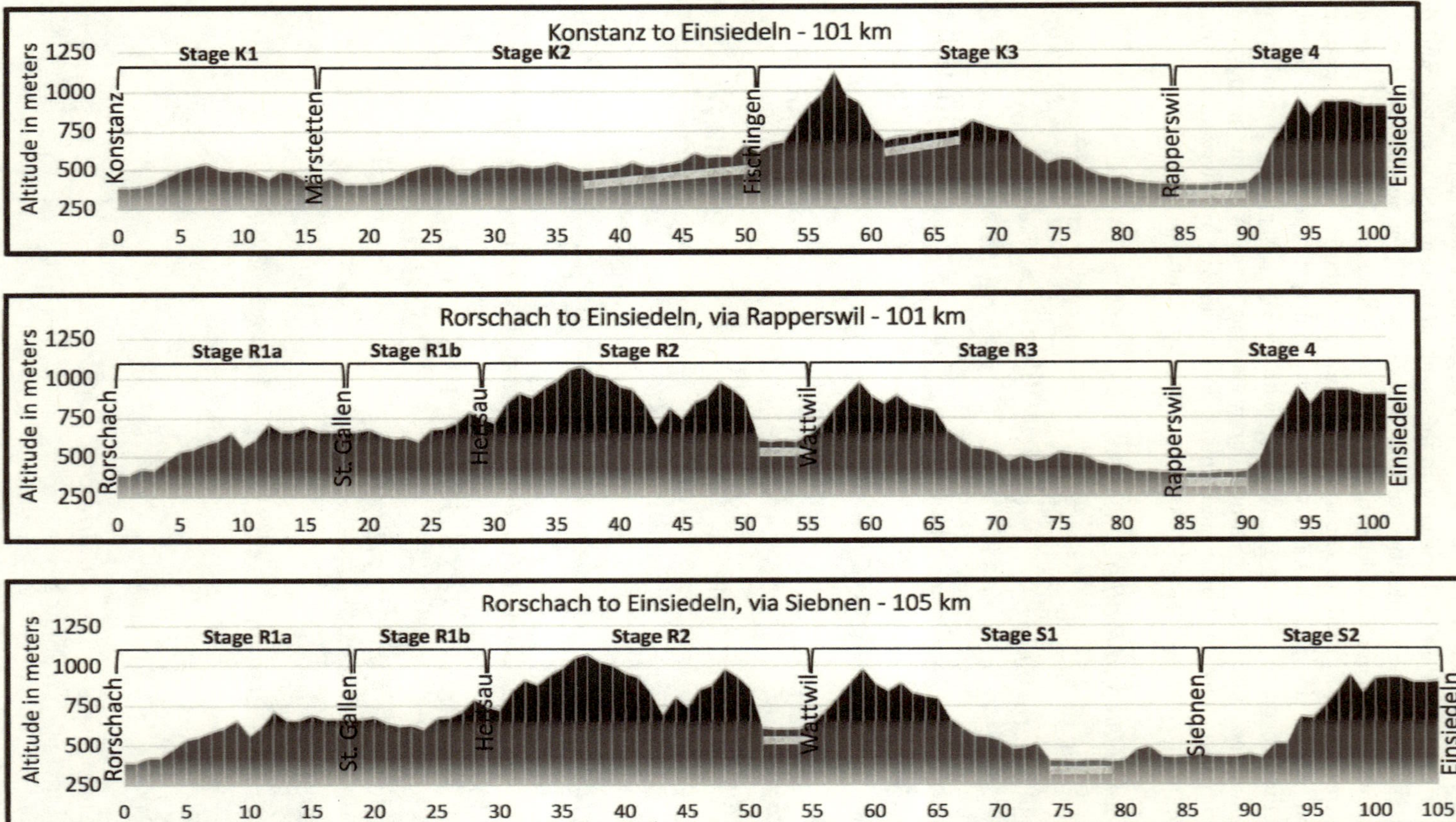
Konstanz to Einsiedeln - 101 km
Altitude in meters
1250
1000
750
500
250
Stage K1
Stage K2
Stage K3
Stage 4
Konstanz
Märstetten
Fischingen
Rapperswil
Einsiedeln
0 5 10 15 20 25 30 35 40 45 50 55 60 65 70 75 80 85 90 95 100
Rorschach to Einsiedeln, via Rapperswil - 101 km
Altitude in meters
1250
1000
750
500
250
Stage R1a
Stage R1b
Stage R2
Stage R3
Stage 4
Rorschach
St. Gallen
Herisau
Wattwil
Rapperswil
Einsiedeln
0 5 10 15 20 25 30 35 40 45 50 55 60 65 70 75 80 85 90 95 100
Rorschach to Einsiedeln, via Siebnen - 105 km
Altitude in meters
1250
1000
750
500
250
Stage R1a
Stage R1b
Stage R2
Stage S1
Stage S2
Rorschach
St. Gallen
Herisau
Wattwil
Siebnen
Einsiedeln
0 5 10 15 20 25 30 35 40 45 50 55 60 65 70 75 80 85 90 95 100 105

# Overview of Cantons

*Understanding the relevant history of the Cantons*

In North-East Switzerland you will be hiking through the following Cantons:

- from Konstanz: Thurgau, Zurich, St. Gallen, and Schwyz
- from Rorschach: St. Gallen, Appenzell Ausserrhoden, and Schwyz

The following sections provide an overview of the above-mentioned Cantons, highlighting their religious history. Read the background information provided below, whenever you enter a new Canton. This will provide the appropriate social, cultural, and religious context of the churches, monasteries, and points of interest.

In the chapters of the individual stages you will find a reference to the Canton and changes from one Canton to the other. As you come across such references, you can flip back to these pages.

## *Canton Thurgau*

From Konstanz, the stages K1, K2, and the beginning of K3 are in Canton Thurgau.

In Canton Thurgau the car license plates start with TG and the people speak Swiss-German (greeting with *Grüezi*). The Canton was named after the Thur River and was declared a Canton in 1798 (at the formation of the Helvetic Republic by Napoleon of France). The capital city is Frauenfeld. Its coat-of-arms with the two lions originates from the House of Kyburg, who ruled the territory of Thurgau in 13th century. The Canton consists mostly of rolling pre-Alp hills with agricultural fields and many apple and pear orchards. The Canton has about 280'000 inhabitants (3 percent) and covers about 2 percent of Switzerland's land area.

The religious Reformation came from Zurich in 1524, and during the subsequent five years all Thurgau's catholic parishes converted to Protestantism. From 1529 until 1531 the lands of Thurgau forbade all catholic worship. The victory of the catholic Cantons over the Reformed Alliance in the 2nd Kappel War (see Canton Zurich below) resulted in either the re-catholicizing of territories that had converted to Protestantism, or the acceptance of confessional parity (co-existence of both within the same territory) in 1531.

From 1531 the lands of Thurgau allowed both worships. After a few years of forced Protestantism, many parishes converted back to Catholicism. Hence, the Canton has both catholic and reformed churches and chapels, often within close vicinity of each other. After 1531 many old churches from before the Reformation were used in confessional parity by both Catholics and Protestants. By the end of the 19th/beginning of the 20th century most of these parities were cancelled and separate churches were built.

## *Canton Zurich*

From Konstanz, km 5 to 28 of stage K3 are in protestant Canton Zurich.

In Canton Zurich the car license plates start with ZH and the people speak Swiss-German (greeting with *Grüezi*). The Canton was formed in 1351 and was named after its capital city, Zurich. Its coat-of-arms with the blue/white colors was designed in 1220; the diagonal division originates from 1389. The Canton has about 1.5 million inhabitants (18 percent) but covers only about 4 percent of Switzerland's land area.

The Swiss religious Reformation, which started in Zurich, had a big influence on the churches in the Canton. From 1525 all catholic worship was legally forbidden in the whole Canton. This resulted in the blind destruction of nearly all catholic religious icons (statues, altars, paintings, frescos, crosses, and so forth) in all its churches and chapels. This caused a significant loss of medieval religious art, without any consideration for their value and importance over the many preceding centuries.

Under leadership of Ulrich Zwingli, Canton Zurich tried to aggressively enforce the Reformation onto the neighboring catholic Cantons. He formed alliances with the other reformed Cantons (i.e. Bern, Basel, City of St. Gallen) and used military force to spread Protestantism. In 1531 a Reformed Alliance blocked all food deliveries to the catholic Cantons. They went to war over this with the City of Zurich and killed Ulrich Zwingli, the leader of the Swiss Reformation, on the battlefield (2nd Kappel War). The victory of the catholic Cantons over Zurich in the 2nd Kappel War dissolved the Reformed Alliance (1531).

For 270 years only protestant worship was allowed (Catholics were pursued, imprisoned, or fined when practicing their worship). This changed when Napoleon conquered Switzerland in 1798, and founded the Helvetic Republic, which stipulated freedom of religion. However, after the Republic Government stepped down in 1803, Canton Zurich limited this freedom again. It was not until 1848, at the formation of the Swiss Confederate Republic, that the country's constitution declared religious freedom for the whole of Switzerland. The first new catholic church (since 1525) was built in Canton Zurich in 1874.

## *Canton St. Gallen*

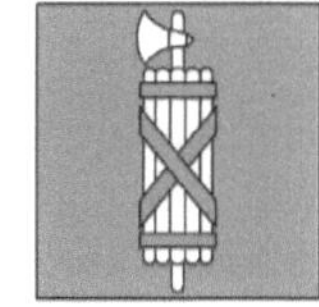

Stages R1a and R3 are completely, and stages R1b, R2, S1, and K3 are partially in Canton St. Gallen.

In Canton St. Gallen the car license plates start with SG and the people speak Swiss-German (greeting with *Grüezi*). The Canton was formed in 1803 and was named after its capital city, Sankt Gallen. The Canton was put together by combining nine territories that formerly belonged to other Cantons or were independent at the time of the creation of the Helvetic Republic (after the French invasion in 1798). About half of its territory originated from lands that were acquired over a period of more than 1'000 years by the Abbey-Kingdom of St. Gallen. The Canton's coat-of-arms (designed in 1803/1843) depicts a bundle of wooden rods with an axe in the middle, representing law and governance. This symbol dates from before the Roman Empire and is nowadays widely used by governments and law enforcers; for example, it can be found in the seal of the US Tax Court, in the emblems of the Spanish Civil Guard and Swedish Police, and on one side of the US 10-cent coin (1916-45). The Canton has about 0.5 million inhabitants (6 percent) and covers about 5 percent of Switzerland's land area. The city of St. Gallen encompasses a large agglomeration with several suburbs and has a population of around 80'000.

At the time of the religious Reformation in the 1520s-30s, the lands of St. Gallen (which were united into a new Canton in 1803) consisted of nine independent territories around the Abbey of St. Gallen. The Swiss Way of St. James passes through five of these former territories: territories owned by the Abbey-Kingdom of St. Gallen (stages R1a and R1b); City-Republic of St. Gallen (stages R1a and R1b); Toggenburg (stages R2 and R3); Uznach (stage R3); and the City-Republic of Rapperswil (stages R3 and K3).

The victory of the catholic Cantons over the Reformed Alliance in the 2nd Kappel War (see Canton Zurich above) resulted in either the re-catholicizing of territories that had converted to Protestantism, or the acceptance of confessional parity (co-existence of both within the same territory) in 1531. Consequently, the Reformation had a different impact on each of the territories of Canton St. Gallen:

- most of the territories of the Abbey-Kingdom stayed catholic, though some initially converted to Protestantism (1528), but converted back to Catholicism in 1531;
- the City-Republic of St. Gallen converted to Protestantism (1528);
- Toggenburg allowed confessional parity;
- Uznach initially converted to Protestantism (1528), but converted back to Catholicism in 1531;
- the independent City-Republic of Rapperswil stayed catholic: under patronage of the catholic House of Habsburg-Austria, the City resisted the Reformation forces coming from Zurich.

## *Canton Appenzell Ausserrhoden*

From Rorschach, the last 2 km of stage R1b and the first 9 km of stage R2 are in protestant Canton Appenzell Ausserrhoden.

In Canton Appenzell Ausserrhoden the car license plates start with AR and the people speak Swiss-German (greeting with *Grüezi*). Canton Appenzell was formed in 1513, when it made itself independent from the Abbey-Kingdom of St. Gallen. The name Appenzell originates from 'abbot's cell', meaning estate of the abbot, from the time that the St. Gallen Abbey owned the lands. In 1597 the Canton split in two half-Cantons: Appenzell Innerrhoden (AI) and Appenzell Ausserrhoden (AR). The name 'Inner Rhoden' translates to inner districts, and 'Ausser Rhoden' to outer districts. Canton Appenzell Ausserrhoden does not have a formally named capital city, but its government is based in Herisau. Its coat-of-arms depicts a male bear with the letters U and R. The male bear dates from 1403, when it was identical to the coat-of-arms of the Abbey of St. Gallen. The letters U and R were added in 1835: U stands for Ussere (outer) and R for Rhoden (district). The Canton has about 55'000 inhabitants (0.6 percent) and covers about 0.6 percent of Switzerland's land area. The half-Canton is the 6th smallest of the 26 Swiss Cantons.

At the time of the religious Reformation in 1525, Canton Appenzell split in two opposing beliefs. The territory that later became Appenzell Ausserrhoden converted to Protestantism, while the territory that later became Appenzell Innerrhoden remained catholic. This caused increasing religious tensions and opposite views on their politics and representation outside the Canton. In 1597 these tensions were resolved with the split of the Canton in two half-Cantons. During the Reformation in Appenzell Ausserrhoden, all catholic icons such as altars, paintings, crucifixes, and statues were removed from its churches.

## *Canton Schwyz*

Stages 4 and S2 are completely and stage S1 is partially in catholic Canton Schwyz.

In Canton Schwyz the car license plates start with SZ and the people speak Swiss-German (greeting with *Grüezi*). The Canton was formed in 1291 and was named after its capital city, Schwyz. Together with the Cantons Uri and Unterwalden (nowadays split in Nidwalden and Obwalden) the Canton founded the first Swiss Confederation (a defensive alliance) in 1291. For this reason, these Cantons are called the original Cantons or Ur-Cantons. Its coat-of-arms dates from 1240, when it was a fully red war-flag. The small white cross was added in 1815. The Canton has around 160'000 inhabitants (2 percent) and covers about 2 percent of Switzerland's land area.

At the time of the religious Reformation in the 1520s-30s, Canton Schwyz, being conservative catholic, strongly rejected the Protestantism coming from Zurich. Canton Schwyz remained catholic and forbade Protestantism. By 1650 the Canton was pursuing and imprisoning Protestants on its territory and confiscating their assets when they fled to Canton Zurich.

The Canton's strive for independence from the protestant Cantons of the Swiss Confederation culminated in the formation of an alliance with six other catholic Cantons (*Sonderbund*) in 1845. This caused a civil war (***Sonderbund* War**) based on a religious dispute. The *Sonderbund* wanted to defend their catholic autonomy against a centralization of authority by the liberal Swiss Confederation, mainly consisting of protestant progressive Cantons led by Bern. Fifteen Confederate Cantons put together an army and defeated the *Sonderbund* alliance in 1847 (in a battle with only very few casualties). Up to that time Switzerland as a country consisted of loosely organized and independent Cantons. The victory resulted in the Confederates solidifying their power through a new Federal Constitution in 1848, limiting the autonomy of the Cantons and bringing them under one modern roof; the Swiss Federal State was born.

At the formation of the Swiss Confederation freedom of religion for the whole of Switzerland was declared in the country's constitution. Still, Canton Schwyz remained conservative catholic: you will come across many catholic chapels and churches, but hardly any protestant ones on its territory.

# KONSTANZ
# TO
# EINSIEDELN

# Stage K1: Konstanz to Märstetten 16 km

*The Way of the Schwaben*

## *Route stats*

| | *Distance in km* | *Time in hrs:min* |
|---|---|---|
| *Route in Konstanz (DE)* | 1.0 | 0:10 |
| Signposted route nr. 4 | 12.8 | 2:30 |
| Churches/chapels | 1.6 | 1:00 |
| Points of interest | 0.2 | 0:15 |
| Rest | | 0:15 |
| Stage K1 | 15.6 | 4:10 |

In case you hike this stage as a daytrip, you need to add 500 meters in Konstanz and 1.4 km in Märstetten (from and to the train stations). The above duration assumes a start at around 12:30, after sightseeing at the basilica of Konstanz and a lunch break.

| | |
|---|---|
| Ascent/descent/total | +257 / -227 / 484 altitude meters |
| Lowest/highest altitude | 400 / 551 meters |
| Pathway/condition | easy / easy |
| Churches/chapels | Konstanz (2), Kreuzlingen, Bernrain, Märstetten |
| Monasteries | none |
| Points of Interest | Schnetz Gate, Ruins Castle of Schleifenrain, Caste of Altenklingen |

## *Route summary*

Stage K1 is in **Canton Thurgau**, which allowed confessional parity.

Stage K1 guides you out of the Lake Constance basin, over the rolling foothills of the pre-Alps, to Märstetten near the Thur River valley.

With less than 16 km this first stage of the Way of St. James through Switzerland is relatively short, because of the time needed to visit the basilica (former cathedral) in Konstanz, which only opens for sightseeing at 10:00 in the morning. It is easy to spend two hours there, so that the day's hike starts around 12:30 (after lunch). With only the afternoon left for hiking, the 16 km ensure a relaxed warm-up for the tougher hiking days to come.

Stage K1 starts at the former Cathedral of Konstanz and goes through the shopping streets of the historical center. The route crosses the small German-Swiss border to Kreuzlingen and leaves the Konstanz/Kreuzlingen agglomeration at km 3.4. From Kreuzlingen the route gradually ascends a hill range called the *Seerücken* ('back of the lake'), which stretches from east to west, south of Lake Constance. It is the first hill of the pre-Alps, with an average elevation of 500 to 600 meters. The Way of St. James crosses over the *Seerücken* (in a southern direction) at an elevation of 551 meters at km 7. From this highest point of the day the route gradually descends to the Kemmen River valley (*Kemmental*). A short ascent on the western flanks of the *Ottenberg* leads out of the Kemmen valley. On the southern side of the Ottenberg lies the wide Thur River valley. The end of stage K1 in Märstetten lies halfway the descent from the Ottenberg to the Thur River valley.

With only 484 altitude meters the route is on gradually ascending and descending pathways. The pathways are easy, on gravel and tarmac country roads through open fields and patches of forest. The signposted route nr. 4 avoids the towns and only goes through small settlements. The route does not even pass through Märstetten. You will need to make a detour from the signposted route nr. 4, and go towards the west for 1 km, to get to the endpoint of stage K1, at the reformed St. James church in Märstetten.

## *Getting to the starting point*

Konstanz in Germany is easily accessible by train from Zurich Airport. A direct train (IR 75 – direction *Konstanz*) departs every 46 minutes past the hour and gets you to Konstanz in 1hr:4min. An indirect train (IC 8 – direction *Romanshorn*) leaves the airport every 16 minutes past the hour and takes 1hr:20min (with a change in *Weinfelden* to the S14 – direction *Konstanz*). A ticket costs CHF 30, which you can buy at the Zurich Airport train station. For the up-to-date timetable and further details please refer to *https://www.sbb.ch/en/buying/pages/fahrplan/fahrplan.xhtml.*

Konstanz has adequate accommodation possibilities to arrive the evening before the start of your pilgrimage. An inn in the historic town offers low-priced accommodation (Glückseeligkeit Herberge; Neugasse 20, 78462 Konstanz; tel. 07531 9911366; www.herberge-konstanz.de; anfrage@herberge-konstanz.de). Tourist information at the Konstanz train station may also help you find the right accommodation (www.konstanz-tourismus.de).

Alternatively, you can arrive by train in the morning. The Tourist Information Office (at the Konstanz train station) opens at 09:00 in the morning, and the sightseeing areas and the information counter at the Konstanz basilica open at 10:00 in the morning (mid of March until end of October). So, there is no need to arrive extra early; though it would provide an opportunity to have a good breakfast at one of the many cafes before starting your pilgrimage. Do not forget to bring your passport as you will be crossing the Swiss-German border.

The start of the Way of St. James is at the basilica. Tourist Information can give you directions and a map, or simply follow the signaling to the *Münster* from the train station. The basilica is about 500 meters north of the train station.

## *Route Map and Profile*

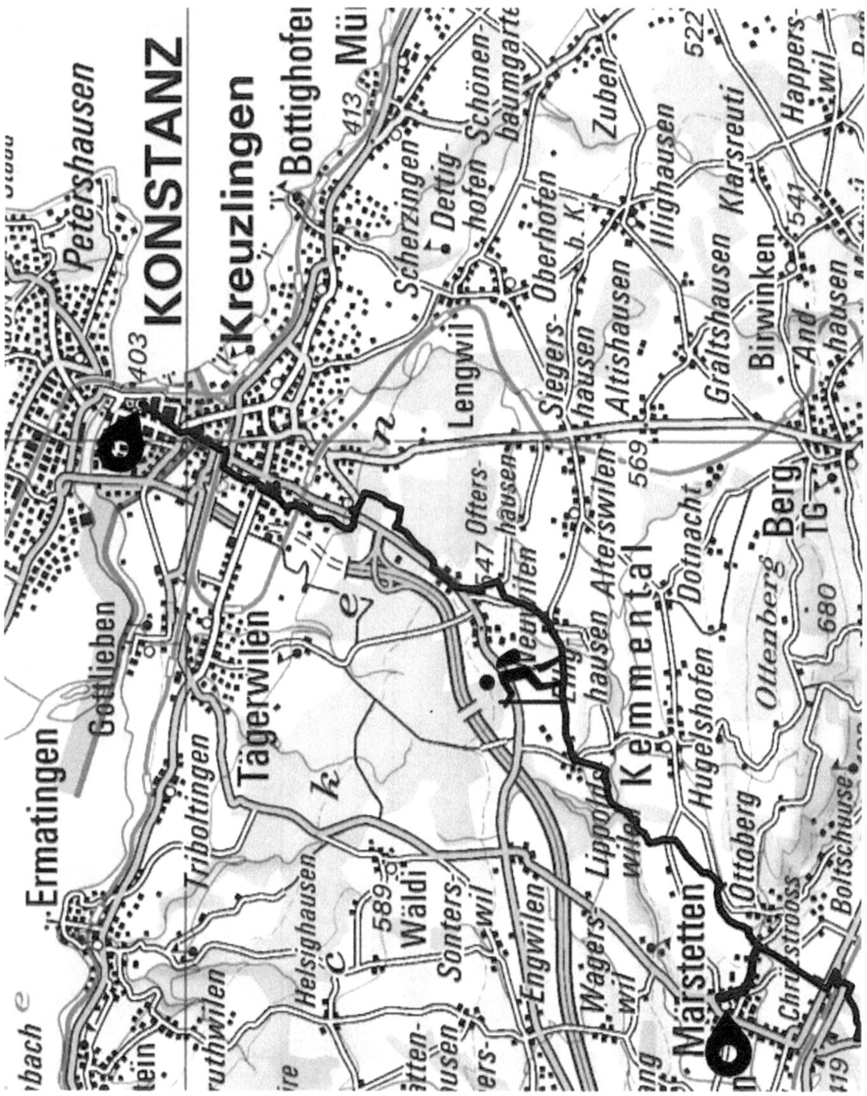

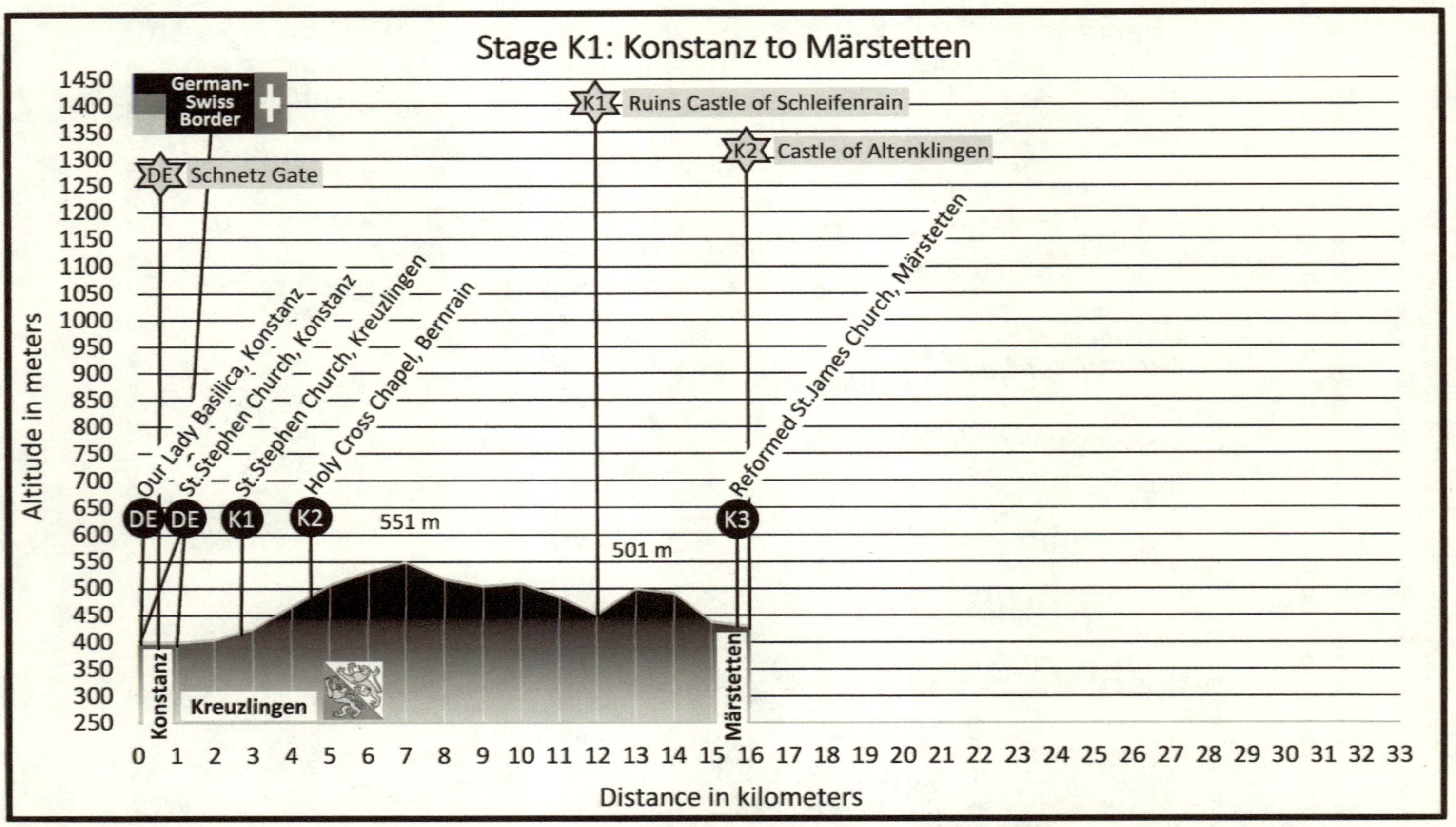
Stage K1: Konstanz to Märstetten
German-Swiss Border
DE Schnetz Gate
K1 Ruins Castle of Schleifenrain
K2 Castle of Altenklingen
Our Lady Basilica, Konstanz
St.Stephen Church, Konstanz
St.Stephen Church, Kreuzlingen
Holy Cross Chapel, Bernrain
Reformed St.James Church, Märstetten
DE
DE
K1
K2
K3
551 m
501 m
Konstanz
Kreuzlingen
Märstetten
Altitude in meters
1450
1400
1350
1300
1250
1200
1150
1100
1050
1000
950
900
850
800
750
700
650
600
550
500
450
400
350
300
250
0 1 2 3 4 5 6 7 8 9 10 11 12 13 14 15 16 17 18 19 20 21 22 23 24 25 26 27 28 29 30 31 32 33
Distance in kilometers

## *Hiking the Route*

Although the basilica opens its doors early in the morning, the areas of interest for sightseeing are only accessible from 10:00 until 18:00 (Sundays 12:30 until 18:30). These are also the opening times of the tourist counter and souvenir shop inside the basilica (on the right, immediately after entering through the main entrance doors). The counter and the tower are open from mid of March until end of October. You can easily spend two hours (from 10:00) sightseeing at the basilica. Information tables in German and English explain the history of the features and the area.

### **Our Lady Basilica, Konstanz** (Unser Lieber Frau Basilika) **DE**

Münsterplatz, 78462 Konstanz, Germany

Our Lady

The stamp of the basilica, preprinted on a tiny sticker, lies on a bookshelf left of the main entrance. The Way of St. James (*Jakobsweg*) stamp can be obtained at either the tourist counter of the basilica or the Konstanz Tourist Information Office at the train station. You need to ask for it at the counters.

The former cathedral has a Gothic architecture and is dedicated to the Virgin Mary. A church was first mentioned in the 7th century and parts of the cathedral were built as early as 940, with main reconstructions and extensions undertaken during the five subsequent centuries. The cathedral, with the attached monastery, was overseen by the Konstanz Bishops between 940 and 1821. In 1821 the Bishop's seat in Konstanz was dissolved and relocated to the German town Freiburg in 1827 (after which the designation of cathedral was removed). In 1955 Pope Pius XII granted the former cathedral the title Basilica.

Between 1414 and 1418 Konstanz and the cathedral hosted the **Council of Constance** (*Konstanzer Konzil*), making the city the religious, scientific, and cultural center of Europe during those years. It was the most important medieval assembly of the Catholic Church. Since 1378 two and from 1410 even three men simultaneously named themselves Pope, and were claiming to be the earthly representative of God. This Papal Schism resulted in a split of the Catholic Church. The Council of Constance aimed to resolve this schism by having a conclave elect one Pope in 1417. This was the only Conclave ever held north of the Alps, and resulted in the election of Pope Martin V.

The basilica has many interesting features:

- the wood carvings of the two main entrance doors. Notice the metal scallop inlay in the floor in front of the two doors.

- the many paintings, sculptures, and other catholic artwork.

- the view over Konstanz and its lake from the top of the bell tower. The admission fee is EUR 2, to be paid at the tourist counter. A stairway with 193 steps leads to the first level observatory at a height of 40 meters, and another 54 steps lead to the second level at a height of 52 meters. The tower's massive bells toll every 15 minutes; it might be best to avoid them when tolling the whole hour.

- the St. Margaret chapel, dating from the year 1000, with its frescos and sarcophagus.
- the crypt subterranean level, believed to have been part of the first stone church built in the 8th century. The crypt contains the tomb of St. Pelagius, with relics believed to have been brought from Rome to Konstanz around

850. A unique artwork of a two-meter-high round copperplate from the 10th century depicts Christ in an unusual way.

- the cloisters, dating from around 1300, with its walls decorated with memorial paintings, and the two large sandstone sculptures (1855) of St. Conrad and St. Pelagius.
- the many colorful stained-glass windows.

- the St. Conrad chapel, the burial chapel of Bishop Conrad of Konstanz (975); the St. Peter and Paul chapel; the St. Sylvester chapel; the St. Barbara chapel; and the St. Blasius chapel with its winged altar from 1524.
- the St. Maurice rotunda, a round burial chamber containing a twelve-sided sandstone structure surrounding a sarcophagus, believed to date from around 1250. Statues of the Twelve Apostles, with their books and symbols, stand on the twelve sides at the top of the structure. One of them is St. James, holding six pilgrim walking canes and six pilgrim bags decorated with scallops.

After sightseeing leave the basilica through the southern doors to go to a square (*Pfalzgarten*). That square contains the famous Way of St. James signpost, indicating 2'340 km to Santiago de Compostela. From here the route is also signposted as the **Schwabenweg**. The route derived its name from a region in the south of Germany called Schwaben. Originating from the medieval Duchy of Swabia, the people from southern Germany were called 'Schwaben', hence the Way of the Schwaben (*Schwabenweg*).

From the square follow the first sign of the Schwabenweg in the direction of Märstetten. It guides you to a shopping street where, after 100 meters, you see the St. Stephen Church on your right. To enter it you need to walk around to the western main entrance.

**St. Stephen Church, Konstanz** (St. Stephans Kirche) **DE**

Sankt-Stephans-Platz, 78462 Konstanz, Germany

St. Stephen

The present church was built in the 15th century. It is believed that a predecessor church was already built in the 7th century. From the perspective of timelines and major events and construction, the church shares a similar history with the former cathedral. Whereas the former cathedral was used by Konstanz's Bishops, the common people visited the St. Stephen church (which was the city church).

The church has artful stained-glass windows, wall and ceiling frescos, woodwork, ironwork, and statues.

After leaving the church turn back to the shopping street and continue to follow the route for 600 meters, until you arrive at a medieval town gate.

The **Schnetz Gate** (*Schnetztor*) and connecting walls are 14th century fortifications that protected the southern side of the medieval town Konstanz. Together with two other towers these are the only remaining medieval fortifications of Konstanz. The half-timbered northern facade of the tower matches the architectural style of the house south of the gate. The fresco fragments inside the gate date from the 17th century.

After the gate cross the street at the zebra crossing, go straight, and at the road split keep to the right. One kilometer from the basilica you arrive at the small border crossing, where you enter Switzerland in **Canton Thurgau**.

At the **German-Swiss border crossing** there is hardly any checking of travel documents, because Switzerland is part of Schengen. The custom officials mostly focus on Swiss shoppers bringing lower priced goods from Konstanz into Switzerland (up to a value CHF 300 per person the Swiss obtain VAT refunds amounting up to 19 percent of the price of a product). On weekends you will see long queues of cars with Swiss number plates at this border crossing (all getting their VAT-refund forms stamped by the customs officials).

After crossing the border, you see an information table explaining the **hiking signaling** along the Swiss Way of St. James. The table explains (in German) the general yellow hiking signs indicating the direction, time, and destination. The yellow arrows or diamonds confirm the route. The ViaJacobi green nr. 4 signs with blue border indicate the direction of the Way of St. James through Switzerland. The yellow scallop against a blue background indicates the direction towards Santiago de Compostela. The white signs indicate the Schwabenweg (only in Canton Thurgau). In stage K1 you will mostly follow the small white signs indicating the Schwabenweg. At critical locations or direction changes you will usually see the bigger white Schwabenweg signs together with the yellow signs and the green/blue nr. 4 squares of the Swiss ViaJacobi.

At this border crossing **Road Nr. 1** starts. This road nr. 1 leads from the German-Swiss border in Konstanz/Kreuzlingen via Zurich and Bern to the Swiss-French border south of Geneva. The Swiss Way of St. James closely follows this road in the first half of stage K1, in stages 16 to 20, and in stage P2. Road nr. 1 continues 343 km from here to the French border, south of Geneva. The Swiss Way of St. James will continue nearly 500 km, taking a different route until converging with road nr. 1 in Moudon (at the end of stage 15).

The route follows road nr. 1 southward towards the Kreuzlingen train station. When the road makes a sharp right curve, the route crosses the street and takes the underpass to the other side of the railway station. After the underpass you turn right, cross the roundabout (of road nr. 1), and after 200 meters turn left. The next

1.3 km you walk on pavement through an urban area of Kreuzlingen, past houses and industry, until you reach a forested narrow valley.

Hidden behind the trees on the left is the St. Stephen church of Kreuzlingen. You need to make a 200-meter detour from the signposted route nr. 4 to get to this church. A narrow footpath on your left leads through a small patch of trees and crosses the small *Saubach* stream. Follow the footpath up a small hill to arrive at the St. Stephen Church in Kreuzlingen (at km 2.7).

**St. Stephen Church, Kreuzlingen** (St. Stefan Kirche) **K-1**

- Bernrainstrasse 8, 8280 Kreuzlingen
- St. Stephen
- In a plastic slip hanging on the notice board, in a recess left of the entrance
- Before the political separation of Kreuzlingen and Konstanz, the local Catholics attended services at the St. Stephen church in Konstanz. After the official border was established in 1818, they attended services at the chapel in Bernrain (see below). When this chapel became too small, the St. Stephen church was built in 1900-03.
- The church has unique interior decorations made of majolica, i.e. tin-glazed ceramics with a shiny finish. Majolica was very popular for the decoration of pottery in the Renaissance period; its name is believed to be derived from the Mediterranean Island Majorca, which was a transit station for the transport of such merchandise in the 15th century. Normally majolica is applied to small pottery such as plates; in this church it is applied on a large scale to the pulpit, baptismal font, high-altar, side-altars, and crucifixion way stations.

  These are all unique masterpieces of ceramic art, nowhere else found along the Way of St. James through Switzerland. Have a closer look at the reliefs of the high-altar: below the altar table a Christmas manger relief; above the altar a Sacred Heart relief (initially the church was to be dedicated to the Sacred Heart of Jesus – *Herz-Jesu*).

After walking back the same 200 meters to the route, the trail continues to pass underneath elevated railway tracks, after which the path enters a forest. The forest is very narrow, following a small and shallow stream (*Saubach*). The trail through the forest gradually slopes up and ascends 55 meters over 1 km. Without noticing you passed by two chateaus on the hills left and right of the forested valley (one on the eastern side called Bernegg and one on the western side called Ebersberg). Nowadays they are residential houses, without fortifications, in private ownership.

You are on the **Crucifixion Way** (*Kreuzweg*) that leads up to the Holy Cross chapel of Bernrain. The 15 crucifixion way stations were created to commemorate the 100-year existence of the St. Stephen church of Kreuzlingen in 2003. They connect the church to the chapel, along a row of thirteen 1.5-meter-high sequentially numbered stations, each 50 meters apart on the pathway through the forest. After a wooden bridge and up steps, the path turns right, and at the end of the forest trail you cross road nr. 1 (here called *Bernrainstrasse*). Station 14 of the crucifixion way (Jesus' body is placed in the tomb) is on the right side of the gravel front yard. The final and 15th station (Jesus' resurrection) is right of the chapel's entrance. You arrive at the Holy Cross Chapel in Bernrain at km 4.5.

**K-2 Holy Cross Chapel, Bernrain** (Heiligkreuz Kapelle)

- Bernrainstrasse 69, 8280 Kreuzlingen
- On a shelf fixed to the right wall, just behind the entrance door. The stamp is preprinted on a sticker and depicts the Holy Cross of the high-altar.
- The chapel was built on the site of a road cross in 1388, based on the legend of the Wonder Cross. In 1384 boys from Konstanz were collecting firewood in the nearby forest. When they rested at the road cross, one boy started making fun of

the road cross and insulting God. According to legend, this boy's hand was suddenly stuck to the cross and he was not able to free himself anymore. Only after his mother and other people from Konstanz prayed to God, promising a pilgrimage to Einsiedeln, was the boy's hand freed from the cross. The chapel was built on the site of the road cross and became a medieval pilgrimage destination.

During the Reformation in 1527 the Wonder Cross was removed and kept at the St. Catherine Convent in Konstanz. It was returned in 1647.

The chapel belonged to the St. Stephen parish of Konstanz until 1818 (when the political border was established that separated Konstanz and Kreuzlingen). Between 1819 and 1903 the chapel served as the parish church of Kreuzlingen, until the new St. Stephen church was built (see above). Since 1903 it has also served as the cemetery chapel of the St. Stephen church of Kreuzlingen (the cemetery is next to the chapel).

The oil painting (1598) on the left wall tells the legend of the Wonder Cross (*Wunderkreuz*). Nowadays the crucifix is at the center of the altar. Notice the Gothic masonry at the top of the windows, not seen very often in a baroque chapel.

From the chapel continue the route by turning left and immediately crossing the road. You enter the Bernrainhau forest and walk on a gravel path for 2 km, parallel to road nr. 1. Be on the lookout for the signposts, as not all of them are clearly visible; some are a bit hidden behind the trees and easy to overlook. The trail is mostly broad, though some parts are narrow in between bushes. The route crosses road nr. 1, which you follow for 500 meters to the village Schwaderloh. There you reach the highest point of this stage at 551 meters at km 7. The signpost directs to the left, where you follow a tarmac country road between agricultural fields for 3.3 km. You pass by several small settlements, but they offer no possibilities for refreshments. There is hardly any traffic on these rural roads, so hiking is relaxed, while enjoying the wide views over the fields. Canton Thurgau is well known for its apple and pear orchards.

At the settlement Lippoldswilen the trail leaves the country road. You make a left turn towards a forest. You are in the forest for about 1 km, first descending, then ascending. The trail descends to a low point of 453 meters, where you cross the

Kemmen stream (*Kemmenbach*) in the middle of a patch of forest. A narrow metal bridge covers the small stream and on your right is a small area for barbequing. At this location, 11.5 km from the basilica of Konstanz, a white signpost indicates 1hr:20min to Märstetten. A brown sign points left to castle ruins. With a small detour up the hill in the forest, you arrive at the ruins of the castle of Schleifenrain.

K-1

Not much is known of the history of the **ruins of the Castle of Schleifenrain** (*Burgruine Schleifenrain im Kemmental*). It is believed that a 12th century fortified tower stood on this site. This residential tower may have belonged to the Lords of Hugelshofen (first mentioned in 1176), who were in service of the Bishops of Konstanz. It is believed that the tower was used only for a short time and was abandoned after it burned down. It was never rebuilt, which explains the lack of medieval documentation about the castle. Excavations were carried out in the 1960s, when the wall foundations were conserved. These revealed the remnants of a nearly square tower (13.7 by 10.6 meters) with 2-meter-thick walls. East of the tower a defensive moat existed; with its dug-out dirt the castle hill was elevated by 3 to 5 meters, thereby protecting its foundations from being undermined by attackers. Between the moat and the tower even older wall foundations were found, which must have belonged to a predecessor fortified tower. Similar ruins of other medieval fortified towers, also without a documented history, are in close vicinity along the Kemmen stream valley.

About 500 meters after the forest you cross a small road in the settlement Riet. In the yard of a house on the right, dogs may start growling and barking while jumping against the fence. Fortunately, the fence is high enough. The next 2 km the route alternates between gravel and tarmac country roads that provide wide views over the agricultural landscape of Thurgau. You walk past sunflower fields, corn fields, wheat fields, meadows, and several half-timbered houses (*Fachwerkhäuser*).

The route gradually ascends to 501 meters on the Ottenberg, after which the path descends more steeply, until a sign directs you to the St. James church (*Jakobskirche*) and pilgrim inn (*Pilgerherberge*) of Märstetten. The town is to the right, whereas the signposted route nr. 4 continues straight down the hill. At this location you need to leave the signposted route nr. 4. A tarmac road leads to the northern part of Märstetten, where you arrive at the reformed St. James Church at km 15.6. Notice the municipal office in the medieval dark-wooden building with its geraniums, next to the church.

## **Reformed St. James Church, Märstetten** (Evangelische Kirche) K-3

- Kehlhofstrasse 5, 8560 Märstetten
- St. James the Greater
- On a table left of the entrance
- The first chapel was built by the Barons of Märstetten. Their lineage died out by the end of the 11th century, after which it is likely that their lands and chapel became the property of the Cathedral of Konstanz. The small chapel was first mentioned as a subsidiary of the Cathedral in 1155. The original chapel was replaced by the present church in the 13th or 14th century, when the chancel and bell tower were built; the chancel is in the base of the bell tower. The tower was heightened and the nave lengthened in 1487-89, determining its present-day appearance.

  During the Reformation in 1529 the church converted to Protestantism; all religious icons were removed, the walls were whitewashed, and its dedication to St. James was removed. The fact that it used to be dedicated to St. James indicates Märstetten's importance as a medieval pilgrimage station along the Swiss Way of St. James. During the Reformation the organ was removed as well, as religious chanting was not condoned.

  The lands of Thurgau partially reversed the influence of the Reformation, and from 1594 until 1795 the church was also shared with the catholic parish in confessional parity. Nowadays the church is still protestant, but also used for catholic services, as a good example of ecumenical collaboration.

Apart from the choir stalls and baptismal font, the chancel is empty; the nave only has pews, a pulpit, and a small organ).

The pale fresco on the arched wall, which separates the nave and the chancel, dates from 1460-70 and depicts the Last Judgement. Together with the frescos in the chancel (depicting the Christmas manger), they are the oldest and only decorations from before the Reformation, which were uncovered during renovations in 1975 (when the whitewash was removed).

The town Märstetten is small, with about 2'400 inhabitants. Since the middle ages it has been an agricultural town under three main rulers: the Barons of Märstetten, the Lords of Klingen, and the Cathedral of Konstanz. The Barons of Märstetten owned a castle (Altenburg) in the Kemmen valley, about 1.4 km northeast of the church. Similar to the Schleifenrain ruins, little is known of its history and nowadays only some wall foundations can be seen. The Lords of Klingen built their castle in the Kemmen valley about 1.2 km north of town.

The **Castle of Altenklingen** was first built by the Lords of Klingen in the 12th century. Like the former Castle of Schleifenrain, it was located in the Kemmen valley as part of a line of fortified towers in relatively close distance of each other. Wiborada of Klingen was a family member who was canonized as a Saint in 1047 (see stage R1a, church nr. R-10 in St. Gallen for her story). By the 16th century the castle was in ruins (just like the other ones). In 1585 Leonhard Zollikofer from St. Gallen acquired the castle ruins, demolished the last remains, and built the present castle. Today it is still owned by the Zollikofer family. Since it is private property, it cannot be accessed.

## *From the ending point*

The reformed St. James Church is the ending point of stage K1, about 1 km aside the signposted route nr. 4.

In case you are a day-hiker, you need to walk about 1.4 km from the church to the Märstetten train station. Walk to main road nr. 16, called *Kreuzlingerstrasse* (west of the church), and follow it southward along the *Bahnhofstrasse* until you get to the train station.

In case you are a thru-hiker and spend the night in Märstetten, you can stay at the pilgrim inn (300 meters south of the church). Follow the road southward and after 150 meters turn right. The pilgrim inn is at the town's square with the fountain. The building dates from the 18th century, but was used as a school until 1811, and by a blacksmith and other craftsmen from 1889 until 2003. Only since then has it served as a pilgrim inn again (Pilgerherberge Märstetten; Hubstrasse 2; tel. 071 657 29 74). Visit the website of the municipality (www.maerstetten.ch, page *Pilgerweg*) for more information. The pilgrim inn is open from 1 April until 31 October, daily from 17:00. An information leaflet at the door provides contact numbers, also for accommodation outside these periods. Check out www.jakobsweg.ch or www.viajacobi4.ch for the accommodation possibilities in Märstetten.

The pilgrim inn is a beautifully restored half-timbered house, of which there are many in Märstetten. Märstetten has several restaurants and guesthouses. You can buy provisions at the small Volg supermarket opposite the pilgrim inn.

## *The next Stage*

Stage K2 guides you from the Thur River valley over rolling hills to the foot of the Hörnli mountain. With 35 km, it is one of the longest hikes of all the stages of the Swiss Way of St. James. Read the next chapter to find out why and what that entails.

# Stage K2: Märstetten to Fischingen 35 km

*The Way to Saint Idda*

## *Route stats*

| | Distance in km | Time in hrs:min |
|---|---|---|
| Signposted route nr. 4 | 28.6 | 5:50 |
| Churches/chapels | 6.6 | 3:10 |
| Points of interest | | |
| Rest | | 1:00 |
| Stage K2 | 35.2 | 10:00 |

In case you hike this stage as a daytrip and start at the church of Märstetten, you need to add 1.4 km in Märstetten (to go from the train station to the church). In Fischingen you can take the bus to the Sirnach train station (14-minute drive).

Only four churches are directly along the signposted route nr. 4 (before arriving in Fischingen). The long distance of stage K2 is caused by detours to eight additional churches that are away from the signposted route. You can of course decide to skip certain detours to reduce the time required for stage K2.

| | |
|---|---|
| Ascent/descent/total | +582 / -387 / 969 altitude meters |
| Lowest/highest altitude | 416 / 666 meters |
| Pathway/condition | easy / difficult |
| Churches/chapels | Kaltenbrunnen, Affeltrangen (2), Tobel, St. Margarethen, Münchwilen (2), Sirnach (2), Oberwangen, Dussnang (2), Fischingen (3) |
| Monasteries | Former Commandry of the Knights of St. John Tobel, Benedictine Monastery Fischingen |
| Points of Interest | none |

## *Route summary*

Stage K2 continues in **Canton Thurgau**, which allowed confessional parity.

Stage K2 guides you from the Thur River valley over rolling hills to the foot of the Hörnli mountain.

Similar to stage K1, the second stage passes through several towns' outskirts and goes over rolling pre-Alp hills with agricultural fields and apple orchards. The total number of 969 altitude meters are spread over a long distance, without any steep ascents or descents. The closer you are getting to Fischingen, the narrower the valleys, the more forested, and the higher the elevation becomes (as you get closer to the foothills of the Hörnli mountain).

Only four churches are directly along the signposted route (before you arrive at the Abbey of Fischingen). If you also want to visit the churches in the towns along the route, you will need to make detours, away from route nr. 4, to eight additional churches (in Affeltrangen, Tobel, Münchwilen, Sirnach, and Dussnang). These add an extra 6.6 km. Because of the relatively long distance and the time needed at the 15 churches and chapels (including the Abbey in Fischingen), you will need to manage your pace, breaks, and visits to the churches. You may consider to skip a detour into a town to save time.

Stage K2 starts in Märstetten and, after an initial descent, the route crosses the flat plains of the Thur River valley for 3 km. Until km 16 the route follows road nr. 16 southwards over gently rolling hills. From km 21 (St. Margarethen) until km 35 (Fischingen) the route closely follows the Murg River (and road nr. 468.1). The first 5 km are directly alongside this river. This is relaxed hiking on shaded gravel pathways that gradually slope upwards. From km 29 the altitude meters increase, as the route becomes steeper, going up and down two hills through patches of forest. This is a prelude to stage K3; during the day you can already see the Hörnli mountain in the distance, coming closer and closer as you approach Fischingen. The Benedictine Abbey of Fischingen at the end of the stage is the highlight of the day and well worth the long-distance hike. This abbey has an exquisite baroque church and a beautifully decorated baroque chapel that contains the tomb of St. Idda.

## *Getting to the starting point*

In case you hike stage K2 as a daytrip, you can arrive by train at the Märstetten station. From there you have two possibilities. You can walk 1.4 km along the *Bahnhofstrasse* (road nr. 16 to the north) to the starting point at the reformed church. Alternatively, you can cross to the southern side of the railway station and follow road nr. 16 (*Amlikonerstrasse*) for 700 meters in a southern direction towards Amlikon, until you get to the signposted route. This is the shortest way to the signposted route nr. 4, which can save 4.3 km from your day hike and may serve as a buffer to visit the churches that require a detour from the signposted route.

In case you spent the night in Märstetten, just make your way back to the signposted route, the way you came the night before.

## *Route Map and Profile*

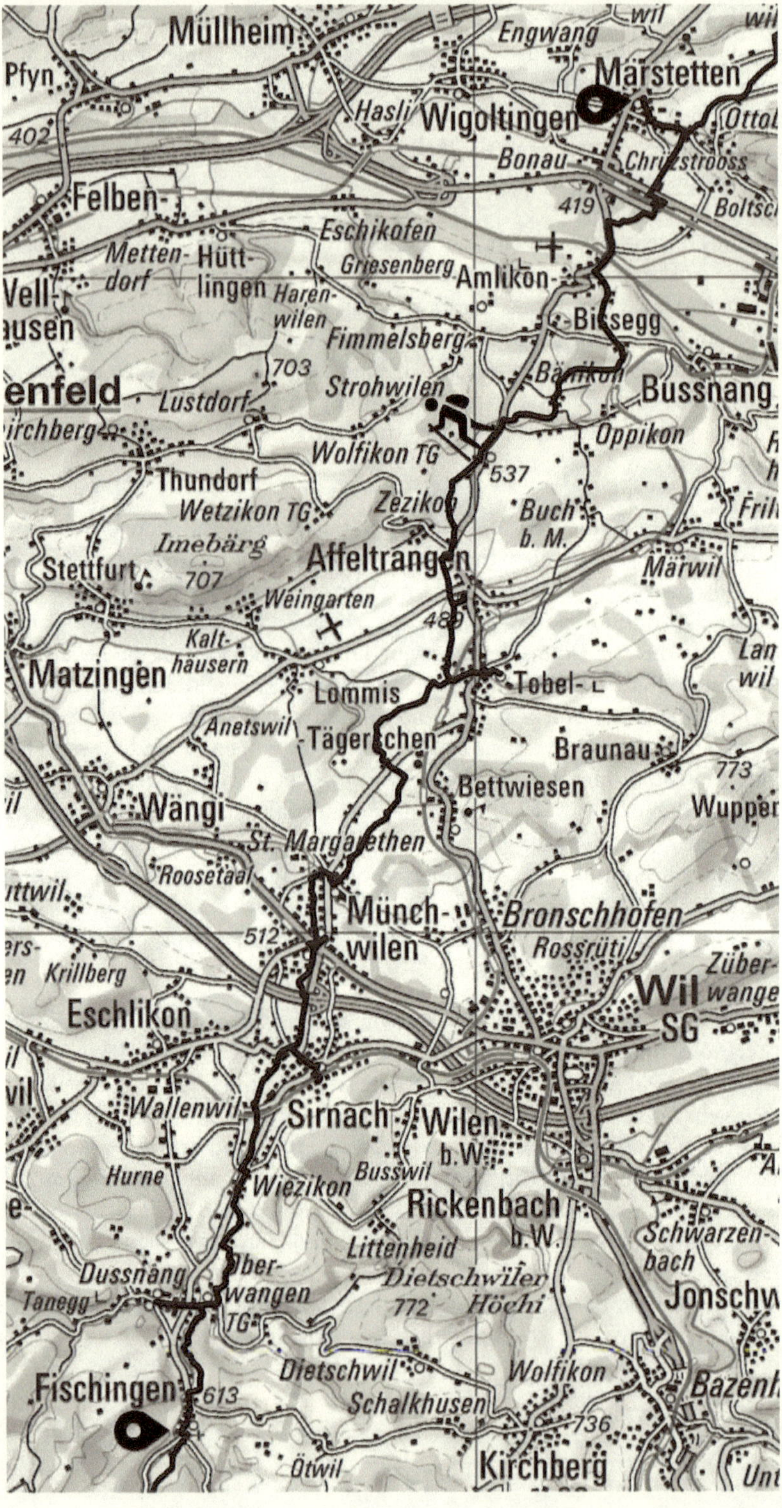
Müllheim
Engwang
Pfyn
Märstetten
Hasli
Wigoltingen
402
Bonau
Felben
419
Eschikofen
Metten-
dorf
Hütt-
lingen
Griesenberg
Amlikon
Haren-
wilen
Fimmelsberg
703
Strohwilen
Bussnang
Lustdorf
Oppikon
Wolfikon TG
537
Thundorf
Wetzikon TG
Buch
b. M.
Imebärg
Affeltrangen
Märwil
Stettfurt
707
Weingarten
Kalt-
häusern
Matzingen
Tobel-
Lommis
Anetswil
Braunau
773
Bettwiesen
Wängi
St. Margarethen
Roosetaal
Münch-
wilen
Bronschhofen
512
Rossrüti
Krillberg
Züber-
Wil
SG
Eschlikon
Wallenwil
Sirnach
Wilen
b.W.
Hurne
Busswil
Wiezikon
Rickenbach
b.W.
Schwarzen-
bach
Littenheid
Dussnang
Dietschwiler
Tanegg
772
Höchi
TG
Dietschwil
Wolfikon
Fischingen
613
Schalkhusen
736
Ötwil
Kirchberg

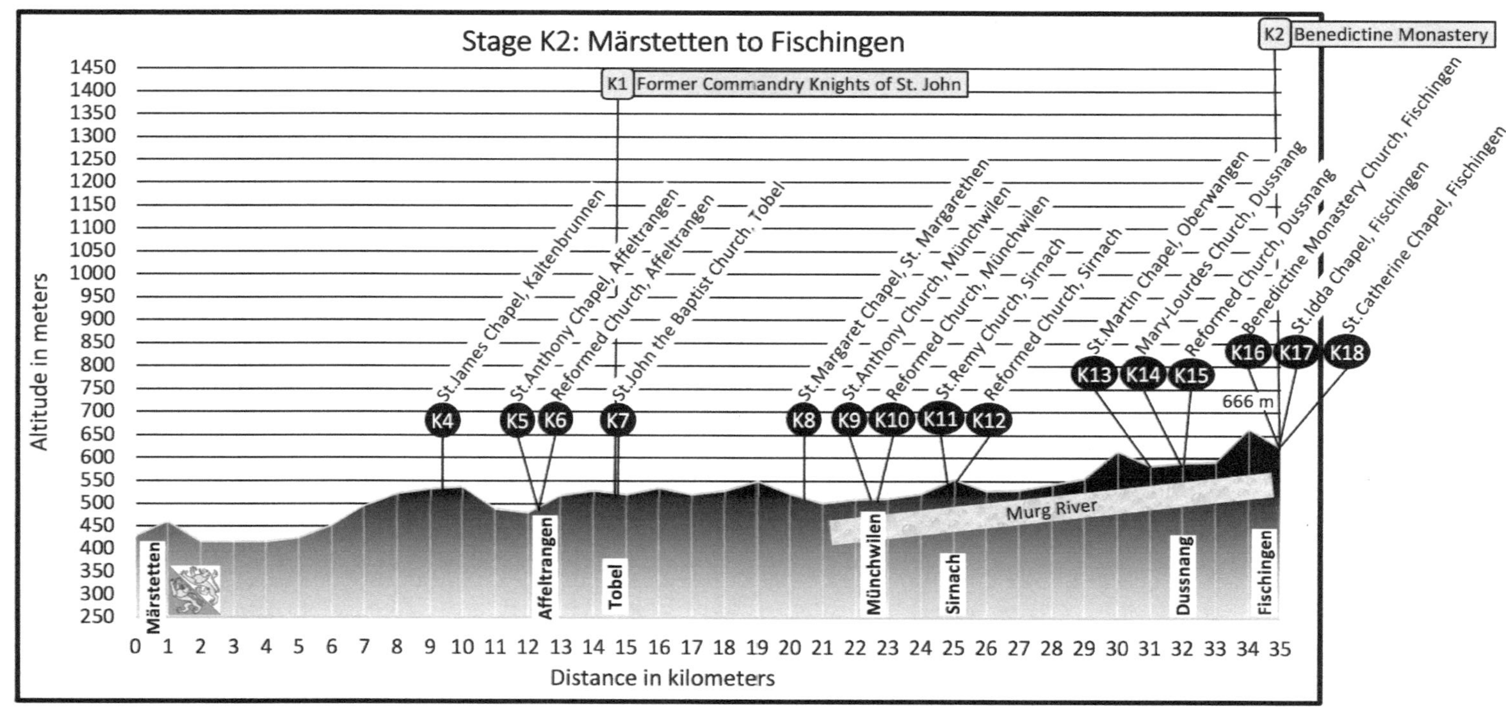
Stage K2: Märstetten to Fischingen
K1 Former Commandry Knights of St. John
K2 Benedictine Monastery
K4 St.James Chapel, Kaltenbrunnen
K5 St.Anthony Chapel, Affeltrangen
K6 Reformed Church, Affeltrangen
K7 St.John the Baptist Church, Tobel
K8 St.Margaret Chapel, St. Margarethen
K9 St.Anthony Church, Münchwilen
K10 Reformed Church, Münchwilen
K11 St.Remy Church, Sirnach
K12 Reformed Church, Sirnach
K13 St.Martin Chapel, Oberwangen
K14 Mary-Lourdes Church, Dussnang
K15 Reformed Church, Dussnang
K16 Benedictine Monastery Church, Fischingen
K17 St.Idda Chapel, Fischingen
K18 St.Catherine Chapel, Fischingen
666 m
Märstetten
Affeltrangen
Tobel
Münchwilen
Sirnach
Dussnang
Fischingen
Murg River
Altitude in meters
1450 1400 1350 1300 1250 1200 1150 1100 1050 1000 950 900 850 800 750 700 650 600 550 500 450 400 350 300 250
Distance in kilometers
0 1 2 3 4 5 6 7 8 9 10 11 12 13 14 15 16 17 18 19 20 21 22 23 24 25 26 27 28 29 30 31 32 33 34 35

## *Hiking the Route*

From the reformed church in Märstetten follow the tarmac road for 1 km towards the east to get back to the signposted route. From there the route continues its descent from the western flanks of the Ottenberg, until you get to the plains of the Thur River valley. The following 3 km are flat. The route goes through an underpass below the railway tracks, through a small patch of forest, some grassland, along road nr. 16, and across the Thur River to the village Amlikon.

The **Thur River** has a length of 131 km and flows into the Rhine River at the Swiss-German border. It is the main river in northeastern Switzerland; Canton Thurgau was named after it. Until 1727 pilgrims crossed here by ferry; it was not until 1727 that the first bridge was built. A covered bridge from 1821 was destroyed by a flood in 1910. The present concrete bridge dates from 1995.

A small supermarket is located on the corner, where you have to turn left. It is one of the few opportunities directly along today's route (without having to make a detour) to buy provisions. After having turned left, follow the tarmac road for 3 km, steadily ascending to an altitude of 515 meters when you reach the settlement Holzhäusern. At the beginning in Amlikon the route is marked by red-colored tarmac pavement on the right of the road. Soon you walk on the road itself, but there is hardly any traffic. The road follows the Hünikerbach (a small stream), alternating between its left and right bank, on the edge of patches of forest, apple tree orchards, and through farmlands.

After Holzhäusern the trail turns right onto a gravel road through farmlands (for 900 meters), until you get back to road nr. 16 in Maltbach. Turn left on the road and after 700 meters you arrive at the St. James Chapel in Kaltenbrunnen, 9.4 km from the church in Märstetten.

## St. James Chapel, Kaltenbrunnen (St. Jakobus Kapelle) K-4

- Kaltenbrunnen 4, 8514 Affeltrangen
- St. James the Greater, St. John the Baptist
- On the last right-side pew. The stamp lies next to four blue-covered volumes of pilgrim guestbooks, the oldest dating from August 2007. It is interesting to flip through the pages, and read the prayers and comments of other pilgrims who visited over the years.
- The catholic chapel was built by a private person called Lauchenauer in 1662. He purposely put the chapel in a private foundation to ensure the protestant church of Affeltrangen would not be able to turn it into a reformed chapel (at that time Affeltrangen did not have a catholic priest). The foundation contained enough funds for the maintenance and hiring of a catholic priest for monthly services at the chapel. This first chapel was dilapidated when the curator of the foundation had it demolished and a new one built in 1780. This is the current chapel, which was renovated several times since.
- The chapel has a simple interior. Two beautiful stained-glass windows (dating from 1951) in the chancel light up the chapel in a bright array of colors. The left window depicts St. James, the right St. John.

After the chapel the route turns right, away from road nr. 16. The trail is parallel to the road past corn fields and apple trees on a tarmac underground for about 1.6 km, before turning back to road nr. 16. At the highest point of this parallel road you have a view of a mountain range (with the Hörnli mountain) at the southern horizon. You will be passing over the Hörnli mountain in stage K3 from Fischingen to Rapperswil.

You turn right past a gas station and follow road nr. 16 for about 250 meters. The route crosses the Lauche stream and immediately turns right. You walk past a newly built residential area. On the right you find five newly carved stones with themes from the Way of St. James. At the end you turn left and continue on a gravel road parallel to road nr. 16. In the distance you can already see the steeple with the colored tiles of the church in Affeltrangen. At a settlement with a few farmhouses called Kreuzegg, a farm road leads to the left (east). At this location you need to briefly leave the signposted route to go to a chapel and a church. After 200 meters you pass by a large chapel on the left corner of the *Kreuzeggstrasse*. At km 12.3 you arrive at the St. Anthony Chapel of Affeltrangen.

**K-5 St. Anthony Chapel, Affeltrangen** (St. Antonius Kapelle)

- Kirchweg 16, 9556 Affeltrangen
- St. Anthony of Padua
- The catholic chapel was built in 1933-34, to serve the Catholics of Affeltrangen. Until that time, they had to use the protestant church, 50 meters down the road (see below), in confessional parity. Building their own chapel gave the Catholics of Affeltrangen independence from the Protestants and enabled them to restore the religious icons, statues, paintings, and altars, which had not been possible in the reformed church.
- The chapel has a baroque interior. The chapel's doors are locked; it is only accessible during the services.

Continuing for 50 meters around the corner, you arrive at the reformed Church of Affeltrangen (at km 12.4).

**Reformed Church, Affeltrangen** (Evangelischer Kirche) **K-6**

- Kirchweg 5, 9556 Affeltrangen
- At the parish office (*Pfarramt*), in the white building south of the church
- The church was first mentioned in 1275. The lower part of the bell tower and parts of its fundament originate from the 13th/14th century. The chancel dates from the 15th century, while the stained-glass windows were placed in 1508 (restored in 1882). The catholic icons, statues, paintings, frescos, and altars from these centuries were all removed at the time of the Reformation in 1529. Until 1934 the church was also used for catholic services in confessional parity. The bell tower can be seen from afar, due to its colored tiles on the spire.
- The church has a typical protestant interior, limited to pews, pulpit, baptismal font (1696), and organ. The latter is located in the chancel instead of in the nave. The most beautiful and oldest pieces in the church are the two stained-glass windows. They are the restored originals from 1508 (see the date at the bottom-right). Have a closer look; they were financed by the former Commandry of the Knights of St. John in Tobel (see below).

From the church it is 250 meters back to the signposted route. The gravel road passes through open grasslands, wheat and corn fields, and apple orchards.

Near the town Tobel you reach a Schwabenweg signpost in white and blue, typical for Canton Thurgau. The signpost indicates it is still 2'315 km to Santiago de Compostela.

The signposted route nr. 4 does not pass through Tobel; it passes about 600 meters west of the town. If you want to visit Tobel's church and former Commandry of the Knights of St. John, you should not follow the sign towards the train station. Instead, you need to walk to the next signpost 100 meters down the trail, which directs to Tobel-Affeltrangen. From this post it is 1 km (with an ascent of 47 meters) in a western direction to the St. John church (*St. Johannes Kirche*). Cross the single train track, along the sports fields, until you get to road nr. 16. Cross the road and turn right along the Hartenauer stream. In front you see an unkept open space with grass, a large tree, and several buildings. To the left on a hill you see the church tower. At km 14.6 you arrive at the former Commandry of the Knights of St. John.

**K-1 Former Commandry of Knights of St. John, Tobel** (Johanniter Komturei)

- Komturei, 9555 Tobel
- Order of Knights of St. John
- The Commandry of the Knights of St. John in Tobel was established based on donations of lands (and income derived from these lands) by the Counts of Toggenburg in 1228. The location in Tobel was an important station along the pilgrimage route from Konstanz to Einsiedeln. Medieval pilgrims would have visited the commandry's church (see below), hospital, and accommodations. Here they would have prayed for a safe pilgrimage, gotten treated when ill, received meals, and spent the night under the protection of the local Knights of St. John. In medieval times Tobel (and most of Canton Thurgau) were the backlands of Konstanz and under authority of its Bishops and Cathedral.

  The commandery prospered for several centuries, but was severely weakened by the Reformation in 1529. The local population plundered the church and destroyed all altars, paintings, statues, and other catholic icons. During the ban of catholic worship in 1529-31, the Order left the commandry, but returned in 1532. They reconstructed the interior of the church and placed new altars and catholic icons in the subsequent decades. But this time was different from the time before the Reformation. The pilgrim streams had strongly reduced (as pilgrimage was not condoned by the Protestants), many of their fellow commandries in Switzerland had closed, and several parishes surrounding Tobel remained Protestant, causing friction. Decline set in, the number of Knights reduced, and by the end of the 17th century its buildings were in poor condition. In 1744-47 the present three-winged building was constructed to replace the old commandry that comprised an administrative building, hospital, and accommodations. The old church on the site had already been demolished and replaced by a new church on the hill in 1707 (see below). The commandry was surrounded by a fortified wall with a watchtower. At the time the new church was constructed in 1706, the moat around the watchtower was filled. Nowadays only the fortified watchtower remains, used as the base of the church's bell tower.

As Napoleon conquered Switzerland and Malta (with the seat of the Order), the last commander left Tobel in 1798. Their extensive lands and sources of income became the property of the newly formed Canton Thurgau in 1809, putting an end to the 581-year-long history of the Knights of St. John in Tobel. This windfall wealth significantly helped Canton Thurgau finance its organization during the founding years.

By 1809 the commandry's former church possessions were allocated to the catholic church of Tobel, making it one of the largest parishes of the Canton. The Canton had a large three-winged building at its disposal and, after reconstruction, turned it into a prison. It was used as a prison (with forced labor) between 1809 and 1973. By 1973 the facilities were outdated and poorly maintained, and the prison was closed.

Since then the Canton looked for alternative uses of the buildings. It temporary housed a pilgrim inn (closed in 2014) and was regularly used for cultural and social events. Nowadays the buildings and areas around them are dilapidated, reflecting decades of neglect.

From the grounds of the former commandry walk up the hill to the St. John the Baptist Church (at km 14.8).

**St. John the Baptist Church, Tobel** (St. Johannes der Täufer Kirche) **K-7**

- Kirchstrasse, 9555 Tobel-Tägerschen
- St. John the Baptist, St. Innocence
- In an envelope stuck to the backside of the entrance door

The catholic church was built by the Knights of St. John in 1706-07. It replaced their old church, also dedicated to St. John, at the foot of the hill, which had become dilapidated and too small for the growing parish. It is not surprising that the commandry dedicated the new church to St. John. After all, they were called the Knights of the Hospital of St. John of Jerusalem.

Notice that the bell tower is detached from the church. This tower was originally a watch- and defense-tower, built at the time of the establishment of the commandry in the 13th century. Its walls are 2 meters thick. During its early years a small group of Knights of St. John probably lived there, until their commandry in the valley was built. During the middle ages the Order also used the tower as a prison. Until 1706 this tower stood alone on the hill (after which the new church was built next to it). In 1717 the church's bell housing was built on top of the 13th century tower, after which the bells of the commandry's old church in the valley were relocated to the top of the tower.

At the time the former commandry housed the Cantonal prison (19th-20th centuries), the prisoners had to use a passage from the tower to the upper gallery of the church (this avoided a commingling with the parishioners).

Until 1984 the church had two galleries above the entrance; the upper one was disassembled to make room for the new organ. The interior of the church is richly decorated in a baroque style. The ceiling frescos date from 1865, while most of the interior dates from the renovations in 1913-14 and 1984-85.

Above the right-side door a tall stained-glass window depicts St. James (*St. Jakobus*) holding a pilgrim cane and carrying a scallop.

Church music automatically plays upon entering the church.

On the left side of the chancel lies a decorated skeleton in a glass vitrine, below a wall fresco. The wall fresco depicts St. Innocence and dates from 1787; it was uncovered during the renovations in 1984.

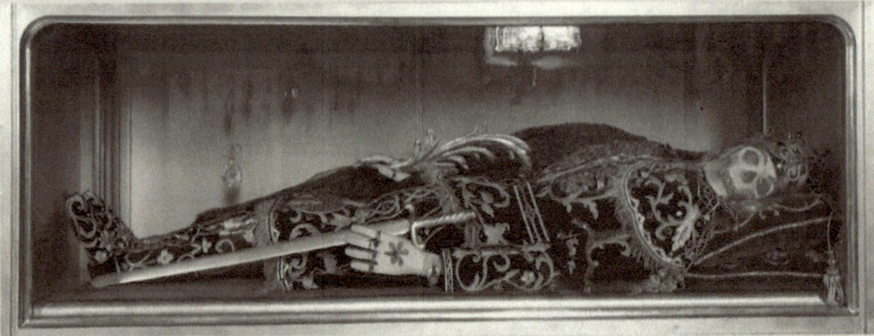

The skeleton is a catacomb saint venerated as St. Innocence, which came from the catacombs in Rome in 1731. The skeleton, mostly made of plaster, has been decorated with an embroidered red tunic, a crown, and many precious stones. A sword and palm branch complete the ensemble of a Theban Legion martyr.

Most of the time this vitrine is covered by a painted front. In case you want to see the relics, you may have to ask the caretaker (if he is around) to remove the front.

From the church it takes 1 km to descend 47 meters to go back to the signposted route nr. 4. The route follows a narrow trail through grasslands for 300 meters. After a left and right turn the route continues on a gravel road, slowly descending. The route provides wide views over the agricultural landscapes of Thurgau. At a crossing with a large metal road cross and a red bench you go straight. The following 1.7 km the road goes through a small patch of forest and follows the edge of the forest, until the route turns left and slightly ascends to the village Thürn. You cross road nr. 354 and 260 meters later the path turns right. You are more or less parallel to road nr. 354 for the next 2.2 km.

You walk between agricultural fields and past grasslands with cows, half-timbered farmhouses, and a small roadside chapel (*Wegkapelle*). The route enters the village St. Margarethen and at km 20.4 you arrive at the catholic St. Margaret Chapel.

**St. Margaret Chapel, St. Margarethen** (St. Margarethen Kapelle) **K-8**

- Trungerstrasse 6, 9543 Münchwilen
- St. Margaret, Fourteen Holy Helpers, St. Idda

Left of the entrance on a wooden shelf attached to the wall. You can leave a comment in the pilgrim guestbook.

The chapel was built in 1642 and renovated several times since. A predecessor chapel, which was first mentioned in official documents in 1316, already stood in the area. This chapel was probably close to the nearby Murg stream, making it susceptible to flooding. The old chapel was demolished and a new one was built on an elevated position in a safe distance from the stream in 1642. The chapel was frequently used by medieval pilgrims: the outside staircase led to a sleeping area.

You can still see the texts the medieval pilgrims left on the inner walls at the entrance. In 1900 these walls were whitewashed, covering these historical scribblings. They were uncovered during a later renovation and are nowadays visible again to the modern-day pilgrim.

The left side-altar painting depicts the Fourteen Holy Helpers and the right side-altar St. Idda.

The route goes north for 300 meters, crosses road nr. 354, and makes a turn to the west (left). After leaving St. Margarethen the trail is alongside a street, until you cross the **Murg River** 250 meters later. There you turn left (south) and stay on a broad gravel footpath alongside the river for the next 850 meters. On your right you pass by a BMX cross-bike parkour while you enter the outskirts of Münchwilen. At a small park surrounding **Villa Sutter** (the former residence of a local industrial tycoon – nowadays housing a library, café, and seminar rooms) the Schwabenweg sign directs to the park, through a small gate, with the Murg River on the left.

The route makes a wide curve around the villa and its gardens, until you get to a road. On the other side of the road, directly on the route, you see the reformed Church of Münchwilen. About 300 meters to the left is the catholic Church of Münchwilen. Walk towards the left and at the roundabout turn left into the *Waldeggstrasse*. You arrive at the catholic St. Anthony Church of Münchwilen at km 22.5.

## St. Anthony Church, Münchwilen (St. Antonius Kirche) K-9

Waldeggstrasse 9, 9542 Münchwilen

St. Anthony of Padua

On a shelf left of the main entrance, together with a guestbook

The catholic church was built in a modern style in 1966-68. The chunky concrete bell tower is typical for the 1960s architecture.

Before 1968 Münchwilen did not have its own catholic church: in medieval times the Catholics had to attend services at either the St. Margaret chapel in St. Margarethen (1 km to the north) or the St. Remy church in Sirnach (2 km to the south). The latter was the oldest church in the region, dating from before the 13th century. From the beginning of the 20th century Münchwilen began to grow and the Catholics wanted to have their own church. Their initiative started in 1947, but it took 20 years to get the financing together; the church was built in 1966-68.

The church and its interior are modernly shaped and decorated. The nave is semicircular. The back of the chancel is decorated with orange-colored cloths in the shape of sails. Church music automatically plays upon entering the church.

Follow the same 300 meters back to the signposted route nr .4. After crossing the road, you arrive at the reformed Church of Münchwilen (at km 22.7).

## K-10 Reformed Church, Münchwilen (Evangelisch-reformierte Kirche)

- Kirchstrasse 2, 9542 Münchwilen
- On a table together with a guestbook, right of the church's entrance portal. The phrase 'dona nobis pacem' is Latin, meaning 'grant us peace'.
- The protestant church was built in 1937, and has a similar history as the catholic St. Anthony church. After the Reformation in 1531, the Protestants of Münchwilen had hold their services at the catholic St. Remy church in Sirnach (2 km to the south), which was used in confessional parity by the Catholics and Protestants. In 1933 the parishes decided to end the confessional parity, after which the protestant parish proceeded to build their own churches. Only four years later the reformed church was built in Münchwilen, serving the needs of the Protestants in the area.
- Typical for a protestant church is the absence of religious icons. The large organ fills most of the space of the chancel.

From the reformed church the route follows a small road alongside the Murg River. For the next 900 meters you walk on tarmac and a broad gravel road alongside the river, passing by the Münchwilen recreational grounds that include swimming pools, sports fields, and grass fields. You go around the recreational grounds and make a sharp right to pass underneath Highway A1. For 500 meters you have the river on your left and corn and grass fields on your right, until you reach the outskirts of Sirnach.

The route keeps following the gravel footpath alongside the Murg River. It is hardly noticeable, but the elevation very gradually increases as you follow the western bank of the river. At a crossing of a main road leading into Sirnach you pass by an information table explaining the town's importance along the Schwabenweg to Einsiedeln. The town used to house two pilgrim inns and Sirnach's coat-of-arms includes three scallops (and the municipal stamp includes a pilgrim). As pilgrim you can still obtain a simple meal (e.g. soup) free of charge at the former pilgrim inn called "*Engel*" (Fischingerstrasse 2, 8370 Sirnach – 500 meters from the signpost, on the corner of a street on the right, just before the church). You need to ask for the pilgrim meal and show your pilgrim pass. If you make the detour to the inn you pass by a large Migros supermarket, where you can buy any provisions you might need. Immediately after the inn, further up the hill, you arrive at the catholic St. Remy Church at km 25.0 (600 meters detour from the signposted route along the Murg River).

## St. Remy Church, Sirnach (St. Remigius Kirche) K-11

- Kirchplatz, 8370 Sirnach
- St. Remy
- At the municipal office across the street or at the parish office 200 meters further. Notice the pilgrim and the three scallops on the town's stamp.
- The catholic church, dedicated to St. Remy, was first mentioned in official documents in 1228. During the Reformation in 1529 the parish decided to convert from Catholicism to Protestantism. During its already more than 300-year existence it had accumulated a wealth of interior decorations, but all these religious icons, statues, paintings, and altars were removed, while the walls were whitewashed. Nearly 40 years later (1568) the church converted back to Catholicism and allowed confessional parity. Both the Catholics and Protestants used the catholic church for their services during the subsequent centuries.

  The parishes agreed to build a new shared church in 1872. The 700-year-old church was demolished and a new church in neo-Gothic style was consecrated in 1874, determining its present-day appearance. In 1933 the parishes of Sirnach decided to end the confessional parity, after which the protestant parish built their own churches. After 366 years the dual use ended, which gave the catholic parish the opportunity to renovate the church, and design and decorate it to their liking.

  Donations were collected and a big renovation was undertaken in 1937-39: six new bells were installed (the biggest bell weighs 6'071 kg and is the heaviest in Canton Thurgau); a new organ was purchased; the church was expanded; and several catholic icons and statues were placed. However, the 'cleansing' of the church at the time of the Reformation and the centuries of dual use still determine its interior appearance today.
- Apart from the four statues and the crucifix in the chancel, the interior resembles the austerity of a protestant church (not one of an 800-year-old catholic church).

From the church walk southward into the *Fischingerstrasse* (road nr. 468) between the church and *Gasthaus Engel*. Take the first street on the left to pass underneath the railway tracks. Follow the curve in the *Hochwachtstrasse* and at km 25.3 you arrive at the reformed Church of Sirnach.

**K-12 Reformed Church, Sirnach** (Evangelisch-reformierte Kirche)

Hochwachtstrasse 4, 8370 Sirnach

The church was built in 1937, and has a similar pre-history as the reformed church of Münchwilen. After the Reformation in 1531, the Protestants of Sirnach had to hold their services at the catholic St. Remy church in confessional parity. In 1933 the parishes decided to end the confessional parity, after which the protestant parish built their own church. Four years later the reformed church was built in Sirnach, only 300 meters away from the St. Remy church. The church was renovated in 2005 (interior) and 2009 (exterior).

The church has a typical protestant interior. The colors, footprint, ceiling, and placement of the organ in the chancel resemble the interior of the reformed church of Münchwilen, which was built in the same year. The church is only open on Sundays or during services on weekdays.

To return to the signposted route, walk back the same 900 meters down the hill to the information board at the Murg River. The gravel footpath continues to closely follow the Murg River for the next 2.5 km. You pass through the outskirts of Sirnach and underneath railway tracks, while you have wide views over grasslands to the right.

After walking on a dam between the river and a pond, the route turns left and then right again. You walk alongside road nr. 468 through a small settlement for 600 meters. The route turns away from the road and follows a country road more or less parallel to road nr. 468 and the Murg River. You pass by farms and grasslands with apple trees. After a sharp left and right, the route goes into a forest.

In the middle of the patch of forest you pass through a **Sunken Lane** (also called Holloway), indicating that this route was already in use during the middle ages. The sunken lanes were created by erosion of the soft and humid forest underground, caused by the traffic of carriages, carts, and horses over many centuries. At the time of heavy use, the sunken lanes had more or less straight walls on the left and right side (U-shape). Because these sunken lanes were dirt roads, they made traveling difficult during rainy periods. The development of bigger and heavier carriages made traveling these soft roads increasingly problematic. Wooden boards were used to stabilize the road, when stones or gravel were not available. After the route was abandoned for newer, faster roads that could carry heavy carriages (such as the mail coach), the sidewalls collapsed and the path got a wide V-shape. Erosion and vegetation growing on the sides finally reduced the path to a hollow footpath.

The trail ascends and descends again over 800 meters. Coming out of the forest you can already see the St. Martin chapel in the distance, on top of a small hill. At the outskirts of the small town Oberwangen, the first road crossing is confusing. There are no signs pointing you in any of the four directions. Here you must turn left (south), to walk with the chapel on your right (though going straight would also get you to the chapel). After making another right, you arrive at the foot of the chapel hill with a red bench and a fountain with potable water. Though a narrow grass trail goes up the small hill, it is easier to walk another 20 meters on the road and use the gravel path with steps and a railing that wind up the chapel's hill. At km 31.1 you arrive at the catholic St. Martin Chapel of Oberwangen.

## K-13 St. Martin Chapel, Oberwangen (Martinskapelle)

- Martinsbergstrasse, 8374 Oberwangen
- St. Martin
- Left of the entrance on a small table
- The chapel was first mentioned in official documents in 1494, but it is believed that a chapel already existed since the 10th century. During the Reformation in 1529 the chapel was secularized, used for different purposes, and its religious icons were destroyed. About 10 years later (1540) the chapel was dedicated to catholic worship again. The chapel burned down after it was hit by lightning in 1685. Eight years later (1693) the chapel was rebuilt in a baroque style. The eight-sided dome and the entrance portico were added in 1728-30, while the ceiling decorations, marble pulpit, and inside gallery were installed in 1811-18.
- The high-altar and the two side-altars are beautiful examples of baroque colored-marble art. Statues of winged angels bless the visitors in the chancel. Exquisite are the relief paintings of the high-altar (1693), depicting St. Martin as a Bishop and Roman soldier.

Walk down the hill of the chapel and continue to the west. About 70 meters from the chapel the route turns left. However, to visit the next two churches in Dussnang, you need to make a 1.5 km detour from the signposted route. One of these churches is the oldest Romanesque church in Canton Thurgau. Continue on the same road through the village Oberwangen (where you cross road nr. 468) into a narrow valley between forested hills. Along the *Kurhausstrasse* you arrive at the town Dussnang. On the right side of the street, after the physical rehabilitation Clinique, is the catholic Mary-Lourdes Church (at km 32.0).

## K-14 Mary-Lourdes Church, Dussnang (Maria-Lourdes Kirche)

- Kurhausstrasse 36, 8374 Dussnang
- Mary-Lourdes
- The catholic church was built in 1889-1890, ending nearly 350 years of confessional parity. Until that time the Catholics used the medieval Romanesque protestant church across the street (see below). The catholic church was built in the neo-Gothic style of the Lourdes church and was the first Swiss church constructed with concrete.

The church is richly decorated with the typical neo-Gothic spires above the pulpit, crucifixion way stations, and altars. The walls and vaulted ceiling have been painted in color with artful decorations of flowers, leaves, and other symbols. Statues of saints line the pillars in the nave and stand at the altars. The high-altar contains a statue representing Our Lady of Lourdes, dressed in white. The chancel has a corridor that allows you to walk around the high-altar area. The stained-glass windows in the chancel depict biblical scenes in beautiful colors. A small chapel right of the entrance has a life-size Pietà statue.

On the other side of the street is the reformed Church of Dussnang.

## Reformed Church, Dussnang (reformierte Kirche) K-15

Frohsinnstrasse 2, 8374 Dussnang

The church has the oldest tower of Canton Thurgau and is one of the few remaining Romanesque buildings in northeastern Switzerland. The low tower and the tiny elevated windows in the nave are typical for Romanesque churches of the 11th/12th century. Notice how the small chancel is in the base of the tower.

The church was dedicated to the Holy Cross (*Heilig Kreuz*) in 1523, which is why it is still called the Cross Church (*Kreuzkirche*). During the Reformation in 1529 the parish converted to protestant worship and all catholic icons were destroyed while the walls were whitewashed. From 1542 until 1890 the Protestants allowed the Catholics to the use the church in confessional parity. In 1890 the Catholics built their own church in Dussnang (see above), ending the parity.

Significant constructional changes were made in the 18th century: the nave was lengthened by two windows; the small Romanesque windows were bricked up and replaced by tall and wide windows in the nave; the gallery was built; and the tower was heightened with the dark-wooden construction. When you look at the outer walls you can clearly recognize the extension and the bricked-up small windows.

The partially uncovered frescos (that were whitewashed in 1529) in the nave date from before the 16th century. Go up the stairs to the gallery if you want to have a closer look at them.

The gallery at the back of the nave is quite unusual: it is very low at a downward angle and has additional pews (instead of the usual organ). Compared to the catholic church across the street, the reformed church has an austere and simple interior.

From the church walk back the same 800 meters to the signposted route. Shortly before reaching the hill of the St. Martin chapel turn right and on a steeply ascending road past some houses you get to a forest trail. For 800 meters a narrow and winding forest trail ascends to the highest point of the day at 666 meters. About 200 meters later you leave the forest and walk on a tarmac road between grasslands. You can already see the Abbey of Fischingen in the distance when you come out of the forest. The first thing that attracts attention is the pink/white painted St. Idda chapel and bell tower.

The road descends into the narrow Murg River valley and curves to the west where you reach the *Hauptstrasse* (road nr. 468) and the Murg River. Turn left on the road and after 700 meters through the village Fischingen (around 2'800 inhabitants together with surrounding villages) you reach the abbey. The route approaches the Abbey of Fischingen from the north. The village road takes you straight to the abbey, which is built on a hill overlooking the village. You can ascend the stairs up the hill or continue along the road for another 150 meters to the front entrance of the monastery complex. At km 35.2 you arrive at the Benedictine Abbey of Fischingen, the end of stage K2.

## Benedictine Monastery, Fischingen (Benediktiner Kloster) K-2

Kloster, 8376 Fischingen

Benedictine Order

The monastery was established by Bishop Ulrich II of Konstanz in 1138, when the first church and accommodations for monks, nuns, and pilgrims were built (1138-44). The abbey flourished during the first 100 years, but the convent already closed in the 13th century, while not more than 10 monks were left during the 13th-16th centuries. The monastery was located deep in the forests of the northern foothills of the Hörnli mountain. Typical for a Benedictine monastery of that time, it was isolated from society.

During the Reformation in 1526 the prior and the remaining monks converted to Protestantism and the monastery was closed. Six years later (1532), catholic priests tried to re-establish the monastery. In 1540 a new prior was appointed and several difficult decades followed, during which they converted the surrounding parishes from Protestantism back to Catholicism.

Between 1575 and 1798 the monastery flourished again and at its peak housed more than 30 Benedictine monks. Under the protection of the Bishops of Konstanz and the lands of Thurgau, the abbey gathered wealth, lands, and income, enabling them to beautify and rebuild their church and monastery.

In 1798 the French invasion and the subsequent establishment of the Helvetic Republic caused the closure of the monastery. The monks had to leave and could only return in 1803, after the Helvetic Republic was dissolved. The lands of Thurgau became a Canton and at the inception of the Swiss Federal Constitution in 1848, a radical-liberal Cantonal government closed all eight monasteries on its territory (these had already been under administrative control of the Canton since 1836). The medieval library was transferred to Canton Thurgau and the buildings were sold to a textile tycoon and used as dyeing and weaving factory. In 1879 the buildings were sold again, after which it housed a boarding school and orphanage.

As recent as 1977, 129 years after it was closed, the monastery was re-established.

Nowadays nine monks live and work at the monastery. They derive their income from several sources: brewery, wood workshop, pilgrim inn, restaurant, and seminars with accommodations and meeting rooms. The brewery's beer is called Pilgrim beer, which is available in several flavors and alcohol percentages. The wood workshop sells commercial woodwork products. The monastery's green center courtyard is surrounded by buildings that include a school, seminar and meeting rooms, restaurant, hotel rooms, and pilgrim dorms. They even offer free WIFI. Concerts are organized every month, either at the church, the center courtyard, or the abbey's library.

For more than 750 years the abbey served as a place of security, prayer, and shelter for pilgrims on their way from Konstanz to Einsiedeln, and it still does to this day.

For a pilgrim on the Way of St. James the monastery offers three main points of interest: the St. John church, the St. Idda chapel, and the St. Catherine chapel. The monastery is built on the north-south axle of the valley. On the northern side you find the church, the St. Idda chapel, and a small cemetery; in the middle the St. Catherine chapel and the main entrance; on the southern side the brewery and wood workshop.

## K-16 Benedictine Monastery Church, Fischingen (Kloster Kirche)

- Kloster, 8376 Fischingen
- St. John the Baptist
- At the front desk of the monastery, at their restaurant, or at the pilgrim blessing in the St. Idda Chapel in the morning
- The church was first built in a Romanesque style in 1138-44, immediately after the establishment of the monastery (around the same time as the Romanesque church in Dussnang). This first church burned down (together with the monastery) in 1440, after which a second Gothic church was constructed. The church tower dates from 1587 and was heightened in 1727 and 1751. The eight-sided onion-dome was added during the first heightening. The Gothic church was replaced by the present baroque church in 1685-87. The exquisite decorations of the chancel were added in 1753-61.
- The church has a beautiful baroque interior. Walk to the rood screen and you can admire splendid details, including the decorations on the organ pipes.

On the northern side of the nave a passage with a beautifully styled iron gate leads to the St. Idda Chapel.

## St. Idda Chapel, Fischingen (St. Idda Kapelle) K-17

Kloster, 8376 Fischingen

St. Idda

The chapel was originally built as a small free-standing chapel at the end of the 15th century. As the pilgrimage to St. Idda increased during the late middle ages, the chapel was extended in 1595 and renewed in 1625. In 1704-18 the chapel was completely rebuilt and attached to the St. John church. Its interior received the same baroque style as the church. This is what you see today.

The St. Idda chapel is the treasure of the monastery and one of Switzerland's most beautiful baroque chapels. Its decorations are unique for a chapel along the Swiss Way of St. James: notice the marble altars, paintings, and artistic decorations, many of them in gold. The chapel was named after the Swiss female Saint Idda. Before becoming a nun at the Fischingen abbey, she lived in a cell at the church in Au (see church nr. K-19, stage K3).

One of the Benedictine monks provides a pilgrim blessing in the St. Idda chapel at 07:45 on weekdays and at 08:15 on weekends (from 1 March until 31 October). Do not miss that if you spent the night at the monastery's pilgrim inn.

The tomb of St. Idda is a big grey stone sarcophagus. It was erected in 1496 and is nowadays the oldest monument in the church and monastery. The tomb does not contain any relics of St. Idda; these were lost because of a fire and the Reformation. You can find the tomb on the left, after entering the chapel. It is below the gold-colored and richly decorated statue of St. Idda, behind the gold/green iron fence. A small bench and a cubic stone with a cushion are in front of it. According to legend, if you put your feet in the hole underneath the tombstone (sit on the cubic stone with cushion), you will be relieved from foot pains.

Upon exiting the church, turn left. Shortly before the entrance to the monastery you arrive at the St. Catherine Chapel. The chapel is located in the main front building; it is easy to overlook its green entrance door.

**K-18 St. Catherine Chapel, Fischingen** (St. Katharina Kapelle)

Kloster, 8376 Fischingen

St. Catherine

The simplicity and modesty of the chapel is in stark contrast to the opulence of the St. Idda chapel and the church.

The monks prefer to perform their prayers at regular times during the day at this chapel. You can join the monks for prayers at 05:30, 11:45, 17:45, and 19:30 on weekdays.

The abbey offers a unique certificate called the **Compostela Fischingensis**. The certificate can be obtained upon request by the pilgrims who chose to end their pilgrimage at the abbey. This may be applicable to older pilgrims or families with children who do not want to make the strenuous ascent up the Hörnli Mountain (in the next stage K3).

The certificate has a photo of the St. Idda altar on the front side and a pilgrim's-blessing text in German on the back side. The certificate will be stamped, dated, and signed by the abbey, with the owner's name handwritten at the front.

## *From the ending point*

The Benedictine Abbey of Fischingen is the ending point of Stage K2, directly on the signposted route nr. 4.

In case you are a day-hiker, you will need to take bus nr. 734 (bus stop in front of the monastery) to get to the train station of Sirnach. The bus departs twice an hour in the afternoon (2 and 32 minutes past the hour), but only once an hour (32 minutes past the hour) at other times of the day and on weekends. The bus ride takes 14 minutes.

In case you are a thru-hiker, you can stay at the monastery. Information about the pilgrim accommodation can be obtained at the front desk of the monastery or at their restaurant. You get to the front desk (of the seminar hotel) via the main entrance, up the stairs, and then to the right. Apart from it being a seminar hotel (individual rooms), the monastery also provides low-priced pilgrim inn accommodations (individual rooms or shared rooms with bunkbeds) and has a restaurant (Kloster Fischingen; Kloster, 8376 Fischingen; tel. 071 978 72 11; info@klosterfischingen.ch; www.klosterfischingen.ch; www.pilgerinfischingen.ch or reservation online on their website). The pilgrim inn is open from 1 April until 31 October, daily from 16:00. Check out www.jakobsweg.ch or www.viajacobi4.ch for the alternative accommodation possibilities in and around Fischingen.

## *The next Stage*

Stage K3 guides you over the Hörnli mountain and across a highland valley and plateau, from where the route descends to the Lake Zurich basin. Stage K3 is one of the toughest hiking sections of the Swiss Way of St. James, because of its distance (33 km) and number of altitude meters (1'815). Read the next chapter to find out what that entails.

# Stage K3:
# Fischingen to Rapperswil
# 33 km

*The Way over the second-highest altitude*

## Route stats

| | *Distance in km* | *Time in hrs:min* |
|---|---|---|
| Signposted route nr. 4 | 31.6 | 7:00 |
| Churches/chapels | 1.0 | 1:30 |
| Points of interest | 0.4 | 0:30 |
| Rest | | 1:00 |
| Stage K3 | 33.0 | 10:00 |

In case you hike this stage as a daytrip, you can take the bus from the Sirnach train station to the Abbey in Fischingen (14-minute drive). In Rapperswil you need to add 500 meters to go to the train station.

| | |
|---|---|
| Ascent/descent/total | +799 / -1'016 / 1'815 altitude meters |
| Lowest/highest altitude | 409 / 1'132 meters |
| Pathway/condition | moderate / difficult |
| Churches/chapels | Au, Fischenthal (3), Rapperswil (4) |
| Monasteries | Capuchin Monastery Rapperswil |
| Points of Interest | Ruins Castle of Baliken, Castle of Rapperswil, Einsiedeln House |

## Route summary

Stage K3 continues in **Canton Thurgau**, but after about 5 km changes to Canton Zurich. This occurs in a dense forest high-up the northern slopes of the Hörnli mountain (about 700 meters before the pass level).

The Swiss Way of St. James passes through protestant **Canton Zurich** for only 23 km; apart from these 23 km, the route does not pass through it anymore. These 23 km are situated in the most eastern part of the Canton, made up of the peak of the Hörnli mountain, its southern slopes, and the Fischenthal highland valley, until shortly before Rapperswil. This region has beautiful nature and forests, but is relatively isolated and has limited economic activity.

At km 28 of stage K3 the route passes from Canton Zurich to **Canton St. Gallen**. This happens shortly before reaching the Rapperswil-Jona agglomeration.

Stage K3 guides you over the Hörnli mountain and across a highland valley and plateau, from where the route descends to the Lake Zurich basin. It is one of the toughest hiking sections of the Swiss Way of St. James, because of its distance (33 km) and number of altitude meters (1'815).

Stage K3 starts in front of the monastery of Fischingen and via a relatively easy ascending forest path leads to the church of Au 2 km later. This path is more or less parallel to the Au stream (*Aubach*) and the road. From the church the route steeply ascends the forested northern slopes of the Hörnli mountain over 4 km. The pass level at 1'132 meters (the second-highest point on the Swiss Way of St. James) is reached after 6 km. This is followed by a steep descent (with regular panoramic views over the southern valley and Alps) to Steg over 4 km. After 10 km the toughest part of stage K3 is over. The remaining 21 km, though long, are less strenuous. From Steg the route closely follows road nr. 15 and a train track through the Fischenthal highland valley for 6 km, offering easy trails that gradually ascend. Soon after Gibswil the route makes a short but steep ascent to arrive at the second-highest point of the day (821 meters). From there it is basically 16 km downhill to reach Rapperswil. The first 4 km you hike on a highland plateau, with road nr. 15 and the town Wald in the valley below (left). The highland route provides wide views over the valley, Lake Zurich, and the Alps. The last 8 km gradually descend to Rapperswil, where the final 3 km are through the city and its agglomeration.

## *Getting to the starting point*

In case you hike stage K3 as a daytrip, you need to take bus nr. 734 from the train station of Sirnach to get to the abbey of Fischingen. The bus takes 15 minutes and departs twice an hour in the early morning (14 and 44 minutes past the hour), but only once an hour (14 minutes past the hour) after 08:14 and on weekends.

In case you spent the night at the abbey's pilgrim inn in Fischingen, you are already at the right location to start stage K3.

## *Route Map and Profile*

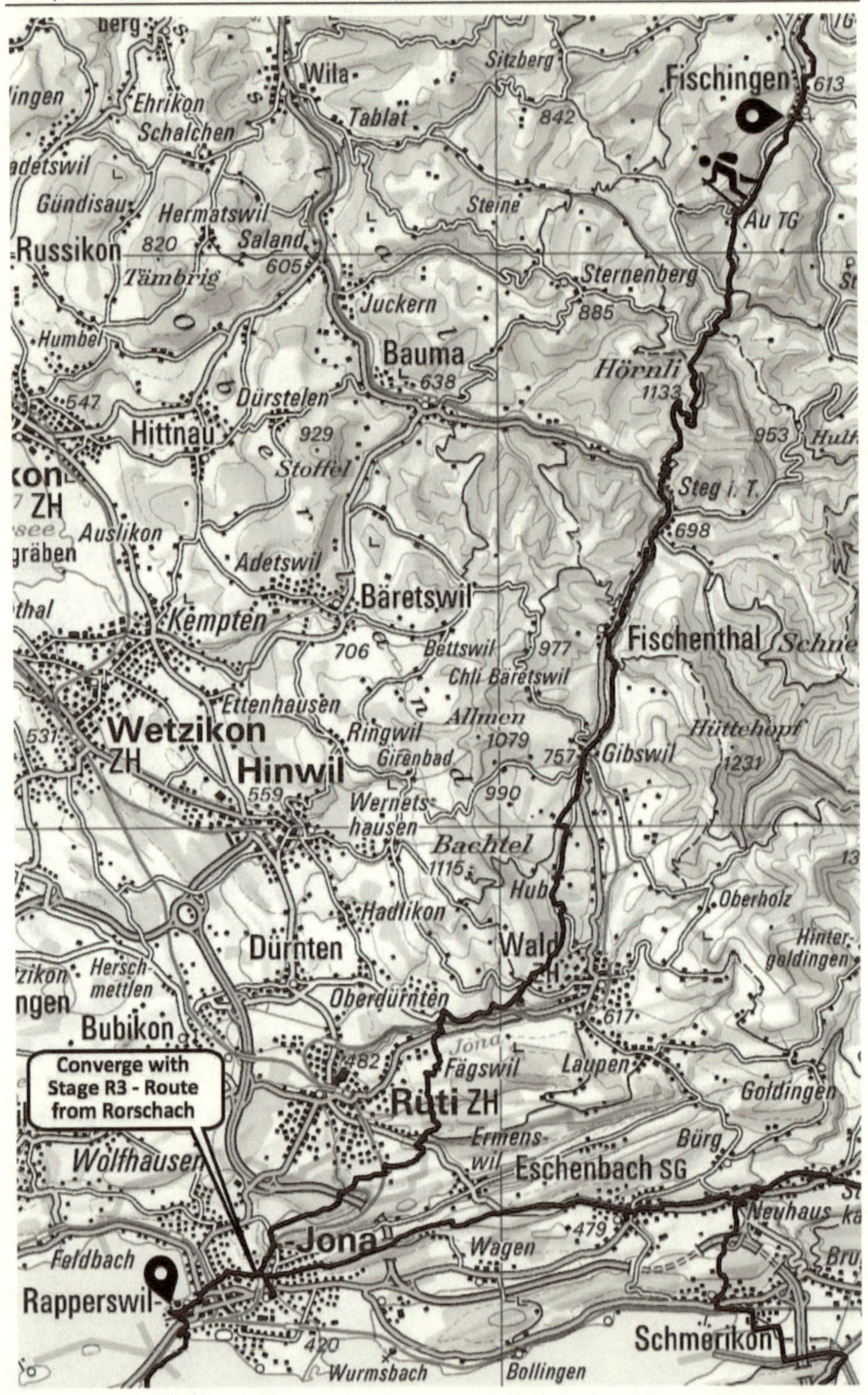
Fischingen
Au TG
Sternenberg
Hörnli
Steg i. T.
Bauma
Wila
Tablat
Sitzberg
Steine
Juckern
Russikon
Hittnau
Dürstelen
Bäretswil
Kempten
Wetzikon ZH
Hinwil
Fischenthal
Gibswil
Bachtel
Wald ZH
Dürnten
Oberdürnten
Bubikon
Fägswil
Rüti ZH
Laupen
Goldingen
Eschenbach SG
Neuhaus
Wolfhausen
Jona
Wagen
Feldbach
Rapperswil
Schmerikon
Wurmsbach
Bollingen
Converge with Stage R3 - Route from Rorschach

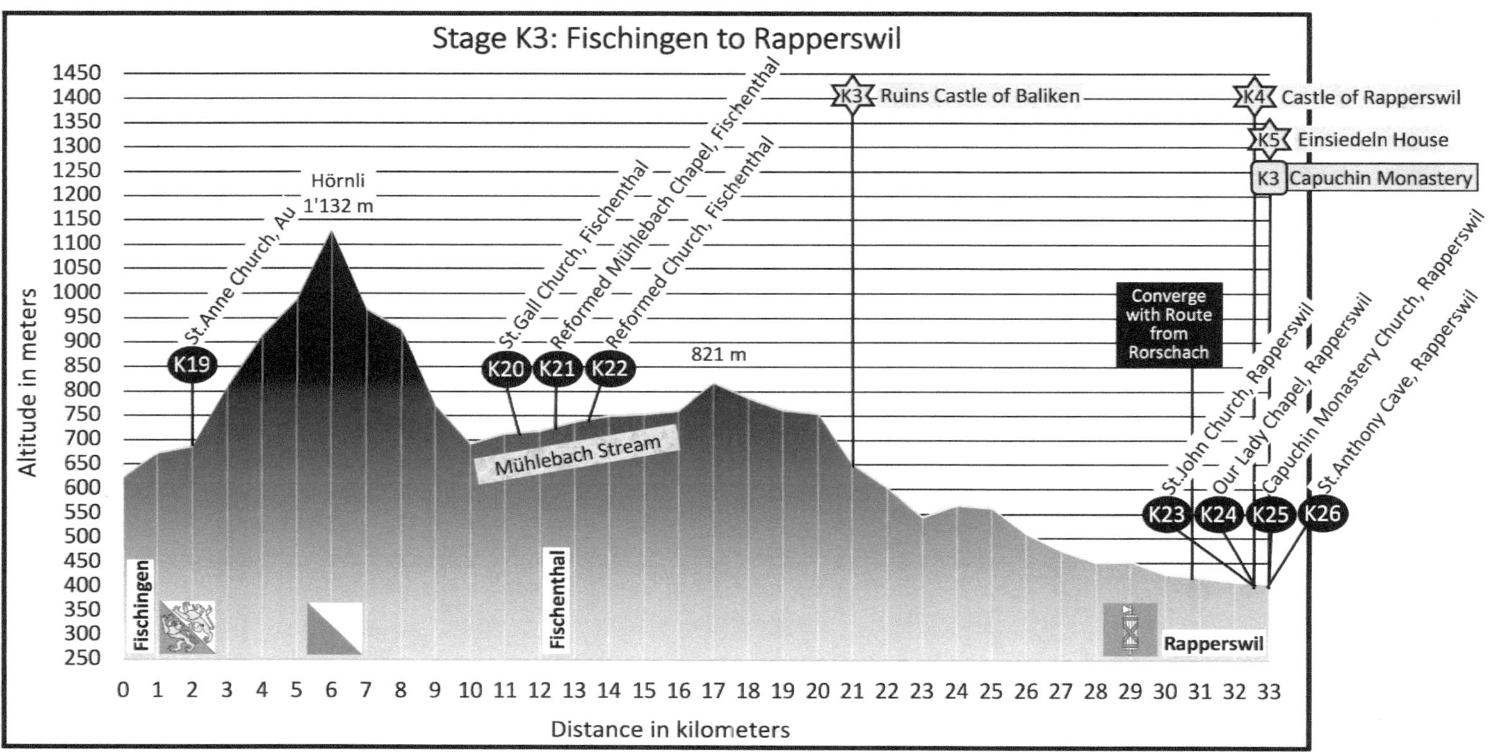
Stage K3: Fischingen to Rapperswil
Altitude in meters
Distance in kilometers
Hörnli
1'132 m
821 m
Fischingen
Fischenthal
Rapperswil
Mühlebach Stream
K19 St.Anne Church, Au
K20 St.Gall Church, Fischenthal
K21 Reformed Mühlebach Chapel, Fischenthal
K22 Reformed Church, Fischenthal
K3 Ruins Castle of Baliken
Converge with Route from Rorschach
K23 St.John Church, Rapperswil
K24 Our Lady Chapel, Rapperswil
K25 Capuchin Monastery Church, Rapperswil
K26 St.Anthony Cave, Rapperswil
K4 Castle of Rapperswil
K5 Einsiedeln House
K3 Capuchin Monastery

## *Hiking the Route*

The hiking signs in front of the road entrance to the monastery direct to many locations. The Schwabenweg sign indicates 3 hours to Steg and 2'300 km to Santiago de Compostela. From this signpost the road slightly descends to the Murg River, which you cross for the last time. The road forks and signs direct to the left road. You ascend on a tarmac road between farmland and some isolated houses over 850 meters. A farm with speakers at the stables plays Swiss folk music for the cows. You pass by a shooting range and an apple orchard before getting to a forest. The forest trail is an easy broad gravel path with very gradual ascents and some descents. It is parallel to the road and the Au stream (*Aubach*), and you are never far away to hear the traffic. After 1.2 km in the forest the trail returns to the road.

Coming out of the forest you see a church to your right. Here you need to briefly leave the signposted route, cross a parking lot and pass by a small fountain, before you cross the street and arrive at the catholic St. Anne Church at km 2.2.

### K-19 St. Anne Church, Au (St. Anna Kirche)

- Hörnlistrasse 1, 8376 Fischingen
- St. Anne, St. Joachim, St. Mary, St. Idda, St. Francis of Assisi
- Left of the entrance on a shelf attached to the wall
- The church was first built as a small chapel in the 11th/12th century. This chapel was probably built to commemorate the location where St. Idda had lived as a hermit in a cell, before becoming a nun at the Fischingen convent. The church

was structurally rebuilt in 1647 and 1802. During the last reconstruction a new chancel was attached to the nave and the church received its present-day baroque style.

📷 The small church has beautiful ceiling frescos: the large square fresco in the nave depicts St. Anne and St. Joachim with their daughter Mary on a cloud above them; the round frescos depict St. Idda and St. Francis of Assisi. The left side-altar painting (1844) depicts St. Anne and St. Joachim with their daughter Mary again. The right side-altar painting (1717) depicts St. Idda. The three altars are made of artfully styled colored marble. Fourteen oval paintings depict the crucifixion way (*Kreuzweg*). Notice how the access to the pulpit is from the base of the bell tower, outside of the nave.

From the chapel (at 692 meters) it is a steep climb to the peak of the Hörnli mountain (at 1'132 meters) over 4 km. Continuing to the south, the first 200 meters are along the road and still flat. You pass by a cheese factory and a pig farm; the loud snorting sounds and the smell of pig dung penetrate the farm's walls. The steep ascent starts on a tarmac road and soon after the pig farm you pass by a small St. Idda road chapel. The route follows a gravel road and keeps going up between meadows over the next 500 meters.

You reach the edge of a forest. The trail starts with 90 steps steeply ascending deep into the forest. The narrow trail in the forest alternates between gravel and soft underground. Notice that the diamond route signs painted on the trees are not yellow but blue for the next couple of kilometers. After 700 meters through the forest and a steep ascent you reach an open field. Up ahead in the distance you can see the Allenwinden guesthouse (at 916 meters) further up the mountain.

The forest trail changes into a tarmac road. You pass by the guesthouse and a bit later a turkey farm, while only slightly ascending over 350 meters. Right after the turkey farm the route turns left and then right. For 400 meters the gravel road ascends steeply. You have panoramic views towards the north and east, and can see distant mountain ranges.

At km 4.6, before entering into a forest again, you pass by a stone marker indicating the change of Canton. After having walked 56 km through Canton Thurgau, you are entering Canton St. Gallen. Though your presence in Canton St. Gallen is very short; 600 meters later (at km 5.2) the route enters Canton Zurich.

With the change of Canton, the Way of St. James signaling changes too. The white Schwabenweg signs and the white signs with the distance to Santiago de Compostela only exist in Canton Thurgau; you will not see these anymore for the remainder of the Way of St. James through Switzerland. Instead, the regular yellow signs, the nr. 4 signs, and a few brown *Jakobsweg* signs indicate the way from here.

The route turns to the right through a short patch of forest. On the other side of the patch of forest the route continues on a dirt road along the edge of the forest. In the distance you can already see the antenna sticking out over the forested top of the Hörnli mountain.

About 700 meters before the top of the Hörnli mountain you enter **Canton Zurich**, where the ascent to the pass level is steep and through a forest. The final ascent starts on broad trails, whereas the last 200 meters are narrow with winding steps leading to the pass level.

At km 6 you arrive at 1'132 meters, where a guesthouse and panoramic views welcome you. The **Hörnli mountain** is the second-highest peak of the Swiss Way of St. James (you cross over the highest peak in stage 5). The guesthouse offers the possibility to relax and recover from the strenuous ascent. To the side of the terrace they offer fresh spring (drinking) water for your bottle, which you can tap from an old-fashioned big metal milk container. The panoramic views are towards the east and south. In the east you see the Alpstein mountain range with the Säntis peaking at 2'502 meters; towards the south you see the Alps in the distance and closer by the town Steg and the Fischenthal highland valley between mountain ranges. The route passes through that highland valley, leading you closer to Rapperswil.

From the Hörnli Pass the route to Steg takes about 4 km to descend from 1'132 to 695 meters. The first 260 meters are on a small road, after which the route turns right, going down steeply along a narrow path on the edge of a small patch of forest. About 450 meters later the path converges with a broad gravel road, which winds down the mountain in a very gradual descent over 1.6 km. The road provides wide views of the Fischenthal highland valley and you pass by a typical Swiss chalet with colorful geraniums at all its windows and its pots in front of it. The trail goes down rather steeply through and along patches of forest for 1 km, until you get to a tarmac road that leads you into Steg.

In Steg (at 695 meters) the trail leads to the local street, about 100 meters from the Steg train station (on the right). The Way of St. James sign directs to the left, where you cross the Töss River and main road nr. 15 (*Tösstalstrasse*). The warm and dry summer of 2018 completely dried up the river. To the right you pass by the local inn, with its colorful geraniums underneath each window. It is an old pilgrim inn called *Landgasthof zum Steg*. Its history dates back to the 15th century, when they already accommodated pilgrims en route to Einsiedeln.

A little later you pass by a bakery and cafeteria called Voland in a long orange building, offering possibilities to buy food and beverages. For another 500 meters the route is on the pavement along road nr. 15, until it turns left, and then immediately right again. The route is now parallel to the road, while you pass by the local outdoor swimming pool. You cross the Töss River again and the trail becomes a broad gravel road, going up a hill towards the left. At the top you have a nice view back to Steg. The route briefly follows a narrow path along the edge of the forest, parallel to the railway track, until it crosses the track and a small stream called Mühlebach. Back on road nr. 15 you need to make a small detour to visit the next church. Turn right (north), back into the direction of Steg, and after 150 meters you reach the catholic St. Gall Church (at km 11.4).

## St. Gall Church, Fischenthal (St. Gallus Kirche) K-20

Tösstalstrasse 156, 8497 Fischenthal

St. Gall, Brother Klaus

Until the Reformation in 1524 the Catholics used the old Romanesque St. Gall church in Fischenthal (see below), which converted to Protestantism in 1524, when all catholic worship was forbidden.

It was not until 446 years later that a catholic church was built again in Fischenthal (1970-71). The present church, just like the former catholic church from before the Reformation, is dedicated to St. Gall.

The building looks like a residential house. On the roof the small cross is hardly noticeable and the three bells are integrated in the edge of the roof below the cross.

The interior is modern and marked by the red-bricked walls and red tiles on the floor. Fourteen modern crucifixion way stations, a large canvas depicting Brother Klaus' meditation wheel (in the kids play corner), and an embroidered image of St. Gall with bear (behind the communion table) decorate the walls.

The following kilometer the route is next to road nr. 15 (*Tösstalstrasse*), with the railway track on your left. You walk in the highland valley with green hills on your left and right. Houses are scattered along the road. You pass by the reformed Mühlebach Chapel, on your right across the road, at km 12.4.

## K-21 Reformed Mühlebach Chapel, Fischenthal (Mühlebach Kapelle)

Tösstalstrasse 304, 8497 Fischenthal

The chapel can easily be overlooked, as it hardly looks like a place of worship from the outside. There is no cross, no bell tower, and it looks like a regular building standing a little aside the road. The only things that might give it away are the long narrow windows and of course the name *Mühlebach Kapelle* on its facade. The chapel was built in 1898 and used as an Evangelic-Methodist church until 1968. From 1969 to 2003 it housed a painter's workshop. In 2003 the reformed Church of Fischenthal (see below) acquired the building and made the space available for a multipurpose use; nowadays it houses a youth center.

Its interior shows no signs of it ever being a religious place (it was never restored to a place of worship after it was used as a painter's workshop). The door is locked.

After the chapel the trail makes a small side-tour to pass by the Fischenthal train station. After 300 meters, to your right across the street, you see a church tower above the tree line. At the corner is a restaurant/inn (*Gasthaus Blume*), behind it the municipal hall (*Gemeindesaal*) of Fischenthal, and to the left the church. You need to briefly leave the signposted route and walk up the hill to arrive at the reformed Church of Fischenthal (at km 13.4).

## K-22 Reformed Church, Fischenthal (Reformierte Kirche)

Kirchstrasse 2, 8497 Fischenthal

St. Gall

Left of the entrance, in a tin can on the piano

The church was originally built as a Romanesque chapel in the first decades after the year 900. This first chapel was dedicated to St. Gall, after the local landowner donated these lands to the Abbey of St. Gallen in the year 878.

The Reformation in 1524 had a big influence on the church. Catholic worship was legally banned in Canton Zurich and the church converted to Protestantism: all catholic religious icons that had been accumulated over 600 years were removed.

Significant reconstruction took place during the middle ages and the current nave was built in 1711. The bell tower has maintained part of its Romanesque style in that it has the small and rather dark chancel in its base and a relatively low height (the steeple was added later). Similarly, the chancel's windows are small and narrow. The building was renovated in 1936 and 1995.

Its interior is typical of protestant churches, displaying no religious icons apart from a cross. The stained-glass windows in the chancel date from 1933.

From the short street of the church the route goes straight, across road nr. 15. You can refill your water bottle at a small fountain with potable water. For 400 meters the route passes by some houses scattered between road nr. 15 and the railway track. The route crosses the track and is parallel to it for 900 meters. You walk with the railway track, a moor, and road nr. 15 to your right. The route switches to the other side of the train track and becomes a narrow gravel path leading through the moor (a nature protected area), until you get back to road nr. 15.

The next kilometer the route follows road nr. 15. You pass by a Volg supermarket and a restaurant (in a yellow building to your right) in the village Gibswil. On your left you see a large and a small ski jump halfway the forested mountain. They are the Bachtelblick Ski Jumps built in 1997 and 2005 respectively, enabling jumps of distances up to 68 meters. To your right you pass by a former pilgrim inn *zum Weissen Kreuz* (At the White Cross), dating from 1777.

In the village Ried the route splits from road nr. 15 (you will cross road nr. 15 again after about 7 km). The split occurs at a small building that looks like a chapel. However, it is not; it is a garage or storage building. From there the route starts ascending and follows a highland road. You pass by a farm with Scottish highland cattle, after which the route forks to the right. From tarmac it changes to concrete and then becomes a narrow trail through grasslands. In the settlement Büel (1 km from Ried) you are at an elevation of 821 meters, the second-highest peak of the day. The route follows the tarmac highland road for the next 2.8 km, while gradually descending to 761 meters. You pass underneath high-voltage power lines and can hear the electricity crackle.

The signs have you make a 350-meter detour to the left, only to end up at the same highland road again (this detour does not seem to make any sense). To your right you look up at the 1'000-meter-high forested Bachtel mountains, while to your left you look down at the Jona valley (*Jonatal*), where the Jona River, road nr. 15, and the railway track pass through small villages. At the other side of the valley you see a 1'200-meter-high forested mountain range and the Alps in the far distance. At a settlement called Tänler (at 751 meters) you have three wonderful views. First, of the town Wald in the valley to the left. Second, of the Alps in the distance. Third, you can see Rapperswil, the lake dam, Lake Zurich, and the Etzel mountain in the distance for the first time. Rapperswil is the destination of this stage, whereas the lake dam and Etzel mountain are on the route of stage 4.

From Tanler the direction changes to southwest. The trail goes right onto grassland and quickly changes to a forest trail. Passing by several houses it continues on a road through the village Blattenbach. You pass by a former pilgrim inn called 'At the Red Sword' (*zum Roten Schwert*) from 1621. About 200 meters later a yellow sign points left, to the ruins of the former Castle of Baliken (a 160-meter detour). Walk down the hill and turn left at the barrier into a patch of forest. Cross a steel plate bridging a small stream, continue steeply down a forest trail, and go up a small hill on your right. Hidden behind trees you see the ruins of a fortified tower (at km 20.9).

Not much is known of the history of the **Castle of Baliken** (*Burgruine Oberes Baliken*). It is believed that a small 12th century fortified residential tower stood on this site. The thick lower walls probably had a wooden construction on top. The five-sided tower foundations, with 1.5-meter-thick walls, were excavated and conserved in 1936-40. Most likely this tower was abandoned in the 14th or 15th century. The ruins of the Baliken tower are the only remnants of a handful of fortified towers that existed in this region along the Jona River valley.

After climbing back up the hill to the signposted route and continuing on the route, the road changes to a gravel path at the edge of a forest, goes through the forest, and back on a road through a settlement. The route turns back to a gravel trail, until it makes a sharp left. The following 400 meters until road nr. 15 are on a historical pilgrim path going down to the Jona River valley. The route turns in a southward direction again and steeply descends on steps through a patch of forest to a road.

About 100 meters later you cross the railway track (be careful of traffic coming around the corner when you cross the road). A steep 100-meter descent on a tarmac footpath leads you back to road nr. 15 in the Jona River valley. At this location the valley is narrow; in medieval times pilgrims crossed the Jona River on a footbridge. The area is called **Pilgersteg**, where *Steg* means footbridge. But nowadays only the name Pilgersteg has remained. The historical pilgrim footbridge over the Jona River was about 400 meters upstream (north). Do not bother to look for it; it was replaced by the concrete road bridge that you cross on the right (south).

After crossing road nr. 15 and the Jona River, the trail goes into a forest. Pay attention at this location, as the trail-head (left-side of the road, immediately at the end of the railing after crossing the river) is a narrow opening underneath high bushes that is easy to overlook.

Steep steps take you up a hill and out of the valley. You get to farmland and follow a grass trail between agricultural fields and pass underneath high-voltage power lines again.

The next 1.4 km the route stays on a plateau between 550- and 570-meters, with some gradual ascents and descents. You walk mostly on gravel roads and pass by farmhouses with geraniums at the stable windows, apple orchards, and agricultural fields with wide views. Shortly before entering the Föriholz forest you pass by a settlement with five houses called New York (*Neu York*) – it is a bit smaller than its twin city nicknamed the 'Big Apple'. Over 1 km the forest trail descends about 50 meters, making it a relaxed hike in the coolness of the forest.

At the next settlement called Weier you pass by a small pilgrim-refreshment-store in the bay window of a house. Colorful geraniums are hanging underneath the low windows.

A narrow path between bushes down the hill leads you to a road. You cross the road and have a nice view of the next 1 km. The route goes down the hill on a gravel farm road along grasslands and the edge of a small patch of forest. The gravel turns to tarmac road when you make a left turn. The road slightly ascends, underneath high-voltage power lines, to cross the railway track, where you turn right (this is the same train track you already followed from Steg through the Fischenthal highland valley). The tarmac road takes you towards the west for 500 meters, past a small settlement. After a left turn the route follows a gravel path for 300 meters, until you cross the Jona River (*Moosbrugg*, at 449 meters) at the edge of the forest. At the bridge over the river you change from Canton Zurich to **Canton St. Gallen**.

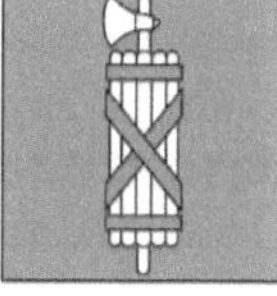

The route goes into a forest and crosses over Highway A53. A broad gravel path takes you through the forest, along a moor, where you cross the Jona River again. The forest is a main recreational area for the population of Rapperswil-Jona and you pass by several playgrounds and barbeque and campfire sites. On a slightly descending path you cross an open field (the Grunau military shooting range is on your right) and go through another patch of forest, until you reach a car park (*Grunau Parkplatz*). Water springing from a tree trunk into a cut-out tree creates a natural fountain. You can refill your drinking bottle. The water is cold and fresh.

From the parking lot the route turns left and you walk on a pavement next to a road for 250 meters. You cross the single railway track (again) and turn right to cross the Jona River (again), and enter a residential area. The route switches to the other side of the railway track after which you pass by a zero-energy house (*Nullenergie-Haus*), deriving its full electricity supply from solar panels.

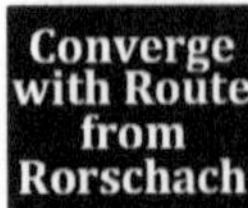


About 300 meters later you arrive at the Jona-Rapperswil Electricity Company (*Elektr. Werk Jona-Rapperswil*). At km 30.8 you find an information board explaining the convergence of the Way of St. James from Konstanz with the route from Rorschach (stage R3).

The route follows a road (*Hanfländerstrasse*) on the northern suburban outskirts of Rapperswil and turns left into the *Attenhoferstrasse* after 600 meters. You walk on a pavement and pass by a school with a large grass and sports field in front of it. The route passes over a train track and at the end of the street you get to a shopping center (*Sonnenhof*). The shopping center, with 38 stores, is a good place to get any sports, pharmacy, supermarket, or other provisions you might need. About 200 meters from the shopping center you cross a busy street and another 250 meters later through the historical cobbled streets of Rapperswil you arrive at the St. John Church (at km 32.6).

## K-23 St. John Church, Rapperswil (St. Johann Kirche)

- Herrenberg 50, 8640 Rapperswil
- St. John the Baptist, St. Catherine, St. Lawrence
- Ask the caretaker (busy somewhere in or around the church) or go to the parish office (*Pfarramt*), 50 meters before arriving at the church
- The church was built by the Counts of Rapperswil around 1220-29, at the same time as the castle was constructed. This first Romanesque church had a rectangular footprint, with one bell tower (the northern one). In 1383 the nave was extended towards the castle by 8 meters, while the second (southern) tower was built in 1441. This southern tower was wider and higher than the older northern tower (notice they have no clock).

During reconstruction in 1493-97 the nave was changed to a Gothic style and a Gothic three-sided vaulted chancel was attached to the eastern side, between the two towers.

As the Reformation swept over Switzerland in the 1520s-30s, the City-Republic of Rapperswil remained catholic. Being on the border of Canton Zurich, the other conservative catholic Cantons strongly supported Rapperswil as a spearhead in the resistance to Protestantism. Though the City-Republic of Rapperswil rejected the Reformation, its close vicinity to Canton Zurich resulted in protestant reformers causing substantial destruction of the church's catholic interior in 1531.

A devastating fire burned down most of the 650-year-old church in 1881; only the two towers survived. The church was rebuilt in a neo-Gothic style in 1882-85, while the towers were heightened by 1.2 meter and the nave was lengthened by several meters. From the outside you can still clearly see the architectural differences between the towers and the chancel in the middle.

Noteworthy in its interior are: the wooden two-winged retables (folding altars; 1533) in the side-chapels, depicting St. Catherine (left) and St. Lawrence (right); the brass-silver Madonna statue (left side-chapel; 1835); and the life-size crucifix (1496) hanging from the chancel arch.

North of the church's entrance is the Our Lady Chapel.

## **Our Lady Chapel, Rapperswil** (Liebfrauenkapelle) K-24

Herrenberg 45, 8640 Rapperswil

St. Mary, St. Mary Magdalene

The chapel consists of a lower ossuary (*Beinhaus*) with a prayer chapel above it (they each have a separate entrance). The ossuary was probably built by the Counts of Rapperswil around 1253, when the city cemetery inside the medieval town walls, next to the castle, was established. The chapel above it was built in a Gothic style around 1489. Several of the interior decorations date from around 1530. From the outside you can clearly see that the chancel is a separate construction; it was attached to the nave in 1675.

Special are the beautiful wall frescos in the nave and chancel, and the paintings, dating from the renovation in 1916-17. In these years the interior underwent an extensive renovation (removing baroque elements) to bring its style in line with the neo-Gothic St. John Church that had been newly built in 1885. A tall statue representing the Virgin Mary with baby Jesus, with beaming golden rays, stands at the altar. The frescos on the outer wall depict St. Mary and St. Mary Magdalene, and date from the construction in 1675.

The stone statue on the pillar (representing Mary) in front of the chapel was made for the National Exhibition in Bern in 1914. It was purchased by locals and donated to the parish.

Across from the church and chapel is the Castle of Rapperswil (at km 32.7).

K-4

The **Castle of Rapperswil** with its fortified walls was built by the Counts of Rapperswil around 1220-29, and coincides with their founding of the town Rapperswil. The Counts of Rapperswil had already established a castle (called old-Rapperswil) on the southern side of Lake Zurich (near present-day Altendorf) in the 11th century. The Way of St. James that follows the route in stage S2 passes by this location (see point of interest nr. S-2). The Counts of Rapperswil also built other castles in the region, for example the Castle of Grynau. You pass by this castle in stage S1 (see point of interest nr. S-1).

Around 1220 the Counts decided to relocate to the peninsula on the northern side of the lake and established a new castle and town (Rapperswil). The castle probably was a residential living tower that was expanded in the subsequent decades.

As the lineage of the Counts died out in 1283, the castle became the property of the Kingdom of Habsburg-Laufenburg (a strong opponent of the early Swiss Confederation). From 1336 the Habsburg granted political refugees, coming from Zurich, accommodation and protection in Rapperswil. In the following decades these exiles tried to undermine the leaders of Zurich. In 1350 Zurich troops attacked the exiles in Rapperswil and destroyed the city and castle. Four years later (1354) ownership of the city and castle changed to the House of Habsburg-Austria, who had the castle rebuilt as a stronghold against the Swiss Confederation. It is believed that the construction of that period resulted in the castle's unusual triangular footprint. Three secret subterranean passages provided the occupants of the castle with safe escape routes to the city at the foot of the hill.

In 1415 the town became an independent City-Republic within the Kingdom of Habsburg-Austria. Regular battles between the Swiss Confederate Cantons and the Kingdom of Habsburg occurred, where Zurich attacked the small City-Republic, severely damaging the town and castle. The Habsburg of Austria were too far away to provide protection, so in 1458 the City changed its patronage to the catholic Ur-

Cantons (Uri, Schwyz, Unterwalden), thereby becoming part of the Swiss Confederation and relinquishing its status as a territory of the Austrian Kingdom. The patronage of the catholic Cantons ended when the reformed Cantons Zurich and Bern assumed patronage of the City-Republic in 1712.

Napoleon's troops conquered Switzerland and plundered part of the castle in 1798. At the inception of the Helvetic Republic, after the French invasion, the Republic of Rapperswil was dissolved. The town was allocated to the newly created Canton St. Gallen in 1803. From 1803 until 1820 the castle housed a Cantonal prison, was for rent, and temporarily housed military barracks until 1869. It subsequently housed the Polish National Museum (erected by Polish emigrants) until 1927. The castle was renovated in 1988-89, and nowadays houses the Polish museum again.

You can access the inner court of the castle, which is regularly used for concerts and is nowadays covered by an artistic transparent plastic rain cover. The Polish museum is also accessible, but not the remainder of the 650-year-old building. Though these other historical rooms, such as the Knights Hall, can be rented for weddings, events, or banquets.

The castle on the hill of the Rapperswil peninsula is one of the most important and well-maintained historical buildings along Lake Zurich. The castle served as a stronghold for the trade and pilgrim routes east of Lake Zurich, from southern Germany to Einsiedeln. It is likely that the Romans already built their fortification on that same site on the hill. Nowadays the town Rapperswil (including Jona) has about 26'000 inhabitants. The castle and the St. John church, constructed in the same style, still dominate the skyline of Rapperswil to this day.

The castle walls extend towards the west, offering magnificent views over the medieval town, its small port, Lake Zurich, and the Alps. On the southern side of the wall you see a small vineyard (first mentioned in 981), as well as the famous rose gardens with over 15'000 roses (created in 1965).

When you return to the route at the location of the St. John church, the sign nr. 4 directs you down the steps, descending from the hill onto a long square (*Hauptplatz*) filled with cafes, restaurants, and terraces with white umbrellas. Make a short stop down the first flight of stairs. You will see a metal St. James scallop inlaid in the pavement, in front of a recess with a moss-covered wall.

The signposted route continues in a southward direction towards the train station of Rapperswil. However, to visit the Capuchin monastery's church you need to briefly leave the signposted route. At the bottom of the stairs take the first street on the right (*Hintergasse*), after 150 meters turn right (*Endingerstrasse*), and another 100 meters later you are at the western end of the peninsula.

K-5

On the left you pass by the so-called **Einsiedeln House** (belonging to the Benedictine Abbey of Einsiedeln). This is probably the oldest building in Rapperswil, as its foundations may date from around 981. Around that time, it housed a ferry station to transport travelers and pilgrims from Rapperswil to Hurden and the Island of Ufenau. This was before the first footbridge was built in 1360 (see stage 4). The Einsiedeln House was part of the city's fortifications at the side of the lake. When you walk to the lakeside promenade you will see the house's massive lower walls and a buttress. Notice that the windows are high up the fortified wall.

The Abbey of Einsiedeln still owns the whole peninsula, including the Einsiedeln House, the land on which the Capuchin monastery was built, and even parts of the lake.

Nowadays the house is occupied by a music school and is not publicly accessible.

After the Einsiedeln House go up the steps to the right and you arrive at the Capuchin Monastery of Rapperswil (at km 33.0).

## Capuchin Monastery, Rapperswil (Kapuziner Kloster) K-3

Endingerstrasse 9, 8640 Rapperswil-Jona

Capuchin Order

The monastery was established on the initiative of the patrons of the City, the catholic Ur-Cantons (Uri, Schwyz, Unterwalden), in 1602. Their aim was to create a catholic counterforce to stave off the Reformation that Canton Zurich tried to expand since the 1520s. Rapperswil was relatively close to Zurich and under continuous reformation pressures. The monastery had the task to firmly anchor Catholicism and care for the remaining Catholics in the eastern highlands of Canton Zurich (such as Fischenthal).

The construction of their buildings lasted several years because the rocky peninsula first had to be leveled (1603-06). The construction was financed by the City of Rapperswil and the buildings are presently still owned by the City (not the Capuchin Order).

The first buildings stood outside the city walls and were small, housing only a few friars. After Zurich attacked Rapperswil, fortified walls were built around the monastery that made it part of the city's western fortifications in 1662. This made the Order part of the city and close to the societal and cultural developments in the City-Republic.

Further extensions and modernizations were undertaken in 1734, 1922-24, and 1967.

Nowadays seven friars and two sisters live in the monastery and provide guided tours, church services, and extended stays for self-reflection and meditation.

The monastery generates income from a small shop, weddings at its church, events, and seminars.

The Capuchin monastery's church is on the right of their small front square.

## K-25 Capuchin Monastery Church, Rapperswil (Kapuziner Kirche)

- Endingerstrasse 9, 8640 Rapperswil-Jona
- At the monastery's shop (*Klosterladen*), left of the church's entrance. Pull the cross that rings a bell and ask for the pilgrim stamp at the shop's counter.
- The church was built as part of the monastery in 1603-06. It was renovated and the chancel was enlarged in 1734. The interior was restyled in 1923.
- As one would expect from a mendicant Order that vowed to poverty, the church has an austere interior (and is not even owned by the Order). There are no marble altars, no gold-painted statues, no colorful frescos on the ceiling or walls, and no stained-glass windows from famous artists (compare this to the opulent decorations in the Benedictine monastery's church in Fischingen). The interior resembles a protestant church. Only the four statues, crucifixion way stations, and the large crucifix in the chancel indicate it being a catholic place of worship. The church has a small bell steeple on its roof (above the chancel).

Inside the church follow the signs to the front-right and you arrive at the St. Anthony Cave.

## K-26 St. Anthony Cave, Rapperswil (Antonius Grotte)

- Endingerstrasse 9, 8640 Rapperswil-Jona
- St. Anthony of Padua
- The cave was hewn into the rocks in 1923. It is a place of worship of St. Anthony of Padua and attracts mostly regional pilgrims.

📷 A statue on an altar at the back wall of the small cave represents a kneeling and praying St. Anthony.

Backtrack the same 150 meters through the *Endingerstrasse* and turn right to arrive at the lake promenade. The promenade at the lake's yachting port and the fish market are always bustling with life. The many cafes, restaurants, and terraces provide an excellent ending of your hiking day in this historical traffic-free medieval town.

## From the ending point

The St. Anthony cave is the ending point of stage K3, about 200 meters aside the signposted route nr. 4.

In case you are a day-hiker, you have easy access to the Rapperswil train station; from the St. Anthony cave it is about 500 meters, from the lake promenade 300 meters, and from Tourist Information 100 meters.

In case you are a thru-hiker, you can stay at the pilgrim inn (*Pilgerherberge Rapperswil*) in the historic center, only a few meters from the promenade (Seestrasse 5, 8640 Rapperswil; tel. 079 886 73 37; www.pilgerherberge.ch; reservation online on their website). A blue pilgrim sign and flag mark their building. The pilgrim inn is open from 1 April until 31 October, daily from 16:00. Of course, there are many more accommodation possibilities. Check out www.jakobsweg.ch or www.viajacobi4.ch for the accommodation possibilities in Rapperswil. At the end of the fish market square, at the lakeside, you find the Tourist Information Office (Fischmarktplatz 1, 8640 Rapperswil; tel. 055 255 77 00; www.rapperswil-zuerichsee.ch; info@rzst.ch).

## The next Stage

Stage 4 guides you across the Lake Zurich basin, over the Etzel mountain, to the highland plateau of Einsiedeln. The next stage is short and will provide relief from the long distances of stages K3, K2 and R3, R2. Read the next chapter to find out what that entails.

# Stage 4: Rapperswil to Einsiedeln 18 km

*The Way to Saint Meinrad*

### *Route stats*

| | *Distance in km* | *Time in hrs:min* |
|---|---|---|
| Signposted route nr. 4 | 16.1 | 3:30 |
| Churches/chapels | 1.4 | 1:40 |
| Points of interest | | 0:20 |
| Rest | | 0:30 |
| Stage 4 | 17.5 | 6:00 |

In case you hike this stage as a daytrip, you need to add 100 meters in Rapperswil and 600 meters in Einsiedeln (from and to the train stations). The visit to the Island of Ufenau, with its chapel and church, is not included in the above time and distance, nor are the last three points of interest.

| | |
|---|---|
| Ascent/descent/total | +710 / -215 / 925 altitude meters |
| Lowest/highest altitude | 406 / 951 meters |
| Pathway/condition | easy / moderate |
| Churches/chapels | Rapperswil, Hurden, Ufenau Island (2), Pfäffikon (2), Etzel Pass, Egg, Einsiedeln (5) |
| Monasteries | Benedictine Monastery Einsiedeln |
| Points of Interest | Site of Neolithic Pile Houses, Wooden Footbridge, Island of Ufenau, Castle of Pfäffikon, Devil Bridge, Site of former Gallows, Our Lady Fountain, Guided Monastery Tour, Diorama Bethlehem, Panorama Crucifixion |

### *Route summary*

Stage 4 starts in Canton St. Gallen, but after about 1.5 km enters catholic **Canton Schwyz**.

Stage 4 guides you across the Lake Zurich basin, over the Etzel mountain, to the highland plateau of Einsiedeln.

From the Rapperswil castle's grounds you have a good view of the first 10 km of stage 4. Looking over the rooftops, you see the famous wooden bridge and dam crossing (left side) and the town Pfäffikon on the other side of Lake Zurich. In the distance you see the Etzel mountain, peaking at 1'096 meters. Stage 4 takes you over the wooden bridge and land tongue, through Pfäffikon, and over the Etzel Pass at 951 meters (east of the summit).

Stage 4 starts with an easy walk across the wooden bridge and the land tongue to the town Pfäffikon, crossing Lake Zurich. These first 6 km are flat. After the Pfäffikon train station underpass the route goes through the town for about a kilometer and passes over Highway A3. From there the ascent becomes steep, as the trail crosses a few grass fields, but most of the time the route is through the forest. After 10 km it reaches the Etzel Pass at 951 meters. From there the route steeply descends over one kilometer to the Devil Bridge that crosses the Sihl River. Climbing out of the river valley, the route reaches the highland plateau offering panoramic views of Einsiedeln, the Sihl Lake, and the Alps. More than 85 percent of the route is on hardened surfaces (tarmac roads, trails with cement or gravel).

There are two reasons why stage 4 is relatively short, only half a day's hike. First, sufficient time for sightseeing in the Abbey of Einsiedeln is needed. The Einsiedeln Tourist Information Office offers a guided tour around the abbey and its historical library, which starts at 14:00. Without the tour, there is no access to the library and limited insight in one of Switzerland's most important abbeys. Second, stage K3/R3 was tough and stage 5 is equally tough; it is good to have a relaxing day in between.

## *Getting to the starting point*

The starting point in Rapperswil is at the St. Antonius cave of the Capuchin monastery. In case you spent the night at the pilgrim inn in Rapperswil, you are already at the right location to start stage 4.

In case you hike stage 4 as a daytrip, you can start at the route nr. 4 signpost at the zebra crossing of road nr. 8 (behind the Tourist Information Office), about 100 meters from the station.

*Route Map and Profile*

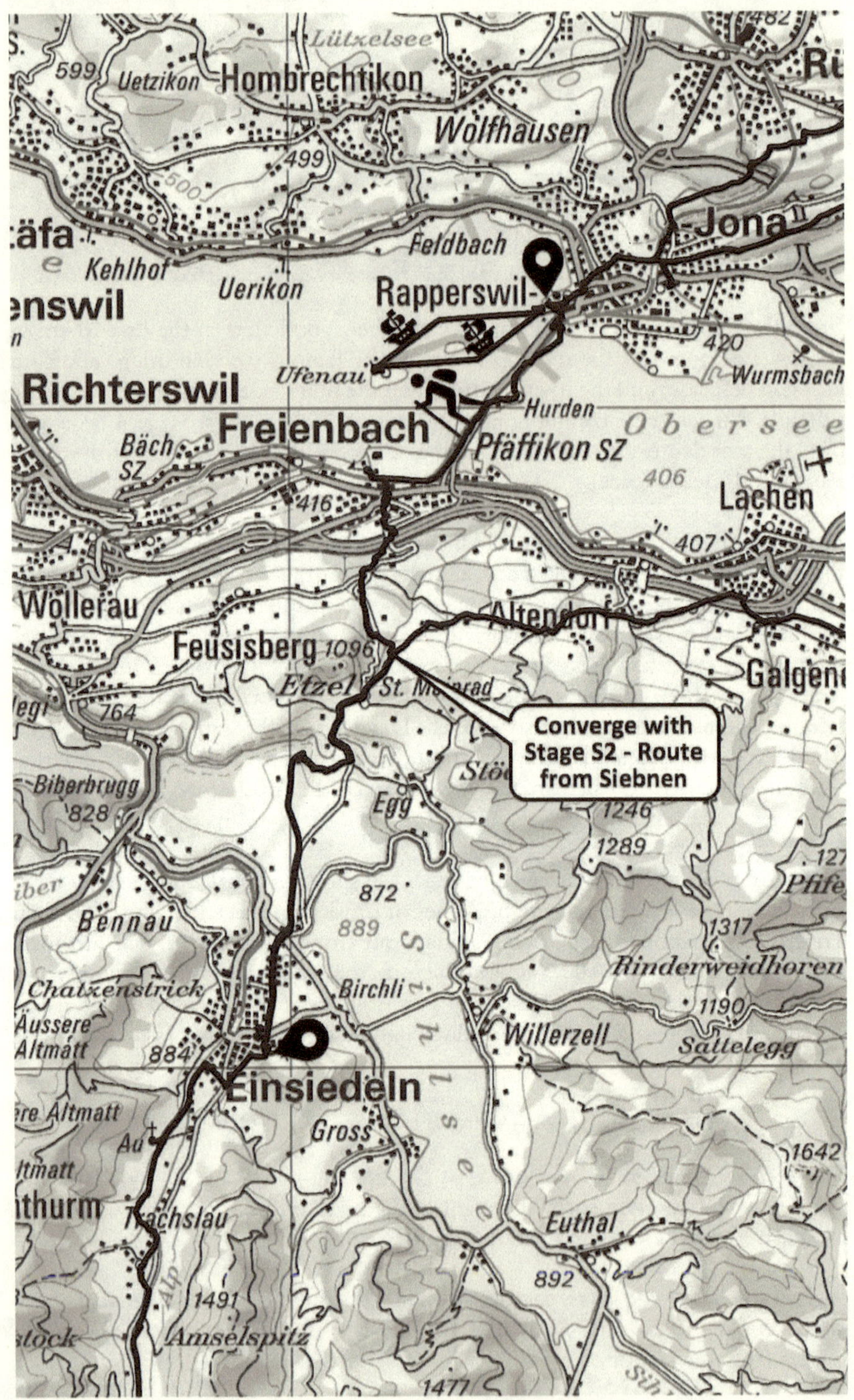

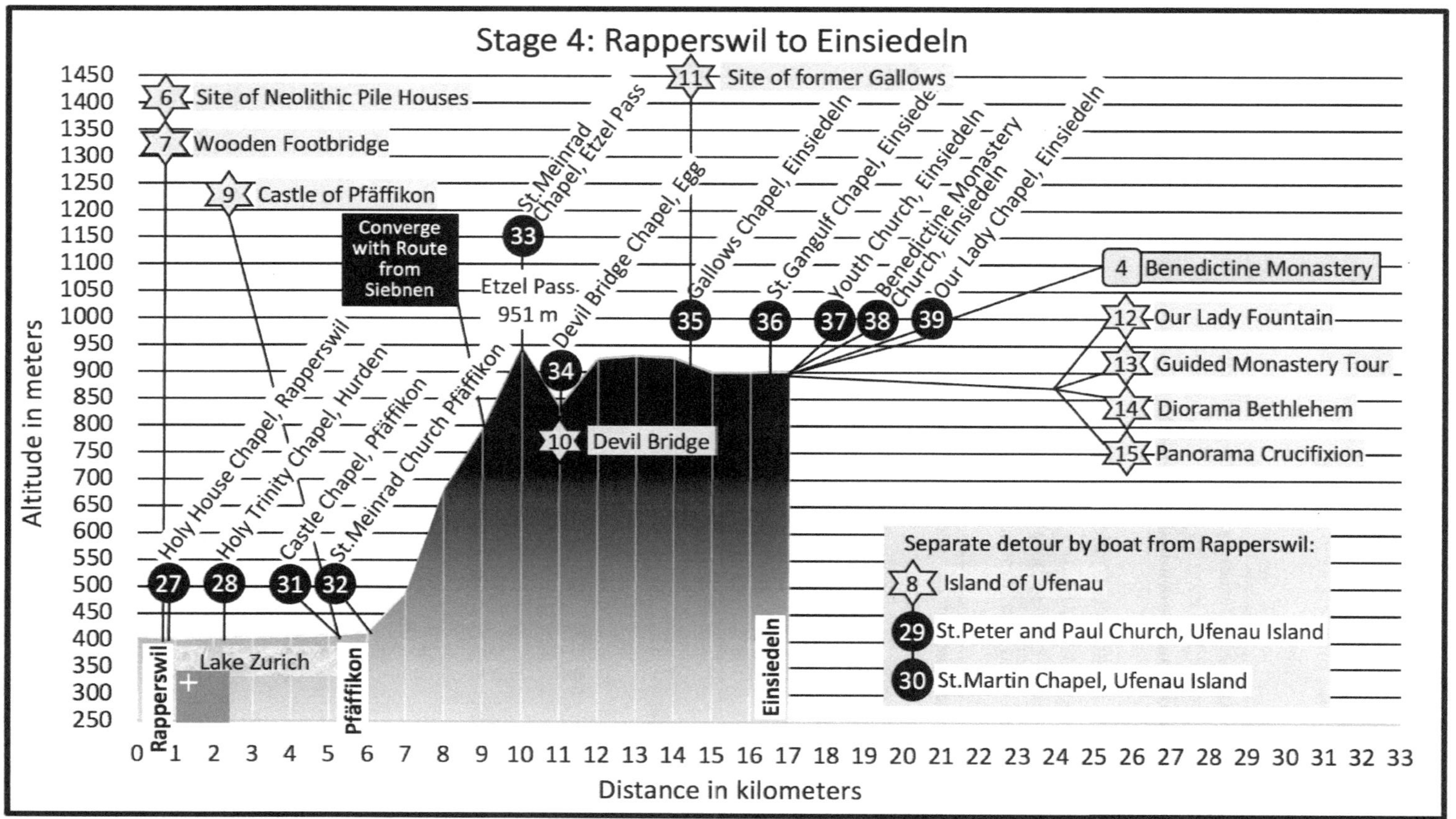
Stage 4: Rapperswil to Einsiedeln
Altitude in meters
1450 1400 1350 1300 1250 1200 1150 1100 1050 1000 950 900 850 800 750 700 650 600 550 500 450 400 350 300 250
6 Site of Neolithic Pile Houses
7 Wooden Footbridge
9 Castle of Pfäffikon
Converge with Route from Siebnen
33 St.Meinrad Chapel, Etzel Pass
Etzel Pass 951 m
11 Site of former Gallows
27 Holy House Chapel, Rapperswil
28 Holy Trinity Chapel, Hurden
31 Castle Chapel, Pfäffikon
32 St.Meinrad Church Pfäffikon
34 Devil Bridge Chapel, Egg
10 Devil Bridge
35 Gallows Chapel, Einsiedeln
36 St.Gangulf Chapel, Einsiede
37 Youth Church, Einsiedeln
38 Benedictine Monastery Church, Einsiedeln
39 Our Lady Chapel, Einsiedeln
4 Benedictine Monastery
12 Our Lady Fountain
13 Guided Monastery Tour
14 Diorama Bethlehem
15 Panorama Crucifixion
Separate detour by boat from Rapperswil:
8 Island of Ufenau
29 St.Peter and Paul Church, Ufenau Island
30 St.Martin Chapel, Ufenau Island
Rapperswil
Lake Zurich
Pfäffikon
Einsiedeln
0 1 2 3 4 5 6 7 8 9 10 11 12 13 14 15 16 17 18 19 20 21 22 23 24 25 26 27 28 29 30 31 32 33
Distance in kilometers

## *Hiking the Route*

From the route nr. 4 signpost at the zebra crossing of road nr. 8 (behind the Tourist Information Office), you walk 200 meters along road nr. 8, turn left to use the underpass, and turn left again to walk half a circle, until you get to the beginning of the wooden bridge across Lake Zurich.

**Lake Zurich** is Switzerland's 6th largest lake, with an average depth of 49 meters (maximum depth 136 meters) and a surface elevation of 406 meters. It has a length of 40 km and a maximum width of 3 km.

Pfäffikon, at the southern side of Lake Zurich, has a natural land tongue extending towards Rapperswil, covering about 2 of the 3 km distance between the two towns. The remaining 1 km gap between Hurden and Rapperswil is nowadays bridged by a dam with a road and train tracks.

Archaeological excavations along this land tongue and the area between Hurden and Rapperswil discovered several stilt house settlements dating from 3500-500 BC. These were wooden houses built on poles in the marshlands and shallow water of the lake. They have been designated UNESCO World Heritage Site of **Neolithic Pile Houses** around the Alps in 2011 (see also stage P1 in Volume III for an area close to Fribourg that received the same designation). Because the lake has expanded over the millennia, the remnants of the stilt houses are nowadays about 4 meters below the water surface.

Further archaeological excavations have revealed that the 1 km gap between Hurden and Rapperswil was first bridged during Neolithic times around 1525 BC. This first **Wooden Footbridge** connected Hurden, the pile dwellings, and Rapperswil, and was solid enough to carry cattle and carts. This confirms that this area at Lake Zurich was already a transport and travel intersection between the Rhine and the Alps several millennia ago. The discovery of the remains of a 3'500-year-old bridge made this the oldest bridge of Switzerland and Central Europe, and was therefore also included in the UNESCO World Heritage Site mentioned above.

Further excavations discovered that the Romans had also built a wooden bridge on poles (around the year 165).

During the middle ages another wooden footbridge was built (1358-60), replacing the ferry. The Count of Habsburg-Austria initiated the construction of this bridge (1358), only four years after he had purchased the city and castle of Rapperswil (1354). This wooden bridge (destroyed and renewed many times over the centuries) existed for more than 500 years, until the dam was built.

A full dam (*Seedamm*), allowing train tracks and road traffic (road nr. 8) to pass easily between the northern and southern shores, was constructed in 1875-78. As soon as this dam was opened for traffic in 1878, the medieval wooden footbridge was demolished.

In 2000-01 a new wooden footbridge was constructed east of the dam. Standing on 233 piles it has a width of 2.4 meters and a length of 841 meters, making it the longest wooden bridge in Switzerland.

One hundred meters onto the bridge is the Holy House Chapel (at km 0.9).

## Holy House Chapel, Rapperswil (Heilig Hüsli) 27

Holzsteg, 8640 Rapperswil

St. Mary

The chapel was part of the wooden bridge that existed from 1360, and was located at the northern end of the lake's crossing. A wooden bridge chapel was first mentioned in 1485 (but had probably already existed since 1360), and was used for prayers by pilgrims on the Way of St. James before they crossed the lake. The present chapel was built in a late-Gothic style in 1551, and is the only remaining part of the medieval bridge. In 1563 a nun from Rapperswil was convicted of being a witch and was drowned in the lake at this chapel. After the lake's dam was built in 1878, the wooden footbridge was dismantled; it was not until 2001 that a new footbridge was built. For 123 years (1878-2001) the Holy House chapel stood isolated in the lake, only accessible from the water.

You cannot access the small chapel; you can only peek in through the grating. The fresco depicting the Virgin Mary is a reproduction from 2001; the original from 1568 is in the City Museum of Rapperswil. The walls and vaulted ceiling indicate remains of old frescos. It is clear that the walls were whitewashed, covering the medieval frescos. A transparent PVC depicts images of medieval pilgrims. People still throw in coins to ask for a safe passage on their Way of St. James, as pilgrims did in the middle ages.

The water around the bridge is shallow and crystal clear. You can see big fish in the water of the lake. The bridge provides panoramic views of Lake Zurich and the mountains beyond, but also back to the Castle of Rapperswil.

About 100 meters before the end of the footbridge (at km 1.5) the Way of St. James enters catholic **Canton Schwyz**. At the end of the wooden bridge the route turns left on a gravel path, east of the road and railway tracks. After 200 meters a small road to the left leads to the Hurden chapel. At this location you need to briefly leave the signposted route to get to the chapel that stood at the southern end of the medieval wooden bridge. At km 2.2 you arrive at the Holy Trinity Chapel, situated opposite of the hotel-restaurant Rössli.

## 28 Holy Trinity Chapel, Hurden (Kapelle Hurden)

Hurdnerstrasse 139, 8640 Hurden

The chapel was built by the abbey-administrator of Einsiedeln in the year 1497. It stood at the southern end of the wooden bridge that existed from 1360. Soon after the construction of the chapel the first inns were built in Hurden, accommodating pilgrims who passed over the wooden bridge on their way to Einsiedeln. In the 16th-18th centuries the small chapel was damaged several times by local wars.

In 1798 French troops destroyed much of the building; it was provisionally repaired by 1809, but it took another 56 years (1865) until the chapel was completely renovated. Since the dam was built and traffic was diverted, the chapel has been standing a bit lost between hotels and restaurants on the edge of the land tongue.

The Gothic chapel is dedicated to the Holy Trinity (*Heilige Dreieinigkeit*) and has a simple interior. Holy Trinity stands for the concept that God is one, yet represented by three Divine Persons, the Father, the Son Jesus Christ, and the Holy Spirit.

From the chapel continue on the *Hurdnerstrasse* southwards and after 200 meters you get back to the signposted route nr. 4. The signpost directs you to the underpass of road nr. 8 and the railway tracks to get to the western side of the land tongue. To the west you see two small islands in Lake Zurich (both are part of Canton Schwyz).

---

The smaller island is called Lützelau, the bigger one **Ufenau Island**. The Benedictine Abbey of Einsiedeln has owned both islands since the year 965 (through donation by Roman-German Emperor Otto I). Ufenau Island is also called Monastery Island (*Klosterinsel*). It is known for its small vineyard (renewed in 1986) from which monastery-wine (*Klosterwein*) is produced, as well as its 1'100-year-old St. Martin chapel and 880-year-old St. Peter and Paul church. Ufenau is Switzerland's largest island, which is gradually getting smaller as the water level of Lake Zurich has been rising for many centuries.

From Hurden a wooden bridge used to connect to Ufenau island. This footbridge existed between 1430 and 1670 (though it was destroyed and rebuilt several times during these centuries), and was called the **Church Way to Ufenau** (*Kirchweg in die Ufenau*). Medieval pilgrims would have used this bridge to get to the chapel and church on the island, say their prayers, and continue on their way to the Benedictine Abbey of Einsiedeln. Already before the existence of this bridge, Ufenau Island had been an important part of the pilgrimage route. Nowadays the only way to get to the island is by boat.

Boat nr. 3730 (return ticket CHF 12.40) from the Rapperswil boat pier takes you to the small island in 12 minutes. On weekdays the departures are at 12:35, 13:30, 15:30, and 16:35 (only four connections) (on weekends more connections between 11:30 and 18:35). The returns are equally limited. These connections are only available from the beginning of April until mid of October. For details of the boat connections visit *http://online.fahrplan.zvv.ch/* or the Rapperswil Tourist Information Office.

Because of the limited timetable of the public ferry to Ufenau it is hardly possible to fit a visit to the island into the pilgrimage schedule between Rapperswil and Einsiedeln. It may require a separate visit on a different occasion.

From the boat pier at Ufenau Island you first get to the St. Peter and Paul Church.

## 29 St. Peter and Paul Church, Ufenau Island (St. Peter und Paul Kirche)

Insel Ufenau, Zürichsee

St. Peter and Paul, St. Adalrich, St. Christopher, St. Meinrad

The church stands on the ruins of a Gallo-Roman temple dating from around the year 200, when the Roman Empire occupied Switzerland. A first Romanesque church was built in the 10th century. This first church was built by Countess Regelinda of Swabia. Her son Adalrich of Einsiedeln was a Benedictine monk from the Einsiedeln Abbey, who lived as a hermit on the island. When Regelinda got sick with leprosy she retreated to the island, where she died in 958. Her bones were buried at the Abbey of Einsiedeln. They both lived in a house on the island, where Adalrich took care of his ill mother. Adalrich died on the island in 973, and was buried at the church.

The Abbey of Einsiedeln, who had become owner of the island in 965, replaced the first Romanesque church with the present building in 1141.

Until 1308 the St. Peter and Paul church was the parish church of the surrounding villages on the lake's shores. This meant that the people had to use a ferry to attend the services on the island. It was rather unpractical to visit the mother church on the island and once in stormy weather 50 parishioners died when their ferry sank. From 1430 to 1670 the wooden footbridge from Hurden provided an easier and safer access for pilgrims to the grave of St. Adalrich.

You can clearly recognize the Romanesque features of the church: tiny windows that are high up the walls; a low tower (the roofed top was added in 1630); Lombard bands, decorative arches on the tower; and the chancel in the base of the tower.

Special features inside the church are: the restored wall frescos depicting St. Adalrich and his mother Regelinda, who holds the church and chapel in her hands; the tall fresco depicting St. Christopher, for the protection of traveling pilgrims; and the wall tabernacle in the chancel. Most walls have faded frescos (one of them tells the story of the killing of St. Meinrad), with hardly recognizable scenes (dating from the 13th until the 17th centuries).

St. Adalrich's tomb was opened in 1659 (the year he was canonized as Saint) and a new baroque sarcophagus was made to hold his bones. This sarcophagus was opened in 1959, when his bones were taken out and moved to the Abbey of Einsiedeln. Since then his empty sarcophagus has been kept in the St. Martin chapel.

About 100 meters to the east is the St. Martin Chapel.

## St. Martin Chapel, Ufenau Island (St. Martin Kapelle) 30

Insel Ufenau, Zürichsee

St. Martin, St. Adalrich

The chapel was built around 1206, on the site of a first church that was probably built in the 7th or 8th century. It was the catholic center of an extensive parish of the villages along the lake's shores.

You can clearly recognize the Romanesque features of the chapel in the tiny windows that are high up the walls. When you have a closer look at the architecture of the chapel and the church, you can see that the naves of both buildings are exactly the same (in size, roof, placement of doors and windows, and orientation to the east) – they were built around the same time. The main difference between the two buildings is the chancel: at the chapel it is a lower and smaller construction; at the church it is in the base of the tower (and the church has an attached sacristy). The bell steeple on the roof was added in 1869.

Special features in the chapel are: the (empty) baroque sarcophagus of St. Adalrich of Einsiedeln with the date of 973; and the frescos in the chancel dating from the 14th to 17th centuries.

With Ufenau being the burial grounds of the Countess of Swabia and her son St. Adalrich, who also founded the church and chapel, it is easy to understand why pilgrims from southern Germany (Schwaben) would visit this area and why their way is called the Schwaben Way until Einsiedeln. The church with the grave of St. Adalrich was a popular pilgrimage destination during the middle ages.

---

But let us return to the signposted route nr. 4 in Hurden, where you just crossed underneath road nr. 8 and railway tracks to get to the western side of the land tongue. The gravel path passes by a nature protected area with farmland and the lake's moors on the right. Notice small lizards running into the bushes when they hear you approach.

The following 2 km you walk alongside the railway tracks, until you get to the underpass at the Pfäffikon railway station. The signpost directs you underneath the railway tracks. However, at this location it is worthwhile to make a short detour of 300 meters to the Pfäffikon Castle, Castle Tower, and Castle Chapel. Instead of taking the underpass, keep walking straight. As the path curves to the right you see the castle buildings (at km 5.3).

The **Castle of Pfäffikon** originated as a warehouse for storage of the harvests of the surrounding lands, after the Benedictine Abbey of Einsiedeln became owner of these lands (by donation from Roman-German Emperor Otto I in 965). The warehouse was replaced by a nearly square tower around 1250, and was expanded to a fortified tower, with 2-meter-thick walls, and a moat and surrounding walls, in 1299. It functioned as residence, watchtower, and storage. The original elevated entrance to the tower was on the first floor (still visible today), via a retractable ladder. It became the administrative seat to oversee the surrounding lands and store harvests owned by the Abbey of Einsiedeln. In 1435 the abbot of Einsiedeln expanded the tower as his summer residence, by attaching the white-colored lower residence with a small chapel on the western side. These were demolished in the 19th century, but later rebuilt (as you see them nowadays).

At the time of the Reformation (from the 1520s) the castle had an important military function as base of protection and bridgehead against invading reformative troops of Ulrich Zwingli, coming from Zurich. Though the abbey owned the castle, the regional rulers (for example the Counts of Rapperswil and the House of Habsburg-Austria) also used the castle for military purposes during local wars. The castle tower was further expanded in 1566-68, when also the castle's chapel (see below) was constructed and integrated next to the access gate to the castle's grounds. Fortified walls, with several moats, surrounded the granary, tower, and chapel; the gate next to the chapel was the main point of access. In 1577 the abbot and monks from Einsiedeln lived there for seven months, when their abbey was destroyed by a fire. In 1759-60 the harvest storage facility was replaced by a rectangular residential building.

The complex was plundered and partially destroyed during the occupation by French troops in 1798. The ruins were rebuilt in 1805-39, when the surrounding walls were demolished (1820) and the moats were filled (except for the one around the tower). In absence of a dedicated use for the tower between 1820 and 1986, the building had been neglected and became dilapidated. The castle's complex consisting of the fortified tower, chapel, and office buildings was fully renovated in its original style in 1986-88. The Abbey of Einsiedeln still owns the complex today.

Nowadays the rectangular white building houses the municipal offices, while the restored tower is used for weddings, meetings, and cultural events. When you look into the water of the moat, you will see many large carps swimming just below the surface.

## 31 **Castle Chapel, Pfäffikon** (Schlosskapelle)

Unterdorfstrasse 9, 8808 Pfäffikon

St. Eustace, St. Adalrich, St. Clement

The chapel was first mentioned in official documents in 1435, when the abbot of Einsiedeln expanded the tower as his summer residence by attaching the white-colored lower residence on the western side. A Gothic chapel was built at its current location in 1566-68, at the time the castle was expanded. It served as the chapel for the residing Benedictine monks. The small tower on top of the chancel was added in 1606. The chapel was transformed to a baroque style in 1780-85. Most of the chapel was destroyed during the occupation by Napoleon's troops in 1798. It was rebuilt and received its present baroque appearance in 1892-95, which was restored during the renovations in 1986-88.

The high-altar is beautifully decorated with paintings and gold-painted artwork. The two side-altars and communion table have been restored in the same style. Notice the large fresco depicting the archangel Gabriel and Mary surrounded by angels above the door.

The chapel was dedicated to Saint Eustace as his skull was kept as a relic in the Abbey of Einsiedeln. Given the fictional existence of this saint, the skull was of a catacomb saint.

Have a closer look at the two side-altars and the communion table. The left side-altar displays bones of St. Adalrich of Einsiedeln. Given that he died on the island of Ufenau, these are likely his bones. His relics are also kept in the St. Meinrad chapel at the Etzel Pass (see below). The right side-altar displays the bones of the Blessed Basilius Oberholzer. He was abbot of Einsiedeln and initiated a renovation of the chapel that was completed in 1895, the year he died.

The communion table contains decorated bones and a skull of St. Clement M.R. (Roman Martyr), a catacomb saint. As you can see, the bones and skull have been decorated with embroidery, a crown, and many precious stones. These artistic decorations were created by the nuns of the Benedictine Convent of Au, who specialized in such beautifications. You will pass by their convent at the beginning of stage 5.

From the chapel trace back the same 300 meters to the signposted route nr. 4, and turn right. The train station's underpass leads you to the front of the station. From there you walk straight to road nr. 8. You cross the road and pass by a COOP supermarket on your right. It is not clearly visible, but the next church is 50 meters to the right, behind the supermarket. Up the broad steps you arrive at the St. Meinrad Church at km 6.1.

**St. Meinrad Church, Pfäffikon** (St. Meinrad Kirche) 32

- Etzelstrasse 14, 8808 Pfäffikon
- St. Meinrad, St. Anne, St. Andrew
- Left of the main entrance is a photocopied stamp on a small piece of paper. A red glue stick is provided to glue it in your pilgrim pass. The original stamp can be collected at the parish office (*Pfarramt*), left of the church.
- The catholic church has a modern appearance, exterior and interior, constructed in 1963-65. The surrounding apartment blocks, restaurants, offices, and shops were built at the same time, creating a new town center in the 1960s. The population growth had required Pfäffikon to build its own parish church and renew its center. The church and its tower were built of concrete, in a design very similar to the St. Anthony church of Münchwilen, also built in the 1960s.

  The St. Meinrad church replaced a chapel, dedicated to St. Anne, which stood opposite of the square, next to the town hall. This chapel from 1132 was first dedicated to St. Andrew, but became known as the St. Anne chapel from the 16th century. It was demolished in 1966, a year after the new church was consecrated, as part of the renewal of the town square.

Inside the church, the Gothic wooden cross dates from the 13th century. The wood-carved statue representing Mary with baby Jesus at the right side-altar dates from around 1500.

The artistic crucifixion way stations, made of silver/gold/tin, date from 1998. Notice that there are 16, instead of the usual 14: the 15th station depicts the Last Supper, left of the cross; the 16th station behind the altar depicts Jesus' abandoned burial shroud (symbolizing resurrection). Next to it stands a lance as it was used to wound Jesus when he was at the cross (symbolizing suffering).

From the church return to the signposted route and 250 meters later you leave the residential area of Pfäffikon. The large building on your left houses a school. After steep steps up, the route turns right and on a narrow trail you pass by a small shrine containing a small replica of the Black Madonna of Einsiedeln. Through meadows the route goes southward on a small trail and passes by a farm, and a little later you pass over Highway A3.

Before passing over the highway, you have a viewpoint to the right, offering a panorama over Pfäffikon, the dam, Rapperswil, and Lake Zurich. Behind Rapperswil you can see the Hörnli mountain (and its antenna), over which you crossed in stage K3.

From the highway the trail turns right and then left, steeply up the mountain for 500 meters, until you reach the restaurant Luegeten. The trail is narrow and made of concrete. Many steps lead through patches of forest and grasslands. When you look back, you have more views over Lake Zurich.

From the restaurant you follow the road for about 300 meters, until you turn right into the forest (*Bannwald*). The following 2.5 km are quiet forest trails until you reach the Etzel Pass at 951 meters. The trails are covered with bare tree roots or gravel as the path goes up steeply. Along the climb you cross several small streams and you pass by nature protected areas, a bee farm, and anti-tank obstacles. About 1 km before the pass level the Way of St. James trail from Siebnen (see stage S2) converges with the route.

**Converge with Route from Siebnen**

The St. Meinrad Chapel is right at the Etzel Pass, next to the St. Meinrad Inn (*Gasthaus*) (at km 10). The inn is a historical pilgrim resting place, originally dating from the 14th century, when it was a wooden building. It was rebuilt after a fire in 1759. The pass at 951 meters is the highest point of stage 4.

**St. Meinrad Chapel, Etzel Pass** (St. Meinrad Kapelle) **33**

- Etzel 12, 8847 Egg
- St. Meinrad, St. Adalrich
- Left of the entrance

The chapel was first built in the year 1289. Because of its poor condition, it was demolished and rebuilt in 1697. After a fire at the neighboring pilgrim inn in 1759, part of its roof and bell steeple had to be replaced. The present steeple was constructed in 1896. The latest renovation was undertaken in 2010.

The small chapel has unexpected artful interior decorations and ceiling frescos. The chapel and pilgrim inn were named after the hermit St. Meinrad, who lived in solitude on the site of the chapel. The four ceiling frescos in the nave tell this story.

A tiny bone fragment of St. Adalrich is kept in a black casing in a recess right of the altar. A tiny bone fragment of St. Meinrad is in a similar casing in a recess left of the altar.

From the chapel the path steeply descends on a tarmac road over 1 km. You pass by some typical Swiss farmhouses and can enjoy panoramic views of the mountains in the distance. You get the first glimpse of the two Mythen mountain peaks, which you will pass by in stage 5. At the end of the descent you cross the Sihl River on a narrow bridge (at km 11.0).

The **Devil Bridge** (*Teufelsbrücke*) was first built by the Abbot of Einsiedeln as a wooden construction over the Sihl River in 1117. It was replaced by a stone bridge in 1517, and another new bridge with a roof in 1699. The purpose of the bridge was to enable the transport of building materials from the quarry on the Etzel mountain to the abbey. In 1794 the bridge was renovated and a small niche was built in the middle of the bridge, serving as a chapel (*Kapellnische*). In 1984 the abbey transferred ownership of the bridge to the municipality of Einsiedeln. The latest renovation was undertaken in 1987-92, after which it was placed under protection as a historical monument.

## 34 **Devil Bridge Chapel, Egg** (Tüfelsbrugg Kapelle)

Etzel 3, 8847 Egg

St. Nepomuk

The niche was built in 1794 (date at the foot of the statue). The stone statue represents St. Nepomuk, who is the patron Saint of bridges.

The route ascends out of the Sihl River valley and follows the road for 300 meters, after which the path turns right. The next kilometer you follow a nature trail on gravel and grassland, curving around a southern bend of the Sihl River. The trail provides nice views back to the Etzel Pass and the Devil Bridge. At the end of the grassland you turn left onto a tarmac road. The trail towards the south stays on tarmac for the following 5 km until Einsiedeln. You are walking on a highland plateau with some gradual ascents and descents. The highland offers magnificent views of the mountain ranges and the Sihl Lake. Hiking is easy and relaxed.

The **Sihl Lake** is Switzerland's 16th largest lake, with a maximum depth of 17 meters and a surface elevation of 889 meters. It has a length of 8.5 km and a maximum width of 2.5 km. The lake is Switzerland's largest artificial lake. It was created by a dam in the Sihl River, flooding part of the valley in 1937.

You pass by a tall roadside crucifix with a gold-colored statue representing Jesus and at km 14.3 arrive at the Gallows Chapel.

**Gallows Chapel, Einsiedeln** (Galgenchappeli) 35

Waldweg 1, 8847 Einsiedeln

The gallows chapel stood on the site of the current wooden structure (a covered resting place) between 1505 and 1840. This half-open chapel stood opposite of the gallows and was used by the condemned for saying their last prayers and receiving absolution. Though the gallows were abolished in 1799 (see below), the chapel continued to be used for another 40 years, until around 1840.

The current covered half-open resting place was restored on the site of the former Gallows chapel in 1933. The sandstone pillar dates from 1935, and was carved by the same artist who made the statue representing St. Nepomuk in the Devil Bridge chapel.

11

The former **Gallows** stood on the left side of the street, opposite the chapel. The macabre history of the gallows demonstrates the cruelty of medieval forms of punishment. Death sentences ordered by the Einsiedeln court were executed by: hanging (for thieves); decapitation with the sword (for murderers); burning (for witches and arsonists); or with the wheel (for murderers). Death with the wheel meant that a convicted person's bones were crushed under a big wooden spoked cartwheel with an iron rim. The tortured body was then tied to the wheel, which was mounted on a pole. Finally, the executioner could decapitate the convict, light a fire underneath the wheel, or simply let the person be picked apart by animals and birds.

People who found their death here were for example: a shoemaker who had pretended to be a priest and swindled money from parishioners was hanged; a woman accused to be a witch was burned alive; a woman accused to be a witch was decapitated and then burned; a boy accused of stealing from the abbey was decapitated. Most executions took place in the town Schwyz (through which you pass in stage 5), but severed heads and limbs were brought to Einsiedeln and nailed to these gallows as a warning.

Executions were carried out at this location between 1505 and 1798. After the invasion by Napoleon in 1798, the new constitution of the Helvetic Republic forbade all gallows, except the ones at the Cantonal Courts. In January 1799 the municipality of Einsiedeln removed these gallows.

The route continues southward and passes by a pilgrim statue on a plinth. The location provides good views over Einsiedeln, the abbey, the ski-jump slope, and the two Mythen mountain peaks. Steeply descending away from this viewpoint, you cross the main road towards Einsiedeln and pass by a long double row of the typical Swiss anti-tank obstacles. At the location where the route enters the

*Etzelstrasse*, you pass by the Eremita Zen Temple (Etzelstrasse 38), a Buddhist temple that also serves as a pilgrim inn. Though from the outside it does not look like a temple; it is a somewhat old looking green-colored house. A kilometer down the road you arrive at the St. Gangulf Chapel of Einsiedeln (at km 16.6).

**St. Gangulf Chapel, Einsiedeln** (St. Gangulf Kapelle) **36**

Etzelstrasse, 8840 Einsiedeln

St. Gangulf

The chapel was built in 1030, making it the oldest building in the Einsiedeln highlands. It resembles the St. Martin chapel on the island of Ufenau in size and design. The front porch was attached in 1814. It seems that the Romanesque features of the old chapel were lost during the renovations and reconstruction over the last 1'000 years. Being the oldest chapel in the region, it was an important station for passing pilgrims from 1030 onwards.

The stained-glass windows date from the renovations in 1944-45. Other than that, the interior is plain. The chapel's doors are locked; the chapel is only open on special occasions or by appointment with the Abbey of Einsiedeln (from where you can borrow the key).

You see the northern side of the massive Benedictine Abbey of Einsiedeln right in front of you.

The signposted route nr. 4 leads to the front of the abbey. This abbey is an important station of the Swiss Way of St. James today and was even more so in the past. In medieval times pilgrims came together at this location and often continued in groups to Santiago de Compostela.

Before visiting the abbey, though, it is worthwhile to make a small detour (300 meters) to the Youth Church. At the car park on the right, before arriving at the abbey's square, take a right and after 150 meters you see the church on the left side of the street (at km 17.1).

## 37 Youth Church St. Wolfgang, Einsiedeln (Jugendkirche St. Wolfgang)

- Eisenbahnstrasse 22, 8840 Einsiedeln
- St. Wolfgang
- At the parish office (*Pfarramt*), which is accessed by the door left of the left tower of the Abbey of Einsiedeln. Go up the stairs and ask at the counter of the office.
- From the outside the church has Romanesque features such as its square and low tower, types of stones, and small windows. But the church is not old: it was built in 1949.
- A modernization renovation was completed in 2015; nowadays the pews have seat heating. As its name indicates, it mainly serves as church for schools and children, but it is also used by non-German-speaking pilgrim groups. The interior is austere.

  The tall painting in the chancel immediately draws attention. It depicts the Assumption of Mary and dates from around 1685. The painting is of excellent quality, even 334 years after it was created. It was an important piece of artwork to the Abbey of Einsiedeln: the painting had been at the high-altar of the abbey's church, until the chancel was reconstructed in 1746. In 1949 the painting found a new place in the chancel of the Youth church.

Walk back the same way to the signposted route nr. 4 and turn right to get to the abbey's square at km 17.5.

## **Benedictine Monastery, Einsiedeln** (Benediktiner Kloster) 4

Klosterplatz, 8840 Einsiedeln

Benedictine Order

St. Meinrad

The Benedictine Abbey of Einsiedeln has its roots in the history of St. Meinrad. As described in his biography (see Appendix 2), St. Meinrad was a Benedictine monk from Swabia, who lived as a hermit at the Etzel Pass and moved to a new cell in the remote and dark forests (now called Einsiedeln) in 835. The German word 'Einsiedeln' means hermitage or retreat. After he was killed by two robbers in 861, his remains were taken to the Benedictine Abbey of Reichenau, where he was originally ordained. His remains were returned to the Benedictine Abbey of Einsiedeln in 1039. His skull is now a relic at the high-altar.

After the death of St. Meinrad, other hermits occupied his cell for 73 years, until Eberhard (from Strasbourg in the Alsace, France) founded the Benedictine Abbey in 934. The Abbey of Einsiedeln, or rather the Our Lady Chapel, was built on the site of St. Meinrad's cell. In the subsequent centuries the abbey became a pilgrimage destination and amassed significant wealth, lands, and income through donations by Emperors, Kings, and nobility. During its early days the abbey received religious support from the Benedictine Abbey of St. Gallen (see stage R1a).

The monastery's decline set in from the 12th century. Just like in Fischingen, the abbey lies in a dead-end highland valley, isolated from the major cities in Canton Schwyz, where society developed. After more than 200 years of conflict over the ownership of its extensive lands, the abbey lost more than half of its properties to the City of Schwyz in 1217 (many local and regional rulers believed the abbey was only concerned with generating profits from its extensive lands, not with their religious tasks). Their isolation, poor leadership of abbots, and the practice to only take-in novices from nobility, almost resulted in the closure of the abbey: by 1513 their buildings were in poor condition and the monastery had only two monks, the abbot and a caretaker.

The Reformation in the 1520s-30s resulted in turbulent times that made it increasingly difficult to keep the abbey going. After the last two monks had also left, the City of Schwyz appointed a former deacon of the Benedictine Abbey of St. Gallen. He and his successors put in place many reformations and re-established a strict interpretation of the Rule of St. Benedict. Their renewed focus on religious monastic life, caring for parishioners and pilgrims, and education, led to a second era of growth and prosperity.

During the 17th and 18th centuries the abbey regained wealth and constructed the opulently decorated baroque church (see below). Next to the St. Gallen abbey, Einsiedeln developed as the most important Benedictine abbey of Switzerland. With the cult around the Black Madonna, the abbey seems to have done a lot better than the abbey in Fischingen, with its relatively unknown St. Idda.

Napoleon's invasion in 1798 put an abrupt end to this era. French troops plundered the abbey and destroyed many treasures. During the years of the Helvetic Republic (1798-1803) the abbey was closed and its lands and properties were allocated to the City of Schwyz. However, after the dissolution of the Helvetic Republic in 1803, the abbey was reopened and its lands and properties were returned to them.

The new Swiss Confederation of 1848 led to uncertainties again (it resulted in the secularization of the Benedictine Abbey in Fischingen). The Abbey of Einsiedeln, worried it might undergo the same fate, expanded to the USA as a backup plan for survival in 1852; later it also founded abbeys in South America. Under the catholic government of Canton Schwyz, the abbey was able to maintain its position and continued to flourish.

In its long history the abbey (and village) burned down several times. When the abbey (including its treasures and documents) was destroyed by a fire in 1577, the abbot and monks lived in the Castle of Pfäffikon for seven months. The present buildings were constructed in 1704-35, and are the largest baroque buildings in Switzerland today.

📷 The abbey's 1'100-year-long focus on studying, learning, music, and its extensive library, attracted many scholars that became dignitaries and saints. Since 1848 (the year of the Swiss Federal Constitution) the abbey has also been housing a gymnasium, which is part of the Swiss schooling system.

Nowadays around 65 monks still live and work in the abbey. The abbey's main sources of income are its store, horse breeding, donations, concerts, exhibitions, vineyards, and its ownership of lands and real estate.

For almost 11 centuries the abbey has been a pilgrimage destination. Nowadays nearly one million visitors from all over the world come to the church and the Our Lady Chapel every year. Most arrive by train or touring cars; a minority visits Einsiedeln as a pilgrim on foot along the Swiss Way of St. James.

## Benedictine Monastery Church, Einsiedeln (Kloster Kirche) 38

Klosterplatz, 8840 Einsiedeln

St. Meinrad, Our Lady, St. Mary Magdalene

The church has a long history of destruction by fire and reconstruction. The first building on the site of the cell of St. Meinrad (nowadays the Our Lady chapel) was a small St. Meinrad chapel (934). Later churches burned down and were subsequently rebuilt in the years 1031, 1226, 1465, 1509, and 1577. The present baroque abbey buildings and church were constructed in 1703-35.

The church is one of the spiritual and sightseeing highlights of the Swiss Way of St. James. The extraordinary baroque interior with its side-altars, wood and metal works, marble, plastering, statues, ceiling frescos, and paintings attract many pilgrims and tourists (nearly a million) from all over the world every year.

The most beautifully decorated part of the church is certainly its chancel with the high-altar. To protect these treasures from the tourist masses, it is closed-off and you can only admire it from a distance (it is not even possible to get close to the beautifully decorated rood screen). This is the only church along the Swiss Way of St. James where it is not allowed to film or take photos (they sell a wide variety of books and brochures). It is the most commercial church with the highest number of tourists and pilgrims along the route.

At the front left of the nave a door leads to several non-tourist areas: the Confession Church (*Beichtkirche*) with rows of red-curtained confessionals, of which several are continuously occupied by priests; the St. Magdalene Chapel (*Magdalenenkapelle*); and the crypt (*Unterkirche*) as a place of silence and prayer without the tourist crowds. There is too much to describe in detail; better see the interior of this church with your own eyes.

Many side-altars display relics of Saints, stored in small gold sarcophaguses. On the left side of the nave a side-altar is dedicated to St. Meinrad, also with a small gold sarcophagus. The skull of St. Meinrad is a relic in the high-altar. It was consecrated by Pope John Paul II on the occasion of his visit to Switzerland in 1984. Since you cannot get close to the chancel, this relic is not visible.

The Our Lady Chapel in black marble is in the front part of the church.

## 39 Our Lady Chapel, Einsiedeln (Gnadenkapelle)

Klosterplatz, 8840 Einsiedeln

Our Lady

The Our Lady chapel in black marble is said to have been built on the site of the original altar of St. Meinrad (934) and houses the Black Madonna.

In the 12th century the Benedictine Abbey of Reichenau spread the legend that this chapel had been consecrated by angels, with dedication to the Virgin Mary, in 964; later added to this legend was that Christ himself had consecrated the chapel in dedication to his mother. A papal certificate confirmed this legend, describing a statement by the Bishop of Konstanz, who had seen this consecration by angels in a vision. Successively the Virgin Mary worship replaced the adoration of St. Meinrad. By the 15th century this papal certificate was exposed as a hoax; it was falsified. Still, by that time the legend and the Our Lady chapel had already attracted many pilgrims who wanted to see this wonder dedicated to the Virgin Mary.

The first statue representing the Virgin Mary with baby Jesus was destroyed in the fire of 1465. The second statue was purchased in 1466 (it had been created in Swabia in 1440-65). The statue became black after enduring exposure to the soot and smoke of oil lamps, candles, and incense within the narrow confines of the chapel.

In the 17th century the chapel received its black marble housing, but this chapel was destroyed by French soldiers in 1798. Before their occupation the statue was already removed: it was hidden in the Alpthal valley and buried on the Haggenegg mountain (you pass by both areas in stage 5), after which it was secured in the Benedictine St. Gerold Monastery in the Austrian Alps. There the statue was renovated and the exposed parts of the faces and hands were painted black (1799). It stayed at the St. Gerold Monastery during the years of the Helvetic Republic (1798-1803), when the abbey of Einsiedeln remained closed.

The statue was returned at the reinstatement of the abbey in 1803. The black marble chapel was rebuilt from the old materials in 1815-17, giving it its present-day appearance.

The 117 cm tall statue is clothed in one of its 27 beautifully embroidered colored dresses, which are being changed with the celebrations. Crowns, precious stones, and jewelry complete the ensemble. The lighting on the lusciously decorated gold background gives the statue a radiating appearance. Many pilgrims visit the Black Madonna to pray for healing of an illness. It is the most important place of pilgrimage dedicated to the Virgin Mary in Switzerland, and well-known in Europe and beyond.

The Abbey invites pilgrims to attend their regular church services. A pilgrim blessing can be obtained at 16:15 or after the vesper service (starting at 16:30) at the Sigismund altar (front right in the church). You may have to approach the celebrant of the Holy Mass to ask for it.

The pilgrim stamp is not available at the church itself, but at three other locations (same stamp): the abbey offices, the abbey shop (*Klosterladen*), and the Tourist Information Office (50 meters down the main street – ask at the counter). The abbey offices and shop can be found at the abbey courtyard (*Abteihof*), right of the church. After entering the small courtyard gate, you find the shop on the right and the offices on the left. You can enter the abbey's offices (open on weekdays 08:00 – 19:00, on weekends 10:30 – 19:00) through the abbey's first door on the left, three steps up, after which you need to ascend the indoor stairs to ring a bell at the indoor iron gate. Ask for the stamp when the office worker appears at the gate. You will be guided to a small office. There you can ask for the new and old stamp. The oval stamp with the black Madonna has been in use since 2010. During many decades before this new stamp, a different stamp was used; the round stamp with a pilgrim.

In front of the abbey you find the **Our Lady Fountain** in the middle of the square, surrounded by two arcades. The fountain was first built in 1686 and renovated many times since; its present appearance dates from reconstruction in 1747. The gold-plated statue on top of the fountain, under the crowned open dome, represents the Virgin Mary. The fountain base is a heptagon (seven sides), on each side of which two faucets spout potable water. The 14 taps represent the Fourteen Holy Helpers (a group of saints who were believed to have helped overcome diseases). Many pilgrims believe that the water has healing power and some tourists fill canisters with this water. This is an excellent spot to quench your thirst and refill your drinking bottle.

13 The best way to learn the history and see the treasures of the monastery is to participate in a **guided tour**. This tour (in German) is daily, except Sundays, from 14:00 until 15:45. You can buy the ticket (CHF 15) at the Tourist Information Office (Hauptstrasse 85, 8840 Einsiedeln), which is also the starting point of the tour (no advance reservation required). The guided tour visits the monastery including its historical library (*Stiftsbibliothek*) that includes more than 230'000 books and manuscripts, of which many before the year 1500. The tour also includes a DiaVision show, providing insight in the history, daily life, and spirituality of the Benedictine monastery.

Einsiedeln is the best place to buy **religious souvenirs** of your Swiss Way of St. James pilgrimage. The abbey's shop has an excellent selection of literature, candles, rosaries, cards, holy water, and much more. The small stores on the right side of the square in front of the abbey have good offerings too.

Two more religious attractions in Einsiedeln may be of interest: the Diorama Bethlehem and the Panorama Crucifixion.

14 The **Diorama Bethlehem** (*Benzingerstrasse* 23, about 700 meters from the abbey) is said to be the largest Christmas crib in the world, with around 470 hand-carved and dressed figures in a reconstructed Bethlehem environment (on 80 $m^2$) representing the story of the birth of Christ. It was first opened in 1954. The ticket price is CHF 6 and it is open daily from 13:00 to 17:00 (April until October). For additional details see *www.diorama.ch.*

15 The **Panorama Crucifixion** (end of *Benzingerstrasse*, 200 meters further from the Diorama) is a round painting, 100 meters long and 10 meters high, depicting the Crucifixion of Christ in Jerusalem. The ticket price is CHF 6 and it is open daily from 13:00 to 17:00 (April until October). It was first opened in 1893 and has been visited by over 4.5 million tourists since. For additional details see *www.panorama-einsiedeln.ch.*

The town Einsiedeln has about 15'000 inhabitants and to a large extent lives of the many tourists that visit the Black Madonna. The square in front of the abbey is always bustling with life. The many cafes, restaurants, and terraces provide an excellent ending of your pilgrimage day.

## *From the ending point*

The Our Lady Chapel with the Black Madonna in the Benedictine Abbey Church is the ending point of stage 4, directly on the signposted route nr. 4.

In case you are a day-hiker, you need to walk 600 meters to the train station. From the abbey square follow the main road (*Hauptstrasse*) down the hill. Since Einsiedeln is a terminal station, you need to take the SOB *Südostbahn* back to the shores of Lake Zurich for further connections.

In case you are a thru-hiker, you can stay at the monastery. The guest area of the abbey offers accommodation (limited to six beds) for one night, including dinner and breakfast. Advance reservation is not possible; you can register upon your arrival in the afternoon. You need to organize this through the abbey's office where you obtained the two pilgrim stamps (*Hofpforte* – tel. 055 418 61 57; hofpforte@kloster-einsiedeln.ch; www.wallfahrt-einsiedeln.ch). Alternatively, the Eremita Zen Temple (Etzelstrasse 38, 8840 Einsiedeln; tel. 078 408 10 89; eremita@zen-tempel.ch; www.zen-tempel.net) offers pilgrim accommodations. This Buddhist inn is 1.3 km away from the abbey: you passed by it on your way to the abbey. Of course, there are many more accommodation possibilities. Check out www.jakobsweg.ch or www.viajacobi4.ch for the accommodation possibilities in Einsiedeln or visit the Tourist Information Office (Hauptstrasse 85; tel. 055 418 44 88; www.eyz.swiss; info@eyz.swiss).

## *The next Stage*

Einsiedeln is the end of the routes through North-East Switzerland. The Way of St. James continues from Einsiedeln to Fribourg through Central Switzerland. These stages, together with their churches, chapels, monasteries, castles, chateaus, cities, and other points of interest are described in **Volume II of the Swiss Camino**.

The next stage 5 guides you through the Einsiedeln highland valley, up the Haggenegg Pass, and down to the Lake Lucerne basin. The Haggenegg Pass is the highest point of the Swiss Way of St. James. Please refer to stage 5 in Volume II to find out what that entails.

# RORSCHACH TO EINSIEDELN

# Stage R1a: Rorschach to St. Gallen 18 km

*The Way to the Abbey Kingdom*

Stages R1a and R1b have to be seen in combination with each other. Stage R1a guides you from the starting point of the Swiss Way of St. James (Rorschach) to the Abbey-Kingdom of St. Gallen. The historic city and Abbey of St. Gallen (a UNESCO World Cultural Heritage Site) may require about half a day to take in their religious, cultural, and historical significance. They are an extraordinary highlight, right at the start of your pilgrimage through Switzerland. Depending on your time of arrival in Rorschach and 18 km later in St. Gallen, it is likely you may have to do part of your sightseeing in the morning of the next day. Stage R1b intentionally has a short distance of only 11.3 km to enable a late hiking start on your second day. In case you start early in Rorschach and need limited time in St. Gallen, it may also possible to hike stages R1a and R1b in one day.

## *Route stats*

| | *Distance in km* | *Time in hrs:min* |
|---|---|---|
| Signposted route nr. 4 | 14.8 | 3:10 |
| Churches/chapels | 3.0 | 3:30 |
| Points of interest | 0.4 | 0:40 |
| Rest/lunch | | 0:40 |
| Stage R1a | 18.2 | 8:00 |

In case you hike this stage as a daytrip, you need to add 500 meters in Rorschach and 650 meters in St. Gallen (from and to the train stations). The time and distance of the historical Abbey and City Tour in St. Gallen are not included in the above stats.

| | |
|---|---|
| Ascent/descent/total | +613/ -337 / 950 altitude meters |
| Lowest/highest altitude | 398 / 723 meters |
| Pathway/condition | easy / easy |
| Churches/chapels | Rorschach (5), Untereggen, Halden, St. Gallen (6) |
| Monasteries | Former Benedictine Monastery Rorschach, former Dominican Convent St. Gallen, former Benedictine Monastery St. Gallen |
| Points of interest | St. James Fountain, Castle of Sulzberg, Ruins Castle of Rappenstein, Abbey Library, Historical Abbey and City Tour |

## *Route summary*

Stage R1a is in **Canton St. Gallen**. From Rorschach until the city of St. Gallen (at km 12.5) the churches are mainly catholic. In the city of St. Gallen the churches are protestant, except for the abbey district, which is catholic.

Stage R1a guides you from the Lake Constance basin to the highland plateau and urban agglomerations of St. Gallen.

The first 3 km are in the town Rorschach and are basically flat. The following 4 km the route gradually ascends on tarmac country roads to the village Untereggen. After Untereggen the route ascends through grasslands, after which it descends steeply over 1 km to the bridge over the Goldach River gorge. The following 2 km the route ascends steeply along patches of forest and meadows to reach the highest point of the day at 723 meters at km 12.0. After a descent over a 1 km the route enters the northern agglomerations of St. Gallen. The final 5.5 km are through the St. Gallen agglomeration and are more or less flat.

The highlight of the day is the Abbey of St. Gallen, a UNESCO World Cultural Heritage Site, at the end of the stage.

## *Getting to the starting point*

The starting point of the Swiss Way of St. James is at the port of Rorschach. In case you arrive by train from St. Gallen, it is best to get off at the station *Rorschach-Stadt* (500 meters), being closer to the port than the subsequent station *Rorschach* (1'000 meters). In case you are a thru-hiker arriving by ferry from the northern shore of Lake Constance, you are at the right location.

Depending on the time of your arrival by train or boat, you can either start your pilgrimage right away or you may have to spend the night in Rorschach. The town offers several accommodation possibilities, though no pilgrim inn. Check out www.jakobsweg.ch or www.viajacobi4.ch for the accommodation possibilities in Rorschach. You can also visit the Tourist Information Office at the port train station (tel. 071 841 70 34; info@tourist-rorschach.ch; www.tourist-rorschach.ch) and have them help you.

If you have not pre-ordered your Swiss pilgrim pass, you can buy one (CHF 12.00) at the front desk of hotel Mozart (Hauptstrasse 82, 9400 Rorschach), 100 meters from the port, or at the Tourist Information Office at the port train station.

## *Route Map and Profile*

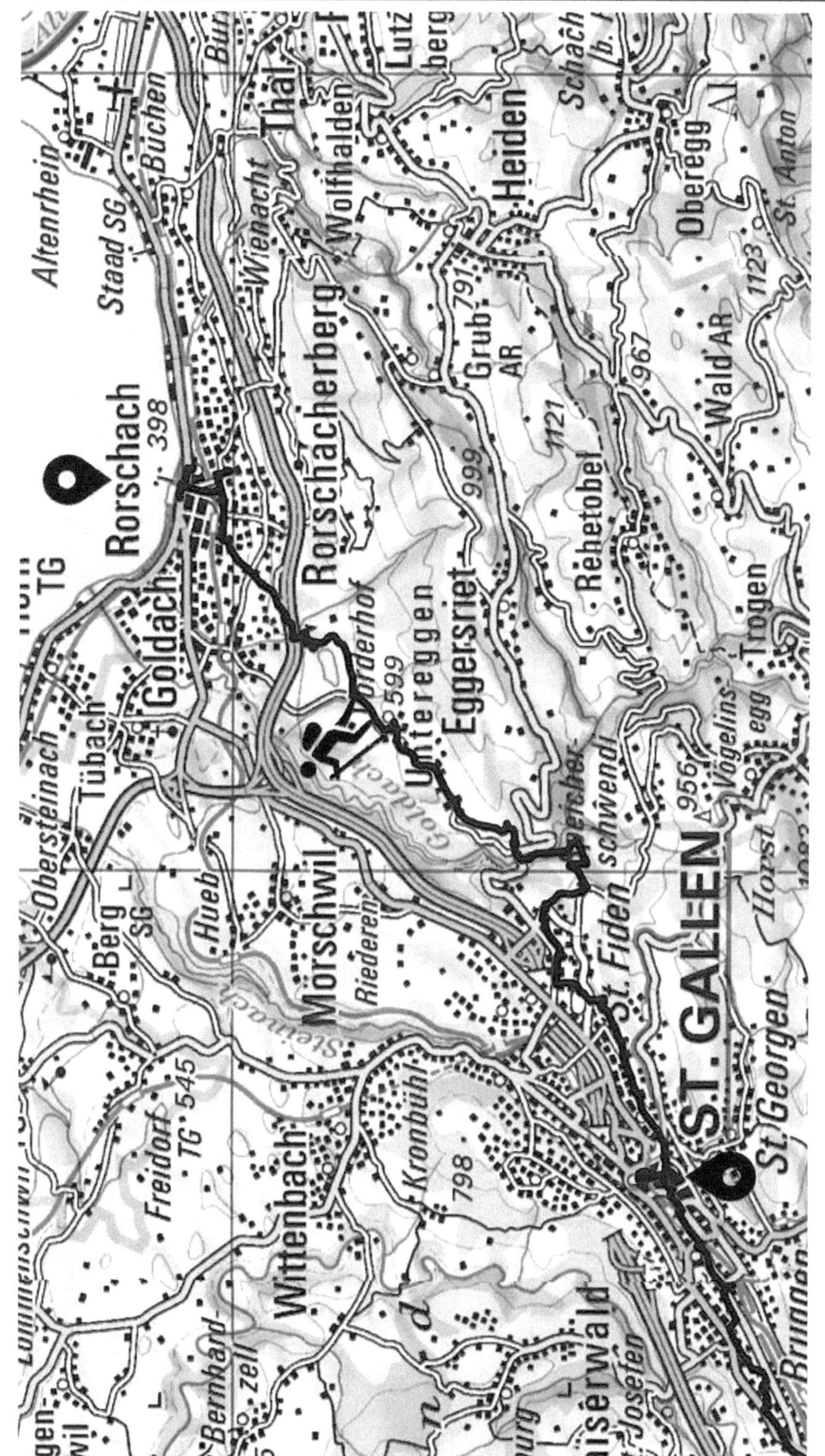
Altenrhein
Staad SG
Buchen
Thal
Wienacht
Wolfhalden
Heiden
Rorschach
398
TG
Rorschacherberg
Goldach
Tübach
Obersteinach
Vorderhof
599
Untereggen
Eggersriet
999
1121
Grub AR
791
Rehetobel
967
Oberegg
1123
St. Anton
Wald AR
Trogen
Vögelinsegg
956
Speicherschwendi
St. Fiden
ST. GALLEN
St. Georgen
Mörschwil
Riederen
Steinach
Goldach
Berg SG
Hueb
Freidorf TG
545
Wittenbach
Kronbühl
798
Bernhardzell
Josefen

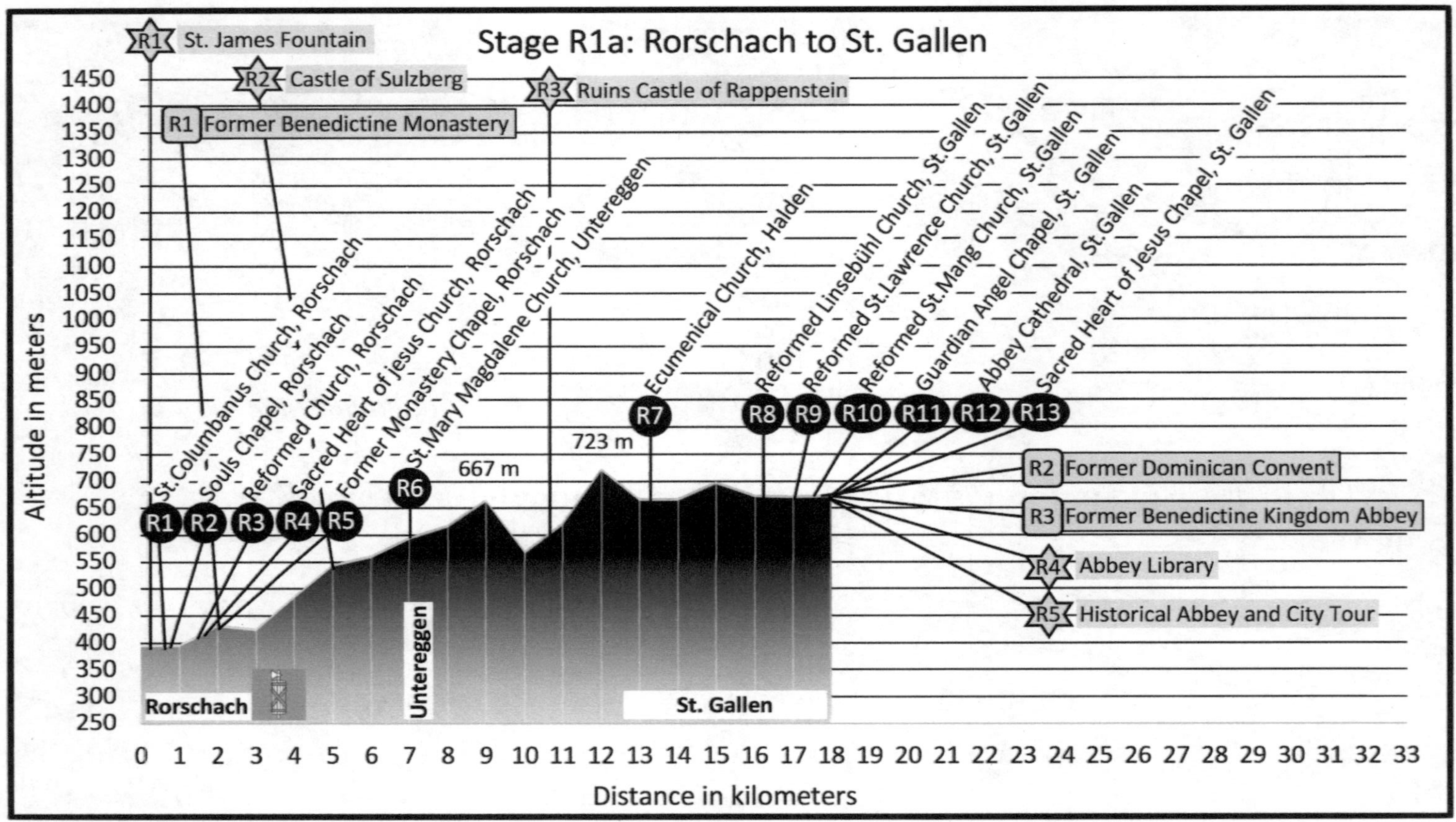
Stage R1a: Rorschach to St. Gallen
R1 St. James Fountain
R2 Castle of Sulzberg
R3 Ruins Castle of Rappenstein
R1 Former Benedictine Monastery
St.Columbanus Church, Rorschach
Souls Chapel, Rorschach
Reformed Church, Rorschach
Sacred Heart of Jesus Church, Rorschach
Former Monastery Chapel, Rorschach
St.Mary Magdalene Church, Untereggen
Ecumenical Church, Halden
Reformed Linsebühl Church, St.Gallen
Reformed St.Lawrence Church, St.Gallen
Reformed St.Mang Church, St.Gallen
Guardian Angel Chapel, St. Gallen
Abbey Cathedral, St.Gallen
Sacred Heart of Jesus Chapel, St. Gallen
R1 R2 R3 R4 R5 R6 R7 R8 R9 R10 R11 R12 R13
667 m
723 m
R2 Former Dominican Convent
R3 Former Benedictine Kingdom Abbey
R4 Abbey Library
R5 Historical Abbey and City Tour
Rorschach
Untereggen
St. Gallen
Altitude in meters
1450 1400 1350 1300 1250 1200 1150 1100 1050 1000 950 900 850 800 750 700 650 600 550 500 450 400 350 300 250
0 1 2 3 4 5 6 7 8 9 10 11 12 13 14 15 16 17 18 19 20 21 22 23 24 25 26 27 28 29 30 31 32 33
Distance in kilometers

## *Hiking the Route*

The **Rorschach port** is the starting point of the Way of St. James through Switzerland. This is where pilgrims from the northern shores of Lake Constance (*Bodensee*) of southern Germany arrive by ferry from Lindau, Langenargen, or Friedrichshafen. Twenty meters from the port, across the railway tracks, there is a small fountain and the typical yellow hiking signs marking the start of stage R1a. The green nr. 4 sign with the scallop and blue border leads in the direction of St. Gallen.

From this post the signposted route goes straight south to the train station *Rorschach-Stadt*, without passing by the churches and former Benedictine monastery of Rorschach. Instead of immediately following the nr. 4 signpost, it is worthwhile to make a brief detour. At the main street (*Hauptstrasse*), road nr. 7, right in front of you, turn right. After 200 meters you pass by hotel Mozart and a few meters later get to the *Kronenplatz* (left, across the street) with the St. James Fountain (at 0.2 km).

The **St. James Fountain** (*Jakobsbrunnen*) dates from 1895. Until 1834 a St. James Chapel (*Jakobskapelle*) stood on this site, marking the official starting point in medieval times. The fountain includes a bell that is still tolled by hand twice a day (11:00 and 18:00) during summer time. The four sides at its base display the St. James scallop and spout fresh drinking water. You can fill your drinking bottle.

From the fountain walk back the same 200 meters to the port and continue along the *Hauptstrasse* in an eastern direction (towards Rorschach train station). About 300 meters from the port, turn right into the *Kirchstrasse* and behind the café you arrive at the catholic St. Columbanus Church (at 0.7 km).

## R-1 St. Columbanus Church, Rorschach (St. Kolumban Kirche)

- Kirchstrasse, 9400 Rorschach
- St. Columbanus, St. Constance
- Preprinted on a sticker, on a table in the front portal. Alternatively, at the Tourist Information Office (Rorschach port train station) or hotel Mozart.
- This is the eighth church building on this site. A first small wooden chapel stood in the middle of a cemetery in the 8th century. It was replaced by a larger stone hall church in the 9th century. This church was enlarged around the year 1000. The fourth church with a bell tower was built in the early 13th century and replaced by another building in 1438. During the Reformation in 1528 the town Rorschach converted from Catholicism to Protestantism, which lasted only six years, as the town converted back to Catholicism in 1534. Though the six years of Reformation impacted the interior of the church (all catholic decorations such as altars, statues, paintings, and frescos were removed), these changes were reversed when the church converted back to Catholicism. Two side-chapels and side-portals were added in 1666-67, while the nave was lengthened by seven meters. In 1782-86 the nave was lengthened again and the church was decorated in a baroque style. Renovations and interior changes in 1921-22, 1966-67, and 1992-94 determined its present-day appearance.
- The church has beautiful baroque interior decorations and frescos. Special features are: the large ceiling fresco in the nave (1876); the five baroque altars in a harmonized design; the gold-colored tabernacle at the high-altar; and the relics of St. Constance. Upon entering the church, go to the right of the front portal. There you will find large information tablets in several languages (including

English). These tablets provide information on the many special features of the church. This is unique and a successful effort of the local parish to make the treasurers of the church better known to international pilgrims and visitors. Take a wooden tablet and follow the numbering around the church.

Number 7 explains the relics of Saint Constance at the St. Constance altar, below the large painting at the right side-transept. Most of the time these relics are hidden behind a screen; they are only uncovered for special celebrations. The relics of the catacomb Saint Constance were brought from Rome in 1674. The beautifully decorated skeleton, in a red Roman legion dress, was completed with plaster and decorated by nuns of the St. Scholastika Convent in Tübach (near Rorschach).

Left of the church, a bit hidden behind the trees, you find the Souls Chapel.

## **Souls Chapel, Rorschach** (Seelen Kapelle) R-2

Kirchstrasse, 9400 Rorschach

St. Michael, St. Gall

The chapel was built in 1686, and served as ossuary, a place of burial and storage of bones of the deceased. During renovations in 1953-54 the interior was restored to its baroque appearance from around 1730.

As in many other cemetery chapels, the archangel Michael is depicted on the main altar. Notice the frescos on the ceiling and the statues left and right of the altar. The statue on the right represents St. Gall with a bear. A cord hangs down the ceiling of the chancel. If you pull it, the bell will toll in the steeple.

From the chapel walk back the same way along the *Hauptstrasse* to the signposted route nr. 4. From the starting signpost at the port follow the route in a southern direction along the *Signalstrasse*. After 300 meters the route leads to a large crossing and goes diagonally to the right (towards the *Rorschach-Stadt* train station). However, at this location you need to briefly leave the signposted route to go to the next two churches and a former monastery. Instead of going diagonally to the right, continue straight uphill along the *Signalstrasse* towards a building that looks a bit like a castle. Go up the wide stairs to arrive at the reformed Church of Rorschach (at km 1.5).

**R-3 Reformed Church, Rorschach** (Reformierte Kirche)

Pestalozzistrasse, 9400 Rorschach

At the time of the Reformation the town was only briefly protestant, but after converting back to Catholicism, no protestant services were held from 1534 until 1854. It was not until 1848, when the new Swiss Federal Constitution declared religious freedom, that protestant services were allowed again. The reformed parish was established in 1854 and the first protestant services were held at the chapel of the former Mariaberg Monastery (see below) in the same year. This chapel soon became too small and a first reformed church was built in 1861-62. In the subsequent decades the town went through a growth phase, due to its success in the textile embroidery industry and its connection to the Swiss railway network. This attracted many protestants and the first church became too small. The second and present church was built next to the old one in 1902-04. Services were held at the old church, while the new one was being constructed. The old church was then demolished in 1904.

The church, with the footprint of a Greek cross with the bell tower on top of the center of the cross, has a typical protestant interior, limited to pulpit, baptismal font, communion table, and organ. Special features of the church are: the fifth-heaviest bell in Switzerland, weighing 8'137 kg (1904); the three stained-glass rose windows (1903) at the arms of the cross; and the four galleries at each end of the cross (three with additional pews, one with the organ).

Exit the reformed church on the southern side and at the street turn left. After 200 meters east on the *Promenadenstrasse* you arrive at the catholic Sacred Heart of Jesus Church (at km 1.7).

## Sacred Heart of Jesus Church, Rorschach (Herz-Jesu Kirche) R-4

Mariabergstrasse, 9400 Rorschach

Twelve Apostles

The church was built in a neo-Gothic style in 1896-98, to serve the growing catholic population of Rorschach. The town went through a growth phase, due to its success in the textile embroidery industry and its connection to the Swiss railway network, and needed a second catholic church. The church is also known under the name Youth Church (*Jugendkirche*), in reference to the many children, as the population was growing at the end of the 19th century.

Special features of the church are the neo-Gothic decorations: the three wood-carved altars with the typical spires; the canopy over the high-altar; the pulpit; the galleries with statues of the Twelve Apostles on the inner side of the nave (can you identify St. James?); and the painted crucifixion way stations.

The interior looks in need of maintenance: paint/plaster has fallen off the walls, cracks show in the masonry, and the steps and floor look worn out.

Relics lie underneath the altar table. Because you cannot access the chancel (a sign indicates there is an alarm), it is not possible to get a close-up view of these relics. The relics are small bone particles of Roman catacomb saints that were decorated by the nuns of the St. Scholastika Convent in Tübach.

From the church turn right into the *Mariabergstrasse* and continue up the hill straight towards the former Benedictine Monastery Mariaberg (km 1.9). Left of the entrance is a statue representing St. Nepomuk, right St. Borromeo.

## R-1 Former Benedictine Monastery Mariaberg, Rorschach (Klosteranlage Mariaberg)

Seminarstrasse 27, 9400 Rorschach

Benedictine Order

St. Nepomuk, St. Borromeo

The former monastery was built by abbot Ulrich Rösch of the St. Gallen Abbey in 1487-89, with the intention to relocate the abbey to Rorschach. The Abbey of St. Gallen had a strained relationship with the City of St. Gallen, causing frequent disputes and tensions. Since the abbey was surrounded by the city, which was growing in population as well as in economic and political power, the abbey saw its position threatened. They had often tried to construct a fortified wall with an access gate around their abbey, but the City of St. Gallen had never allowed this. The abbey owned extensive lands at Lake Constance, so a relocation to Rorschach was considered a better way to separate from the interference and limitations imposed by the City of St. Gallen. In 1483 the abbot received permission from the Pope to build the new monastery.

The first buildings were erected in 1489 and accommodated 80 monk cells, while the space for a church was left open. The monastery's community hall was temporary arranged as a chapel. However, shortly before the interior completion of the buildings, troops of the City of St. Gallen seized the buildings and set them on fire (1489) as a violent display of their disagreement with the abbey's politics. The abbey requested support from its allies (Schwyz, Luzern, Zurich, and Glarus), who sent a large army to Rorschach. In 1490 the City of St. Gallen accepted defeat and signed a peace treaty, with which ownership of most of its lands outside the city were transferred to the Abbey of St. Gallen. The monastery Mariaberg was subsequently rebuilt in 1490. Abbot Ulrich Rösch died the next year. His successor decided not to relocate the abbey to Rorschach. Instead, he intended to make it a residence for the abbot and the governor of the abbey's estates along Lake Constance. The interior of the buildings was completed in the subsequent decades, finishing in 1522. The church was never built.

During the Reformation all catholic interior decorations were removed or destroyed in 1529. When Rorschach converted back to Catholicism in 1536, the interior was redecorated. Between 1624 and 1699 the building housed a gymnasium and theological school. As Rorschach became a major transit hub for trade in the 18th century, the region flourished, and the abbots of St. Gallen changed the interior to a baroque style. During Napoleon's conquests at the end of the 18th century, French troops occupied the monastery. After the inception of Canton St. Gallen in 1803, the Canton closed the Abbey of St. Gallen and secularized all its assets in 1805. The buildings became the property of the City of Rorschach in 1840. Since then many interior construction changes were made, while it housed a school for the education of teachers. Nowadays it still houses the Cantonal teacher's college (*Pädagogische Hochschule St. Gallen*). The building is accessible during school hours.

Special features are: the Gothic cloisters around the central courtyard; the hallways with the former monk cells; and the old chapel. The cloisters around the square courtyard are one of the best maintained Gothic cloisters in Switzerland and the best ones along the Swiss Way of St. James. Notice the exquisite masonry of the keystones in the vaulted ceilings of the eastern and southern cloisters, and the Gothic masonry in many different patterns on the top parts of the windows. This is one of the best examples of craftsmanship of glass cut into Gothic shapes.

The first floor is also worthwhile a visit. A broad hallway goes around the building in a square shape. The walls are made of half-timbered constructions with low doors on both sides. These were the 80 monk cells. Nowadays class rooms hide behind these doors.

The secretarial offices are also on the first floor, where you can kindly ask for the key to the music room. A person from the office might escort you to the former chapel. As you walked through the corridors around the courtyard, you saw a small chapel steeple with an onion dome. Below that steeple is the former chapel. The entrance to the former chapel is marked by text on the vaulted ceiling.

## R-5 Former Benedictine Monastery Chapel, Rorschach (Kloster Kapelle)

Seminarstrasse 27, 9400 Rorschach

The chapel was built at the same time as the former monastery. It was used by the reformed parish of Rorschach in 1854-60. Nowadays the chapel houses the school's music room.

The chapel still has the original Renaissance ceiling frescos from 1564-68 (date painted above the entrance door), covering the whole vaulted ceiling. The walls must have had similar frescos that were whitewashed and only partly recovered. These vaulted ceiling frescos are unique for the Swiss Way of St. James. The chapel and building display the wealth of the former Abbey-Kingdom of St. Gallen, when abbot Ulrich Rösch was planning to relocate the Kingdom's headquarters to this monastery in 1489.

From the former monastery you need to get back to the signposted route. The easiest way is to walk back to the reformed church and continue straight along the *Pestalozzistrasse.* After walking past an industrial complex, you get to the crossing of the *Pestalozzistrasse* and the *Feldmühlestrasse* (about 250 meters from the reformed church), where you are back on the signposted route.

Continue straight along the *Pestalozzistrasse* and keep following the hiking signs. The route follows a gradual ascending tarmac road through the southern suburbs of Rorschach. You arrive at the countryside and cross over Highway A1. When you look back, you have a great view over Rorschach and Lake Constance.

The path steeply ascends a hill and arrives at the Castle of Sulzberg, partly hidden behind the trees left of the trail.

R-2

The **Castle of Sulzberg** was built by the Lords of Sulzberg, who were in service of the Bishops of Konstanz, around 1260. The noble family used it as a residence to oversee the surrounding lands owned by the bishops. The castle stood in a line of fortified towers on the southern side of Lake Constance. Around 1474 the Mötteli family bought the tower. The main residential buildings originate from 1475-1500, built by the Mötteli family. During the subsequent centuries, ownership of the castle changed many times and each owner made constructional changes. By the beginning of the 18th century the buildings were dilapidated. They were reconstructed in 1784-85, resulting in their present-day appearance. In the subsequent centuries the castle changed ownership many times again, until in 1985 a new owner had the buildings renovated. The main residential building was reconstructed to contain six modern rental apartments. In Winter 2018 the castle was for sale for CHF 9.5 million. Because it is private property, you cannot access the castle or its grounds; the iron front gate is closed.

The castle has a square fortified tower annexed by residential buildings. The tower is the only remaining building originating from around 1260. At the foundations its walls are over 3 meters thick. The tower is about 20 meters high. The top construction dates from 1875, when it housed a restaurant. The castle used to have a moat with a drawbridge and used to be surrounded by fortified walls.

The path continues to ascend on the castle grounds. You pass by the castle's pond and cows grazing in the meadows. At the *Untereggerstrasse* the route turns left. Along a tarmac road you enter the village Untereggen. The next church is on a hilltop, clearly visible as you approach the village. The route passes by the church, at the foot of the hill in about 100 meters distance. You need to make a brief detour to go up the hill to visit the catholic St. Mary Magdalene Church at km 7.0.

**R-6 St. Mary Magdalene Church, Untereggen** (St. Maria Magdalena Kirche)

- Vorderhof, 9033 Untereggen
- St. Mary Magdalene
- On the information stand right of the entrance
- The church was first built as a small chapel in 1677. Until that time the local Catholics had to walk 10 km to attend services at the parish church in Arbon. Although their own parish was established in 1703, it took them until 1782-84 to have this church built.
- The church has a typical baroque style. The pulpit and three altars form a unity in design and color. The gold and silver colored tabernacle at the high-altar exhibits beautiful craftsmanship.

From the church walk back down the hill to the signposted route nr. 4. The signs lead you to a path through the grasslands on the western side of Untereggen. After a kilometer the path converges again with the main road. It takes another 500 meters along this tarmac road before the sign directs you to the left, steep up a hill through grasslands. You can barely make out the trail through the meadow. At km 9.0 you reach a first high point of the day at 667 meters. A steep descent through a small patch of forest and grassland leads you back to the main road, at the location where you cross the road bridge (*Martinsbrugg*) over the Goldach River gorge. The current concrete bridge dates from 1968. A first wooden bridge was already built at this narrowest part of the gorge in 1468.

After the bridge the route immediately turns left, following a gravel path through the forest parallel to the Goldach River gorge. This is the medieval road from Rorschach to St. Gallen. The following 1.5 kilometer the path ascends steeply. You pass underneath high-voltage power lines and get to a shooting range with a restaurant called Schaugenbad. In case people are practicing, you will hear the rifle shots long before you see the shooting range. The name Schaugenbad is derived from a natural healing spring that was used for bathing until 1890 (after which the shooting range was established). Shortly before the restaurant you see the ruins of the Castle of Rappenstein on your left. The ruins are high above the Goldach River gorge, opposite steep cliffs that rise on the other side of the river.

The former **Castle of Rappenstein**, Martinstobel, was built by abbot von Montfort of the Abbey-Kingdom of St. Gallen. It was a fortified tower in a series of outposts protecting and controlling the main travel and trade routes. The abbots used it as a second residence for nearly 120 years from 1282. Around 1400 the wealthy merchant family Mötteli purchased the castle. They could not enjoy the castle for long: in 1405 Appenzell troops destroyed the tower in battles with the Abbey-Kingdom of St. Gallen. The Mötteli family never rebuilt the tower. Instead, they purchased the nearby Castle of Sulzberg in 1474. Over the centuries the ruins eroded until not much was left of it. The wall foundations as you see them today were restored in 2007.

The route continues to ascend on a tarmac country road. In a curve the route leaves the road and turns right.

The trail becomes a narrow path steeply up the flanks of a forested hill. Before the trail enters the tree line at the top of the hill, you have a great view looking back. You reach the highest point of the day at 723 meters, when you reach a road at km 12.0. After only 100 meters along the road, the route forks to the right and gradually descends on a tractor path through meadows. To the north you see Lake Constance in the distance. About 500 meters later you are back on a tarmac road, as you enter the northern suburbs of the St. Gallen agglomeration (at km 12.5).

From this point you will be hiking in an urban environment, until you reach the end of stage R1a. For 700 meters you pass through a residential area with apartment blocks. Shortly before the route turns left at the *Martinsbruggstrasse*, you need to briefly leave the signposted route to get to the next church. At the end of the *Reherstrasse* steps go up the hill and 100 meters later, across a retirement home, you reach the Ecumenical Church of Halden (at km 13.2). This is one of only three ecumenical churches along the Swiss Way of St. James.

**Ecumenical Church, Halden** (Ökumenische Kirche) **R-7**

Oberhaldenstrasse 25, 9016 St. Gallen

The church was built in a cooperation between the catholic and protestant parishes of Halden in 1986.

It is an inter-religious church used by both parishes, hence the sparse interior decorations. The chairs and open space of the interior enable a multipurpose use. St. James scallops and information about the Way of St. James and the pilgrim inn St. Gallen indicate the church is frequented by pilgrims.

The solar panels on the roof were installed in 2010, making the building energy self-sufficient.

From the church walk back the same way to the signposted route in the *Reherstrasse.* The route turns left and you enter the Halden suburb, which is known as the northern **Sports District** of St. Gallen. After 300 meters you see a large carpark in front of a public swimming pool on your right. At that location the route turns left, passes by an athletics field, and trails through an area with several soccer fields. The route briefly turns southward towards a forested hill, where it makes a sharp right, and passes by the backside of a college, with the forested hill on the left. After a small patch of green and trees, the route leads to the *Flurhofstrasse.*

You are entering the Linsebühl suburb, which is known as the **Hospital District** of St. Gallen. Behind houses lining the street you first pass by a children's hospital (on your right). About 500 meters later you pass by a geriatric clinic and the Cantonal hospital on your right (only partially visible). In front, the next church tower rises high above the surrounding buildings. At km 16.2 you arrive at the reformed Linsebühl Church. The church is accessible via the right side back-entrance. Take the door on the left after entering the small anteroom. The name Linsebühl was derived from a field of lentils (*Linse* in German) on which this part of town was originally built.

**R-8 Reformed Linsebühl Church, St. Gallen** (Linsebühl Kirche)

- Flurhofstrasse 1, 9000 St. Gallen
- On a lectern in front of a pillar, together with a pilgrim guestbook
- The church was built on the site of two predecessor churches in 1895-97. A first chapel was next to a leprosarium. The leper house already existed since 1219 and stood outside the city walls of St. Gallen, together with a small chapel used by the lepers (preventing them from entering the city). In 1469 this leper house chapel was reconstructed as a larger church. During the Reformation in 1528 the City of St. Gallen converted to Protestantism. As the Linsebühl church was in the city, it also converted to Protestantism and all catholic interior decorations were removed. In 1575 the leprosarium became a psychiatric ward and part of

the public hospital of St. Gallen (nowadays the St. Gallen geriatric clinic and Cantonal hospital complex you just passed by). The church was further expanded in 1603. The present church was constructed on the site of the former cemetery in 1895-97. After the new church was finished, the old one was demolished in 1897.

📷 The church has a typical protestant interior limited to a pulpit, communion table, baptismal font, cross, and organ. Special features are the tall stained-glass window of the chancel and the three wooden galleries. Lampposts on the two side-galleries make them look like elevated streets.

On the church grounds you see a metal Way of St. James (*Jakobsweg*) information board. It provides a brief history (in German) of St. Gallen and its main churches and indicates the points of interest. Some of these are not along the signposted route nr. 4, but are included in this book.

From the church continue along the *Linsebühlstrasse* towards the historical center of St. Gallen. About 250 meters from the church you pass by the pilgrim inn of St. Gallen, in a building on your right (*Linsebühlstrasse 61* – above the store with the bicycles in its windows.). Blue-yellow scallop flags are hanging in the windows on the first floor. In case you plan to spend the night at this pilgrim inn, you will have to return to this location later. In front you can already see the two towers of the St. Gallen abbey.

About 250 meters after the pilgrim inn you get to a large and busy roundabout. The signposts direct straight and across the road you enter the *Spisergasse*, which is the beginning of the historic center of St. Gallen.

As you enter the **Historic City of St. Gallen**, keep the following in mind. The history of the city of St. Gallen was majorly influenced by two factors: the Abbey and Textile Industry, both generating political and economic growth. The city of St. Gallen was established around the abbey from the 10th century. As the city began expanding, the political tensions concerning its independence from the abbey began to grow. For many centuries the abbey had a dominating position over the politics and decisions concerning the City. Because of the abbey's dominating position in St. Gallen, no other male monastic Orders settled in town.

A convent of Dominican nuns existed until the Reformation, while beguines lived in the Linsebühl district (with the leprosarium and hospital). During the Reformation in 1528, the City converted to Protestantism and secularized the Dominican convent, while the abbey remained catholic, which added a source of tensions. In 1566 a wall was built to separate the protestant City from the catholic abbey (the wall was demolished in 1798). After the French occupation in 1798, the City became the capital of the newly established Canton St. Gallen in 1803, when it finally seized the opportunity to dominate the abbey. In 1805 the Canton decided to close the monastery and seized all its assets.

From the 15th century the town became well known for its linen textile manufacturing. From the industrialization at the beginning of the 19th century it changed to embroidery of textiles. By the beginning of the 20th century the St. Gallen region was producing more than half of the world's embroidered textiles. Many of the houses in the old city were built by wealthy textile manufacturers. Nowadays the small textile industry focuses on the high-end embroidery for Haute Couture.

As the town grew over the centuries, several layers of fortified walls, access gates, and moats were built. You will hardly see any remnants today: most were demolished in 1808-43, to make room for the increasing urbanization and textile industry. The historic city of St. Gallen never had a castle. Rather, the abbey served as the castle of the Abbot-King.

The car-free pedestrian center is a maze of small shopping streets where it is easy to lose your sense of direction. It is easy to overlook the hiking signposts, as they are replaced by small yellow stickers on not so obvious places. When many tourists and shoppers surround you, it is easy to miss a sign. It may be easiest to follow the signs to the abbey.

Immediately after entering the *Spisergasse* of the old center, turn left into the *Zeughausgasse*. Follow the street to the right and you walk past the outer buildings of the abbey (on your left). In front you see the bell tower of the next church. At km 17.0 you arrive at the reformed St. Lawrence Church. You enter the church via its side-corridor. Information boards along the walls tell the history of the church and city.

## Reformed St. Lawrence Church, St. Gallen (St. Laurenzen Kirche) R-9

- Marktgasse 25, 9000 St. Gallen
- St. Lawrence
- Ask for the stamp at the information office at the end of the side-corridor
- The church was probably first built around 1150. The church was first mentioned in official documents as the parish church of the early City of St. Gallen in 1235. It belonged to the Abbey of St. Gallen and only received its independence from the abbey in 1413. The City demonstrated its independence by reconstructing the church in 1413-23. Because it was the largest building in town, it was used for communal meetings and its tower served as a lookout (for fire and beleaguering troops). During the Reformation in 1525-28 the City of St. Gallen converted to Protestantism, whereas the Abbey of St. Gallen remained catholic. As the St. Lawrence church was in the city, it had to convert to Protestantism. All catholic interior decorations such as altars, statues, and paintings were removed. In 1528 the City forbade catholic worship. The name reference to the saint was removed, though nowadays the church is still known as St. Lawrence, despite being reformed.

  This protestant church, only a few meters from the catholic abbey, frequently caused tensions between the City and abbey. The tensions were partially relieved when a 10-meter-high wall was built to separate the two in 1566. The church as you see it today is the result of construction during more than 800 years. Four predecessor churches were expanded or reconstructed resulting in the present-day building. In 1774 an earthquake damaged the church, which was provisionally repaired. By 1845 the church was in poor condition. Plans to demolish and replace it with a new building were rejected; instead, the old church was comprehensively renovated and expanded in a neo-Gothic style in 1850-54, determining its present-day appearance. Nowadays the church is still the city's main parish church and is often used for concerts.
- The church has a typical protestant interior, limited to pulpit, baptismal font, and organ. Special features are: the enormous organ filling up the back wall of the chancel, built around the stained-glass window; the three side-galleries that were built in 1513 and 1577 to serve the growing number of parishioners attending services; the Gothic masonry of the baptismal font; the stained-glass window of the chancel, with its Gothic top masonry; and the abstract linear frescos and colorings on the walls.

You may be tempted to turn left at the church and enter the grounds of the Abbey of St. Gallen. However, before visiting the abbey, it is worthwhile to briefly deviate from the signposted route to visit a church with its foundations in the 9th century (the second-oldest church in St. Gallen, after the Abbey's Cathedral).

From the St. Lawrence church turn right into the *Marktgasse* (away from the abbey), one of the city's main shopping streets. After 300 meters you get to a busy street (*Marktplatz*) with bus and tram stops. In the front you see the low white bell tower of the next church. Turn right along the tram tracks and 50 meters later left into the *Katharinengasse*. About 400 meters from the reformed St. Lawrence church you arrive at the former Dominican Convent St. Catherine.

**R-2 Former Dominican Convent St. Catherine, St. Gallen** (Dominikanerinnen Kloster)

- Katharinengasse 11, 9000 St. Gallen
- Dominican Order
- St. Catherine
- The former convent was first established as a community of religious women in 1228. In 1266 the sisters adopted the Rule of St. Augustine and became a monastic Order. In 1368 their church and cemetery were consecrated, at which occasion they changed to the Rule of St. Dominic. This was the only other monastic Order within the city walls (the Abbey-Kingdom did not condone any other Orders). Most of their first building was destroyed in the city fire of 1418. The convent was subsequently rebuilt and a cloister was built that attached the nun's cells with the convent's church in 1504-07. As the City converted to Protestantism in 1527, the interior of the convent suffered gravely. Most of their catholic religious icons, altars, statues, and books were destroyed and the clapper of the bell was removed. A year later the whole bell tower was dismantled. The

convent was closed for a year, but the City allowed the nuns to resume their hermitage under protestant restrictions in 1528. As a result, most of the nuns left the convent to join other Orders outside the city. Three sisters remained but finally also left in 1555.

By 1594 the buildings became the property of the City of St. Gallen, housing a secondary school for boys. From 1615 the city-library occupied part of the buildings. From 1855 the buildings were in private possession. Their present-day appearance is a result of extensive renovations undertaken in 1976-78.

In 2007 the private Bank Wegelin purchased the former convent buildings to house their expanding business. As a result of the Swiss-US banking scandals in 2012, Bank Wegelin ceased to exist; its former properties now belong to the Raiffeisen Bank.

Nowadays the only publicly accessible area is the city's youth library. The former church was turned into a modern conference hall for the bank (only the restored organ was maintained; the room itself was completely emptied out and whitewashed).

From the convent turn left and continue in the *Katharinengasse* (north). At the T-crossing turn left into the *Goliathgasse* and after 50 meters right in the *Magnihalden* you arrive at the reformed St. Mang Church (at km 17.5).

## Reformed St. Mang Church, St. Gallen (St. Mangen Kirche) R-10

Kirchgasse 17, 9000 St. Gallen

St. Mang, St. Wiborada

The church was first built in 898, as a private church by Salomon, abbot of the St. Gallen monastery, who also was Bishop of Konstanz. The church was built next to his residence, outside the abbey. The Abbot/Bishop received relics of St. Mang (his right arm bones) from the Abbey of Füssen (Bavaria, Germany) for his personal church. Salomon gave the church its own lands as a source of income. This income financed the Collegiate (*Chorherrenstift*) that managed the church. In 916 the female hermit Wiborada had herself locked up in a bricked-up cell attached to the church. In 925 she had a vision in which she foresaw her own death and Hungarian troops invading and looting the St. Gallen monastery. The abbey's treasures were brought to safety and when indeed Hungarian troops besieged the city in 926, she was killed when she refused to flee from the approaching troops. The relics of St. Mang and Wiborada made the church a place of pilgrimage during the middle ages (until the Reformation). The church became too small for the increasing number of pilgrims and a new larger one was built around 1100 (which determined its present-day appearance). In the $15^{th}$ century the city walls were extended to include the St. Mang church, on which occasion it became a city-church.

During the Reformation in 1528 the City of St. Gallen forced the St. Mang church to convert to Protestantism. All catholic interior decorations were removed and all metal artefacts were smelted. The relics of the two saints were buried somewhere. The name reference to the Saint was removed, though nowadays the church is still called St. Mang, despite being reformed.

In 1774 an earthquake damaged the church, which was provisionally repaired. By 1837 the church was still in poor condition. Plans to demolish and replace it with a new building were rejected; instead, the old church was comprehensively renovated in 1838-42. The church was on loan to a newly established Christ-Catholic parish in the years 1876-95. After the Christ-Catholic parish built their own church (1895), the protestant parish resumed its use. Since 1979 the church has also been used by the French-speaking protestant community of St. Gallen and region.

📷 The church has an austere protestant interior; its chancel is empty.

From the church walk back 500 meters to the reformed St. Lawrence church and continue straight into the St. Gallen Abbey District.

The **St. Gallen Abbey District** (*Klosterviertel*) is a UNESCO World Cultural Heritage Site and the highlight of stage R1a. The Benedictine Abbey district boasts a magnificent cathedral, abbey grounds, and an abbey library, surrounded by medieval historic houses. The origins date back to the year 612, when the Irish monk Gallus settled as a hermit at this location. In the early $8^{th}$ century his hermit cell developed into a monastery, which had become a medieval center for religion, education, and trade by the $9^{th}$ century. The current baroque abbey buildings were completed in 1767. At the Tourist Information Office, opposite the main entrance of the cathedral, you can obtain the UNESCO stamp for your pilgrim pass.

## Former Benedictine Abbey-Kingdom, St. Gallen (Benediktiner Kloster) R-3

Klosterhof, 9000 St. Gallen

Benedictine Order

St. Gall, St. Othmar

The former Benedictine Kingdom-Abbey of St. Gallen was established by the first abbot Othmar on the site of the hermit cell of St. Gall in 719. Othmar established a monastery for the priests who were caring for the grave. In 747 the abbey adopted the Rule of St. Benedict and became a Benedictine monastery.

The abbey quickly became wealthy from the donations of lands by noble families, whose sons joined the monastery. Around 760 the abbey became dependent on the Bishops of Konstanz (who appointed the abbots). In 845 the German Emperor Ludwig made the abbey an independent monastery (*Reichskloster*) within the German Empire. The abbey's good reputation spread and donations of lands and resulting income continued to increase its earthly possessions. Emperors and Kings regularly stayed at the guesthouse of the monastery. The monks led a school that attracted and educated many religious scholars, artists, and noblemen. By 900 their library already contained more than 600 handwritten books.

The invasion of the Hungarian armies in 926, and a large fire in 937, caused a temporary setback for the monastery. From the second half of the 10th century the abbey flourished again, which resulted in a construction boom. The St. Lawrence church and other churches were built in the region, while the monastery was renewed and its church was newly decorated.

From the end of the 12th century the abbots came from noble families, who focused on politics and expansion/protection of the earthly territories with military force. Several abbots participated in or led battles for their own purposes or to support the German Emperors.

In 1207 the German King Philip of Swabia assigned royal rights to the abbey, which made the abbot an Abbot-King (*Fürstabt*) and the abbey a royal organization (*Fürstabtei*). The monks became feudal overlords. The monastery expanded its territorial kingdom and was ruler of all earthly matters within its territories that reached far into Germany, north of Lake Constance. It became a territorial powerhouse that founded new cities, built roads, and engaged noble families in the supervision and management of its territories. As a royal monastery it maintained an expensive court with entourage, organized extravagant banquets and feasts, and regularly knighted noblemen. Maintaining the royal organization and territory became very expensive, while its involvement in politics and wars drained their treasury.

As the medieval society changed from the 13th century, the monastery's economic decline set in and started a long crisis. Lands were sold, cultural development (teaching, manual copying of manuscripts) was neglected, and the community of monks fell apart. By the middle of the 15th century the Pope ordered reforms and initiated the replacement of several abbots.

Abbot-King Ulrich Rösch reorganized the monastery during his 28-year reign (1463-91). He initiated a strict reinterpretation of the Rule of St. Benedict, refocused the school, sent young monks to universities, expanded the library, remodeled the chancel of the church, promoted pilgrimages, consolidated the lands, issued a unified governmental rulebook for the territories, and built the new monastery Mariaberg in Rorschach.

The Reformation in the 1520s had an important impact on the kingdom of the abbey. In 1528-29 the City of St. Gallen converted to Protestantism and tried to enforce the Reformation on the abbey (since it was enclosed in the center of town). Protestants occupied the monastery and the abbot-king had to flee to his castle in Rorschach. Many of the abbey's territories accepted the Reformation and converted to Protestantism, though some converted back to Catholicism after 1531 (as a direct result of catholic Cantons defeating protestant Cantons in the so-called 2nd Kappel War in 1531). The abbot-king returned in 1532 and started the Counter-Reformation, trying to convert cities and parishes in its territories back to Catholicism.

In the subsequent centuries the kingdom continued to govern the religious and earthly life in its territories. These were increasingly striving for independence, which regularly led to wars with the involvement of protestant and catholic troops from opposing or supporting Cantons. These wars led to a prolonged crisis in the abbey-kingdom. For some years the abbot was exiled to southern Germany, while the royal organization fell apart. Renewed construction led to debts, and internal political turmoil arose as monks questioned the autocratic leadership of the abbot-king.

In the 1790s the French Revolution strongly influenced the revolutionary forces in the abbey's kingdom. The abbot was forced to abolish serfdom and gave up on the feudal rights over the population in its territories, after which several of its territories declared independence. The abbey-kingdom was already falling apart by the time French troops invaded Switzerland and occupied the monastery in 1798. The abbot fled to Vienna (Austria), while a few monks stayed to continue catholic services.

In 1803 Canton St. Gallen was created, put together from former territories of other Cantons, the City of St. Gallen, and former territories of the Abbey-Kingdom. In 1805 the Canton decided to secularize the monastery and liquidate all the abbey's assets. This ended the abbey-kingdom and closed the monastery after 1'086 years of existence. The last abbot remained in exile and tried to regain the kingdom but to no avail. In 1823 the Pope formally accepted the secularization of the abbey.

Nowadays the extensive buildings house Cantonal offices and archives, the bishop's residence and offices, the cathedral's parish offices, the former abbey's historical library and museum, and a school.

Upon entering the abbey's district from the street of the St. Lawrence church, you pass by a square building on the corner to your right. This is the catholic Guardian Angel Chapel (also called the Child Chapel) (at km 18.0).

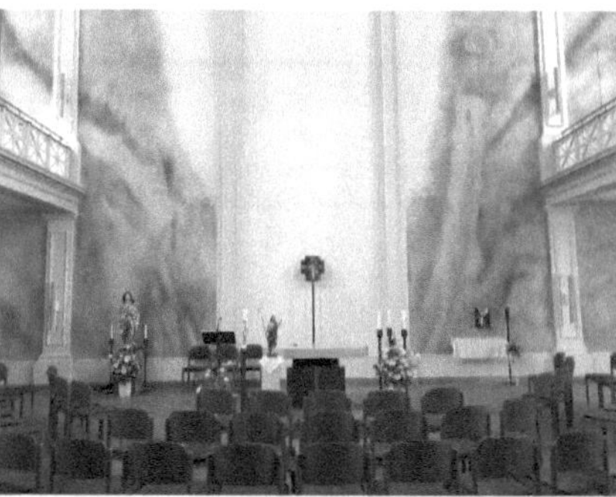

**Guardian Angel Chapel, St. Gallen** (Schutzengel Kapelle) **R-11**

Klosterhof, 9000 St. Gallen

The catholic chapel was built for the catholic civil servants of the administration of St. Gallen City (who occupied the former monastery buildings) in 1843-46. The building replaced an older Guardian Angel chapel from 1764-66, which was demolished in 1807.

The cubic hall chapel has a surprising modern interior. The back wall of the chancel is painted in bright yellow and blue colors within the arches that nearly reach the high ceiling. Three side-galleries provide additional seating, with the organ integrated in the wall above the entrance.

The ceiling has a large fresco depicting the Christmas manger scene with baby Jesus in a crib surrounded by angels and the three Kings from the East. These angels and the crib gave the chapel its names.

The chapel is closed most of the time. It is only accessible during services or on special occasions, for example during concerts.

When approaching the cathedral, notice the two metal St. James scallops set in the pavement. One is located 30 meters before the left-side entrance door, the other is 2 meters in front of its large wooden door.

## R-12 Abbey Cathedral, St. Gallen (Stiftskirche St. Gallus und Otmar)

Klosterhof, 9000 St. Gallen

St. Gall, St. Othmar, St. Mang, St. Wiborada

At the tourist Information Office (Bankgasse 9, 9000 St. Gallen) opposite the main entrance of the cathedral. Ask for the stamp at the counter.

The cathedral has its foundations in 719, when a first church was built as part of the monastery. As the monastery was reconstructed and expanded many times over the centuries, so was the abbey's church. In 1207 the German King Philip of Swabia assigned royal rights to the abbey, which made the abbot an Abbot-King (*Fürstabt*) and the abbey a royal organization (*Fürstabtei*). This resulted in expansion and beautification of the church to make it a royal church, worthy of the visiting Emperors, Kings, and other nobility.

At the time of the Reformation in 1528-29, the city of St. Gallen surrounded the abbey and its church. When the City converted to Protestantism, they tried to enforce the Reformation on the abbey and its church. Protestants plundered the church, destroyed the catholic icons, and occupied the monastery. The abbot-king had to flee to his castle in Rorschach. He could return in 1532 (after the 2nd Kappel War), so that the abbey and its church remained catholic.

By the middle of the 18th century the church was in poor condition. The old nave was demolished in 1755 and a new one constructed in 1756-60. The old chancel served as provisional place of worship during the construction of the nave. After the nave was rebuilt, the chancel was demolished in 1760 and reconstructed over 6 years. The two bell towers were the last to be finished in 1766. The interior decorations such as frescos, statues, paintings, and altars were made in a late-baroque style.

After the secularization of the abbey and its church in 1805, no further significant constructional changes were made; it stayed as you see it today. Interior and exterior renovations were regularly undertaken (the latest one in 2000-03). The Bishopric of St. Gallen was established in 1823, after which the church's designation was elevated to cathedral.

The late-baroque interior of the cathedral is one of the most beautiful along the Way of St. James. Take your time to admire the artistic decorations, woodwork, statues, ceiling frescos, ironwork, altars, stucco, and paintings. The cathedral has several additional special features. The rotunda in the middle splits the cathedral in two. The eastern half is the chancel, the western half the nave, making them of nearly equal size. The nave and chancel are separated by an artfully crafted and decorated green-gold iron gate (rood screen); you cannot access the chancel. The ceiling fresco of the rotunda depicts God surrounded by saints. The frescos of the domes in the nave depict Saints Gall, Othmar, Mang, and Wiborada.

The cathedral has two crypts (not publicly accessible): one with the grave of St. Gall, where part of his skull is kept in a reliquary; and one with the graves of St. Othmar and the Bishops of St. Gallen.

The abbey has three more chapels: the Sacred Heart of Jesus Chapel, the St. Gall Chapel, and the Bishop's Chapel. These chapels are rooms inside the former abbey complex. You get to these chapels by walking around the cathedral to the triangular northern courtyard (with a modern fountain).

The entrance to the St. Gall and Bishop's chapels is flanked by two tall stone statues, representing the 6th century Bishop Desiderius of Vienne (left) and St. Maurice (right). The St. Gall chapel is used as a baptizing chapel by the cathedral's parish, whereas the Bishop's chapel is used by the Bishops of St. Gallen. Both are in private use and not publicly accessible.

You can access the catholic Sacred Heart of Jesus chapel via the wooden entrance door on the southern corner of the triangular courtyard. A brown nameplate left of the door indicates the *Herz-Jesu-Kapelle*. Pass through the first hall and through another door enter the vaulted cloisters. Turn right and you can access the chapel through the doors with the two carved angels at the end of the corridor.

## R-13 Sacred Heart of Jesus Chapel, St. Gallen (Herz-Jesu Kapelle)

Klosterhof 6b, 9000 St. Gallen

The chapel is a room inside the former abbey complex, built in 1666-67.

The chapel has a simple interior with a few baroque style elements on its ceiling. The square chancel contains a communion table in front of the altar.

Leave the triangular courtyard through the passage on the southern side. From there you get to the world-famous Abbey Library.

R-4

The **Abbey Library** (*Stiftsbibliothek*) is the oldest and most precious library in Switzerland, and one of the biggest and oldest monastic libraries in the world. It contains 170'000 books and calligraphic manuscripts, of which 400 date from the period 700-1000. It also contains books that were printed before the year 1500. The library is situated in a hall with elaborate baroque woodwork and ceiling frescos dating from 1758-67 (constructed and decorated in the same period as the church's nave and chancel were remodeled).

The Greek inscription above the library entrance means 'Sanatorium for the soul'. You are not allowed to take photos inside the library. However, you can take a photo of a large poster of the interior of the library, right of the entrance of the building.

In addition to the books and manuscripts exhibited in the Library Hall, a permanent exhibition of St. Gall and the 1'300-year history of the abbey is located in its vaulted cellars. This exhibition includes items from the cathedral's treasures, an exquisitely decorated book from 895, a tracing of the way of St. Gall from Ireland to St. Gallen, and many more historical artefacts demonstrating the abbey's influence on cultural and spiritual development over 1'300 years.

The Abbey Library is open 7 days a week, from 10:00 to 17:00. A combined ticket to the permanent exhibitions in the library and vaulted cellar, and the temporary exhibition in a separate hall, costs CHF 18.

The library counter offers audio guides in several languages (CHF 5). The audio guide can take you on a narrated **historical Abbey and City Tour** through the abbey's library, vaulted cellar, within and around the abbey, inside as well as outside the cathedral, and a tour of the historical city of St. Gallen (including the St. Lawrence and St. Mang churches). Take your time and enjoy this tour. It offers a unique insight in the history of the Abbey-Kingdom of St. Gallen and is an extraordinary highlight of the Swiss Way of St. James.

## *From the ending point*

The Abbey of St. Gallen is the ending point of stage R1a, about 100 meters aside the signposted route nr. 4.

In case you are a day-hiker, you need to walk 650 meters to the St. Gallen train station.

In case you are a thru-hiker and spend the night in St. Gallen, you need to walk back to the pilgrim inn on the *Linsebühlstrasse* nr. 61 (tel. 071 220 00 62; verein@pilgerherberge-sg.ch; www.pilgerherberge-sg.ch; email reservation or advance call in the afternoon).

As a main tourist destination in northeastern Switzerland, St. Gallen offers many hotels and restaurants. Check out www.jakobsweg.ch or www.viajacobi4.ch for the accommodation possibilities in St. Gallen. You can also visit the Tourist Information Office opposite the cathedral (St. Gallen-Bodensee

Tourismus; Bankgasse 9, 9001, St. Gallen; tel. 071 227 37 37; www.st.gallen-bodensee.ch; info@st.gallen-bodensee.ch) and have them help you.

## *The next Stage*

Stage R1b guides you from the highland plateau with the St. Gallen agglomerations to the beginning of the Appenzell hills. This stage is intentionally short, with only 11 km. Read the next chapter to find out what that entails.

# Stage R1b: St. Gallen to Herisau 11 km

*The Way over the shortest distance*

As mentioned in the introduction of stage R1a, the stages R1a and R1b have to be seen in combination with each other. Stage R1b intentionally has a short distance to enable a late hiking start on your second day, providing sufficient time for sightseeing in St. Gallen. In case you start early in Rorschach and need limited time in St. Gallen, it may also be possible to hike stages R1a and R1b in one day.

## *Route stats*

| | *Distance in km* | *Time in hrs:min* |
|---|---|---|
| Signposted route nr. 4 | 8.9 | 1:50 |
| Churches/chapels | 2.4 | 1:20 |
| Points of interest | | |
| Rest | | 0:20 |
| Stage R1b | 11.3 | 3:30 |

In case you hike this stage as a daytrip, you need to add 650 meters in St. Gallen and 300 meters in Herisau (from and to the train stations).

| | |
|---|---|
| Ascent/descent/total | +264/ -179 / 443 altitude meters |
| Lowest/highest altitude | 610 / 798 meters |
| Pathway/condition | easy / easy |
| Churches/chapels | St. Gallen (2), Bruggen (3), Herisau (2) |
| Monasteries | none |
| Points of Interest | Chateau of Waldegg |

## *Route summary*

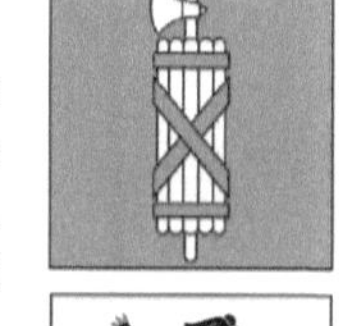

Stage R1b continues in **Canton St. Gallen**. From km 0 to 3 the route is in the protestant city of St. Gallen. From km 3 to 9 the route is in the former catholic territory of the Abbey of St. Gallen. At km 9.0 the route enters protestant **Canton Appenzell Ausserrhoden**.

Stage R1b guides you from the highland plateau with the St. Gallen agglomerations to the beginning of the Appenzell hills.

The first 2 km are through the city of St. Gallen in a southwestern direction. This is followed by a gradual descent through the southern St. Gallen suburb Bruggen over 4 km. At km 6 the route reaches its lowest point of the day on a road bridge crossing the Sitter River gorge. From there the route leaves the St. Gallen highland plateau and ascends over 4 km. About 2.5 km are through fields and past a recreational lake, after which the route enters the northern outskirts of Herisau. There it ascends to the highest point of the stage at 798 meters. Finally, a descent over 1 km leads to the center of Herisau.

## *Route Map and Profile*

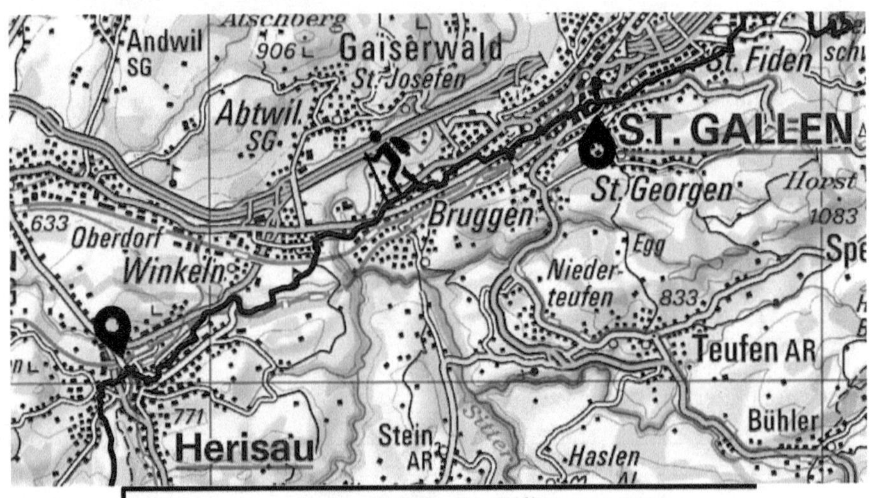


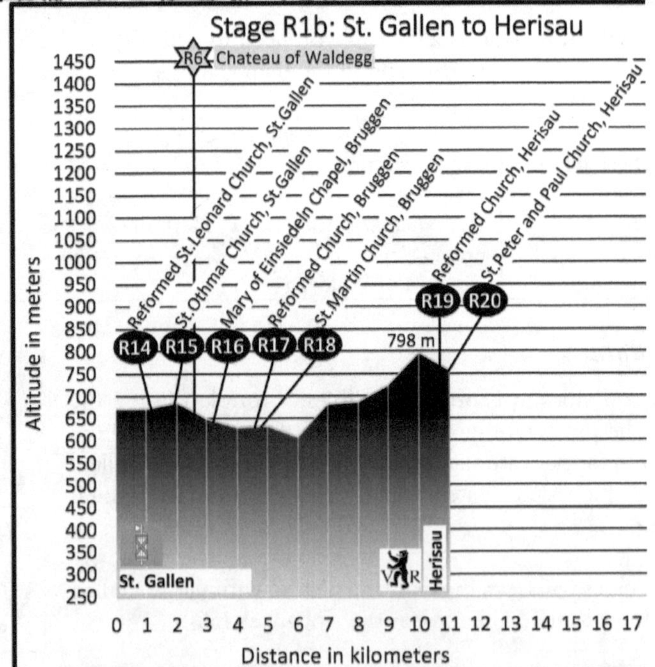

## Getting to the starting point

Today's starting point in St. Gallen is at the reformed St. Lawrence Church (*St. Laurenzen Kirche*), which is where you left the signposted route nr. 4 at the end of stage R1a. In case you hike stage R1b as a daytrip, you need to walk 700 meters from the St. Gallen train station to the church. Alternatively, you can also start at the train station, as the signposted route passes by the train station. Since there are no churches between the St. Lawrence church and the train station, you can save the 700 meters there and back.

## Hiking the Route

From the St. Lawrence church follow the yellow sign into the pedestrian and shopping street of the *Schmiedgasse*. At the end the route turns right and immediately left to cross a main road. Continue diagonally-left into the *Vadianstrasse* (also a pedestrian and shopping street). On your right you pass by the Textile Museum of St. Gallen in the long orange building. At the end of the pedestrian zone the route turns right and the first left into the busy *Sankt-Leonhard-Strasse*. On your right you pass by the main post office building that has a tall tower resembling a bell tower of a church. Behind the post office is the train station. The route continues with the tracks on your right. In front you can already see the bell tower of the first church.

On an elevated road to the right you cross over the tracks and follow a footpath on the right that turns underneath the bridge you just crossed over. You get to a path with the tracks on your left and see a neglected church. Weed and grass are growing on its grounds and the church looks deserted. You are looking at the reformed St. Leonard Church (at km 1.2).

**R-14 Reformed St. Leonard Church, St. Gallen** (Reformierte St. Leonhard Kirche)

Burgstrasse 8, 9000 St. Gallen

St. Leonard

The church was built in a neo-Gothic style by the reformed parish of St. Gallen in 1885-87. The church replaced a smaller one dating from 1654. Rather unusual, the reformed church has the name of a catholic saint, St. Leonard. The church was renovated in 1931 and by 1980 there was a need for renovations again. In the meantime, the number of parishioners was reduced so much that no funding for renovations was available. In 1995 the church was closed for services, but occasionally used for cultural events. In 2004 the church was in poor condition and sold at auction by the protestant parish to an architect. He made plans for renovations, but these were rejected by the local Authorities. In 2007 the roof burned down and collapsed on the nave. The roof was provisionally repaired and the doors of the church were permanently closed. In 2013 the private owner planned to turn the former church into an event- and cultural-center, but these plans were also rejected. Until today (2019) nothing has changed, while the condition of the church keeps deteriorating. The doors to the church remain locked.

From the church continue on the *Burgstrasse*. On your right you pass by a sports hall with soccer fields behind it. At the intersection with the *Vonwilstrasse* the signpost directs to turn right. At this location you need to briefly leave the signposted route. Instead of turning right, turn left and follow the *Vonwilstrasse* for 100 meters to the catholic St. Othmar Church (at km 1.9).

## St. Othmar Church, St. Gallen (St. Otmar Kirche) R-15

Vonwilstrasse 10, 9000 St. Gallen

St. Othmar, St. Mary, Holy Family, Four Evangelists

The catholic church was built in a neo-Gothic style in 1905-08. At that time the southern suburb of St. Gallen, called Straubenzell, was still an independent municipality that wanted to have its own catholic church. The bell tower of 71.5 meters is the highest in St. Gallen.

Before they built their own church, the Catholics had to attend services at either the St. Martin church in Bruggen (see below) or the abbey's cathedral in St. Gallen.

The three altars are decorated with beautiful wood-carved retables in neo-Gothic style. In most churches and chapels winged altars from the middle ages are of relatively small size. In this church the wood-carved altars, created in 1908, are of large size: the largest retables along the Swiss Way of St. James.

The carvings in the two-winged left side-altar are dedicated to Mary and represent scenes from her life. The large center carving represents Mary's coronation as Queen of Heaven by Jesus, flanked by two angels.

The four-winged high-altar represent scenes from the life of Jesus (left to right: entering Jerusalem; washing of feet; Last Supper; and appearance on the road to Emmaus). The center piece is a statue representing Jesus in artistically carved spires.

The carvings in the two-winged right side-altar are dedicated to the Holy Family and represent scenes from the life of Mary and Joseph.

Have a closer look at the neo-Gothic pulpit. It contains a statue representing Jesus as shepherd (with staff and a sheep on his shoulders) inside the spires. The Four Evangelists (Matthew, Mark, John, and Luke) are carved on the base of the pulpit.

The eight tall stained-glass windows are dedicated to Jesus' Sermon on the Mount where he pronounced eight beatitudes. Blessed are: the poor in spirit; those who mourn; the meek; those who hunger and thirst for righteousness; the merciful; the pure of heart; the peacemakers; and those who are persecuted because of their righteousness.

From the church walk back the same 100 meters to the signposted route. At the *Schillerstrasse* the route turns left through a neighborhood with low apartment buildings. At the T-crossing at the end of the street the route turns right into the *Burgstrasse.* When you look to the left you see a chateau beyond a grass field about 150 meters away. You need to consciously look for it, otherwise you will probably miss the Chateau of Waldegg.

The **Chateau of Waldegg** (*Schloss Waldegg*) was built by wealthy St. Gallen merchants as their residence around 1475. They built their chateau on the lands of the Abbey-Kingdom of St. Gallen and sold it to the abbey in 1505. The master of ceremonies of the abbot-king's royal court resided at the chateau. At the time of the secularization of the abbey in 1805, the chateau became the property of Canton St. Gallen.

In 1825 the Canton sold it to a textile industrialist, who turned it into his residence and factory offices, and built a red-dyeing plant next to it. He also built a wooden drying tower on the southern side of the estate. Most of the chateau and attached plant burned down in a fire in 1901. It was subsequently rebuilt, determining its present-day appearance. In 1997-98 renovations restored many of its 19th century features. The chateau is privately owned and cannot be accessed.

Finally you get to a patch of green in the urban agglomeration of St. Gallen. The signposted route continues around the chateau's former pond, along a school and playground, and past the tall wooden drying tower (*Tröckneturm*). About 100 meters after the wooden tower a narrow footpath between bushes on the left leads to the hidden Mary of Einsiedeln Chapel (at km 3.1).

**Mary of Einsiedeln Chapel, Bruggen** (Maria Einsiedeln Kapelle) **R-16**

- Burgweiherweg 33, 9000 St. Gallen
- St. Mary
- The catholic chapel was built on the territory of the catholic Abbey of St. Gallen in 1770. It replaced a small roadside chapel from 1680, which was called the St. James-fountain Chapel (*Jakobsbrunnen Kapelle*), as it served pilgrims on their way to Einsiedeln.
- The chapel is dedicated to the Black Madonna of Einsiedeln and has a copy of the 117-cm statue at its altar, though it is not painted black and has no embroidered dresses. The statue you see today is still the original from 1770. The chapel is only open on Sunday afternoons.

From the chapel the route continues through an industrial area, passes by another grass field, and briefly follows a small stream south of the Lidl supermarket. After turning right and left, you get to a main street called *Zürcherstrasse*. You are back on road nr. 7, on which you started at the port in Rorschach.

You can already see the next church tower in front of you. The route passes through Bruggen (a southern suburb of the St. Gallen agglomeration) where you pass by shops, supermarkets, gas stations, schools, and so forth. After 400 meters along the busy street you arrive at the reformed Church of Bruggen (at km 4.5).

## R-17 Reformed Church, Bruggen (Evangelische Kirche)

- Zürcherstrasse 223, 9014 St. Gallen
- On a cabinet left of the entrance
- The church was built as a hall church in 1904-05, after a new reformed parish was established the year before. The parish separated from the reformed St. Leonard church (see above), which enabled the construction of their own church in Bruggen. The Catholics already had a church in Bruggen since 1600 (see below) and the Protestants wanted to establish their own church too. Significant remodeling took place in 1966-67, when the space in the church was reduced by the construction of a sacristy, wooden ceiling, meeting room on the second floor, and front hall.
- The front hall is separated by a glass wall from the nave and has a small side-chapel on the right. Above it is a gallery with a large organ and additional seats. The nave is a hall with a triangular footprint, without a separate chancel. The back of the nave contains another gallery with additional seats. Underneath this gallery are tables that are covered with tablecloth, just like in a restaurant. The church has a typical protestant interior, without altars, saints, and paintings.

From the reformed church the *Zürcherstrasse* curves to the left and 300 meters later you arrive at the catholic St. Martin Church (at km 4.8). In front of the church notice the statue representing St. Martin with a beggar, depicting the legend of this saint.

## St. Martin Church, Bruggen (St. Martin Kirche) R-18

- Zürcherstrasse 253, 9014 St. Gallen
- St. Martin, St. Leonard, St. Gall, St. Othmar, St. Fidelis, Sorrowful Mother of God
- On a shelf, right of the entrance. The stamp depicts the statue of St. Martin on his horse, next to the road bridge over the Sitter River gorge (see below).
- A first small chapel was built by the Abbey of St. Gallen in 1600. It was outside the city of St. Gallen and served the leprosarium (1567) that was connected via a cloister. The second church considerably expanded the first one in 1672-73. The third church (in a baroque style) was built with yet again a bigger footprint and higher roof in 1783-84. The bell tower was added in 1808. Finally, this church was demolished in 1936 and replaced by the current (fourth) church in a modern style with square and rectangular shapes.
- The first thing that catches your eye are the gold-glitters of the mosaics at the front of the nave. Instead of side-altars, the front walls have two mosaics with figures inside a gold-mosaic rectangular shape. On the left wall the figures represent St. Leonard and St. Martin; on the right wall St. Gall (with bear) and St. Othmar. The round wall of the pulpit depicts four saints also set in gold-colored mosaics. One would expect the wall of the chancel to have a similar style mosaic, but is does not. A large tapestry depicts the resurrection of Christ.

Even more remarkable are the colorful stained-glass windows.

On the right side of the nave, nine angels shine in the most beautiful illuminative red, blue, and yellow glass colors. The three in red on the left depict devotion to God, the three blue in the middle the mediation between God and people, and the three yellow on the right the approach to people.

On the left side of the nave, a long row of narrow stained-glass windows depicts the 14 stations of the crucifixion way.

From the front of the nave, look back to the main entrance. Above it you see a large (4.4-meter diameter) stained-glass rose window in the similar illuminative coloring as the angel windows. The inner circle in yellow/orange/blue depicts Mary with baby Jesus, the second circle in pink depicts the Seven Sorrows of Mary. These are seven events that caused intense suffering to Mary (see Appendix 2 under 'Sorrowful Mother of God'). These Seven Sorrows are often depicted as seven swords piercing the heart of Mary (in this case the seven lines into the center circle).

The third special feature of the St. Martin church is a catacomb saint, venerated as St. Fidelis. You find the vitrine with the skeleton in a red Roman dress and sword in the left side-nave, behind the pulpit. Notice the small silver chalice at the feet. This was supposed to contain the blood of the martyr Saint Fidelis. The bones were brought from Rome to the Abbey of St. Gallen in 1782.

The nuns of the Capuchin Convent of Notkersegg (on a hill northeast of St. Gallen) reassembled the received bones and skull, and filled up missing parts with plaster. They made the dress and decorations and assembled the lying relics as you see it now. In 1789 the Abbey of St. Gallen donated the relics to the newly built baroque St. Martin church.

From the church the *Zürcherstrasse* curves to the right and 400 meters later you leave road nr. 7 again. The signposted route forks to the left and gradually descends to a bridge over the Sitter River gorge.

The **Sitter River** has a length of 49 km and flows from the Appenzell Cantons, through Canton St. Gallen, to Canton Thurgau where it flows into the Thur River.

From the *Kräzernbrücke* you look down at a few houses in the valley and to your right look up at the *Zürcherstrasse* road bridge crossing the valley.

About 400 meters after the bridge the route turns left. In between some houses the path ascends steeply up a hill after which the Way of St. James finally leaves the urban St. Gallen agglomeration behind. You pass over railway tracks and through open fields you walk towards a recreational lake (*Gübsensee*). The route half-circles the lake and passes underneath high-voltage power lines and along a large power station. After an s-curve through a patch of forest, the trail starts ascending again through meadows.

At km 9.0 the route converges with road nr. 8 and railway tracks. At this location you pass from Canton St. Gallen into **Canton Appenzell Ausserrhoden.** After 100 meters on road nr. 8 the route turns left, crosses the railway tracks, and through a meadow continues to ascend towards Herisau. Passing a farm, the route turns right into the *Kreuzstrasse* and continues to ascend on a tarmac road. On your left you overlook a valley with sports fields, schools, industry, and residential houses. After passing by the cemetery of Herisau (with a cemetery chapel) you reach the highest point of stage R1b at 798 meters.

From this high point the *Kreuzstrasse* descends into the town Herisau. You pass by a hospital, after which the route turns left and subsequently circles to the right through the old part of town. The route turns left and left again into the *Bahnhofstrasse*, where you see the reformed church of Herisau in front of you. After a right turn you arrive at the village square (*Dorfplatz*) and the entrance of the reformed Church of Herisau (at km 10.8).

## R-19 Reformed Church, Herisau (Evangelisch-reformierte Kirche)

- Platz 1, 9100 Herisau
- St. Lawrence
- Right of the main entrance, next to a pilgrim guestbook
- A first catholic church was mentioned in 907 (established by the Abbey of St. Gallen), which was replaced by another church in 1225. St. Lawrence was the patron Saint of the church at that time, similar to the city-church of St. Gallen. The present church was built in a late-Gothic style in 1516-20. During the Reformation in the 1520s Canton Appenzell Ausserrhoden converted to Protestantism and the town Herisau followed in 1529; all catholic interior decorations were destroyed and the name of the patron Saint was removed.

  After a devastating fire the church was rebuilt in 1559. This occurred again in 1606. In 1741 the bell tower was strengthened and received a new steeple.
- In 1782-83 renovations resulted in the rococo-stuccos at the ceiling, a new pulpit and baptismal font, and the two galleries (on the left and back side of the nave).

  In 1807 the parish purchased a bell (made in 1756) with a weight of 9'120 kg from a secularized monastery north of Lake Constance. This is the second-heaviest church bell in Switzerland (the heaviest is hanging in the reformed St. Vincent Cathedral in Bern – see stage L4, Volume II).

  In the chancel, have a closer look at the left wall. It has a wall tabernacle from before the Reformation. In 1782 it was covered, but restored to its original late-Gothic appearance, including the masonry above it, in 1960.

  During renovations a new organ was installed on the gallery and stained-glass was placed in the three windows of the chancel in 1959-61. The austere interior is typical of a protestant church.

The signposted route nr. 4 continues south of the church and leaves Herisau. To end stage R1b, however, you should still visit the catholic church of Herisau, for which you need to leave the signposted route. The church is in the direction of the train station, 500 meters away. From the *Dorfplatz* return to the *Bahnhofstrasse* and turn left towards the train station. After 250 meters the road forks in front of hotel Herisau (right continues down the hill towards the train station). Take the left fork into the *Alte Bahnhofstrasse/Gossauerstrasse* and follow it for 250 meters until you arrive at the catholic St. Peter and Paul Church of Herisau (at km 11.3).

## St. Peter and Paul Church, Herisau (St. Peter und Paul Kirche) R-20

Gossauerstrasse 62a, 9100 Herisau

St. Peter and Paul

At the parish office (the white building west (right) of the church)

The catholic church was first built in 1879. Since the new Swiss Constitution of 1848 declared freedom of religion, the first catholic services in protestant Herisau were held in a house in 1867. The new catholic parish built its first church in 1879, 350 years after the former catholic church of Herisau had converted to Protestantism and all catholic services had been prohibited.

This first church had structural weaknesses in its fundament, causing subsiding of the floor of the nave. These construction weaknesses and the growing size of the catholic parish led to the decision to build a new church. In 1936 the first church was demolished and rebuilt as the church you see today in 1936-37.

The church has a modern and austere interior, without the lusciously decorated altars you see in the older churches. Frescos from 1937 decorate the walls.

Rather unusual for a 20th century church, it contains a small space of worship below. The subterranean space was created during the construction of 1936, when the foundations required strengthening, and an extra underground space was created.

The underground chapel is used for additional services and only accessible during such times. The small space has a modern decoration, a bit similar to the Guardian Angel chapel of the Abbey of St. Gallen.

**Herisau** is the main city of Canton Appenzell Ausserrhoden. For many centuries the city and area belonged to the Abbey-Kingdom of St. Gallen, while it was governed on their behalf by the Lords of Rorschach. They had two castles on elevated positions north (Rosenberg) and west (Rosenburg) of town. From the beginning of the 15th century the town Herisau joined other towns in the Appenzell region in opposition against the Abbey-Kingdom of St. Gallen. During a revolt against the kingdom, Appenzell troops destroyed the two castles in 1403 (nowadays only ruins are left). In 1433 Herisau became part of the lands of Appenzell, and in 1529 accepted the Reformation and converted to Protestantism.

Herisau never housed a monastic Order due to its closeness to the Abbey of St. Gallen before the Reformation and its Protestantism after the Reformation. Most of the old town was rebuilt after the city fire of 1606. From the 16th century the town's prosperity grew and declined with the economic cycles of the textile industry, as it became heavily dependent on textile manufacturing. Many of the old houses were built by wealthy textile manufacturers after 1730.

Nowadays Herisau has a population of about 16'000, of whom many commute daily to St. Gallen. The textile industry is virtually non-existent and economically the town has become an extended part of the western agglomerations of St. Gallen.

## *From the ending point*

The St. Peter and Paul Church is the ending point of stage R1b, about 500 meters aside the signposted route nr. 4.

In case you are a day-hiker, you need to walk 300 meters downhill to the Herisau train station.

In case you are a thru-hiker and spend the night in Herisau, there are four hotels and several private accommodations to choose from, but no pilgrim inn. Check out www.jakobsweg.ch or www.viajacobi4.ch for the accommodation possibilities in Herisau. The Herisau Tourist Information Office is at the front desk of the hotel Herisau (Bahnhofstrasse 14, 9100 Herisau; www.hotelherisau.ch; tel. 071 354 83 83). They can assist you too.

### *The next Stage*

Stage R2 guides you over the Appenzell and Toggenburg hills west of the Alpstein mountain range to the town Wattwil in the Thur River valley. Stage R2 is probably the toughest hiking section of the Swiss Way of St. James. Read the next chapter to find out what that entails.

# Stage R2: Herisau to Wattwil 26 km

*The Way over the third-highest altitude*

### *Route stats*

| | *Distance in km* | *Time in hrs:min* |
|---|---|---|
| Signposted route nr. 4 | 23.8 | 6:00 |
| Churches/chapels | 1.7 | 1:00 |
| Points of interest | | |
| Rest/lunch | | 1:00 |
| Stage R2 | 25.5 | 8:00 |

In case you hike this stage as a daytrip, you need to add 650 meters in Herisau and 500 meters in Wattwil (from and to the train stations).

| Ascent/descent/total | +927/ -1'051 / 1'978 altitude meters |
|---|---|
| Lowest/highest altitude | 611 / 1'083 meters |
| Pathway/condition | difficult / difficult |
| Churches/chapels | St. Peterzell (3), Wattwil (4) |
| Monasteries | Former Benedictine Monastery St. Peterzell, Former Capuchin Convent Wattwil |
| Points of interest | Ruins Castle of Iberg |

### *Route summary*

Stage R2 continues in protestant **Canton Appenzell Ausserrhoden**. At km 9.0 the route enters **Canton St. Gallen** again, where you are in the former lands of Toggenburg, which allowed confessional parity since the Reformation.

Stage R2 guides you over the Appenzell and Toggenburg hills west of the Alpstein mountain range to the town Wattwil in the Thur River valley.

Stage R2 is probably the toughest hiking section of the Swiss Way of St. James. Most of the pathway is through farm grasslands with nearly 2'000 altitude meters. The profile is straightforward: 1 km down, 7 km up, 6 km down, 5 km up, and 3 km down. The final 4 km in Wattwil are more or less flat. The trail goes up and down two mountains, peaking at 1'083 and 989 meters. In between these two peaks the trail descends to 703 meters, when crossing the Necker River at St. Peterzell.

From Herisau to St. Peterzell, a distance of 14 km, the trail follows a high-altitude mountain crest, geographically parallel to road nr. 8 in the valley in the east (left).

After St. Peterzell the trail follows a rural path, through grasslands and patches of forest that alternate with hard surfaced farm roads. Whereas road nr. 8 from St. Peterzell to Wattwil makes a northern detour around the Köbelisberg mountain, the trail crosses over its southern foothills. At the higher parts of the trail there are panoramic views of the rolling hills and the Alpstein mountain range in the east, with the Säntis mountain peaking at 2'502 meters. The final descent to Wattwil is steep and mostly through grasslands.

Compared to stage R1 (a and b), the possibilities to buy provisions during today's stage are limited, as more than 80 percent of the trail is through agricultural landscapes. Nevertheless, after hiking through the urban areas in stage R1, it is a relief to finally be out in nature in stage R2.

There are no churches or chapels while crossing over the two mountains, making the day mostly a hiking day. Only in the valleys of St. Peterzell and Wattwil the route passes by churches and monasteries. The signposted route does not pass by the churches in Wattwil (it immediately leaves Wattwil again in a western direction). To visit two churches and a monastery, the end of stage R2 describes a 1.7 km detour through Wattwil (aside the signposted route nr. 4). This detour has only a few gradual altitude meters.

## *Getting to the starting point*

Today's starting point in Herisau is at the reformed Church. In case you hike stage R2 as a daytrip, you need to walk 650 meters from the Herisau train station to the church.

## *Route Map and Profile*

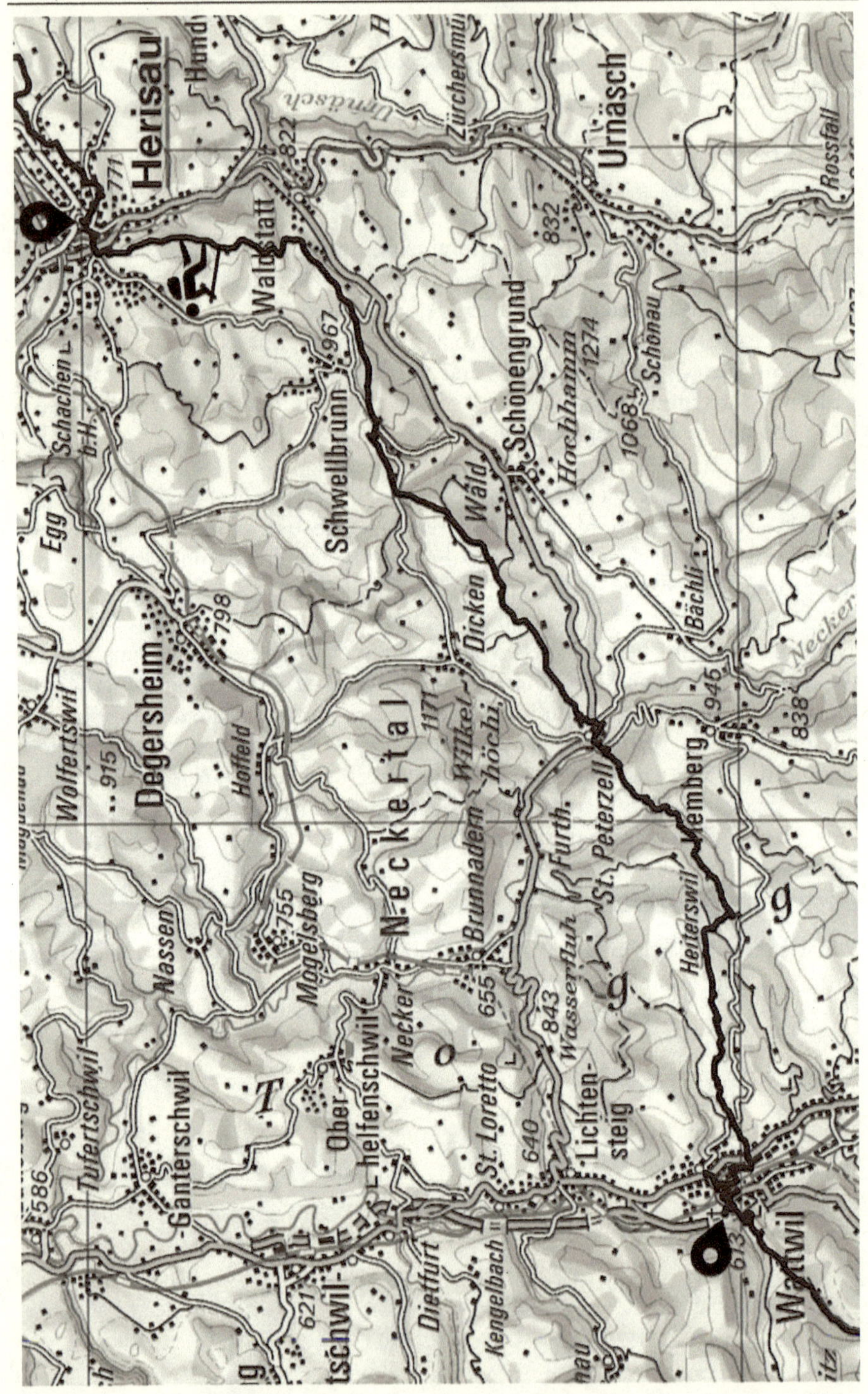
Herisau
Urnäsch
Waldstatt
Schwellbrunn
Schönengrund
Hochhamm
Schönau
Zürchersmühle
Urnäsch
Rossfall
Schachen
Egg
Degersheim
Wolfertswil
Hoffeld
Dicken
Wald
Wilkethöchi
Neckertal
Bächli
Necker
Hemberg
St. Peterzell
Furth
Brunnadern
Mogelsberg
Wassen
Heiterswil
Wasserfluh
Necker
Helfenschwil
Ober-
St. Loretto
Lichten-
steig
Tufertschwil
Ganterschwil
Dietfurt
Kengelbach
Wattwil

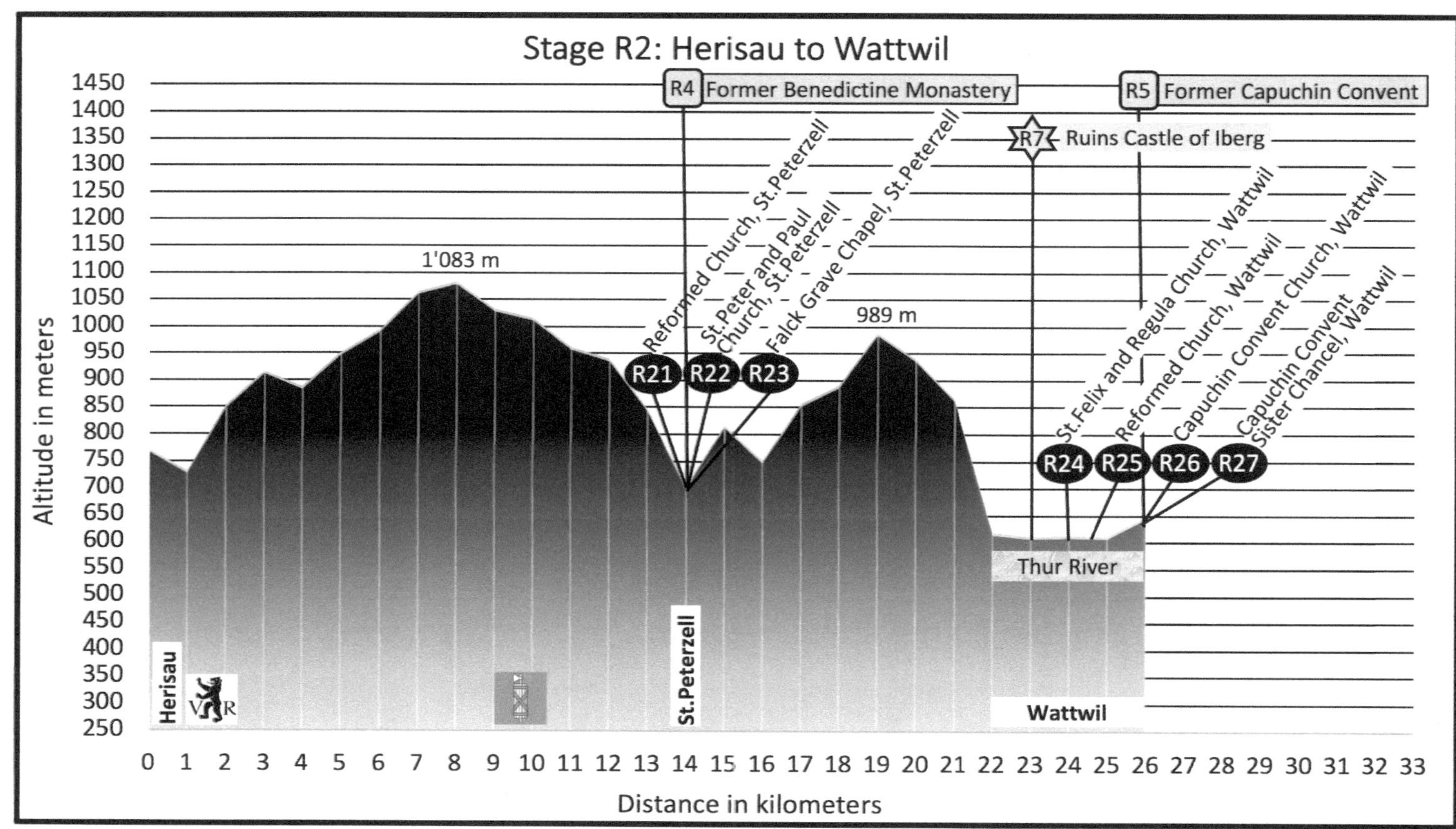
Stage R2: Herisau to Wattwil
R4 Former Benedictine Monastery
R5 Former Capuchin Convent
R7 Ruins Castle of Iberg
Reformed Church, St.Peterzell
St.Peter and Paul Church, St.Peterzell
Falck Grave Chapel, St.Peterzell
St.Felix and Regula Church, Wattwil
Reformed Church, Wattwil
Capuchin Convent Church, Wattwil
Capuchin Convent Sister Chancel, Wattwil
R21
R22
R23
R24
R25
R26
R27
1'083 m
989 m
Herisau
St.Peterzell
Thur River
Wattwil
Altitude in meters
Distance in kilometers

## *Hiking the Route*

From the church cross the square and take the road on the southwestern corner. In between houses the route descends relatively steep. You cross the railway tracks and after a roundabout you cross road nr. 8 and a small stream. A brown '*Jakobsweg*' sign directs to a concrete footbridge over the stream.

From the valley of this small stream the route will continuously ascend over the next 7 km. Turning left you pass by some more houses and after some trees you enter a grassland trail, which goes up steeply. While briefly on a tarmac country road, you have a great view back to the town Herisau.

The route passes through meadows on ascending grass trails for 700 meters, after which it follows an 800-meter ascending trail through the Nieschberg forest. The route continues through grasslands, along or through patches of forest, and is regularly alternated with farm roads, with either tarmac, concrete, or gravel surfaces. Along the way you see signs for snowshoe hiking trails.

Hiking through the grasslands is tough. Most of the time you hike at a steep or moderate angle up or down a hill. The grasslands are often very uneven and cow trails make the surface even harder to traverse. It is easy to confuse cow trails with the existing pilgrimage trails. Be aware, following a cow trail, instead of the pilgrimage trail, will get you away from the route. The grass may be knee-length high, which makes it impossible to see the holes and unevenness of the surface below the grass. The route is not always clear, as the signaling on the grasslands is limited. Often the only guidance to the route is a narrow trail of flattened high grass. Sometimes a farmer has mowed a narrow path through his meadow.

Most of the grasslands are fenced by (low-voltage) electrified wires that keep the cows contained in a specific patch of meadow. Frequently the trail crosses such patches, meaning you have to cross the electrified wires. That is not always obvious. Be aware that on several occasions you need to cross the electrified wire, instead of walking alongside it. Following a trail that may be a cow trail along the wire, may lead to a dead end. This is where the GPS function of the SwitzerlandMobility App is useful to get back on the trail. However, most of the time there are fixed locations where the trail crosses from one meadow onto another. These crossings are revolving gates, small wooden pass-through gates, big cattle fence gates, or electrified wiring with a plastic handle to detach/attach the wire. These crossings provide easy passage, while at the same time avoid that cows are able to go through these gates. Be careful not to step into the cow pies. When cows are suckling and have their calves with them in the meadow, be careful, as they may become aggressive when you get too close to them (several times a year Swiss newspapers report cow attacks). Better avoid getting near to them.

Occasionally you pass by isolated farms or small clusters of farmhouses. Be aware of farm dogs protecting their territory. Though most of them only bark, some will run towards you, only held back by their chain. On occasion a farm dog may chase you, barking and viciously baring his teeth. Your hiking stick can offer protection if you need to fend off a dog. When you are resting or standing still to take photos of the panoramic views, be aware of stinging insects, such as horseflies, particularly around the farms and cows.

At km 8 you arrive at the highest point of stage R2: 1'083 meters. The guesthouse/restaurant Sitz provides relief, where you can rest, relax, eat and drink. From its terrace you can enjoy the panoramic views of the Alpstein mountain range, with its highest peak (Säntis) at 2'502 meters. The Säntis mountain peak is only 16 km away. But these views are not always clear. The weather in the mountain ranges can be unpredictable and often clouds rise up the side of the mountains, blocking the view of its peaks. In closer distance you see the rolling hills of the Appenzell countryside. These views are a nice reward for the strenuous hike.

About 700 meters after the guesthouse/restaurant Sitz the route changes from Canton Appenzell Ausserrhoden back to **Canton St. Gallen**. The change occurs unnoticed in a meadow after passing restaurant Landscheide (at the bottom of the

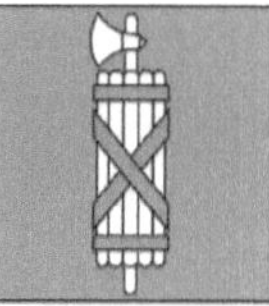

ski lift). At the change of Canton, you pass from the Appenzell rolling hills to the Toggenburg rolling hills. This is, however, purely a political distinction. The landscape and the views stay the same: you are surrounded by rolling hills covered with meadows and small patches of forest.

The following 6 km lead you down to the village St. Peterzell at an altitude of 703 meters. The descent is as the ascent: through grasslands, regularly alternated with farm roads, with either tarmac, concrete, or gravel surfaces. Occasionally you pass by isolated farms or small clusters of farmhouses. In the valley on your left (east), road nr. 8 follows the same southwestern direction. The last kilometer of the descent is steep, through meadows and along a small patch of forest. During the descent you have a great view of the village St. Peterzell. The last 300 meters the route descends on a road through a residential area. At km 14.0 you arrive at the reformed Church of St. Peterzell.

## Reformed Church, St. Peterzell (Reformierte Kirche) R-21

Dorf, 9127 St. Peterzell

After the Reformation the protestant parish used the Benedictine monastery church (see below) in confessional parity for 26 years (1538-64). During the following 145 years (1564-1709) the Protestants had to attend services at the reformed church in Hemberg (about 3 km south). This was during the time that the (catholic) lands of Toggenburg were autonomous and did not belong to the

Abbey-Kingdom of St. Gallen. From 1709 until 1963 the Protestants used the catholic church in St. Peterzell in confessional parity again.

In 1964 the Protestants ended the parity and built their own church. The architecture of the church is typical of the 1960s, with a triangular shape and a free-standing bell tower. The building has two floors: the upper floor is the church, the lower floor the parish hall.

The church has a modern protestant interior, with decorations limited to a cross, pulpit, and communion table. The stained-glass windowpane on the left depicts baptizing and communion (1991), the one on the right the Christmas manger (1994). Notice the weather cock on top of the bell tower (catholic churches have a cross).

After a 400-meter final descent to the Necker River valley, you arrive at the catholic St. Peter and Paul Church (white building) and the former Benedictine monastery (yellow building) in the middle of the village (at km 14.4).

**R-4 Former Benedictine Monastery, St. Peterzell** (Benediktiner Kloster)

Dorf, 9127 St. Peterzell

Benedictine Order

St. Peter

The former Benedictine monastery was established by the Lords of Illnau (who owned these lands) around 1050. It started as a simple hermit's cell dedicated to St. Peter. This is how the small town got its name in 1227, combining St. Peter with cell (*St. Peter* and *zell* in German). The monastery was first mentioned in official documents in 1178, when it was listed as a subsidiary of the Benedictine monastery of Alt St. Johann (about 25 km southeast). The hermit cells in St. Peterzell were designated as monastery from 1214. The monks maintained the St. Peter church and provided pastoral care for the Catholics in the region. During the middle ages the monastery also took care of the passing pilgrims.

At the time of the Reformation in 1524-31, the monastery was closed. In 1555 the Abbey of St. Gallen seized control over the monastery of Alt St. Johann and thus also became the owner of the priory in St. Peterzell. By the middle of the 18th century the building was in poor condition. The old building was torn down and a new one was constructed in 1763-64. The new building was occupied by the monks for around 40 years only.

When Napoleon's troops occupied Switzerland in 1798 and during the time of the Helvetic Republic in 1798-1803, the monastery was closed. In 1805 the new Canton St. Gallen was formed. As the abbey of St. Gallen was closed and secularized, so was the small priory in St. Peterzell. The last monks left and their assets became the property of Canton St. Gallen.

The building subsequently housed the catholic parish office, guest rooms, meeting rooms, and an archive. The former monastery building was completely renovated in 2005 and since then houses a local event organization (*Verein Ereignisse Propstei St. Peterzell*).

## St. Peter and Paul Church, St. Peterzell (St. Peter und Paul Kirche) R-22

- Dorf 9, 9127 St. Peterzell
- St. Peter and Paul
- At the convenience store (across the road – ask the cashier), at restaurant Hörnli, or at hotel Schäfle (across the road – on a table at the entrance).
- The church was part of the small Benedictine priory, who built a first chapel around 1178. The monks used the chapel for their own prayers, as well as for pastoral care for the population in the region. At the time of the Reformation in 1524-31, the church was closed (as the monastery was secularized). From 1533 the church was back in use for catholic worship and was used in confessional parity together with the protestant parish for 26 years (1538-64). In 1709 the confessional parity was reinstated. By the beginning of the 18th century the church had become too small and was in poor condition. In 1721-23 the church was newly built in a baroque style, in a shared effort and financing by both the catholic and protestant parishes. The confessional parity ended when the protestant parish built their own church in 1963; since then the Catholics have the church to themselves again. The church was completely renovated in 2005.
- The three altars have a typical baroque style, with marble columns, angel statues, and center paintings. The left side-altar painting depicts Jesus taken from the Cross, the high-altar painting Jesus at the Cross, and the right side-altar Jesus' Resurrection. Much of the art dates from the predecessor churches. The pulpit in Renaissance style dates from 1660.

There is one more small chapel to visit. You can reach the Falck Grave Chapel via the door at the front-right of the nave of the church, or the green door behind the outside stairs left of the former monastery.

## R-23 Falck Grave Chapel, St. Peterzell (Falck Grab Kapelle)

- Dorf 9, 9127 St. Peterzell
- The chapel was part of the small Benedictine priory, built in 1763-64. The chapel commemorates graves of the Falck family. One branch of this family resided at the Benedictine monastery of St. Peterzell, through which they came in service of the Abbey-Kingdom of St. Gallen.
- Part of this story is told with inscriptions on the walls. A statue representing Mary with baby Jesus is at the center of the small baroque altar.

On your way through the center of St. Peterzell, you pass by several old inns. They are housed in 17th century buildings that have been providing accommodations to pilgrims along the Swiss Way of St. James for more than 350 years. Continuing on the signposted route nr. 4, you cross over the Necker River. The river flows through the village, making this the lowest point between today's two mountains. After crossing the Necker River, you immediately leave the village and start an ascent to the second peak of the day over 5 km. About 200 meters into the ascent you have a good view back to St. Peterzell.

This time you do not hike on a mountain crest parallel to a valley, like in the first half of stage R2. Instead, you go up and over a mountain, without a parallel main road in the same direction. Road nr. 8 from St. Peterzell to Wattwil goes north around the Köbelisberg (1'146 m), whereas the trail goes over its southern hills. One kilometer after leaving St. Peterzell you reach a first high point (815 m), from where the route gradually descends over 1 km, while crossing several small streams. The following 3 km the route continues the ascent to the second-highest point of the day at 989 meters. The trails are similar to the first half of stage R2: grasslands, patches of forest, and farm roads.

At the higher parts of the trail you are rewarded with panoramic views of the Toggenburg landscape, with its typical rolling hills. At the highest point, 989 meters, you can rest and treat yourself at restaurant Churfirsten. From this location the trail descends steeply over 3 km, until you reach Wattwil. Particularly the last kilometer down the meadows is very steep. In case you need to walk through meadows with freshly cut grass, it is likely that the beaten path will have disappeared, making it difficult to recognize the route. Not only that, the cut long grass can be quite slippery and stick to your shoes.

Before finally descending into Wattwil you have a panoramic view of the city in the Thur River valley. Three things stand out: the valley with the river in the middle; a medieval castle tower on a hill on the other side of the valley; and a monastery complex on a low hill, also on the other side of the valley. The town

Wattwil lies in the valley against the backdrop of high forested mountains (which you will cross over in stage R3).

You arrive at a main street in Wattwil, directly from a steep descent through a meadow. The route crosses the street and continues to a road bridge over the Thur River.

The **Thur River** has a length of 131 km, springs at the Säntis mountain range, and flows into the Rhine River at the Swiss-German border near Schaffhausen. It is the 6th longest river in Switzerland and the main river in northeast Switzerland. Canton Thurgau was named after it.

The route immediately turns right after the bridge and follows the western bank of the river for 400 meters. With a sharp left the signs guide you to the train station. On a hill behind the station you can see the former convent that nowadays houses a pilgrim inn. Opposite the train station you pass by a Migros supermarket, which would be a good place to buy provisions for the evening or the next day. The train station is the end of the signposted route in Wattwil. The signposted route nr. 4 continues through an underpass of the train station and enters the forested hills west of Wattwil. Should you want to visit the two churches and the former convent, the end of stage R2 would involve a 1.7 km detour through Wattwil, away from the signposted route.

**Wattwil** has a population of around 9'000. The town was built in the narrow valley of the Thur River. During the middle ages the river regularly flooded, which is why the historical buildings (castle, convent, reformed church) were built on the slopes lining the river valley. In 1907-13 the Thur River was canalized, eliminating this flood risk. The medieval history of Wattwil was determined by the Iberg castle, standing on a hill west of town. From the time of the industrial revolution, cotton and textile mills and factories flourished, manufacturing woven, dyed, and printed textiles.

The former **Castle of Iberg** belonged to the Abbey-Kingdom of St. Gallen. It was built, by order of the abbot of the St. Gallen Abbey, by the local Lords of Iberg of Wattwil in 1230-40. The castle consisted of a fortified residential tower surrounded by high walls and a moat on three sides. The tower was square, had six levels, and a height of 25 meters. The lower walls were nearly 2 meters thick and the entrance door was at an elevated position (reachable by retractable ladder).

Over the centuries the castle was expanded with additional residential halls and storage and craftsmen buildings, while it served as the seat of the regional Governor of the abbey's Kingdom. Its purpose was to control trade and traffic over the southern Ricken and Laad Passes, and protect the southern borders of the abbey's Kingdom. During the 470 years the abbey owned the castle, it was often in the center of power battles between the abbey and regional nobility (Counts of Toggenburg). The abbey lost the castle and subsequently regained it several times during its history. This occurred in 1249-55, 1290-92, 1405-08, and 1710-18. During the Thirty Years' War (1618-48), the abbey stored their monastery's treasures within the thick and fireproof walls of the castle.

By 1718 the castle was in poor condition and the abbey leased it out. It was transformed into a farmhouse and inn. During the following 100 years the buildings were neglected and fell into ruins. In 1805 the Abbey of St. Gallen was secularized and the Canton became the owner of the castle. The Canton sold it to a local manufacturer who had the roof, bricks, and all other constructions removed in 1835. The remains quickly fell into ruins. In 1883 the ruins were donated to the municipality of Wattwil, which renovated and re-erected the tower, gate, and part of the fortified walls in 1901-02. The constructions you see nowadays date from 1902 (renovated 2011); only the design dates from the 13th century.

The Way of St. James passes by these castle ruins in stage R3, upon leaving Wattwil. For the end of stage R2, however, continue in Wattwil. From the roundabout in front of the train station follow road nr. 8 (*Bahnhofstrasse*) in a northern direction and cross over the Thur River. From the bridge you can already see a modern church on your left. Immediately after the bridge follow the path (*Grüenauweg*) on your left. At km 24.0 you arrive at the catholic St. Felix and Regula Church of Wattwil.

## R-24 St. Felix and Regula Church, Wattwil (St. Felix und Regula Kirche)

- Grüenauweg 8, 9630 Wattwil
- St. Felix and Regula
- Right of the main entrance
- At the time of the Reformation the catholic church of Wattwil converted to Protestantism (see below). This protestant church was used in confessional parity by the Catholics for 375 years (1593 until 1967). In 1967-68 the Catholics built their own church in Wattwil (the one you are in now). The patron Saints of the church originate from the old catholic church from before the Reformation.

  The church and its tower have a design typical of the 1960s. The use of concrete as building material and the unusual shape of the bell tower demonstrate this. The interior and exterior designs have a high resemblance to the St. Meinrad Church of Pfäffikon (see stage 4), which was built around the same time.
- The interior of the church is as austere as a protestant church. The only thing reminding you of it being a catholic church is the tall wooden crucifix at the back of the chancel.

From the catholic church walk back to road nr. 8, where you crossed the bridge. Turn left (north) and follow the *Poststrasse* past the post office through an s-curve for 500 meters. In front is the reformed Church of Wattwil (at km 24.5).

## **Reformed Church, Wattwil** (Evangelisch-reformierte Kirche) R-25

Kirchenrain 1, 9630 Wattwil

St. Andrew, St. Felix and Regula

In a small red basket that hangs on the information board in the front portal

The church is on the site of a first catholic church that was built around 897 (dedicated to St. Andrew). In 1344 the patronage of the church was changed to the patron Saints of the City of Zurich, St. Felix and Regula. During the Reformation in 1529, the City of Wattwil converted to Protestantism. The catholic church was stripped of its interior decorations and was subsequently used for protestant worship. It was not for another 65 years (1593) that catholic services were re-established in Wattwil. From 1593 until 1967 the church was also used by the Catholic parish in confessional parity.

By 1835 the church was dilapidated and at risk of collapsing. It took several years for the protestant and catholic parishes to agree on a shared reconstruction project. The old church and bell tower were demolished in 1844. In 1844-48 a new church and bell tower were built; this is the church as you see it today.

The 375-year confessional parity ended in 1967, when the catholic parish built their own church (see above). This gave the protestant parish the possibility to restyle the church to their own liking and the church was renovated in 1968-70. The altars and baptismal font were removed and replaced by a pulpit, communion table, and a simple cross. Two years later (1972) a new large organ was installed. In 1992 a baptism-tree was added; on its leaves the names of the baptized were written. The latest renovations were undertaken in 1996-97.

The interior is a typical protestant square hall church with galleries on three sides. The left and right side-galleries have additional pews, while the gallery above the entrance has a large organ filling up the space between three arches.

From the reformed church walk back in the direction of the train station along the *Poststrasse*. After the bridge over the Thur River take the first street on the right (*Alte Bahnhofstrasse*). You can already see the convent complex on the hill in front of you. Go straight into the *Susann-Müller-Strasse*, and at the *Rickenstrasse* turn right and follow it for 300 meters around the u-curve. Then turn right and follow the small street up the hill to the complex. At km 25.5 you arrive at the former Capuchin Convent St. Mary the Angel.

## R-5 Former Capuchin Convent St. Mary the Angel, Wattwil (Kapuzinerinnen Kloster St. Maria der Engel)

Klosterhof, 9630 Wattwil

Capuchin Order

St. Mary

The former convent was built in 1620-21. A fire destroyed their previous building that stood about 2 km south, on a hill (*Pfanneregg*) on the eastern side of the Thur River. A group of religious women (beguines) had already settled in Pfanneregg since 1403. From 1502 they were organized as the Third Order of St. Francis (a religious community, without entering the Order or obedience to their strict rules). During the Reformation in 1525 many sisters converted to Protestantism, and left with most of the possessions. The remaining nuns were left in poverty. Because the lands of Toggenburg allowed both catholic and protestant worship, the convent continued to exist. In 1591 the nuns were newly organized as a Capuchin convent (entering the Order with much stricter rules) but maintained a high level of independence. They built a new convent in Pfanneregg in 1619-20, which burned down five months after its completion. The abbot of the St. Gallen Abbey allowed them to temporarily reside at his Castle of Iberg.

The old site was abandoned and a new convent was built at the present location in 1620-21. The sisters were self-sufficient as an enclosed community, worked in the convent's garden, and ran a small store. At its peak the convent housed around 30 nuns.

During the French invasion in 1798, troops occupied the convent and caused significant damage. Because the convent did not belong to the Abbey of St. Gallen, their secularization by the newly formed Canton St. Gallen did not impact the convent in Wattwil in 1805. During the great famine of 1816-17, the nuns provided soup for up to 100 people daily for a period of five months. In 1980-96 the nuns were in charge of the fire alarm center of Wattwil and two more municipalities.

By 2011 seven nuns lived in the convent. They derived their income from a small store, lease of lands, manufacturing of candles, and laundry services for the parishes. Because of their high age they relocated to other convents and the Capuchin convent was closed after 390 years of service to the local community.

In 2012 an organization called 'Fazenda da Esperanca' (Portuguese for 'Farm of Hope') moved in and occupied part of the buildings with 12 people. They offer a small community for outcast young people (often addicts), preparing them to reintegrate into society. The remaining buildings of the former convent (hall, church, rooms, kitchen, and cafe) are used for various purposes and events. Nowadays the complex is one of the best maintained medieval convents in Canton St. Gallen.

The former convent's corridors and paintings still reflect the century-old atmosphere of the nunnery. Two small bells hang in the corridor close to the church and sister chancel. They were manually tolled to call the nuns to service. The nun's cells (rooms) have been maintained with their original furniture and are nowadays also used as accommodation for pilgrims. Spending the night there is a unique pilgrimage experience.

## Capuchin Convent Church, Wattwil (Kapuzinerinnen Kloster Kirche) R-26

Klosterhof, 9630 Wattwil

St. Leander

The convent church was built at the same time as the convent, in 1620-21. In the 17th/18th century the church was reconstructed and received a baroque interior. Not much was saved from the fire that burned down the previous convent on the Pfanneregg hill in 1620.

The three Renaissance altars have a uniform design and coloring, dating from 1623. The altar paintings date from 1864, when the church was renovated. High up the left wall of the chancel is a bay window, in the same decorative style as the high-altar, from where the nuns could observe the chancel (from the first floor of their convent).

Another special feature is the organ located on the gallery above the entrance. This organ has four winged paintings (two above each other, on each side). When they are closed, the wings cover all 23 pipes of the organ.

The back part of the nave underneath the gallery has a metal grating. Usually the gate is closed and you will not be able to continue further into the nave (and see the organ and bay window). Only when you access the former convent from the inside (when you spend the night there) can you get to the internal corridor accessing the church.

The church has relics of the catacomb Saint Leander (not on display), which were brought from Rome in 1653.

From the inside you can also access the former chancel of the nuns, the Sister Chancel.

**R-27 Capuchin Convent Sister Chancel, Wattwil** (Schwesternchor)

Klosterhof, 9630 Wattwil

The chancel was built at the same time as the convent, in 1620-21. In the 17th/18th century it was reconstructed and received a baroque interior, though a much simpler one than the interior of the church. The former chancel was used solely by the former Capuchin nuns, whereas the convent's church was also accessible to the parishioners. The so-called Sister Chancel is located at the northern end of the church, behind its high-altar. A door connects the two.

The sister chancel is of small size, has a simple interior, an organ, and a dark-wooden Renaissance altar with a painting depicting Jesus at the Cross. A black statue representing the Virgin Mary with baby Jesus stands on a cabinet next to the altar. Nowadays the former chancel is mainly in use as a music room.

## *From the ending point*

The former Capuchin Convent Church in Wattwil is the ending point of stage R2, about 500 meters aside the signposted route nr. 4 (which passes underneath the train station).

In case you are a day-hiker, you need to walk about 500 meters to the Wattwil train station.

In case you are a thru-hiker and spend the night in Wattwil, you are already in the right place (in case you need provisions for stage R3, it is best to pick them up before ascending the hill to the convent, since this avoids having to go back down the hill the next morning). The former Capuchin convent houses a pilgrim inn (tel. 071 985 04 50; www.fazenda.ch/pilger; kontakt@fazenda.ch), offering double and single rooms in the former cells of the Capuchin nuns (no sleeping halls with bunkbeds). Staying in one of these former cells, with the original furniture, is quite a unique experience (the only one along the Swiss Way of St. James). You can spend the night for a suggested voluntary contribution of CHF 40, including dinner and breakfast with the community. Wattwil has two hotels and a few low-cost accommodations at private residences. Check out www.jakobsweg.ch or www.viajacobi4.ch for the accommodation possibilities in Wattwil.

## *The next Stage*

There are two possible next stages on your way to Einsiedeln. One is stage R3 to Rapperswil, the other is stage S1 to Siebnen. For the choice of the route via Rapperswil or Siebnen, see page 52.

Stage S1 guides you from Wattwil in the Thur River valley in a steep ascent to the Laad Pass and in a long descent to the Linth Plain, at the eastern end of the Lake Zurich basin. Stage S1 and the subsequent stage S2 are described from page 270 onwards.

Stage R3 guides you from Wattwil in the Thur River valley in a steep ascent to the Laad Pass and in a long descent to Rapperswil at the Lake Zurich basin. Read the next chapter to find out what that entails.

# Stage R3: Wattwil to Rapperswil 29 km

*The Way over the fourth-highest altitude*

## *Route stats*

| | *Distance in km* | *Time in hrs:min* |
|---|---|---|
| Signposted route nr. 4 | 27.1 | 5:30 |
| Churches/chapels | 1.6 | 2:00 |
| Points of interest | | 0.10 |
| Rest | | 1:00 |
| Stage R3 | 28.7 | 8:40 |

In case you hike this stage as a daytrip, you need to add 500 meters to the train station in Rapperswil. In Wattwil the route starts at the train station.

| | |
|---|---|
| Ascent/descent/total | +600/ -801 / 1'401 altitude meters |
| Lowest/highest altitude | 410 / 987 meters |
| Pathway/condition | easy / moderate |
| Churches/chapels | Walde, Rüeterswil, St. Gallenkappel, Neuhaus, Eschenbach, Jona, Rapperswil (4) |
| Monasteries | Capuchin Monastery Rapperswil |
| Points of interest | Castle of Rapperswil, Einsiedeln House |

## *Route summary*

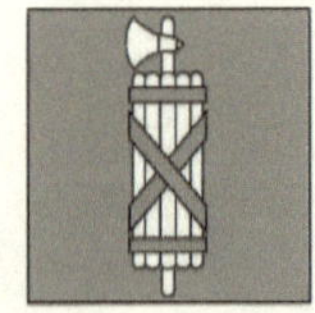

Stage R3 continues in **Canton St. Gallen**. From km 0 to 4 the route is in the former lands of Toggenburg, where confessional parity was allowed since the Reformation. From km 4 to 21 the route is in the former lands of Uznach, which initially converted to Protestantism, but converted back to Catholicism in 1531. From km 21 to 29 the route is in the former lands of the City-Republic of Rapperswil, which remained catholic after the Reformation.

Stage R3 guides you from Wattwil in the Thur River valley in a steep ascent to the Laad Pass and in a long descent to Rapperswil at the Lake Zurich basin.

Stage R3 starts with steep hike up the Ricken mountain to the Laad Pass over 4 km. The trail is a lot easier compared to stage R2. About two-thirds of the route are on hardened surfaces (pavements, streets, farm roads with cement, tarmac, or gravel). The route is on small roads that connect farms and settlements. The highest point of the day at 987 meters is already reached at km 4.

After the highest point the route descends steeply over 2 km, after which it ascends again for about a kilometer. From km 7 it is basically a 22-km hike down to Lake Zurich (*Zürichsee*). Until km 14 the route is mostly on tarmac roads through agricultural fields. As it gets to the lower flanks of the mountain, the route passes through three towns (St. Gallenkappel, Neuhaus, and Eschenbach) in relatively short distances from each other. About 5 km lie between Eschenbach and the next town, Jona. Most of this distance is through or on the edge of several patches of forest. Hiking is easy on gradually descending trails. At km 24.5 the route reaches the outskirts of Jona and the final 4.2 km are through the urban environment of the towns Jona and Rapperswil.

## Getting to the starting point

The starting point in Wattwil is at the signposted route nr. 4 at the train station. In case you hike stage R3 as a daytrip and arrive by train, you are already at the right location.

In case you are a thru-hiker and spent the night at the former Capuchin convent, you do not need to walk down the hill to the train station of Wattwil. You can get to the signposted route nr. 4 from the hill of the convent with a 180-meter shortcut. At the entrance of the convent a nr. 4 sign directs down the hill to the parking lot in the curve of the road. You can already see the top of the tower of Iberg above the trees in front of you. From the end of the gravel parking lot a hiking trail (direction Iberg) enters a small patch of forest and after a short descent of 50 meters bridges the Feldbach stream. Over about 100 meters the forested trail climbs out of the stream's valley and reaches the signposted route nr. 4. On the edge of the patch of forest turn right (up the hill) and you are on the right track. This saves about 1 km going down to the train station and then back up again.

## Route Map and Profile

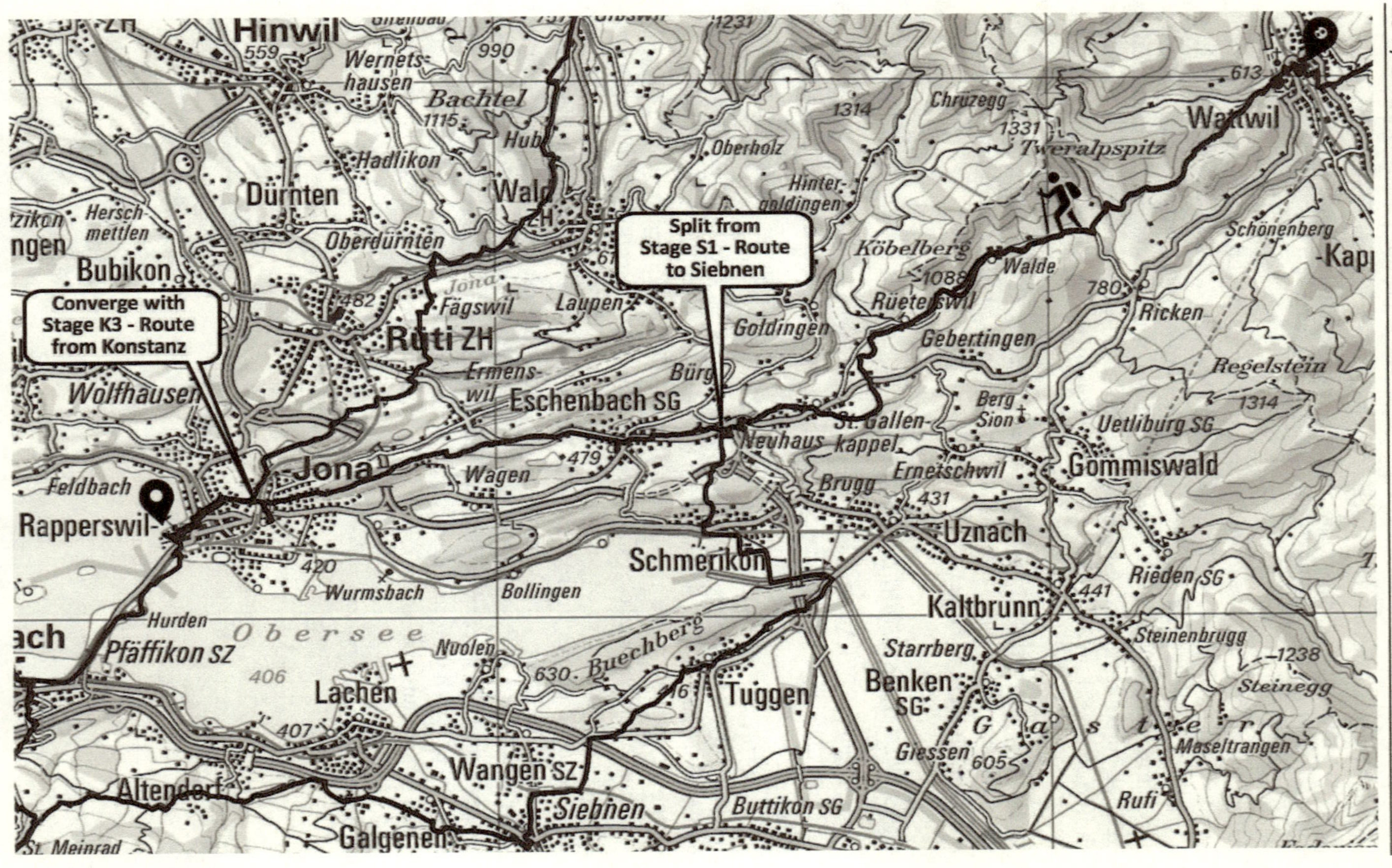
Split from
Stage S1 - Route
to Siebnen
Converge with
Stage K3 - Route
from Konstanz
Hinwil
Dürnten
Bubikon
Wald
Rüti ZH
Eschenbach SG
Jona
Rapperswil
Wolfhausen
Neuhaus
Schmerikon
Uznach
Gommiswald
Kaltbrunn
Benken SG
Tuggen
Lachen
Wangen SZ
Siebnen
Galgenen
Pfäffikon SZ
Altendorf
Obersee
Bollingen
Wurmsbach
Wattwil
Ricken
Tweralpspitz

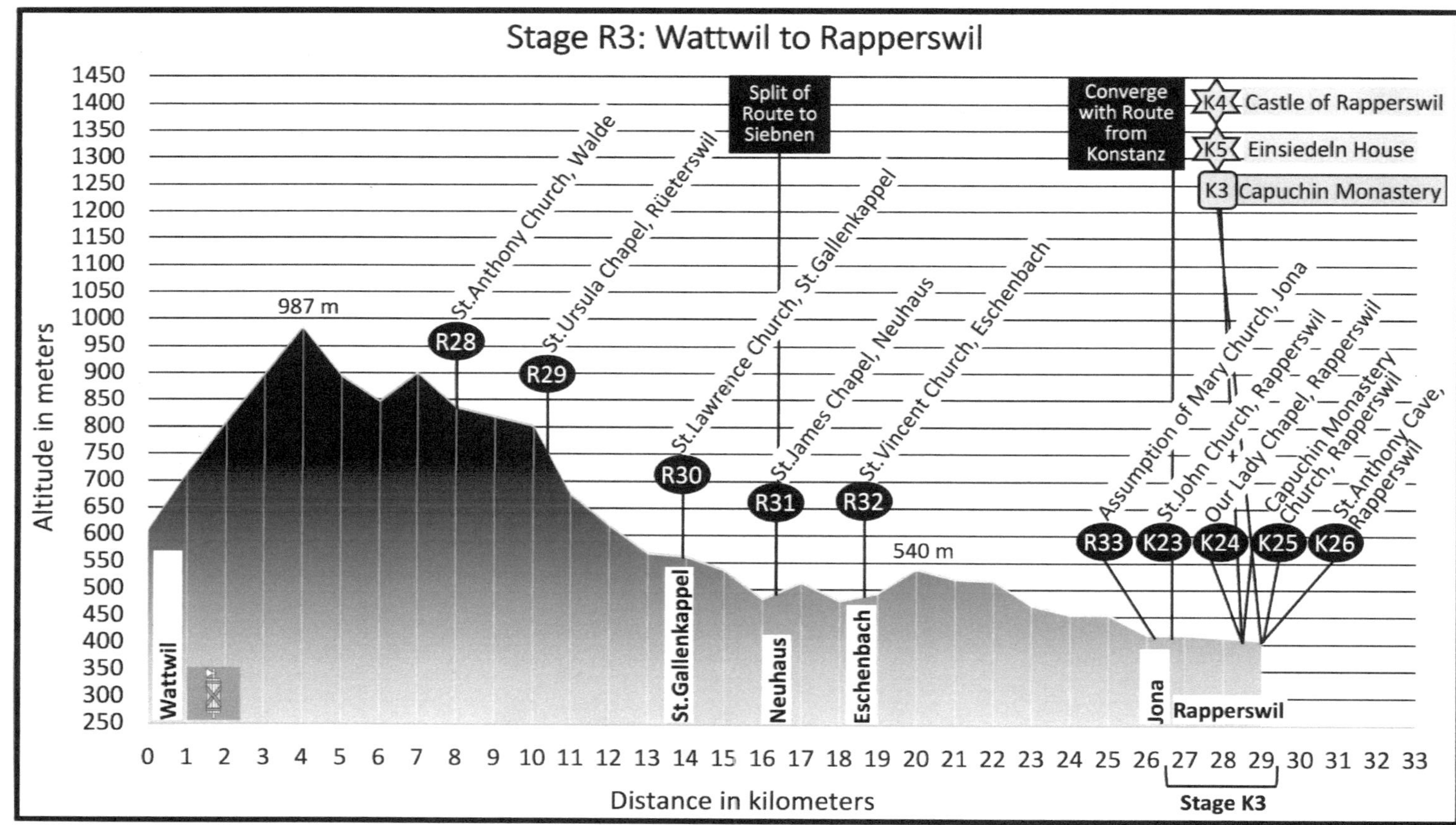
Stage R3: Wattwil to Rapperswil
Altitude in meters
1450
1400
1350
1300
1250
1200
1150
1100
1050
1000
950
900
850
800
750
700
650
600
550
500
450
400
350
300
250
Distance in kilometers
0 1 2 3 4 5 6 7 8 9 10 11 12 13 14 15 16 17 18 19 20 21 22 23 24 25 26 27 28 29 30 31 32 33
987 m
540 m
Wattwil
St.Gallenkappel
Neuhaus
Eschenbach
Jona
Rapperswil
Stage K3
R28 St.Anthony Church, Walde
R29 St.Ursula Chapel, Rüeterswil
R30 St.Lawrence Church, St.Gallenkappel
R31 St.James Chapel, Neuhaus
R32 St.Vincent Church, Eschenbach
R33 Assumption of Mary Church, Jona
K23 St.John Church, Rapperswil
K24 Our Lady Chapel, Rapperswil
K25 Capuchin Monastery Church, Rapperswil
K26 St.Anthony Cave, Rapperswil
Split of Route to Siebnen
Converge with Route from Konstanz
K4 Castle of Rapperswil
K5 Einsiedeln House
K3 Capuchin Monastery

## *Hiking the Route*

From the train station follow the signposted route nr. 4. You walk through the underpass below the tracks to get to the western side. After a sharp right, 100 meters on road nr. 8 (the continuing road from Herisau to Rapperswil), and a sharp left, you immediately leave Wattwil and enter a forest. The trail zigzags and ascends steeply. Early on the path you have a good view back to Wattwil and you see the former Capuchin Convent St. Mary the Angel (*Kapuzinerinnenkloster St. Maria der Engel*) on your right.

One kilometer from the train station you get near the remains of the Castle of Iberg. The route nr. 4 signaling towards the castle is confusing. Following the signs will not get you there, as at a key crossing at the foot of the castle's hill, the signs directing to and from Santiago de Compostela have been switched. At that crossing, follow the sign with nr. 4 without the blue border (the road to the left instead of turning back) to make the final steep ascent to the castle tower (these switched signs should soon be corrected). You could also follow the local signaling, a brown sign with the name *Iburg*; that may be less confusing. For the description and history of the castle, please refer to point of interest nr. R-7 on page 245. There are 97 steps to the top of the tower (in summer open daily between 10:00 and 19:00). The top floor provides a panoramic view of Wattwil (east) and the Ricken mountain range (west).

Back on the trail, the route follows a narrow tarmac road going up the Ricken mountain. On some sections you walk on the road, but where the road makes a wide turn, the trail follows a steep shortcut through grass. Most of the route ascends through landscapes with open fields, offering wide views of the forested hills ahead and to your right (with altitudes up to 1'332 meters). You pass through one small patch of forest. The first 2 km of the ascent are particularly steep.

You pass by isolated farms, where farm dogs may bark at you while passing by. When you look back you have a good view of the tarmac road curving up the Laad Pass and the town Wattwil in the distance. You are surrounded by forested hills dotted with patches of alpine meadows. At km 4 you reach the highest point of the day, called *Heid*, at 987 meters. On a lower altitude on your left (east), about 1 km parallel to where you are, road nr. 8 follows the same direction.

From this high point a concrete and tarmac road steeply descends over the next 2 km. You walk past isolated farmhouses and have wide views of the Alps in the south. Cows graze in the meadows. You pass by an occasional road cross.

In the settlement Bodenwies (at km 6.0) you briefly pass through an area with highland moors and cross small streams. The following kilometer the tarmac road ascends again to reach an altitude of 903 meters at the settlement Oberricken. From Oberricken the route descends and 400 meters later forks to the left, away from the tarmac street. The route follows a gravel tractor trail parallel to the road and passes through a small patch of forest. Ahead is the village Walde.

The route converges back to the tarmac road, enters the village, and at km 8.0 you arrive at the first church of the day, the St. Anthony Church of Walde.

## St. Anthony Church, Walde (St. Antonius Kirche) R-28

Oberrickenstrasse, 8727 Walde

St. Mary, St. Anthony of Padua

On a shelf at the back of the church. A pilgrim guestbook on a lectern invites to leave a comment or prayer.

A first small chapel was built on the site of the church in 1775. Still, the local parishioners had to make their way to the church in St. Gallenkappel to attend services (the next village almost 7 km away). By the beginning of the 19th century they considered the way too long and difficult (especially in winter), and therefore established their own parish. The chapel was expanded and reconstructed into the present church in 1836-37, while the tower was added in 1840. The consecration of the church was not until 1883. Because of limited financial means the bells (1859), organ (1881/1917), and stained-glass windows (1886) could only be installed based on donations in later decades.

The neoclassical side-altars form a unity and include a statue representing Mary with baby Jesus (left) and St. Anthony of Padua with baby Jesus (right). The high-altar has a different style with a painting depicting Jesus taken from the Cross.

From the church in Walde you keep walking on a highland plateau with a very gradual descent over 2 km. The underground alternates between tarmac and gravel. You pass by a road crucifix that is inside a small hut with an open front. The highland plateau offers limited views. At the settlement Allenwinden (at the end of the plateau) you get a first view of Lake Zurich (*Zürichsee*) in the distance.

From Allenwinden (at km 10.0) the tarmac road descends steeply and 400 meters later you arrive at the St. Ursula Chapel in Rüeterswil (at km 10.4).

## R-29 St. Ursula Chapel, Rüeterswil (St. Ursula Kapelle)

Allenwindenstrasse 4, 8735 Rüeterswil

St. Ursula, St. James the Greater, Holy Family, Mary-Lourdes

The chapel was first built in 1696 and rebuilt in 1810. Comprehensive renovations were undertaken in 1918 and 1982-83. The small organ was placed in 1993.

The three altars have the same design. The left and right side-altars depict the Holy Family. The painting of the high-altar depicts St. Ursula and her maidens. Notice the small wooden statue representing St. James at the left wall of the chancel and the white Mary-Lourdes statue on the right. Rüeterswil has been on the Way of St. James since the middle ages, hence the statue of St. James. The ceiling frescos date from 1810.

Right after the chapel is a restaurant, inviting for a rest and refreshments. The route continues to descend through patches of forest, grasslands, and on gravel roads. The route along meadows and agricultural fields provides wide views of Lake Zurich and the northern extensions of the Alps.

In the settlement Betzikon the trail crosses road nr. 8 and goes southward and westward in a wide curve, until it turns back to road nr. 8 in the town St. Gallenkappel. You cross road nr. 8 and arrive at the St. Lawrence Church at km 13.9.

## St. Lawrence Church, St. Gallenkappel (St. Laurentius Kirche) R-30

Kirchweg, 8735 St. Gallenkappel

St. Gall, St. Lawrence, St. Celestine, St. Anthony of Padua

On a shelf left of the main entrance. Like the church's interior decorations, the stamp is artfully designed too, depicting the two patron Saints.

The catholic church stands on the site of a former chapel, which is believed to have been built in the 9th century. This chapel was dedicated to St. Gall as it stood on the lands of the Abbey of St. Gallen. The town was established around this chapel and derived its name from the chapel: St. Gallenkappel (St. Gall Chapel). In 1456 a new church was built in a late-Gothic style with St. Lawrence and St. Gall as the patron Saints. This church was expanded in the 16th and 17th centuries, but demolished to make room for a new church in 1754. The present church was built in 1754-64 and became known under the name of its patron Saint Lawrence. During renovations in 1899-1907 many changes were made to the original interior, for example the ceiling frescos were covered up and painted in a new design. Most of these changes were reversed and the interior received its original appearance during the renovations in 1975-78. The latest exterior renovations were undertaken in 1998-99.

Behind the church is the St. Michael cemetery chapel. It was built in 1667 and completely renovated in its present-day appearance in 1959. The chapel is locked.

The church has a beautiful baroque-rococo interior with harmonizing frescos, statues, altars, paintings, stuccos, and coloring. It is surprising to find such artistic paintings, ceiling frescos, and other artwork in this small town. Have a closer look at the decorations of the pulpit, tabernacle, and three altars. The statue left of the high-altar painting represents St. Lawrence (with metal grating) and the statue right of the painting St. Gall.

In the vitrine of the left side-altar lies a decorated skeleton venerated as St. Celestine. These are relics of a catacomb saint that were brought from Rome in 1795. The bones were assembled as a full skeleton with elaborate decorations by the nuns of the Benedictine Convent of Au, Einsiedeln (see stage 5, Volume II). Notice the many precious stones fitted on the open ribcage; a fine example of the nuns' craftsmanship and reflection of the importance assigned to this catacomb saint. The chalice at the feet of the skeleton is supposed to hold the blood of this martyr. The palm branch in his hand identifies him as martyr.

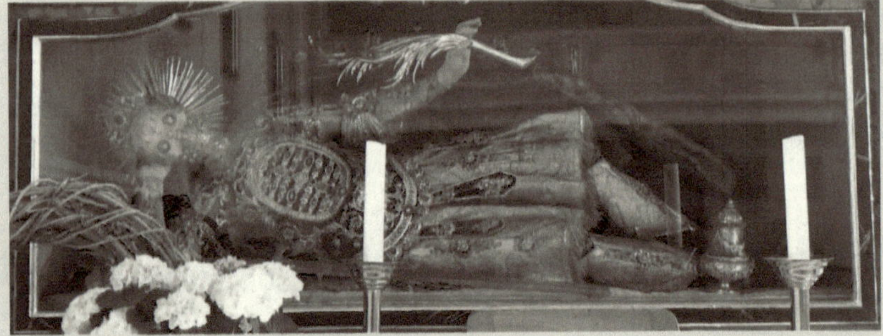

The right side-altar (with a statue representing St. Anthony of Padua) also contains relics. The small metal center piece on the pedestal holds bone particles of St. Gall and dates from around 1700-10. The two wooden vitrines left and right of it date from the late 18th century.

The trail guides you through the outskirts of St. Gallenkappel, staying north of road nr. 8. After a dirt trail on the edge of a patch of forest the route converges back to road nr. 8. You walk over a road bridge across the Goldinger stream gorge. Across the gorge the trail makes a sharp right to turn underneath the road bridge.

You take a left turn and cross an old wooden bridge over the gorge. The route descends into the gorge and after some turns you cross over the Goldinger stream on a low metal footbridge. The path then goes up steeply, underneath the overpass of road nr. 8, and ascends out of the gorge to the village Neuhaus. At km 16.2 you arrive at the St. James Chapel that has already welcomed pilgrims since the middle ages.

## St. James Chapel, Neuhaus (St. Jakobskapelle) R-31

- Jakobstrasse 7, 8732 Neuhaus
- St. James the Greater
- In a plastic slip on the information board left of the entrance
- The chapel was first built in 1585. After a renovation in 1635 the small chapel was dedicated to St. James the Greater as a sign of its importance along the Swiss Way of St. James. By the end of the 17th century the chapel was in poor condition and demolished. A new baroque building was constructed in 1695-97, which is what you see today. The chapel was fully renovated in 2018.
- The oldest parts of the chapel are its bells in the small steeple, dating from 1599. Notice the statue representing St. James above the entrance door and the gold-colored statue representing the Virgin Mary with baby Jesus at the front. Special is the statue representing St. James in a niche above the outside entrance (above the porch, below the sundial). The original dates from around 1585, but is exhibited in a museum in Uznach.

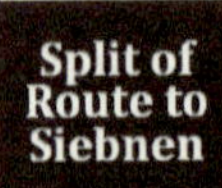


The St. James Chapel is located at Way of St. James crossroads, as explained by the map at the hiking signpost. The route splits at this chapel, until it converges again shortly before the summit of the Etzel Pass, on the way to Einsiedeln. One green/blue nr. 4 sign directs west, whereas another one directs south. The most popular route continues westward to Rapperswil, north of Lake Zurich. The other route turns south and goes around the eastern and southern side of the Obersee to the town Siebnen. See stages S1 and S2 for the description of the route via Sieben (pages 270 to 300). In this stage R3 you continue to Rapperswil.

Continuing on the route to Rapperswil, the trail crosses road nr. 8 in Neuhaus and stays parallel to and north of this main road on a grassland track that is elevated on the flanks of a hill. About 1.4 km later the route joins road nr. 8, as you enter the town Eschenbach. The route stays on road nr. 8 for 500 meters, until the center of town. There the route turns right, from road nr. 8 to road nr. 345. On your left (south) you see a church. At this location you need to leave the signposted route for 200 meters to get to the St. Vincent Church (at km 18.6). Its doors on the northern side are open (the doors from the south are locked).

**R-32 St. Vincent Church, Eschenbach** (St. Vinzentius Kirche)

- Kirchweg, 8733 Eschenbach
- St. Vincent, St. Michael, St. Mary, St. Joseph

At the western end of the nave. The stamp is preprinted on a small piece of paper and lies on a metal shelf below the information board. In case you missed the stamps at the chapel in Neuhaus or the church in St. Gallenkappel, you will also find a preprinted one here.

A church on this site was first mentioned in official documents in 885, though excavations discovered that a first church was probably already built around 800 or earlier. In those days the region belonged to the Abbey of St. Gallen.

Late 13th century the first church was reconstructed in a Romanesque design, with a bell tower. In 1309 the local Lords donated the church to the Premonstratensian (or Norbertine) Monastery of Rüti (Canton Zurich). In 1444 the church and village Schmerikon were burned down during battles with the City of Zurich. The provisionally repaired remnants of the church were demolished and replaced by a Gothic church in 1496. A decade after the Norbertine Monastery of Rüti was secularized by Canton Zurich as a result of the Reformation (1525), the parish of Eschenbach became independent (1537).

The chancel was restyled in a baroque design in 1665-67. The old nave was demolished and reconstructed in a matching baroque style, but without any decorations, in 1723-26. The artistic baroque interior decorations as you see them today were added in 1753-54. Upon completion of the baroque decorations the church changed its patronage from St. Michael to St. Vincent (1755).

As the local population grew, the church became too small. The nave was lengthened by two windows, a front portal was added, and the ceiling frescos were covered in 1875-77. The interior was significantly changed and modernized during renovations in 1955-56. A new pulpit was placed, a gallery was built for the organ, the original baroque ceiling frescos were recovered, the dark stone communion table was placed, and the chancel was nearly emptied. A tall baroque high-altar piece was replaced by a small late-Gothic winged altar. The latest interior and exterior renovations were undertaken in 1995-97.

The beautifully carved retable in the chancel dates from 1507. The retable was made by a medieval artist named Haggenberg (from Winterthur). He also made the wood-carved retables that you will see in the chapels in Galgenen and Altendorf (church nrs. S-9 and S-10). Notice that the retable depicts five female Saints and that two side-wings are missing. This retable is a real treasure, but was not recognized as such by the parish in earlier times. The small altar stood in the former ossuary until 1874, after which it was stored in a humid basement under the nave. In 1909 the Bishop of St. Gallen purchased the altar, had it restored, and placed it in the bishop's personal chapel at the Abbey of St. Gallen. The altar was returned to the church during the renovations in 1955.

Nowadays the church has an unusual combination of contemporary and baroque styles. Modern are the chancel, windows, and nave; baroque are the ceiling frescos and two side-altars (dating from the renovations in 1874). Notice the windows in the chancel that have been bricked up and the wall tabernacle that was used for storage of the Host during the middle ages.

The left and right side-altars have the same design with elaborate wood-carvings, statues, and gold-colored finish. The left side-altar has a painting depicting Mary with baby Jesus, the right side-altar Joseph with Jesus as a boy.

In a vitrine below the left side-altar rests an enshrined catacomb saint venerated as St. Vincent. The relics of St. Vincent were brought from Rome to Eschenbach in 1675. The church changed its patron Saint from St. Michael to St. Vincent in 1585; it was not until a century later that relics of St. Vincent were obtained.

The catacomb skeleton was elaborately decorated with precious stones, pearls, and a red Roman dress (as the one in the St. Lawrence church in St. Gallenkappel) by the nuns of the Capuchin Convent Mary the Angel in Wattwil (see monastery nr. R-5). These decorations were renewed by the nuns of the Benedictine Convent of Au, Einsiedeln in 1877 (see stage 5, Volume II).

Unfortunately, these luscious decorations are not visible anymore. The decorated skeleton was enclosed in the silver effigy during the renovations in 1955.

From the church return to the signposted route and turn left onto road nr. 345. The following 1.1 km you hike along the street to get out of Eschenbach. The route is more or less flat and provides splendid views over Lake Zurich towards the northern Alps.

For 1 km the trail goes north of the street, first steeply up crossing through grassland, and continuing along a small patch of forest, until you get back to road nr. 345. The signs direct you to cross the road, after which the route ascends through the next patch of forest (*Eggwald*). Most of the following 3 km are easy forest trails sloping down until reaching the urban outskirts of Jona.

Out of the forests, the views of Lake Zurich open up as you descend into Jona. From the elevated position you can see the white bell tower of the next church left in front, while right in front you see the dark stone tower of the castle of Rapperswil. For 1.2 km the route follows the descending tarmac street (*Johannisbergstrasse*), until you cross over the Jona River. At this location you need to leave the signposted route to go to the next church (470 meters to the south) that you already saw during the descent into town. After the bridge turn left immediately and follow the small road (*Jonaportstrasse*). Walk past the Jonerhof bakery and café, cross the street, and continue southward with the Jona River on your left. You pass by the hotel and theater *Kreuz Kultur und Gastlichkeit*, after which you arrive at the foot of a hill with the catholic Assumption of Mary Church (at km 26.1).

**Assumption of Mary Church, Jona** (Maria Himmelfahrt Kirche) **R-33**

- Friedhofstrasse 3, 8645 Rapperswil-Jona
- St. Mary
- At the parish office (the white building at the foot of the hill)
- The church is on the site of a first catholic church dated from around 812. It is believed that this first church was built on the foundations of a Roman temple. The churches that stood at this location were frequently damaged during battles, causing significant reconstructions in 1419 and 1480-90. After the Reformation Zurich troops regularly attacked the City of Rapperswil to enforce Protestantism,

which led to significant damage and demolition of catholic icons such as altars, statues, and paintings in 1531 and 1656.

The church was reconstructed and received a new interior in 1675. The nave was newly built and the tower was heightened in 1852 (the Gothic chancel dates from 1480-90). At that time the interior received extensive neo-Gothic frescos, covering the whole ceiling and most of the walls. All these frescos were whitewashed, all three traditional baroque altars were replaced by simple altar tables, and a western side-portal was built to expand the church during renovations in 1936. In 1974 the side-altar tables and pulpit were removed.

The latest renovations were undertaken in 2003-04, which provided the interior an austere and modern look (like a protestant church). The windows in the chancel (bricked up in an earlier century) were broken through the wall again, the high-altar was removed and replaced by a communion table, a new ceiling was put in, and the traditional pews made room for chairs.

Nowadays the 15th century chancel is basically empty, on occasion used for small services. The only indication of the church's 1'200-year history is the beautiful gold-colored statue representing Mary (1656) at the wall of the former left side-altar. The crucifixion group and the Pietà in the Mary side-chapel are of a more recent date.

From the church walk back the same 470 meters north along the Jona River to get back to the signposted route nr. 4. Turn left at the *Werkstrasse*, pass underneath the elevated railway tracks, and 100 meters later you arrive at the location where the

Way of St. James route from Rorschach converges with the route from Konstanz. This occurs at the Jona-Rapperswil Electricity Company (*Elektr. Werk Jona-Rapperswil*) (at km 26.7). An information board explains the convergence of the two routes.

## *Hiking the Route from the Converge point in Jona (km 27-29)*

From the location of convergence, it is an easy hike of only 2 km through the town Rapperswil until the end of stage R3. For the description of the route, four churches, Capuchin monastery, and the castle of Rapperswil along these last 2 km, please refer to pages 146-153 of stage K3.

# Stage 4:
# Rapperswil to Einsiedeln
# 18 km

*The Way to Saint Meinrad*

Stage 4 on the route from Rorschach to Einsiedeln corresponds to stage 4 of the route from Konstanz. This route has already been described in the chapter 'Stage 4 Rapperswil to Einsiedeln' on pages 154 to 181. Please refer to those pages for stage 4 of your pilgrimage to Einsiedeln.

# Stage S1:
# Wattwil to Siebnen
# 31 km

*The Way across the Linth Plain*

## *Route stats*

| | *Distance in km* | *Time in hrs:min* |
|---|---|---|
| Signposted route nr. 4 | 30.9 | 6:30 |
| Churches/chapels | | 1:40 |
| Points of interest | | 0.10 |
| Rest/lunch | | 1:00 |
| Stage S1 | 30.9 | 9:20 |

In case you hike this stage as a daytrip, you need to add 1 km to the train station in Siebnen. In Wattwil the signposted route starts at the train station.

| | |
|---|---|
| Ascent/descent/total | +770/ -934 / 1'704 altitude meters |
| Lowest/highest altitude | 407 / 987 meters |
| Pathway/condition | easy / moderate |
| Churches/chapels | Walde, Rüeterswil, St. Gallenkappel, Neuhaus, Schmerikon, Grynau, Tuggen (2), Kromen, Siebnen (3) |
| Monasteries | none |
| Points of interest | Castle of Grynau |

## *Route summary*

Stage S1 continues in **Canton St. Gallen**. From km 0 to 4 the route is in the former lands of Toggenburg, where confessional parity was allowed since the Reformation. From km 4 to 22 the route is in the former lands of Uznach that initially converted to Protestantism, but converted back to Catholicism in 1531.

At km 22.2 from Wattwil (km 6.0 from Neuhaus) the route enters catholic **Canton Schwyz**.

Stage S1 guides you from Wattwil in the Thur River valley in a steep ascent to the Laad Pass and in a long descent to the Linth Plain, at the eastern end of the Lake Zurich basin.

The first 16 km overlap with the first half of stage R3 from Wattwil to Rapperswil. This starts with a steep hike up the Ricken mountain to the Laad Pass over 4 km. The route reaches the highest point of the day at 987 meters already at km 4. The route is on small roads that connect farms and settlements. After the highest point the route descends steeply over 2 km, after which it ascends again over a kilometer. From km 7 it is basically a 12 km hike down to the Obersee and the Linth Plain. Until km 14 the route is mostly on tarmac roads through agricultural fields. At Neuhaus (km 16) the route splits from stage R3 to Rapperswil.

From Neuhaus the route ascends the Goldberg (521 meters) and descends to the most eastern side of Lake Zurich. Tarmac and gravel paths alternate. The route between Schmerikon and Tuggen (6 km) is flat, going through the Linth Plain and partly along the Linth Canal. From Tuggen the route goes over an extension of the Buechberg to the March Plain.

## *Getting to the starting point*

The starting point in Wattwil is at the signposted route nr. 4 at the train station. In case you hike stage R3 as a daytrip and arrive by train, you are already at the right location.

In case you are a thru-hiker and spent the night at the former Capuchin convent, you do not need to walk down the hill to the train station of Wattwil. You can get to the signposted route nr. 4 from the hill of the convent with a 180-meter shortcut. At the entrance of the convent a nr. 4 sign directs down the hill to the parking lot in the curve of the road. You can already see the top of the tower of Iberg above the trees in front of you. From the end of the gravel parking lot a hiking trail (direction Iberg) enters a small patch of forest and after a short descent of 50 meters bridges the Feldbach stream. Over about 100 meters the forested trail climbs out of the stream's valley and reaches the signposted route nr. 4. On the edge of the patch of forest turn right (up the hill) and you are on the right track. This saves about 1 km going down to the train station and then back up again.

## *Route Map and Profile*

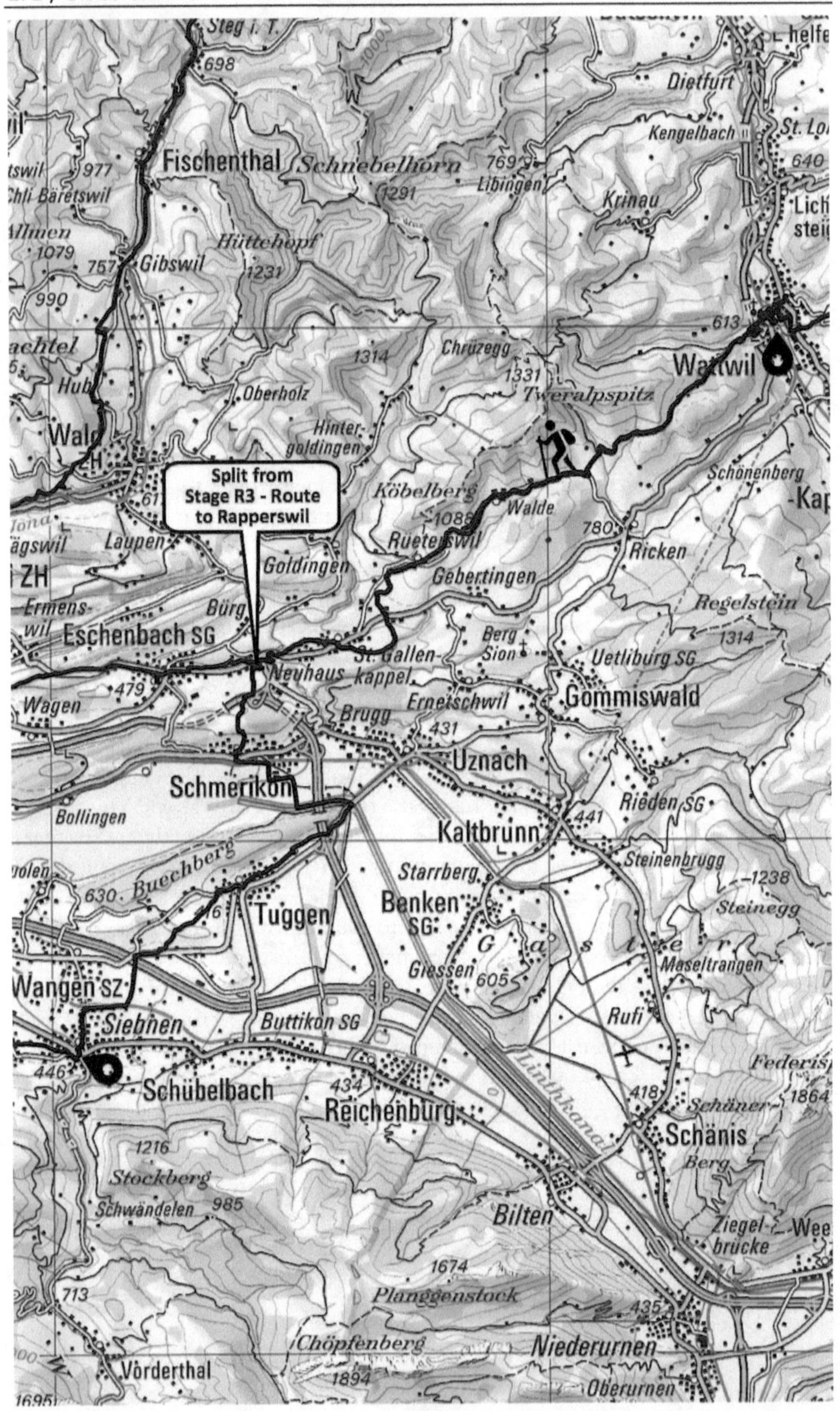
Split from Stage R3 - Route to Rapperswil
Steg i. T.
698
Fischenthal
Schnebelhorn
769
Libingen
1291
Dietfurt
Kengelbach
St. Lo
640
Krinau
Lich
steig
Chli Bäretswil
977
Hüttchopf
1079
757
Gibswil
1231
990
613
Wattwil
Chrüzegg
1314
1331
Hub
Oberholz
Tweralpspitz
Wald
ZH
Hinter-
goldingen
Schönenberg
Köbelberg
Walde
1088
Kap
Laupen
780
Rüeterswil
Ricken
Goldingen
Gebertingen
ZH
Ermens-
wil
Bürg
Regelstein
Eschenbach SG
Berg
Sion
1314
St. Gallen-
kappel
Uetliburg SG
Neuhaus
479
Wagen
Ernetschwil
Gommiswald
Brugg
431
Uznach
Schmerikon
Rieden SG
Bollingen
441
Kaltbrunn
Steinenbrugg
1238
Buechberg
Starrberg
630
Steinegg
Tuggen
Benken
SG
Maseltrangen
Giessen
605
Wangen SZ
Rufi
Siebnen
Buttikon SG
Federis
446
Schübelbach
434
Linthkanal
418
1864
Reichenburg
Schänner
Schänis
1216
Berg
Stockberg
Schwändelen
985
Bilten
Ziegel-
brücke
Wee
1674
713
Planggenstock
435
Chöpfenberg
Niederurnen
Vorderthal
1894
Oberurnen
1695

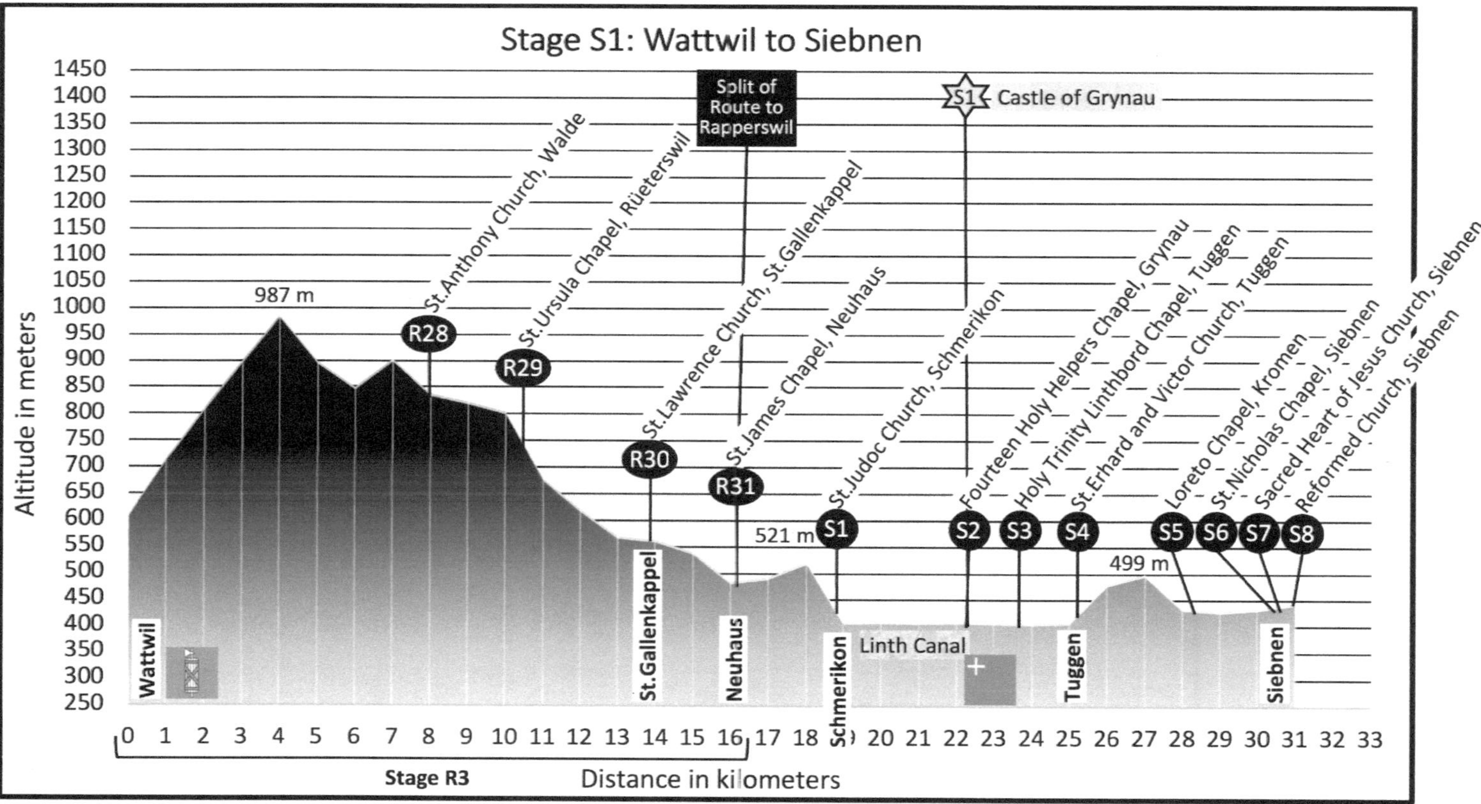
Stage S1: Wattwil to Siebnen
Altitude in meters
1450
1400
1350
1300
1250
1200
1150
1100
1050
1000
950
900
850
800
750
700
650
600
550
500
450
400
350
300
250
Distance in kilometers
0 1 2 3 4 5 6 7 8 9 10 11 12 13 14 15 16 17 18 19 20 21 22 23 24 25 26 27 28 29 30 31 32 33
Stage R3
Wattwil
987 m
St.Gallenkappel
Neuhaus
521 m
Schmerikon
Linth Canal
Tuggen
499 m
Siebnen
Split of Route to Rapperswil
S1 Castle of Grynau
R28 St.Anthony Church, Walde
R29 St.Ursula Chapel, Rüeterswil
R30 St.Lawrence Church, St.Gallenkappel
R31 St.James Chapel, Neuhaus
S1 St.Judoc Church, Schmerikon
S2 Fourteen Holy Helpers Chapel, Grynau
S3 Holy Trinity Linthbord Chapel, Tuggen
S4 St.Erhard and Victor Church, Tuggen
S5 Loreto Chapel, Kromen
S6 St.Nicholas Chapel, Siebnen
S7 Sacred Heart of Jesus Church, Siebnen
S8 Reformed Church, Siebnen

## *Hiking the Route from Wattwil to Neuhaus (km 0-16)*

The 16 km route from Wattwil to Neuhaus overlaps with the first half of stage R3 (Wattwil to Rapperswil). For the detailed description of the route, churches and chapels, please refer to pages 256 to 263 of stage R3.

**Split of Route to Rapperswil**

The St. James Chapel in Neuhaus is located at Way of St. James crossroads, as indicated by the map at the hiking signpost. The route splits at this chapel, until it converges again shortly before the summit of the Etzel Pass, on the way to Einsiedeln. One green/blue nr. 4 sign directs to the west, whereas another one directs to the south. For the continuation of the route to Rapperswil (west) please refer to pages 264 to 268 of stage R3. The route of stage S1 follows the signaling to the south. This route goes around the eastern side of the Obersee to the Siebnen.

## *Alternative: making Neuhaus the starting point of a day-hike*

For a day-hiker there may be an alternative to hiking stage S1 from Wattwil to Siebnen, followed by stage S2 from Siebnen to Einsiedeln. In case you have already hiked stage R3 (Wattwil to Rapperswil) and stage 4 (Rapperswil to Einsiedeln), you can also hike the route from Neuhaus to the Etzel Pass as a separate daytrip. Such a daytrip allows you to hike the route via the Linth Plain and Siebnen without having to walk the distances of the preceding (to Neuhaus) and succeeding (from the Etzel Pass) sections again. This enables you to cover this route in one day, instead of the two days scheduled for stages S1 and S2.

Neuhaus does not have a train station. From the Rapperswil train station you can go to Neuhaus by bus nr. 622 (direction Wattwil), bus stop nr. 23 called Neuhaus Ochsen. Bus 622 departs every 3 and 33 minutes past the hour and takes 15 minutes to bus stop nr. 23. From the Uznach train station you can also go to Neuhaus by bus. The direct bus (nr. 631, direction Rüti ZH) takes 12 minutes and departs every 18 minutes past the hour. Ask the driver to let you know when you need to get off (the bus will not halt without pushing the stop button shortly before arriving at the desired stop). From the bus stop in Neuhaus it is only 100 meters to the St. James chapel (*St. Jakobs kapelle*).

## *Hiking the Route from Neuhaus to Siebnen (km 16-31)(km 0-15)*

The starting point of this section is at the St. James chapel in Neuhaus. From the chapel the route continues southward towards the main road, but makes a sharp right (west) into the grasslands after 130 meters. Halfway the meadow the path turns left (south) and with a gradual descent you reach a hardened road between farmhouses.

Before Highway A53 the route turns right (west) and after 200 meters walking parallel to the highway, you cross over it to the left (south). The trail continues through grasslands ascending steeply until you reach a high point (521 meters) at the *Goldberg* at km 18 (2 km from Neuhaus). After passing by some farmhouses the route turns left and then quickly right again, descending steeply from the *Goldberg*. At the high point and during the descent you have wide views over the Linth Plain, the most eastern part of Lake Zurich (*Obersee*), and the Alps in the distance.

While descending on a tarmac road you enter the outskirts of the town Schmerikon and walk directly towards the St. Judoc Church (at 18.7 km from Wattwil, 2.5 km from Neuhaus).

## S-1 St. Judoc Church, Schmerikon (St. Jodokus Kirche)

Obergasse 44, 8716 Schmerikon

St. Judoc, St. Urban

On a table at the back of the church

The church stands on the site of a pilgrim chapel that was first mentioned in 1448. This chapel was replaced by a Gothic church in 1498-1500. At this time the Bishop of Konstanz split the parish from Eschenbach, through which it became independent.

The Gothic church was replaced by a baroque church in 1774-76, while the bell tower from 1498 was maintained. All Gothic decorations were removed and the bell tower was heightened during renovations in 1884.

The fifth version of the church was constructed in 1906. The nave was newly built and expanded, while the interior decorations received a rococo style. The elaborate ceiling frescos date from 1929 (after the ceiling was strengthened). Finally, the sixth version of the church, as you see it today, was remodeled in 1965: the large front portal was attached to the southern side, the roof was changed, and the tower received a Gothic top.

The church has beautiful baroque interior decorations, altars, ceiling frescos, pulpit, and statues. The interior coloring has been harmonized in shades of brown, gold, and cream. Most of these decorations date from renovations in 1981-82, when baroque and rococo features were restored. The oldest part of the church is the lower half of the bell tower, originating from 1498.

Look for the small statue representing St. Judoc (as reflected on the pilgrim stamp) left of the right side-altar. The center ceiling fresco depicts St. Judoc declining the king's crown. The church's name and depictions of St. Judoc imply the medieval importance of the former chapel/church as a station along the Swiss Way of St. James to Einsiedeln.

The right side-altar contains a beautifully dressed and decorated skeleton venerated as Saint Urban. It is a catacomb saint that was brought from Rome in 1729. The skeleton was prepared, completed with plaster, and decorated by the nuns of the St. Scholastika Convent in Tübach (near Rorschach). Notice the palm branch (identifying him as a martyr), sword (representing the way he died), crown (symbolizing the victory over death), and chalice (supposedly holding the blood of this martyr).

After exiting the church keep following a tarmac road downhill towards the lake. At road nr. 17 the route turns left, crosses the road and railway tracks, and continues to the east. You pass by a small lake port (right) and the Schmerikon railway station (left).

Hiking is easy and relaxed along the lake's promenade. At the most eastern end of the Obersee the route turns right onto a gravel path past sports fields and an indoor and outdoor swimming area. After 300 meters you reach the Aa stream, where you turn left and follow a gravel path along the stream for 450 meters. You reach a wooden roofed bridge, where the route turns right over the Aabach. For almost 600 meters the route continues south on a tarmac road lined with trees, until you reach a bridge over the canalized Steinenbach, leading to the Linth Canal (*Linthkanal*). Cross the metal bridge carefully as it may be slippery.

The **Linth River** has a length of about 50 km and flows from the glaciers of Canton Glarus into the Obersee (the most eastern section of Lake Zurich).

The wide flat valley east and south of the Obersee is called the **Linth Plain** (*Linth Ebene*). This plain was created after the last ice age, when Lake Walen (17 km to the southeast) and Lake Zurich formed one long-stretched lake. The Linth Plain was a lake until the early middle ages. During many millennia the side rivers flowing into the Linth Plain deposited so much sediment that the lake was eventually filled up.

In 1807-23 a national project for the correction of the Linth River canalized 17 km of the river between Lake Walen and Lake Zurich. The **Linth Canal** prevented flooding and improved shipping. From 1937 additional large areas (that were moors and swamps) of the Linth Plain were drained and developed for agricultural purposes.

After the metal footbridge the route turns left (east) and follows the gravel footpath along the Linth canal for 1.1 km. You pass under Highway A53 and pass by a concrete WWII bunker.

At the road bridge over the canal turn right (south) to cross over the canal. At this location you change from Canton St. Gallen to catholic **Canton Schwyz** (at 22.2 km from Wattwil, 6 km from Neuhaus). Across the bridge you arrive at Grynau Castle.

The **Castle of Grynau** (*Schloss Grynau*) consists of two buildings: a bulky square tower and a residential building, separated by a street. The fortified tower was built by the Counts of Rapperswil in the first decades after 1200. These Counts built two more castles in the region: in Altendorf (see point of interest nr. S-2 in stage S2) and Rapperswil (see point of interest nr. K-4 in stage K3).

The Grynau castle tower is standing at a historically strategic location. The Linth River marks the border between the Cantons St. Gallen and Schwyz, and the tower is located at what used to be the only river crossing. The castle was used to control trade and traffic (and taxes) crossing the Linth River from the northeast to central Switzerland.

In 1343-1437 the tower was the property of the Counts of Toggenburg. After 1437 the fortified tower was controlled by Canton Schwyz and housed their regional Governor.

The tower as you see it today dates mostly from 1906. Its interior, roof, and part of the walls burned down in 1906, after which it was reconstructed in its original design.

The tower is square (12.5 by 12.5 meters) and its foundation walls are 2.2 meters thick. Notice the two small entrance doors on the southern side. The original entrance is the one on the first floor (accessible by retractable ladder).

The fortified tower was expanded with a new residential and administrative building on the other side of the street in 1652. Nowadays this building houses a restaurant and guesthouse (*Landgasthof Schloss Grynau*). The fortified tower and the former residential building have been privately owned by the same family for already 140 years (the last Governor bought it in 1879). Descendants of this family still run the restaurant and guesthouse.

The former residential and administrative building also houses a small chapel, which can easily be overlooked in absence of exterior indications (other than a small information plaque). You find the Fourteen Holy Helpers Chapel on the southwestern corner of the guesthouse (on the side of the car park) at 22.3 km from Wattwil (6.1 km from Neuhaus).

**Fourteen Holy Helpers Chapel, Grynau** (Vierzehn Nothelfer Kapelle) **S-2**

Sankt Gallerstrasse, 8856 Tuggen

Fourteen Holy Helpers, St. Mary

The chapel was built as part of the newly constructed residential house in 1652 and served as house-chapel for the residing Governor. The chapel was never consecrated. Though the former castle is privately owned, the chapel's ownership was transferred to the municipality of Tuggen in 1882.

Over time several renovations were undertaken, most recently in 2014.

The chapel is small and simple on the inside. There is no altar; it was stolen in 1965. The small altar painting depicts the Fourteen Holy Helpers below a scene of the Coronation of Mary as the Queen of Heaven.

From the small chapel cross the road and cross the Old Linth stream (*Alt Linth*) on a narrow wooden footbridge. You ascend and descend several altitude meters on a narrow dirt trail on the edge of the Buechberg forest, parallel to the road. Continue on a narrow gravel path alongside the road and walk underneath the blue road sign.

The trail turns right, crosses a small field, and goes through a narrow pedestrian tunnel underneath Highway A53. After the tunnel you walk 600 meters along the southern edge of the Buechberg forest.

Along the pathway are 13 crucifixion way stations, each about 50 meters apart, leading to the Holy Trinity Linthbord Chapel. Across the moors you can already see the small chapel, which you reach at 23.8 km from Wattwil (7.6 km from Neuhaus).

## Holy Trinity Linthbord Chapel, Tuggen (Linthbordkapelle) S-3

Sankt Gallerstrasse, 8856 Tuggen

St. Anthony of Padua, St. John the Baptist

Linthbord was the name of a girl who could not walk from birth, but was miraculously healed after she set out on a pilgrimage to Einsiedeln in 1580. The chapel was built four years later (1584), to commemorate her miraculous healing. This first chapel was replaced by the current one in a baroque style in 1666-67.

The eight wall frescos tell the story of this girl and her pilgrimage to Einsiedeln. The three baroque altars have paintings depicting St. Anthony of Padua (left), Holy Trinity (center), and St. John the Baptist (right). The Holy Trinity doctrine is based on God being one, existing in three persons: Father (God), Son (Christ), and Holy Spirit. The chapel is popular for wedding ceremonies.

From the chapel the trail continues through the grassland until you reach the outskirts of Tuggen. On tarmac roads you pass through Tuggen, where the route makes a right to arrive at the St. Erhard and Victor Church (at 25.3 km from Wattwil, 9.1 km from Neuhaus).

## S-4 St. Erhard and Victor Church, Tuggen (St. Erhard und Viktor Kirche)

Buchbergstrasse 6, 8856 Tuggen

St. Erhard, St. Victor, St. Gall, St. Columbanus, St. Othmar

In an envelope on a table next to the St. Victor altar. The stamp is preprinted on a small piece of paper. Next to the envelope you find a pilgrim guestbook.

The church stands on the site of a first church, which was mentioned around 630. Subsequent churches were mentioned in 1116 (Romanesque) and 1345 (Gothic). The present baroque church was built in 1733-34. The nave was lengthened by one window and the tower heightened during renovations in 1958-59. The frescos in the chancel were recovered during renovations in 1994.

The church has artful interior decorations, paintings, and statues. The three altars, with many statues, are beautiful examples of baroque style; notice that they are made of wood, painted to resemble marble. Special features are the fourth altar and the two loggias in the chancel. The fourth altar is dedicated to St. Victor, who is depicted in his Roman army dress on a large painting.

The high-altar holds four reliquaries with decorated bone fragments, including relics of St. Gall, St. Columbanus, and St. Othmar. They were donated by the Abbey of St. Gallen to several parish churches in the region around 1482.

The last 6 km, from Schmerikon until Tuggen, the route was flat. From the St. Erhard and Victor church the trail goes up again. The following 2 km you ascend almost 100 meters to get to 499 meters. The beginning of the ascent on the pavement along a tarmac road is a bit steep.

After 500 meters you leave the road and continue towards the left on a patch of grasslands along cherry and apple trees. The route continues on tarmac farm roads and at the highest point of 499 meters you turn left. The path quickly descends on a curving road, until you reach a main road behind a bus stop. The descent provides wide views over the valley and the Alps behind it.

At a busy road you turn right and follow it for 400 meters. Watch out for traffic; you need to walk along the edge of the road, as there is no pedestrian path. Subsequently the signs direct to the left (south), in the direction of Siebnen. The tarmac road goes over Highway A3 and after 150 meters you arrive at the Loreto Chapel (at 28.3 km from Wattwil, 12.1 km from Neuhaus).

## **Loreto Chapel, Kromen** (Loreto Kapelle) S-5

Kromenstrasse 10, 8855 Tuggen

Holy Family

The chapel is a so-called farm chapel that was built by a local Governor on his farm estate in 1693 (the farmhouse is nearby). Ownership of the chapel changed to the St. Erhard and Victor church in Tuggen in 1808. The chapel has no windows but a skylight in the roof, similar to the original Loreto Chapel.

The Loreto chapel represents the Holy Family's house in Nazareth, which according to legend, was miraculously transported by angels to Loreto, Italy in 1295. This was just before Christian Crusaders lost the Holy Land and the Holy Family's house was threatened to be destroyed by Muslim soldiers. The Our Lady of Loreto in the Basilica della Santa Casa in Italy is a Black Madonna (like the one in Einsiedeln). The Loreto chapel is often depicted without a roof; the ceiling is usually decorated with stars.

The chapel has two small door openings, one leading to the sacristy, the other to the nave. The small sacristy is separated from the nave by a wooden grating. In front of it is a small altar. The altar received new decorations (statues representing the Holy Family; Mary and Joseph holding hands with a young Jesus in the middle) during renovations in 1986-87. The small niche next to the altar represents the chimney as in the original Loreto chapel. Several vague frescos decorate the red bricks of the nave. These were (partially) uncovered during the renovations of 1986. The doors to the small chapel are locked; you can only get in on special occasions.

The final 2.6 km to the end of stage S1 in Siebnen are flat. The route continues southward on a tarmac road between farmlands, until you pass underneath railway tracks. There you turn right and follow the train tracks for about 900 meters, passing by the Siebnen-Wangen train station.

In case you are a day-hiker and came from Wattwil, you can consider to end stage S1 at the train station. The route continues for another kilometer and passes by one chapel and two churches. From the ending point you would need to walk back the same kilometer to this train station. In case you walk stage S2 as a day-hike another time, you can then simply start at this train station and continue the route as described below.

After the train station the route turns left and follows the main road into Siebnen. You walk south towards the center and can already see the bell tower of the next church. Shortly before that church you arrive at the St. Nicholas Chapel (at 30.5 km from Wattwil, 14.3 km from Neuhaus).

## St. Nicholas Chapel, Siebnen (St. Niklaus Kapelle) S-6

Bahnhofstrasse 20, 8854 Siebnen

St. Nicholas, St. James the Greater, St. Anne

It is believed a first chapel was built around 1200. It was first mentioned in official documents as a farm chapel built by a local patrician family in 1353. In 1370 the chapel was listed as a subsidiary of the parish church St. Erhard and Victor of Tuggen. The chapel was expanded in 1606 and again in 1676, when it received its present appearance. Until 1905 the chapel was the only place for catholic worship in Siebnen. Catholics had to attend services at the churches in the surrounding towns, until their own parish church was built in Siebnen (see below).

The interior of the chapel contains several art treasures of Canton Schwyz: an exquisite altar and colorful wall frescos. The small wood-carved altar dates from around 1623 and includes statues representing St. Anne, flanked by St. James (left) and St. Nicholas (right). Several layers of paint were removed from the altar during renovations in 1986-87, so that it is now in its original color again. The presence of St. James at the altar reflects the importance of this chapel during medieval pilgrimages to Einsiedeln.

Most frescos (1631) on the right wall were renovated; a large spot on the left wall still is white. The frescos depict scenes from the life of St. Nicholas. To protect these treasures, the door of the chapel remains locked. However, you can borrow the key from the parish office, which is just across the street next to the Sacred Heart of Jesus Church.

On the opposite side of the street you arrive at the Sacred Heart of Jesus Church (at 30.6 km from Wattwil, 14.4 km from Neuhaus).

## S-7 **Sacred Heart of Jesus Church, Siebnen** (Herz-Jesu Kirche)

- Kirchweg 1, 8854 Siebnen
- St. Margaret Alacoque
- At the parish office in the building left of the church
- The church was built in 1925-27. There was no other historical church on this site, because the town was too small and most Catholics attended services at churches in the neighboring parishes. As the town grew and needed an own church, a local priest started with catholic services at a school in 1905. It took nearly 20 years to organize the financing and construction of the new church, which was consecrated in 1927. Because no money was left for bells, the reformed Church (see below) tolled its bells during the consecration ceremony. Its own bells were installed in 1931, while the organ was purchased in 1937. The wooden ceiling construction was put in during renovations in 1959-60, when the old ceiling needed replacement because of its bad condition.
- The church has an austere and modern interior. Eye-catchers are the two gold-colored kneeling angels in the chancel and the tall chancel painting. This oil painting depicts St. Margaret Alacoque with Jesus appearing in front of her (it is a replica of a mosaic from the St. Peter's Basilica in Rome). The painting is an original given by French Catholics to Pope Benedict XV upon St. Margaret's canonization in 1920. It came to the church in Siebnen as a gift from the Bishop of Chur, who purchased it from the Bishop of Bologna (its large size made it difficult to place in a chancel).

Follow the signposted route nr. 4 to the southern side of the church, past the cemetery, and you get to the shallow Wägitaler Aa stream. Turn left and you arrive at the reformed Church of Siebnen (at 30.9 km from Wattwil, 14.7 km from Neuhaus).

## Reformed Church, Siebnen (Evangelisch-reformierte Kirche) S-8

Fabrikstrasse 2, 8854 Siebnen

The church was built in 1875-78, when the protestant community was still very small (around 100). The reformed parish was established as the first protestant organization in Canton Schwyz in 1868. In 1868-75 protestant services were held at the local school.

The reformed church was built with the support of a local textile manufacturer and protestant organizations from Zurich (in an effort to enter the catholic stronghold of Canton Schwyz). Newly established textile factories employed protestants coming from Zurich, developing the protestant community in 1840-80.

In 1916 the gallery was built, on which the first organ was placed. In 1985-86 renovations restored the interior to its original condition, while the chandeliers, a new organ, and the three stained-glass windows in the chancel were installed. The last renovations (for the 125-year jubilee) were undertaken in 2002-03. At that time the church received a new baptismal font and baptism tree.

The hall church has a typical protestant interior, with decorations limited to a pulpit, communion table, baptismal font, and cross.

The doors are locked; you cannot enter the church outside the times of services. However, the parish office (50 meters back at the corner of the street) can open the church for you.

The development of the town **Siebnen** was closely linked to the Wägitaler Aa River that flows from the southern mountains through town. A mill was first mentioned in 1178 and a bridge over the river in 1450.

During medieval times this was the only bridge over the Wägitaler Aa River, which made Siebnen a convergence point for trade, travel, and pilgrim routes through the March Plain. So, it is logical that the Swiss Way of St. James passes through Siebnen, thereby following the medieval pilgrimage route over the only bridge. In the 18th/19th centuries the river was canalized and its former flood areas used for agriculture and urbanization.

The modern development of Siebnen started during the industrial revolution from 1830 onwards, when textile manufacturers set up their plants. Further development occurred after the town was connected to the Swiss railway network in 1875. Nowadays the town has a population of around 7'000. Many of the employed people commute to the larger municipalities Lachen, Pfäffikon, or Rapperswil.

## *From the ending point*

The reformed Church in Siebnen is the ending point of stage S1, directly on the signposted route nr. 4.

In case you are a day-hiker, you need to walk back 1 km to the Sieben-Wangen train station.

In case you are a thru-hiker and spend the night in Sieben, you can choose between two hotels. Neither a pilgrim inn nor low-cost private accommodations are available. Check out www.jakobsweg.ch or www.viajacobi4.ch for the accommodation possibilities in Siebnen.

## *The next Stage*

Stage S2 guides you from Siebnen in the March Plain over the Etzel Pass to the highland plateau of Einsiedeln. The stage is relatively short, providing sufficient time to visit the Benedictine Monastery in Einsiedeln and see its treasures. Read the next chapter to find out what that entails.

# Stage S2:
# Siebnen to Einsiedeln
# 19 km

*The Way to Saint Meinrad*

## *Route stats*

| | *Distance in km* | *Time in hrs:min* |
|---|---|---|
| Signposted route nr. 4 | 18.6 | 4:20 |
| Churches/chapels | 0.4 | 1:30 |
| Points of interest | | 0.10 |
| Rest/lunch | | 0:30 |
| Stage S2 | 19.0 | 6:30 |

In case you hike this stage as a daytrip, you need to add 1 km in Siebnen and 600 meters in Einsiedeln (from and to the train stations). The last three points of interest are not included in the above time and distance.

| | |
|---|---|
| Ascent/descent/total | +813/ -354 / 1'167 altitude meters |
| Lowest/highest altitude | 426 / 951 meters |
| Pathway/condition | easy / moderate |
| Churches/chapels | Galgenen, Altendorf, Etzel Pass, Egg, Einsiedeln (5) |
| Monasteries | Benedictine Monastery Einsiedeln |
| Points of interest | Former Castle of old-Rapperswil, Devil Bridge, Site of former Gallows, Our Lady Fountain, Guided Monastery Tour, Diorama Bethlehem, Panorama Crucifixion |

## *Route summary*

Stage S2 continues in catholic **Canton Schwyz**.

Stage S2 guides you from Siebnen in the March Plain over the Etzel Pass to the highland plateau of Einsiedeln. The stage is relatively short, providing sufficient time to visit the Benedictine Monastery in Einsiedeln and see its treasures.

The first 5 km from Siebnen are through the flat March Plain. From km 5 to 6 the route steeply ascends, after which it is more or less flat for another kilometer. From km 7 to 8 the route steeply ascends, after which it is more or less flat for another kilometer. From km 9 to 11 the route steeply ascends on the flanks of the Etzel mountain to reach the point of convergence with the route from Rapperswil at km 11 (about 1 km below the pass level).

Km 11-19 overlap with the second half of stage 4 from Rapperswil to Einsiedeln. From the Etzel Pass the route steeply descends over 1 km to the Devil Bridge that crosses the Sihl River. Climbing out of the river valley, the route reaches a highland plateau offering panoramic views of the Sihl Lake and the Alps. After 5 km on the highland plateau the route reaches Einsiedeln.

## *Route Map and Profile*

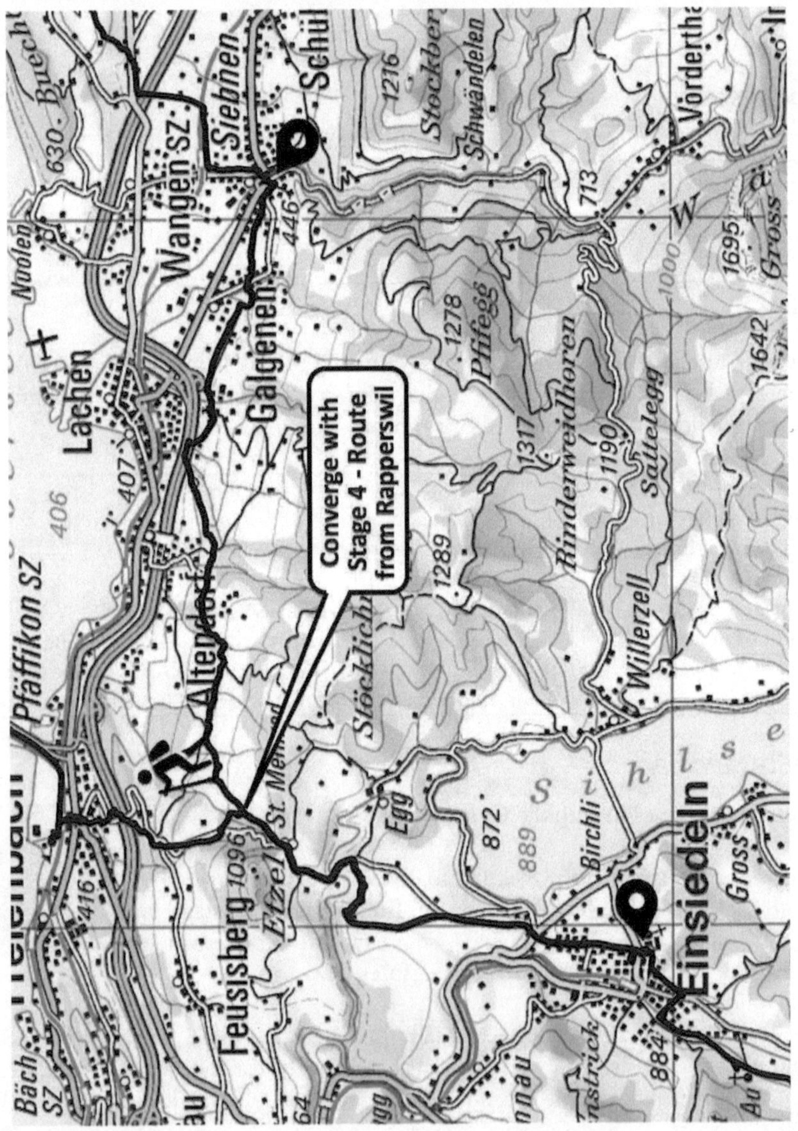

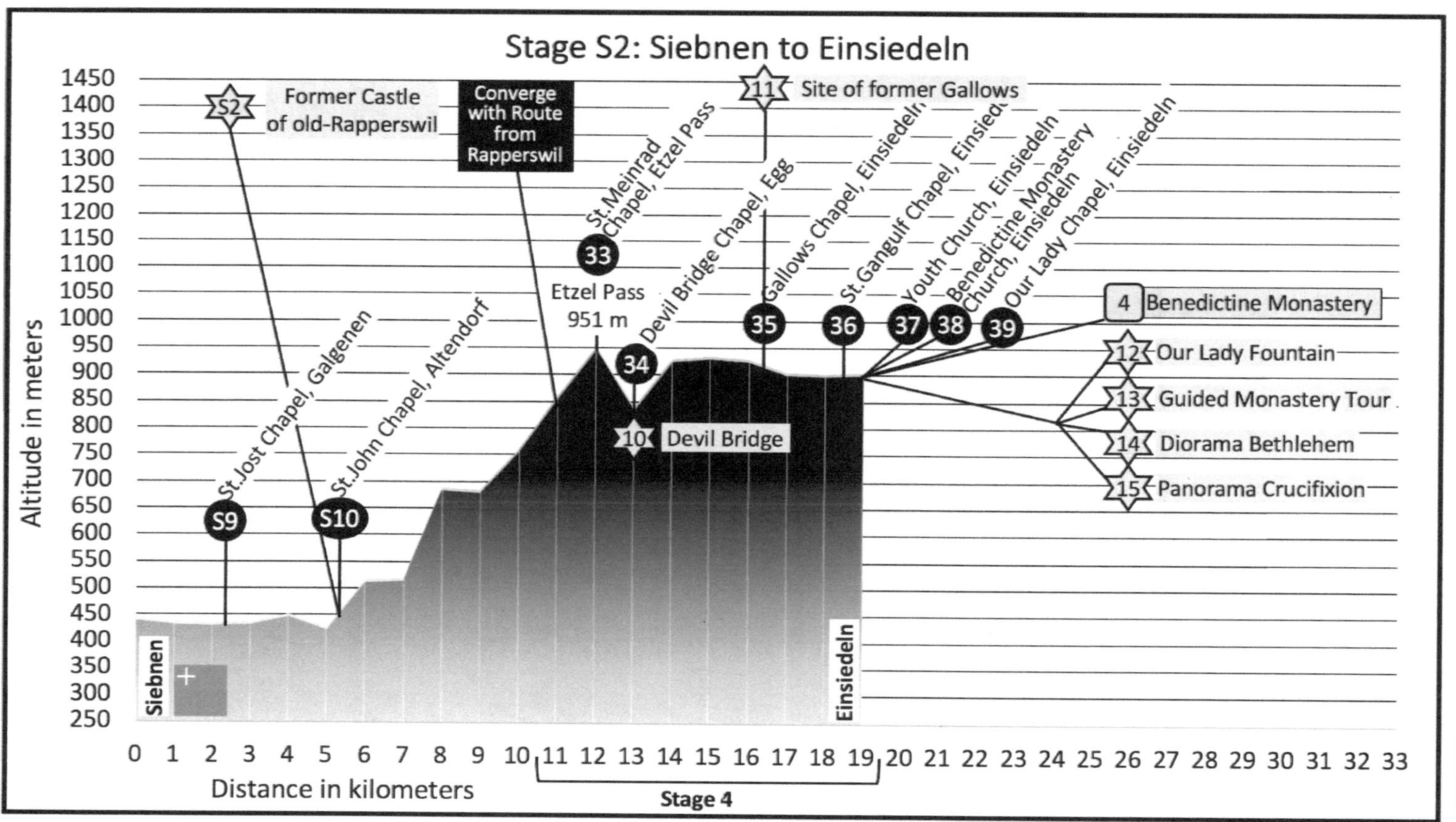

Stage S2: Siebnen to Einsiedeln
Altitude in meters
1450
1400
1350
1300
1250
1200
1150
1100
1050
1000
950
900
850
800
750
700
650
600
550
500
450
400
350
300
250
Distance in kilometers
0 1 2 3 4 5 6 7 8 9 10 11 12 13 14 15 16 17 18 19 20 21 22 23 24 25 26 27 28 29 30 31 32 33
Stage 4
Siebnen
Einsiedeln
S2
Former Castle of old-Rapperswil
Converge with Route from Rapperswil
11
Site of former Gallows
S9
St.Jost Chapel, Galgenen
S10
St.John Chapel, Altendorf
33
St.Meinrad Chapel, Etzel Pass
Etzel Pass 951 m
34
Devil Bridge Chapel, Egg
10
Devil Bridge
35
Gallows Chapel, Einsiedeln
36
St.Gangulf Chapel, Einsiedeln
37
Youth Church, Einsiedeln
38
Benedictine Monastery Church, Einsiedeln
39
Our Lady Chapel, Einsiedeln
4
Benedictine Monastery
12
Our Lady Fountain
13
Guided Monastery Tour
14
Diorama Bethlehem
15
Panorama Crucifixion

## *Getting to the starting point*

The starting point is at the reformed Church in the center of Siebnen, directly on the signposted route nr. 4. In case you hike stage S2 as a daytrip and arrive by train at the Siebnen-Wangen station, you need to walk 1 km to the starting point.

## *Hiking the Route from Siebnen to Etzel Pass (km 0-11) (from Neuhaus km 15-26)*

On the corner of the main street the route turns right, and crosses the road and the Wägitaler Aa stream. The signs direct you between houses and after making a right turn the route alternates between small patches of grass field and tarmac road in the western outskirts of Siebnen. On a gravel path between apple trees you leave the town behind you.

After a 600-meter crossing of a meadow you reach the outskirts of the town Galgenen. The route continues along residential areas, on grasslands and tarmac roads. You pass by a small roadside chapel (*Wegkapelle*).

The road ends at a T-crossing, where you can already see the St. Jost Chapel from the last curve. The first thing you notice as you come closer to the chapel (at 2.2 km from Siebnen, 16.9 km from Neuhaus) are the exterior wall frescos.

## St. Jost Chapel, Galgenen (St. Jost Kapelle) S-9

- Kapellstrasse, 8854 Galgenen
- St. Jost, Brother Klaus, St. Anne
- At the house opposite the chapel
- The chapel was first mentioned in 1362 and consecrated in 1398. It was built by the local parish priest to serve the growing pilgrim streams to Einsiedeln. The present chapel still has the original footprint and walls from 1362. For a 14th century chapel it is relatively large, an indication of the number of pilgrims passing by at that time.

After the Reformation in the 1520s-30s, the pilgrim streams significantly reduced (as pilgrimage was not condoned by Protestantism) and a local family acquired the chapel around 1600. They made it their private family chapel and renovated it in 1622-23 (new gallery, windows, doors, winged altar; Gothic frescos replaced by frescos with scenes from the life of St. Jost and Brother Klaus).

Additional renovations were undertaken in 1760 (curved ceiling with paintings, new left side-altar), 1910, 1953, and 1960 (recovery of the Gothic frescos). The latest comprehensive renovations were undertaken in 2011-12. The chapel is one of the few that was not changed to a baroque style, which was so popular during the 18th century.

The winged altar (retable) is a beautiful piece of woodcarving dating from around 1500. A statue representing St. Jost is in the center. Have a closer look at the left-side retable (from around 1500) dedicated to St. Anne. Notice how the two outside wings are missing. Both retables were made by the artist Haggenberg, who also made the retables in the church of Eschenbach (church nr. R-32) and the chapel in Altendorf (see below).

The wall frescos on the left side of the nave depict scenes from Brother Klaus (you will visit his birthplace and hermit cell, and read about his historical significance in stage 7, Volume II). The frescos on the right side of the chancel depict the life of St. Jost.

The other pale frescos in the chancel and its windowsills were recovered during earlier renovations and are the original ones from 1362.

Nowadays the chapel is more than 650 years old; it is remarkable how its treasures have survived the centuries. It has many similarities with the St. Nicholas chapel in Siebnen, which was built around the same time.

From the chapel you follow the westward road between meadows for about 1.3 km. At the T-crossing you turn left and then immediately right to cross a road bridge over the rocky and shallow Spreiten stream (*Spreitenbach*). After a left turn you make an almost immediate right turn (be aware that the sign directing to the right is missing). The trail is between two apartment blocks, at the end of which is another small roadside chapel. From there the route follows a straight road for 500 meters. In the distance you see a small chapel on top of a hill, surrounded by grapevines. You are getting closer to Highway A3; the sound of speeding traffic intensifies.

You pass by a small industrial area and at another T-crossing the route goes right, and 80 meters later left. The route is next to Highway A3 for 200 meters, after which it turns left and goes steep up the hill to the chapel. Over 450 meters on the narrow tarmac road you ascend almost 70 meters. From the road a small gravel path leads you to the St. John Chapel (at 5.2 km from Siebnen, 19.9 km from Neuhaus).

## St. John Chapel, Altendorf (St. Johann Kapelle) S-10

Burgweg, 8852 Altendorf

St. Mary, St. John the Baptist, St. John the Evangelist, St. Anne, St. Vitus, St. Wolfgang

The chapel was built on the ruins of a destroyed castle (see below). Hence, its name 'St. John on the Castle' (*St. Johann auf der Burg*). It is believed that a first chapel was built together with the castle in the 11th century. After the castle and chapel were destroyed in a battle in 1350, the chancel was reconstructed around 1370-80. Notice that the chancel is round, with a low arched opening to the nave. It is rather unusual to still find such an original round shape, as over the centuries most chancels were changed to semicircular with a wide opening to the nave. It is believed that the round footprint was inspired by the shape of the Holy Sepulcher Church in Jerusalem (around the empty tomb of Jesus), which the Counts of Rapperswil (who owned the former castle) must have seen during their crusades to the Holy Land. Additionally, the round shape of the chancel is exactly on the foundations of the former round fortified castle tower.

The round chancel stood alone for more than 100 years. The nave was built in 1476, while the bell tower was attached seven years later (1483). Significant renovations were undertaken in 1891-92 (wooden ceiling, windows renewed).

Eye-catchers are the three wooden winged altars (retables) that are artfully carved, painted, and decorated with gold leaf. These extraordinary winged altars are catholic artefacts (made by Haggenberg) that date from 1490-1520.

The left winged side-altar has a center statue representing St. Anne, though the altar is dedicated to St. Vitus; the backside contains paintings that depict 14 scenes from the life of St. Vitus, which are revealed when the altar wings are closed. Notice the two reliquaries at the foot of this retable.

The retable in the chancel depicts Mary with baby Jesus, flanked by St. John the Baptist and St. John the Evangelist.

The right winged side-altar is dedicated to St. Wolfgang, who is closely connected with the early history of the Abbey of Einsiedeln.

Left of the entrance stands one of the smallest organs along the Swiss Way of St. James.

Enjoy the wide views over Lake Zurich towards the west and north. You can see the towns Lachen, Pfäffikon, and Rapperswil, and the dam (*Seedamm*) across the lake. This was a strategic location for a castle to oversee the surrounding region.

As mentioned above, the chapel was built on the ruins of a former **Castle of old-Rapperswil**. The Counts of Rapperswil had already established this castle in the 11th century (before 1100). This former castle was known under the name old-Rapperswil, to distinguish it from a later castle they built in Rapperswil, which was called new-Rapperswil. The Counts of Rapperswil had their residence at the old-Rapperswil castle, from where they controlled trade and traffic along the route from Zurich to Chur (from where the route continued to Venice and Rome, using Switzerland's eastern mountain passes to the south).

This trade route structurally changed when the north-south passage over the Gotthard Pass was opened around 1220. This passage was enabled when the Schöllenen Gorge was made accessible to horses and carts through the construction of a wooden bridge. From then on major trade and pilgrimage routes passed by Zug/Luzern and further south to the Gotthard Pass, instead of via Altendorf and Chur. This would have been reason enough for the Counts of Rapperswil to relocate their residence. Around 1220 they relocated to the peninsula on the northern side of Lake Zurich and established a new castle and town (called new-Rapperswil).

The castle of old-Rapperswil was destroyed in a battle by troops from the City of Zurich in 1350 and was never rebuilt. The remaining ruins have long since disappeared (only some foundations were excavated underneath the chancel of the chapel in 1972).

The first 5 km from Siebnen were flat, until the foot of the hill. From here the route enters the northern flanks of the pre-Alps and goes up to the Etzel Pass. Over the next 7 km the route ascends 512 altitude meters until the Etzel Pass. The strenuous part of the stage begins. About 300 meters further up the hill you pass by restaurant Johannesburg. Its terrace provides splendid views. The route continues on a tarmac road, with vineyards on the slope of the hill. After 900 meters and some ascending and descending, the trail changes to grassland.

You cross the Altendorf military shooting range through a meadow; in case of shooting exercises, you will have to follow a detour around the shooting range. A little later you cross over the Chessi stream (*Chessibach*) on a metal footbridge and pass through an arched gate made of rose branches. The owners of the nearby house hung many white St. James scallops around the arch. A nice confirmation that you are on the Swiss Way of St. James trail.

The trail changes from grass to road (ascending steeply), which you follow for 500 meters. At a curve in the road the route turns right and follows the edge of a forest. The forest trail ascends steeply: 90 altitude meters over 530 meters. The trail returns to the same road you were on before and follows it, in a more gradual ascent over 600 meters, to restaurant Bilstenhof at 700 meters altitude. You pass by a small roadside chapel, after which the trail turns onto a gravel path and then grassland. You walk underneath and aside several high-voltage power lines. You can hear the crackling of electricity.

Back on the road at the Schwändi settlement you pass by another small roadside chapel, after which you turn left onto a gravel road. The trail goes up steeply and shortly before reaching Oberschwändi across a ridge, you have a wide view looking back to Lake Zurich. The gravel path has an appropriate name: pilgrim path (*Pilgerweg*). At Oberschwändi you are at 768 meters. At a small water fountain, with potable water, and a signpost underneath overhanging branches of a cherry tree, the route makes a sharp left.

The route steeply ascends on a short stretch of tarmac road, along cherry trees and below the power lines. The next 600 meters ascend gradually and are not so steep anymore. The trail goes through grasslands and you have a view of the Etzel mountain in front of you.

The last 100 meters are through a moor, almost flat, after which you reach the point where the route from Siebnen converges with the trail coming from Rapperswil. You are at 822 meters at 11 km from Siebnen, 26 km from Neuhaus.

The location where the Siebnen route converges with the Rapperswil route is in the forest, 1 km before the Etzel Pass level.

### *Hiking the Route from the Converge point below the Etzel Pass to Einsiedeln (km 11-19)*

The 8 km route from the point of convergence below the Etzel Pass to Einsiedeln overlaps with the second half of stage 4 (Rapperswil to Einsiedeln). For the detailed description of the route, churches, chapels, monasteries, and points of interest, please refer to pages 169 to 181 of stage 4.

### *From the Converge point below the Etzel Pass (daytrip from Neuhaus)*

The point of convergence is in the forest, without any nearby transportation connections. As a day-hiker you have two possibilities: ascend the last kilometer to the Etzel Pass or descend towards Pfäffikon.

Taking the reverse route nr. 4 (just follow the green signs) to Pfäffikon is the simplest way. It involves a descent of 412 altitude meters over 4 km, until you reach the Pfäffikon train station. You could also wait for the bus when you get to restaurant Luegeten (halfway the descent); in summer bus nr. 190 from Luegeten to Pfäffikon train station departs from the restaurant at 2 and 37 minutes past the hour in the afternoon (from 15:37 onwards) and takes 11 minutes.

In case you still have energy after 26 km and 1'081 altitude meters, you can continue your hike to the Etzel Pass (1 km distance, 127 meters ascent). At the pass level there is no public transportation either. You are left with two options: continue the hike to Einsiedeln and take the train from there, or hike to the nearest train station. The hike to the Einsiedeln train station is 7 km with 346 altitude meters (mostly descending).

The nearest train station is in Schindellegi (which is the second stop of the train coming from Einsiedeln), taking 6 km and 412 altitude meters (mostly descending). When you follow the yellow hiking signs to Schindellegi you first go up the Etzel mountain to an altitude of 1'015 meters before descending to Schindellegi. The elevated route on the southern side of the Etzel mountain provides panoramic views (to the east and south) of the Alps, Mythen, Sihl Lake, and Einsiedeln. Once you are descending on the western side of the Etzel mountain you have panoramic views (to the west) of Lake Zurich towards Zurich. This makes it a long hiking day, covering 32 km and 1'493 altitude meters, with a worthwhile ending of the alternative day-hike from Neuhaus to the Etzel Pass.

# APPENDICES

# Appendix 1: List of Churches

Appendix 1 lists all churches and chapels along the Way of St. James in North-East Switzerland, with references to the locations, stages, and page numbers.
The descriptions of their history and special features are included in the chapters of the respective hiking stages.

## *Churches from Konstanz to Einsiedeln*

| Nr. | Name | City | Stage | Page |
|---|---|---|---|---|
| DE | Our Lady Basilica | Konstanz | K1 | 91 |
| DE | St. Stephen Church | Konstanz | K1 | 95 |
| K-1 | St. Stephen Church | Kreuzlingen | K1 | 97 |
| K-2 | Holy Cross Chapel | Bernrain | K1 | 98 |
| K-3 | Reformed St. James Church | Märstetten | K1 | 101 |
| K-4 | St. James Chapel | Kaltenbrunnen | K2 | 109 |
| K-5 | St. Anthony Chapel | Affeltrangen | K2 | 110 |
| K-6 | Reformed Church | Affeltrangen | K2 | 111 |
| K-7 | St. John the Baptist Church | Tobel | K2 | 113 |
| K-8 | St. Margaret Chapel | St. Margarethen | K2 | 115 |
| K-9 | St. Anthony Church | Münchwilen | K2 | 117 |
| K-10 | Reformed Church | Münchwilen | K2 | 118 |
| K-11 | St. Remy Church | Sirnach | K2 | 119 |
| K-12 | Reformed Church | Sirnach | K2 | 120 |
| K-13 | St. Martin Chapel | Oberwangen | K2 | 122 |
| K-14 | Mary-Lourdes Church | Dussnang | K2 | 122 |
| K-15 | Reformed Church | Dussnang | K2 | 123 |
| K-16 | Benedictine Monastery Church | Fischingen | K2 | 126 |
| K-17 | St. Idda Chapel | Fischingen | K2 | 127 |
| K-18 | St. Catherine Chapel | Fischingen | K2 | 128 |
| K-19 | St. Anne Church | Au | K3 | 134 |
| K-20 | St. Gall Church | Fischenthal | K3 | 139 |
| K-21 | Reformed Mühlebach Chapel | Fischenthal | K3 | 140 |
| K-22 | Reformed Church | Fischenthal | K3 | 140 |
| K-23 | St. John Church | Rapperswil | K3 | 146 |
| K-24 | Our Lady Chapel | Rapperswil | K3 | 147 |
| K-25 | Capuchin Monastery Church | Rapperswil | K3 | 152 |
| K-26 | St. Anthony Cave | Rapperswil | K3 | 152 |
| 27 | Holy House Chapel | Rapperswil | 4 | 159 |
| 28 | Holy Trinity Chapel | Hurden | 4 | 160 |
| 29 | St. Peter and Paul Church | Ufenau Island | 4 | 162 |
| 30 | St. Martin Chapel | Ufenau Island | 4 | 163 |
| 31 | Castle Chapel | Pfäffikon | 4 | 165 |
| 32 | St. Meinrad Church | Pfäffikon | 4 | 167 |
| 33 | St. Meinrad Chapel | Etzel Pass | 4 | 169 |

| Nr. | Name | City | Stage | Page |
|---|---|---|---|---|
| 34 | Devil Bridge Chapel | Egg | 4 | 170 |
| 35 | Gallows Chapel | Einsiedeln | 4 | 171 |
| 36 | St. Gangulf Chapel | Einsiedeln | 4 | 173 |
| 37 | Youth Church St. Wolfgang | Einsiedeln | 4 | 174 |
| 38 | Benedictine Monastery Church | Einsiedeln | 4 | 177 |
| 39 | Our Lady Chapel | Einsiedeln | 4 | 178 |

## *Churches from Rorschach to Jona and Etzel Pass*

| Nr. | Name | City | Stage | Page |
|---|---|---|---|---|
| R-1 | St. Columbanus Church | Rorschach | R1a | 190 |
| R-2 | Souls Chapel | Rorschach | R1a | 191 |
| R-3 | Reformed Church | Rorschach | R1a | 192 |
| R-4 | Sacred Heart of Jesus Church | Rorschach | R1a | 193 |
| R-5 | Former Benedictine Monastery Chapel | Rorschach | R1a | 195 |
| R-6 | St. Mary Magdalene Church | Untereggen | R1a | 198 |
| R-7 | Ecumenical Church | Halden | R1a | 201 |
| R-8 | Reformed Linsebühl Church | St. Gallen | R1a | 202 |
| R-9 | Reformed St. Lawrence Church | St. Gallen | R1a | 205 |
| R-10 | Reformed St. Mang Church | St. Gallen | R1a | 207 |
| R-11 | Guardian Angel Chapel | St. Gallen | R1a | 211 |
| R-12 | Abbey Cathedral | St. Gallen | R1a | 212 |
| R-13 | Sacred Heart of Jesus Chapel | St. Gallen | R1a | 214 |
| R-14 | Reformed St. Leonard Church | St. Gallen | R1b | 220 |
| R-15 | St. Othmar Church | St. Gallen | R1b | 221 |
| R-16 | Mary of Einsiedeln Chapel | Bruggen | R1b | 223 |
| R-17 | Reformed Church | Bruggen | R1b | 224 |
| R-18 | St. Martin Church | Bruggen | R1b | 225 |
| R-19 | Reformed Church | Herisau | R1b | 228 |
| R-20 | St. Peter and Paul Church | Herisau | R1b | 229 |
| R-21 | Reformed Church | St. Peterzell | R2 | 239 |
| R-22 | St. Peter and Paul Church | St. Peterzell | R2 | 241 |
| R-23 | Falck Grave Chapel | St. Peterzell | R2 | 242 |
| R-24 | St. Felix and Regula Church | Wattwil | R2 | 246 |
| R-25 | Reformed Church | Wattwil | R2 | 247 |
| R-26 | Capuchin Convent Church | Wattwil | R2 | 249 |
| R-27 | Capuchin Convent Sister Chancel | Wattwil | R2 | 250 |
| R-28 | St. Anthony Church | Walde | R3 | 259 |
| R-29 | St. Ursula Chapel | Rüeterswil | R3 | 260 |
| R-30 | St. Lawrence Church | St. Gallenkappel | R3 | 261 |
| R-31 | St. James Chapel | Neuhaus | R3 | 263 |
| R-32 | St. Vincent Church | Eschenbach | R3 | 264 |
| R-33 | Assumption of Mary Church | Jona | R3 | 267 |
| S-1 | St. Judoc Church | Schmerikon | S1 | 276 |
| S-2 | Fourteen Holy Helpers Chapel | Grynau | S1 | 279 |
| S-3 | Holy Trinity Linthbord Chapel | Tuggen | S1 | 281 |
| S-4 | St. Erhard and Victor Church | Tuggen | S1 | 282 |
| S-5 | Loreto Chapel | Kromen | S1 | 283 |
| S-6 | St. Nicholas Chapel | Siebnen | S1 | 285 |
| S-7 | Sacred Heart of Jesus Church | Siebnen | S1 | 286 |
| S-8 | Reformed Church | Siebnen | S1 | 287 |
| S-9 | St. Jost Chapel | Galgenen | S2 | 293 |
| S-10 | St. John Chapel | Altendorf | S2 | 295 |

# Appendix 2: Biography of Saints

Appendix 2 lists, in alphabetical order, all the names of saints represented along the Way of St. James in North-East Switzerland, with references to the church numbers.

A short biography of these saints, in alphabetical order, is provided on the next pages. Their biography should be read in the context of the background of saints and Roman catacomb relics, as described in the chapter Religious Context of the General Introduction to the Swiss Camino in Volume I.

## *Saints from Konstanz and Rorschach to Einsiedeln*

| Name | Church nr. |
|---|---|
| St. Adalrich | 29, 30, 31, 33 |
| St. Andrew | R-25, 32 |
| St. Anne | K-19, S-6, S-9, S-10, 32 |
| St. Anthony of Padua | K-5, K-9, K-26, R-28, R-30, S-3 |
| St. Borromeo | R-5 |
| Brother Klaus | *See St. Nicholas of Flüe* |
| St. Catherine | K-18, K-23 |
| St. Celestine | R-30 |
| St. Christopher | 29 |
| St. Clement | 31 |
| St. Columbanus | R-1, S-4 |
| St. Constance | R-1 |
| St. Erhard | S-4 |
| St. Eustace | 31 |
| St. Felix and Regula | R-24, R-25 |
| St. Fidelis | R-18 |
| Four Evangelists | R-15 |
| Fourteen Holy Helpers | K-8, S-2 |
| St. Francis of Assisi | K-19 |
| St. Gall | K-20, K-22, R-2, R-12, R-18, R-30, S-4 |
| St. Gangulf | 36 |
| Holy Family | R-15, R-29, S-5 |
| St. Idda | K-8, K-17, K-19 |
| St. Innocence | K-7 |
| St. James the Greater | K-3, K-4, R-29, R-31, S-6 |
| St. Joachim | K-19 |
| St. John the Baptist | K-4, K-7, K-16, K-23, S-3, S-10 |
| St. John the Evangelist | S-10 |
| St. Joseph | R-32 |
| St. Jost | S-9 |
| St. Judoc | S-1 |

| Name | Church nr. |
|---|---|
| St. Lawrence | K-23, R-9, R-19, R-30 |
| St. Leander | R-26 |
| St. Leonard | R-14, R-18 |
| (Mary-) Lourdes | K-14, R-29 |
| St. Mang | R-10, R-12 |
| St. Margaret | K-8 |
| St. Margaret Alacoque | S-7 |
| St. Martin | K-13, R-18, 30 |
| St. Mary | K-19, K-24, R-15, R-16, R-26, R-28, R-32, R-33, S-2, S-10, 27, 38, 39 |
| St. Mary Magdalene | K-24, R-6, 38 |
| St. Meinrad | 29, 32, 33, 38 |
| St. Michael | R-2, R-32 |
| St. Nepomuk | R-5, 34 |
| St. Nicholas of Flüe | K-20, S-9 |
| St. Nicholas (of Myra) | S-6 |
| St. Othmar | R-12, R-15, R-18, S-4 |
| Our Lady | *See St. Mary* |
| St. Paul | R-20, R-22, 29 |
| St. Peter | R-20, R-22, 29 |
| St. Remy | K-11 |
| Sorrowful Mother of God | R-18 |
| St. Stephen | K-1 |
| Twelve Apostles | R-4 |
| St. Urban | S-1 |
| St. Ursula | R-29 |
| St. Victor | S-4 |
| St. Vincent | R-32 |
| St. Vitus | S-10 |
| St. Wiborada | R-10, R-12 |
| St. Wolfgang | S-10, 37 |

## *Biography of Saints*

### St. Adalrich

St. Adalrich of Einsiedeln (or of Swabia) was a Benedictine monk from the Einsiedeln Abbey who lived as a hermit on the island Ufenau in Lake Zurich (near Rapperswil). When his mother Regelinda fell ill with leprosy she retreated to the island, where she died in 958. They both lived in a house on the island, where Adalrich took care of his ill mother. Adalrich died on the island in 973 and was buried there in the church. He was canonized in 1141.

### St. Andrew

St. Andrew was one of the Twelve Apostles and the brother of St. Peter. As his brother, St. Andrew was a fisherman before becoming a follower of Jesus. According to legend he traveled to eastern European countries such as Turkey, Ukraine, and Russia to preach and convert pagans to Christianity. He was said to have established the Bishopric of Byzantium (Constantinople or Istanbul) and to have been martyred in Greece. From the middle ages he was said to have been crucified (tied with ropes) to an X-shaped cross, now known as the St. Andrew's Cross. St. Andrew became the patron Saint of many countries and cities, of which several have the X-shaped cross in their flag (e.g. Scotland).

**St. Anne**
St. Anne was married to St. Joachim and was the mother of Mary and the grandmother of Jesus. She died in 12 AD. She became the patroness Saint of grandmothers and miners. Her womb was considered the source from which silver (representing Mary) was mined, while gold (representing Jesus) was mined from Mary's womb.

**St. Anthony of Padua**
St. Anthony of Padua was a Portuguese friar (from Lisbon) in the Franciscan Order, well known for his teaching and preaching. He died from an illness in Padua, Italy in 1231. He became the patron Saint of lost souls, lost people, and lost things. A novice stole his psalm book, which was returned to him after he prayed for it to be found.

**St. Borromeo**
St. Charles Borromeo came from a noble Italian family north of Milan (his uncle was Pope Pius IV) and was Bishop of Milan in 1564-84. He was one of the leaders of the Roman-Catholic resistance against the Reformation and initiated significant reforms in the Catholic Church. He was known for the 19th Ecumenical Council of Trent (in northern Italy) in 1562-63, which resulted in important Counter-Reformation activities and reforms of Catholic doctrines. The Pope appointed him apostle to Switzerland, for which he made several trips to the Catholic Cantons (Unterwalden, Schwyz, Luzern) to help them strengthen their Counter-Reformation activities and implement the required reforms. During famine and the plague in Milan he organized care and support for the local population and tried to feed more than 50'000 people, after the Authorities had fled the city in 1576. He became the patron Saint against illnesses and the plague. He died in 1584 and was canonized in 1610.

**Brother Klaus**
See St. Nicholas of Flüe.

**St. Catherine**
St. Catherine (of Alexandria, Egypt) was imprisoned and tortured, but refused to give up her belief, for which she was beheaded in 305. She became the patroness Saint of the condemned. St. Catherine was one for the Fourteen Holy Helpers and also the patroness Saint of students and educators (she devoted herself to study and was a strong debater).

**St. Celestine**
St. Celestine I was a Roman Pope in the years 422 to 432. Not much is known of his person, other than that he spent his 10-year papacy fighting ideologies that were not reconcilable with the Church. He sent missionaries to England, Scotland, Ireland, and Gaul (France) to convert pagans and strengthen Christianity in these regions.

**St. Christopher**
St. Christopher probably lived in the 3rd century. Nothing is known of his life or death, and some historians doubt he really existed. His broad popularity as a Saint originated from legends created in the 6th century. By the 9th century his legends spread through

Europe and he became a popular Saint of travelers and children. This despite the fact that he was never recognized by the Church, nor canonized as a Saint. He was one of the Fourteen Holy Helpers. The name Christopher was derived from 'Christ-bearer', linked to the following legend.

Christopher was a tall and strong man, born in Arabia. He wanted to serve the most fearless King. After he saw that the King was afraid of the devil, he went to search for the devil. He met the head of a bandit gang, who called himself the devil. He started serving him, but soon found out that this bandit was afraid of Christ. Christopher continued to look for Christ, who supposedly was the most fearless person. A hermit advised him to serve Christ by carrying people across a dangerous river, where many had died in the currents. After doing so for a while, a young boy asked him to be carried across. While Christopher was crossing the river, the water level rose and the boy's weight increased to become almost impossible to carry. He asked the boy why he was so heavy. The child responded that he was Christ and carried the weight of the world. Christopher converted to Catholicism and subsequently converted many pagans. He was beheaded upon his refusal to make offerings to pagan Gods.

**St. Clement**
St. Clement I (or Clemens) was the fourth Pope of Rome at the end of the 1st century. Little is known of his person. According to legend he was exiled to the Crimea and put to work in a stone quarry at the end of his papacy. Allegedly he was martyred by being tied to an anchor and thrown in the Black Sea. He became the patron Saint of masons and mariners.

**St. Columbanus**
St. Columbanus was an Irish missionary who established several monasteries in France and Italy in 590-615. During his travels through Europe he also stayed in Tuggen (Switzerland) and Bregenz (Austria). He had several followers, one of them the Irish missionary St. Gall, with whom he preached in Bregenz. St. Columbanus died in Italy in 615.

**St. Constance**
St. Constance (or Constantius) may refer to several saints. It is not known to which saint the relics at the St. Columbanus church in Rorschach relate. A likely candidate is St. Constance of Perugia. He was considered the first Bishop of Perugia, Italy. He died for his Christian faith after torture and decapitation by the Romans around the year 170.

Lake Constance and the German city Konstanz were not named after this Saint. They most likely derived their name from the Roman Emperor Constantius II (317-361). Konstanz was a military base for Roman battles against the Alemanni and Emperor Constantius' stay in Konstanz may have given the town its name.

**St. Erhard**
St. Erhard (of Regensburg, Germany) lived in the 7th century. Little is known of his person. He probably was an Irish missionary who became Bishop of Regensburg and died around 686. He became the patron Saint of farm animals and was invoked against cattle diseases.

**St. Eustace**

St. Eustace was a Roman general who upheld his catholic faith, even when it was severely tested. According to legend, when he refused to make offerings to pagan gods he and his family were roasted to death inside a bronze statue of an ox in 118. This made him the patron Saint of firefighters. However, his existence and torture were believed to be fictional; his feast day was removed from the Roman calendar in 1969.

**St. Felix and Regula**

St. Felix and Regula were Roman soldiers in the Theban Legion of St. Maurice. They were siblings and both escaped the executions of the members of the Theban Legion in St. Maurice, Canton Valais. They fled to Zurich, where they were captured and executed in 286. According to legend, after their decapitation they picked up their head, walked 40 paces, and prayed before dropping down. The Cathedral of Zurich was built on the location where they prayed and lay down.

**St. Fidelis**

St. Fidelis (of Sigmaringen) was a German Capuchin friar who strongly supported the Counter-Reformation in Switzerland and Austria. He was killed by protestant soldiers in eastern Switzerland in 1622, after he refused to denounce Catholicism. He was canonized in 1746.

**Four Evangelists**

The Four Evangelists were Matthew, Mark, Luke and John, accredited with writing the four Gospel accounts of the New Testament. Matthew (a former tax collector) and John (a former fisherman) were two of the Twelve Apostles, whereas Mark was a travel companion and interpreter of St. Peter, and Luke was a former physician. Matthew was often symbolized as a winged man, Mark as a winged lion, Luke as a winged ox, and John as an eagle. The four Gospels, probably written in 66-110, gave an account of the life of Jesus.

**Fourteen Holy Helpers**

The Fourteen Holy Helpers were a group of Saints who were believed to have helped overcome diseases, particularly the Black Plague. This group was formed in the 14th century (around 1347, at the time the plague spread through Europe, after it had arrived in Italy on a merchant ship from Asia). The fourteen Saints were: Agatha, Barbara, Blaise, Catherine of Alexandria, Christopher, Denis, Erasmus, Eustace, George, Giles, Margaret of Antioch, Pantaleon, Syriac, and Vitus.

Each of these Saints was invoked against specific physical diseases and their symptoms. Collectively they were assigned the holy power to overcome even the worst of medieval diseases, the Bubonic Plague. The Plague, transmitted by rats because of the poor hygienic circumstances in which most of the medieval population lived, killed between 40 to 60 percent of the European population in the 14th century, and reoccurred regularly in later centuries.

**St. Francis of Assisi**

St. Francis of Assisi was an Italian friar, who lived in 1182-1226. He became one of the most well-known religious figures and was canonized in 1228. He became the patron Saint of animals; he prayed to birds and persuaded a wolf not to attack a village.

He was the first one to arrange a live nativity (birth) scene (nowadays known as the Christmas manger) in 1223. St. Francis established the Franciscan Order in 1209.

**St. Gall**

St. Gall (or Gallus) was an Irish missionary who followed St. Columbanus to northern Switzerland around the year 610. St. Columbanus continued his travels to Italy, whereas St. Gall remained in Switzerland. Together with several other monks he lived in the isolated forests south of Lake Constance, where they built a small chapel near a waterfall around 612. St. Gall died in Arbon around 645, after which his remains were brought to his former cell in the forest. The City of St. Gallen was named after him and the St. Gallen Abbey Cathedral was built on the site of his cell. The sarcophagus in the cathedral still contains parts of the skull of the Saint. He became the patron Saint of birds. He spoke with animals who helped him survive as a hermit. St. Gall was often depicted with a small bear. According to legend, St. Gall talked a bear into bringing him firewood and accompanying him during his years of hermitage in the dense forests. St. Gall became one of the patron Saints of Switzerland.

**St. Gangulf**

St. Gangulf was a dedicated Christian and nobleman from Burgundy (France), who renounced his wealth to become a hermit. He died of wounds caused by a spear, when a priest, who had committed adultery with Gangulf's wife, tried to kill him in 760. He was invoked against marital problems and adultery.

**Holy Family**

The Holy Family consisted of Joseph, Mary, and Jesus.

**St. Idda**

Saint Idda (also named Ida of Toggenburg) lived in a cell on the site of the present church in Au, before becoming a nun at the Abbey of Fischingen. She became the patroness Saint of pregnancy and was invoked against bodily pains and lost cattle. She died around 1200 and was canonized in 1724.

According to legend, a raven stole her wedding ring. A young man found the ring in the nest and put it on his finger. Under suspicion of adultery her husband (Lord of Toggenburg) cast her out, after which she lived as a hermit in a cave at the foot of the Hörnli mountain (Hörnli translates as horn) close to the Abbey of Fischingen. A deer with 12 lights in its antlers showed her the way through the dark forest when she was going to morning prayers every day. St. Idda was always depicted with a deer or with antlers.

**St. Innocence**

St. Innocence was one of the martyrs of the Theban Legion of the Roman Empire in the 3$^{rd}$ century. He was a soldier who served with St. Maurice, and was executed when refusing to slay Swiss Christians.

**St. James the Greater**

St. James (the Greater or the Elder) was one of the Twelve Apostles. He was called the Greater (or Elder) to distinguish from James the Lesser, who was also one of the Twelve Apostles and the first Bishop of Jerusalem. St. James the Greater was either taller or older than the other James. King Herod had James (the Greater) beheaded by the sword in Jerusalem in the year 44; he was considered the first apostle who died for his faith in Christ. He became the patron Saint of Spain and pilgrims.

The legend that the remains of St. James were kept in Spain (Santiago de Compostela) arose around 900. According to this legend, St. James was a missionary in Iberia and after his execution in Jerusalem, his remains were miraculously shipped from Jerusalem to Santiago de Compostela. His remains were allegedly discovered in Spain in the 9th century (although he had died in the 1st century). In the 9th century the Spanish hermit Pelagius was said to have had a revelation of the location of the tomb of St. James. The then bishop of the region identified the tomb, the Spanish King Alfonso II had a church built for the relics in Santiago de Compostela, and Pope Leo XIII officially recognized this legend in 1884. Several versions of the legend were told: some said that St. James was an apostle in Spain before going back to Jerusalem (this version surfaced in the 9th century); others said he was never in Spain. It is, however, likely that his remains were spread over several locations in Europe, amongst others Santiago de Compostela.

**St. Joachim**
St. Joachim was the husband of St. Anne and father of Mary. He came from Nazareth and married St. Anne from Bethlehem. He was usually depicted as a wealthy man. According to legend, he and Anne had difficulties conceiving a child. As penance he spent 40 days fasting in the desert, where angels appeared to promise a child. Mary was born around the year 18 BC. St. Joachim died in the year 15 AD in Jerusalem.

**St. John the Baptist**
St. John the Baptist was considered a prophet, as he announced the coming of Jesus. He was born around the same time as Jesus: a pregnant Mary visited his pregnant mother Elisabeth, known from the scene of the Mary Visitation. St. John baptized Jesus when He was around 30 years of age. King Herod had St. John beheaded around 28-36, after St. John had criticized the King for divorcing his wife and taking the wife of his brother.

**St. John the Evangelist**
St. John the Evangelist was one of the Twelve Apostles, also called John the Apostle. He was the younger brother of St. James the Greater. He died of old age around the year 100 and was the only Apostle who was not martyred.

**St. Joseph**
St. Joseph was married to Mary and was Jesus' foster father. He became the patron Saint of fathers and carpenters (he raised Jesus and was a carpenter).

**St. Jost**
See St. Judoc

**St. Judoc**
St. Judoc (also called Jost or Joyce) was born in a noble family in Breton (France) in the 7th century. Around 636 he renounced the family fortune and went on a pilgrimage to Rome, became a priest, established a monastery, and lived as a hermit in northern

France until he died in 668. Though he was never canonized, he was considered a Saint. In the middle ages he was an important Saint for pilgrims, together with St. James.

**St. Lawrence**

St. Lawrence was born in Spain, but moved to Italy where he became a deacon (a member of clergy responsible for charity) for the Pope in Rome. In 258 Emperor Valerian ordered all Christian Church officials in Rome to be executed, after which Lawrence was imprisoned. As a deacon Lawrence had been responsible for safekeeping the treasures of the church and giving to the poor. Thus, the Roman Authorities asked him to hand over the treasures. According to legend, instead of presenting the treasures, he presented the poor and ill people as the real treasures of the Church. He was executed by being roasted on a metal grating above hot coal. He became the patron Saint of cooks and firefighters.

**St. Leander**

St. Leander (of Seville) was a Bishop of Seville (Spain). He came from a wealthy family, was a Benedictine monk, and became Bishop in 579. The local King exiled him after he converted the King's son to Christianity in 579. He spent several years in exile in Byzantium (Constantinople or Istanbul), but returned after the King died and continued to convert pagans in Spain. He died around 600.

**St. Leonard**

St. Leonard (of Noblac) was a French nobleman who was converted to Christianity by St. Remy, Bishop of Reims, together with King Clovis I. Leonard asked the King the right to free prisoners. He became a hermit and founded the Abbey of Noblac, where he died in 559. He became the patron Saint of prisoners. He enabled the release of prisoners and prisoners who prayed to him had their chains miraculously broken.

**(Mary-) Lourdes**

Mary-Lourdes, or Our Lady of Lourdes, is a title of the Virgin Mary at the location of Lourdes. Lourdes (France) is the site where the Virgin Mary was reported to have appeared 18 times in 1858. The Virgin Mary appeared to a local 14-year-old girl called Bernadette Soubirous, who was canonized in 1933 (Saint Bernadette of Lourdes). The spring water of the Lourdes cave is said to have healing powers and the Catholic Church has officially recognized several dozens of miraculous healings. Every year millions of pilgrims visit the Lourdes cave and drink the spring water.

**St. Mang**

St. Mang (of Füssen), also called Magnus, was a missionary to Allgäu, southern Germany. He became a monk at the Abbey of St. Gallen, after which the first abbot of St. Gallen, Othmar, sent him to Allgäu to establish a subsidiary abbey in Füssen and become a missionary to convert local pagans to Christianity. He died around 750 and became the patron Saint of cattle.

**St. Margaret**

St. Margaret (also known as Margaret of Antioch or Margaret the Virgin) was one of the Fourteen Holy Helpers. In 304 she was tortured to death at a young age, after she refused to give up her virginity and Christianity to marry a Roman Governor of Antioch, Turkey. She became the patroness Saint of pregnant women and child birth.

**St. Margaret Alacoque**

St. Margaret Alacoque (1647-90) was a French nun in the Convent of the Visitation Sisters. She had visions of Jesus, relating to the adoration of his Sacred Heart and started this devotion, which was officially recognized by the Pope in 1765. Margaret was canonized in 1920. The 'Sacred Heart of Jesus' devotion symbolizes Christ's love and compassion for countering the suffering of humanity.

**St. Martin**

St. Martin (of Tours) was a cavalry soldier in the Roman army, for which he traveled through France and Germany. According to legend, during his army presence in France he cut his army cape in two and gave one half to a barely dressed beggar outside the gates of Amiens (150 km north of Paris) on a cold winter day. Subsequently he dreamt that Jesus wore the half-cape he had given to the beggar. This vision made him convert to Christianity, renounce the fighting, and leave the army. After becoming a monk, traveling, and living as a hermit for a while, he had to be persuaded to become the Bishop of Tours (275 km southwest of Paris) in 371. He established a monastery in Tours (372), but kept traveling through France, converting pagans and freeing prisoners. He died in Tours in 397.

The Abbey of Marmoutier became an important pilgrimage destination during the early middle ages, because of the shrine of St. Martin. According to legend, the half-cape he had kept was a precious relic of this abbey. The location in the abbey where this half-cape was kept was called the Chapelle, or sanctuary for the little cape. The word chapel was derived from the medieval Latin word for little cape, Capella, translated into medieval French as Chapelle. This became Chapel in English and Kapelle in German.

**St. Mary**

St. Mary was the mother of Jesus and known under many different names, such as Virgin Mary, Our Lady, Mother of God, Madonna, and Queen of Heaven. She was the daughter of St. Joachim and St. Anne, and was born in Nazareth around 18 BC. According to tradition, Jesus was conceived through the Holy Spirit, while she remained a virgin. She was married to Joseph. Besides the adoration of Jesus, the adoration of Mary became the most widespread in Christianity.

**St. Mary Magdalene**

St. Mary Magdalene was one of the main and closest followers of Jesus in the 1st century. She came from a wealthy family and helped finance the travels of Jesus, while she traveled with him across Galilea. Jesus cured her of a physical disorder (called the cleansing of 'seven demons'). She was present at Jesus' crucifixion and burial, and was the first person who saw Jesus after his resurrection. She was one of the main, and first female, apostles after Jesus' death. She became the patroness Saint of converts and women. There is no reliable history of when, how, and where she died.

The important role attributed to her in the 1st century was quite special, given the male-dominated patriarchal society of that time. However, her image was changed during the middle ages (particularly around the Reformation), when she was (untruly) branded to have been a repentant sinner as a prostitute. This image change was created by the male-dominated celibate monks, who considered women to be sinners for tempting men. She became the patroness Saint of prostitutes.

**St. Meinrad**

St. Meinrad came from Swabia (southern Germany) and was educated as a monk at the Benedictine Monastery of Reichenau, situated on an island in Lake Constance. He spent some time in a subsidiary abbey east of the Obersee (Benken), before he retreated as a hermit at the Etzel Pass around 828. He brought a statue of the Virgin Mary from Benken to his cell at the pass. Because of the many pilgrims who visited him for advice, he moved his retreat to the remote forests seven kilometers to the south (present location of the Abbey of Einsiedeln) in 835. Although the location was isolated and difficult to reach, he was still frequently visited by pilgrims looking for his advice. There he spent 26 years as a hermit leading an ascetic life, until he was killed by two robbers in the year 861. According to legend, Meinrad had two black ravens who followed his two killers all the way to Zurich. In Zurich the ravens pointed to the location were the killers were hiding, which led to their capture and punishment. To this day two ravens are in the coat-of-arms of the City of Einsiedeln. The Abbey of Einsiedeln was built on the site of his cell. He became the patron Saint of hospitality, based on his hospitality to strangers in the remoteness of the dark forest.

**St. Michael**

St. Michael was not a saint, though he was called that; he was never canonized. It is unlikely that he existed as a living person. St. Michael was one of the three archangels (together with Gabriel and Raphael); an archangel was the highest-ranking angel, always depicted with wings. He became the patron Saint of soldiers: in The Bible he was the leader of God's army that protected the Church and defeated Satan (often depicted as a dragon or serpent). For this reason, he was often chosen as the patron Saint of castle churches and chapels.

According to Roman-Catholic scriptures, St. Michael is the angel who is present at the hour of death and accompanies the soul to heaven where he weighs the good vs. bad deeds of the soul in their last judgement (deciding whether the soul goes to heaven or hell). For this reason, he was often chosen as the patron Saint of funeral and cemetery chapels.

**St. Nepomuk**

St. John of Nepomuk was a priest in 14th century Bohemia (nowadays Czech Republic) and confessional of the Queen of Bohemia. In 1393 he was drowned in the Vltava River by the King of Bohemia, when Nepomuk refused to disclose the confessions of the Queen. He became the first martyr of the Confessional Seal and the patron Saint of defamation and bridges, and was invoked against flooding and drowning. He was canonized in 1729.

**St. Nicholas of Flüe**

St. Nicholas of Flüe (also called Brother Klaus, *Bruder Klaus*, or *Niklaus von Flüe*) was born in 1417 and served in the Swiss Confederate Army of Unterwalden until the age of 37. He subsequently served as a judge and counselor for the Canton. After a vision he retreated from his wife Dorothee and 10 children, and became a hermit in a gorge close to their house. He lived an ascetic life, allegedly living of Eucharist for 20 years. He was sought after for his wisdom and counsel, by pilgrims and Authorities. Many pilgrims visited him in his cell to ask for advice. In 1481 he had a decisive consulting role that prevented a civil war, which would likely have caused a split of the Swiss

Confederation. He died in 1487 and was canonized in 1947. He became the patron Saint of Switzerland and the Swiss Guard at the Vatican. He is Switzerland's most well-known medieval hermit, mystic, and counselor.

**St. Nicholas (of Myra)**

St. Nicholas (of Myra) was a Bishop of Myra (Turkey) in the Roman Empire. He died in 342. Though not much is known of his historical person, there are many legends about him. The most famous legends are: secret gift-giving, such as giving three purses of money as dowry for three neighboring virgin girls (so that they could get married), or secretly leaving coins in shoes; staving off a storm and waves that threatened to sink the ship he was on; and reviving three children that had been killed by a butcher, their flesh intended to be sold as ham during a time of famine. These legends made him the medieval patron Saint of children, sailors, and fishermen.

The legend of the secret gift-giving has survived nearly 1'700 years, though nowadays it is called Santa Claus (a popularization of the name Saint Nicholas). Santa Claus has its origins in Dutch traditions, where on 5th/6th December, the commemorative day of St. Nicholas' death, Sinterklaas (or Sint Nikolaas; Dutch derived from Saint Nicholas) would leave small presents in the shoes of children. When the Dutch established New Amsterdam (nowadays named New York) in 1625, they continued this tradition. Under the American commercialization of Sint Nikolaas in the 19th century, he was renamed Santa Claus and the timing of the gift-giving shifted to 24th/25th of December.

**St. Othmar**

St. Othmar was the first abbot of the Abbey of St. Gallen, where he introduced the Rule of St. Benedict in 747. He built the abbey's church at the location of the hermit cell of St. Gall. He died around 759 and was canonized in 864.

**Our Lady**

Our Lady, see St. Mary. In German *Unser Liebe Frau*, in French *Notre Dame.*

**St. Paul**

St. Paul was also known as St. Paul the Apostle, though he was not one of the Twelve Apostles. He lived in the first century (5-65). According to legend, he was persecuting followers of Jesus, but was converted to Christianity when a resurrected Jesus appeared to him while he was on the road to Damascus. He started preaching the word of God and traveled extensively through the Roman Empire, where he established churches. According to legend he was decapitated in Rome by order of Emperor Nero. He became the patron Saint of missionaries and authors.

**St. Peter**

St. Peter (originally named Simon) was one of the Twelve Apostles and the brother of St. Andrew. He was a fisherman before becoming a follower of Jesus. He was the first Pope of Rome and was crucified by Emperor Nero around the year 66. He became the patron Saint of fishermen and clergy. The St. Peter's Basilica in the Vatican was built on the site of the grave of St. Peter. This basilica became one of the most well-known churches of Christianity, after which many other churches chose St. Peter as their patron Saint.

**St. Remy**

St. Remy (also called Remigius) was a Bishop of Reims (France) and baptized King Clovis I, resulting in the conversion to Christianity of the entire Frankish population of the 6th century. St. Remy died in 533 and became the patron Saint of meditation, providing the worshipper with a clear mind and openness of their thoughts toward God.

**Sorrowful Mother of God**

The Sorrowful Mother of God – also Our Lady of Sorrows, the Suffering Mother of God, Our Lady of the Seven Sorrows – refers to the Virgin Mary and her suffering during her life. Seven events relating to Jesus caused intense suffering to Mary:

(1) when Jesus was presented as a baby to a temple in Jerusalem, Simeon prophesied that Mary would suffer, as her son's life would be one of suffering;
(2) when King Herod ordered all boys below two years killed, she, Joseph, and baby Jesus had to flee and undertake a long journey to Egypt;
(3) when Jesus was 12 years old He went missing for three days, but they found him in a temple in Jerusalem debating with Jewish teachers;
(4) when witnessing Jesus carrying his Cross on his way to Calvary (Golgotha);
(5) when seeing Jesus' Crucifixion;
(6) when Jesus' lifeless body was taken from the Cross and laid in her lap (this is what a Pietà depicts); and
(7) when Jesus' lifeless body was laid in the tomb.

These Seven Sorrows were often depicted as seven swords piercing the heart of Mary.

**St. Stephen**

St. Stephen was a deacon (a member of clergy responsible for charity) in the early Church in Jerusalem. He was considered the first martyr of Christianity. In the year 34 he was stoned to death after he denounced the Jewish Authorities, who accused him of blasphemy. He became the patron Saint of masons.

**Twelve Apostles**

The Twelve Apostles were 12 men chosen by Jesus to be sent out on apostolic missions. Initially they were sent out in pairs. These 12 men were: St. Peter (Simon) and his brother St. Andrew, St. James the Greater and his brother St. John the Evangelist, St. Bartholomew, St. James the Lesser, St. Judas, St. Matthew, St. Philip, St. Simon the Zealot, St. Thaddaeus, and St. Thomas.

**St. Urban**

There are several Saints with the name Urban; one of the better known is 3rd century Pope St. Urban. Not much is known of this Pope, other than he was a Pope in Rome in 222-230.

**St. Ursula**

St. Ursula most likely lived in the 4th century. Not much is certain of her story. According to legend, she was a Christian of British nobility who went on a European pilgrimage before (or to avoid) marrying a pagan Lord. She was accompanied by a few maids. In Cologne (Germany) besieging Huns killed them in 383.

In the 9th/10th century a fabulous legend around St. Ursula was created, which told that she had been accompanied by 11'000 virgin maids who had been killed together with her in Cologne. Because of the unreliability of this story, her feast day was removed from the Roman Calendar in 1969. St. Ursula became the patroness Saint of female students upon the foundation of the Order of Ursulines (1535), which was dedicated to the education of girls.

**St. Victor**

St. Victor was a soldier in the Theban Legion of St. Maurice, but escaped the executions at Saint-Maurice and fled to Solothurn (about 40 km north of Bern). St. Victor could not escape the martyr's fate of the Theban Legion: he was tortured and beheaded by Roman executioners in Solothurn in 303.

**St. Vincent**

St. Vincent (of Saragossa) was a spokesman of the Bishop of Saragossa, Spain (who was speech impaired) and a deacon of the church. When the Romans started persecuting Christians in Spain, he and the Bishop were imprisoned. St. Vincent died, after severe torture, from the shards of broken pottery on the floor of his prison cell (around 303). His body was thrown in the sea, but was later recovered by sailors. He became the patron Saint of masons and sailors.

**St. Vitus**

St. Vitus was born in Sicily around 290. He died during Christian persecutions in 303, when he was only 12 years old. According to legend, his feast day was celebrated in Germany by dancing in front of his statue. He subsequently became the patron Saint of dancers and entertainers. He became one of the Fourteen Holy Helpers invoked against neurological disorders, such as epilepsy, based on the legends of the dancing.

**St. Wiborada**

St. Wiborada (of Klingen) was a female hermit, who had herself locked up in a bricked-up cell attached to the St. Mang church in St. Gallen in the year 916. She had one window to the outside through which pilgrims asked for her advice, and one window on the inside to receive food and water. In 925 she had a vision of invading Hungarian troops looting the St. Gallen monastery and she foresaw her own death. Hungarian troops indeed besieged the city in 926. She was killed after she refused to flee from the approaching troops. Her bones were displayed as relics in the St. Mang church from around 950. She was canonized as the first Swiss female Saint in 1047, based on numerous accounts of miraculous healings.

**St. Wolfgang**

St. Wolfgang (of Regensburg, Bavaria, Germany) was educated as a monk in the Benedictine Abbey of Reichenau (around 100 years after St. Meinrad trained there). He joined the Abbey of Einsiedeln in 964 (around 100 years after St. Meinrad had died there) in the early stages of the monastery. From 972 until his death in 994 he was the Bishop of Regensburg. Towards the end of his life he became a hermit living in the forests of upper Austria. In order to choose where to build his cell, he threw an axe and asked God to decide the spot. He became the patron Saint of carpenters. He was canonized in 1052.

# Appendix 3: History of Monastic Orders

Appendix 3 lists all monasteries and convents along the Way of St. James in North-East Switzerland, with references to the locations, stages, and page numbers.
The descriptions of their history and special features are included in the chapters of the respective hiking stages.

A short history of these monastic Orders, in alphabetical order, is provided on the next pages. Their history should be read in the context of the medieval monastic world, as described in the chapter Religious Context of the General Introduction to the Swiss Camino in Volume I.

## *Monasteries from Konstanz to Einsiedeln*

| Nr. | Name | Location | Stage | Page |
|---|---|---|---|---|
| K-1 | Former Commandry of the Knights of St. John | Tobel | K2 | 112 |
| K-2 | Benedictine Monastery | Fischingen | K2 | 125 |
| K-3 | Capuchin Monastery | Rapperswil | K3 | 151 |
| 4 | Benedictine Monastery | Einsiedeln | 4 | 175 |

## *Monasteries from Rorschach to Jona and Etzel Pass*

| Nr. | Name | Location | Stage | Page |
|---|---|---|---|---|
| R-1 | Former Benedictine Monastery Mariaberg | Rorschach | R1a | 194 |
| R-2 | Former Dominican Convent St. Catherine | St. Gallen | R1a | 206 |
| R-3 | Former Benedictine Abbey-Kingdom | St. Gallen | R1a | 209 |
| R-4 | Former Benedictine Monastery | St. Peterzell | R2 | 240 |
| R-5 | Former Capuchin Convent St. Mary the Angel | Wattwil | R2 | 248 |

## *History of Monastic Orders*

**Benedictine Order**

The Benedictine Order, also called the Order of Saint Benedict, was founded by Benedict of Nursia in Italy in 529. The Order revolved around prayer and physical labor ('Ora et Labora') under the Rule of St. Benedict. Each Benedictine abbey was independent and governed by their own abbot. A supervising abbot was often appointed by local noblemen, with the assignment to control and protect a monastery's assets. The monasteries were autonomous; there was no mother house that set a policy or appointed the abbots. Monks had to vow to stay within the same community and be obedient to the abbot and the Rule of St. Benedict. This gave the abbot full control over the monks: he set the rules for silence, reading, prayer, meals, sleep, and work. They would spend most of their time in prayer (eight times a day), several hours reading, and working the fields (to be self-sufficient). Application of these foundational rules resulted in tight communities of monks, who stayed in one location their whole (monastic) life. This resulted in stability and productivity; they amassed significant wealth in assets (donations of lands and income by noblemen) and knowledge (from studying and copying handwritten books). Monks were often the few people (apart from noblemen) who could read and write. This enabled them to collect and contain knowledge, often resulting in extensive libraries (for example the libraries of the Abbeys of St. Gallen and Einsiedeln). These monasteries created the first universities that collected and transferred knowledge (though within their Order, not to the public in general).

The Benedictine monasteries flourished and dominated the western monastic landscape until the 12th century. They are considered the foundation of western monastic life. They became wealthy through extensive ownership of lands, towns, and income. The medieval Christian doctrine focused on heaven and hell, in which the monasteries and their churches played a central role. Donations were considered a good way to attain salvation for a person's soul. It was the monastery as a community or institution that received the donations, not the individual monks. So long as the community continued to exist through succession of abbots, the monastery would keep accumulating wealth. After several centuries, these Benedictine monasteries had amassed so much wealth (lands, rights, and knowledge) that they often became the center of power of large territories. Their increasing wealth, knowledge, and land ownership resulted in increasing resistance from monarchs, noblemen, and state governors who saw their own territories and rule undermined.

During the 11th and 12th centuries society was changing and the population increasingly concentrated in towns. This set in the decline of the Benedictine monasteries. The application of the Rule of St. Benedict (already 600 years old) often resulted in inflexibility and isolation from the developing society and cities around them. They became complacent as a result of the wealth they had accumulated over the many centuries, and focused more on earthly than spiritual matters. Other Orders arose, such as the Franciscans and Augustinians, which were better adapted to the changing society, the development of cities, and were based on a vow of poverty (instead of amassing wealth) and care for the ill and poor (instead of staying within their own monastery). The Benedictines stayed in their monasteries, which became isolated from society and cities that developed in new areas and territories, while the new Orders participated in supporting the needy. As you can still see today, the Fischingen and Einsiedeln abbeys are located in an isolated forested dead-end highland valley at the northern foothills of a mountain, away from the larger cities that developed in other regions.

Nowadays the Order maintains eight monasteries and 12 convents in Switzerland (of which two and one respectively along the Swiss Way of St. James).

**Capuchin Order**

The Order of Friars Minor Capuchin is a branch of the Franciscan Order. The Capuchin Order was established by Matteo de Bascio, who sought a stricter reinterpretation of the Rule of St. Francis of Assisi, in Italy in 1525. This entailed a simpler life of austerity and poverty, and preaching to and caring for the poor. The Capuchin Order was a mendicant Order, established during the Counter-Reformation. Since they were a beggar-order, they had to be close to the population. Pastoral care and caring for the elderly, ill, and poor required them to be in the towns. The male members of the Order were called friars instead of monks. They dressed in a brown long pointy hooded habit that was tied around the waste with a white cord with three knots, and wore sandals on their feet. Customarily they had a long untrimmed beard. Their name was derived from the hoods, which were called capuchins (in Italian). The Italian coffee cappuccino was named after the shade of brown of their habit.

Nowadays the Order maintains 11 monasteries and 12 convents (of the Capuchin Order of Poor Clares) in Switzerland (of which three and one respectively along the Swiss Way of St. James).

**Dominican Order**

The Dominican Order, also called the Order of the Preachers, was established by the Spaniard St. Dominic of Guzman in 1216. He recruited priests, brothers, and nuns to preach the true teachings of Christianity. They were not bound by the usual monastic rules of being assigned to one location for life. With their apostolic missions they went out in the world, following the example of the Twelve Apostles. Their focus on preaching, studying, prayer, and meditation made them a leading force of theological intellect during the middle ages. As mendicant Order the Dominicans preached to the poor in a language they understood (instead of the difficult Latin or liturgical words).

Nowadays the Order maintains three monasteries and 11 convents in Switzerland (of which two convents along the Swiss Way of St. James).

**Knights of St. John Order**

The 'Order of Knights of the Hospital of Saint John of Jerusalem' is better known as the Maltese Order or the Hospitaller Order. The Order was established at the time of the Crusades in Jerusalem around 1048. Their task was to build a hospital to care for the ill and wounded pilgrims, and secure their safety at the times of military battles for the Holy Land. It was a military organization made up of Knights of noble background with Christian faith. After Islamic troops conquered Jerusalem, they relocated their base to Cyprus (1291), Rhodes (1310), and finally Malta (1530). This last location gave them their name under which they became more popularly known. The Order was seriously weakened by the Reformation that swept over Europe from the 1520s, and the conquests by Napoleon around 1798. They had to give up many of their commandries, and the Order was disrupted when Napoleon conquered the Island of Malta.

Between 1180 and 1456 the Order of the Knights of St. John maintained 20 commandries in Switzerland, which were situated at strategic locations enabling care for the ill and pilgrims. The Swiss Reformation had a devastating impact on the commandries, causing the closure of many of them between 1523 and 1536. The remaining commandries were closed or secularized from 1798, after Napoleon conquered Switzerland.

Nowadays the Order maintains one commandry in Switzerland (which is not along the Swiss Way of St. James).

# Appendix 4: List of Points of Interest

Appendix 4 lists all points of interest along the Way of St. James in North-East Switzerland, with references to the locations, stages, and page numbers.
The descriptions of their history and special features are included in the chapters of the respective hiking stages.

## *Points of Interest from Konstanz to Einsiedeln*

| Nr. | Name | Location | Stage | Page |
|---|---|---|---|---|
| DE | Schnetz Gate | Konstanz | K1 | 95 |
| K-1 | Ruins Castle of Schleifenrain | Kemmental | K1 | 100 |
| K-2 | Castle of Altenklingen | Märstetten | K1 | 102 |
| K-3 | Ruins Castle of Baliken | Wald | K3 | 143 |
| K-4 | Castle of Rapperswil | Rapperswil | K3 | 148 |
| K-5 | Einsiedeln House | Rapperswil | K3 | 150 |
| 6 | Site of Neolithic Pile Houses | Hurden | 4 | 158 |
| 7 | Wooden Footbridge | Hurden | 4 | 158 |
| 8 | Island of Ufenau | Lake Zurich | 4 | 161 |
| 9 | Castle of Pfäffikon | Pfäffikon | 4 | 165 |
| 10 | Devil Bridge | Egg | 4 | 170 |
| 11 | Site of former Gallows | Einsiedeln | 4 | 172 |
| 12 | Our Lady Fountain | Einsiedeln | 4 | 179 |
| 13 | Guided Monastery Tour | Einsiedeln | 4 | 180 |
| 14 | Diorama Bethlehem | Einsiedeln | 4 | 180 |
| 15 | Panorama Crucifixion | Einsiedeln | 4 | 180 |

## *Points of Interest from Rorschach to Jona and Etzel Pass*

| Nr. | Name | Location | Stage | Page |
|---|---|---|---|---|
| R-1 | St. James Fountain | Rorschach | R1a | 190 |
| R-2 | Castle of Sulzberg | Rorschach | R1a | 197 |
| R-3 | Ruins Castle of Rappenstein | Martinstobel | R1a | 199 |
| R-4 | Abbey Library | St. Gallen | R1a | 214 |
| R-5 | Historical Abbey and City Tour | St. Gallen | R1a | 215 |
| R-6 | Chateau of Waldegg | St. Gallen | R1b | 222 |
| R-7 | Ruins Castle of Iberg | Wattwil | R3 | 245 |
| S-1 | Castle of Grynau | Grynau | S1 | 279 |
| S-2 | Former Castle of old-Rapperswil | Altendorf | S2 | 296 |

# Bibliography and Copyrights

**Icons**

Hiking Icon, Church Icon, Castle Icon, Camera Icon, Underground Icon, Raincloud Icon, Moneybag with dollar symbol Icon, and Medicine Briefcase Icon, Angel Icon, Antique Building Icon, Skeleton Icon, Rubber Stamp Icon, Shell Icon, all made by Freepik from www.flaticon.com, 2019

Monastery Icon, Route Icon, and Pin Icon, Placeholder 2 Icon, all made by Smashicons from www.flaticon.com, 2019

Pray Icon made by FJStudio from www.flaticon.com

SwitzerlandMobility name and logo used with copyright approval from Stiftung SchweizMobil, 2019

Flags of Cantons from Swiss Cantonal Authorities, 2019

**Photos**

Cover and pages 71, 177: Kloster Einsiedeln. Bild vom Black Madonna, 2019

Page 25: Bild Beumer Hans. Copyright vom Pilgerpass bei Jakobsweg.ch

Page 110: Weber, Norbert. Fotograf vom Bild des äusseren und inneren der Kapelle in Affeltrangen, 2019

Page 139: Nuspliger, Susanne. Fotografin des innere der Mühlebach Kapelle, Fischenthal, 2018

Page 191: Jehle, Peter. Fotograf vom Bild des Katakomben Heilige Konstantius in der St. Kolumban Kirche in Rorschach, 2019

Page 220: Cerfada, Melina. Fotografin vom Bild des inneren der St. Leonhard Kirche in St. Gallen, 2019

Page 223: Wunderlin, Stephan. Fotograf vom Bild des äusseren und inneren der Maria Einsiedeln Kapelle in St. Gallen. Pfarramt St. Otmar, St. Gallen, 2019

Page 229: Oberholzer, Reto. Fotograf vom Bild des inneren der Unterkirche in Herisau. Pfarramt Katholische Kirche Herisau, 2019

Page 283: Trummer, Paul. Fotograf vom Bild des inneren der Loreto Kapelle, Tuggen, 2019

**Geographical Maps**

Page 28: Europäische Jakobswege, 2019, vom https://camino-europe.eu/en/eu/homepage-jakobswege/

Pages 55, 60, 77, 79, 89, 106, 132, 156, 187, 218, 234, 254, 272, 290 and cover: Geographical Maps from Swiss Federal Office of Topography, 2019

**Biographies of Saints**

Catholic Online, 2018, www.catholic.org

Commission on Tourism, Leisure and Pastoral Care for Pilgrims, 2018, www.chkath.ch

Schäfer, Joachim. Ökumenisches Heiligenlexikon, 2018, www.heiligenlexikon.de

**Historical Information (in geographical order of the chapters/stages)**

<u>Introduction</u>

Bischof, Franz Xaver. Jesuiten, in: Historisches Lexikon der Schweiz (HLS) 2011, URL: http://www.hls-dhs-dss.ch/textes/d/D11718.php

Ettlin, Leo. Benediktiner, in: Historisches Lexikon der Schweiz (HLS) 2008, URL: http://www.hls-dhs-dss.ch/textes/d/D11707.php

Morerod, Jean-Daniel. Cluniazenser, in: Historisches Lexikon der Schweiz (HLS) 2003, URL: http://www.hls-dhs-dss.ch/textes/d/D7153.php

Müller, Franz. Dominikaner, in: Historisches Lexikon der Schweiz (HLS) 2012, URL: http://www.hls-dhs-dss.ch/textes/d/D11714.php

Nuwer, Rachel. The Smithsonian Institute, 01.10.2013, https://www.smithsonianmag.com/history/meet-the-fantastically-bejeweled-skeletons-of-catholicisms-forgotten-martyrs-284882/

Schnyder, Caroline. Reformation, in: Historisches Lexikon der Schweiz (HLS) 2013, URL: http://www.hls-dhs-dss.ch/textes/d/D13328.php

Schweizer, Christian. Franziskusorden, in: Historisches Lexikon der Schweiz (HLS) 2014, URL: http://www.hls-dhs-dss.ch/textes/d/D11715.php

Schweizer, Christian. Kapuziner, in: Historisches Lexikon der Schweiz (HLS) 2009, URL: http://www.hls-dhs-dss.ch/textes/d/D11708.php

Siegwart, Josef. Augustiner Chorherren, in: Historisches Lexikon der Schweiz (HLS) 2001, URL: http://www.hls-dhs-dss.ch/textes/d/D11706.php

Ziegler, Peter. Johanniter, in: Historisches Lexikon der Schweiz (HLS) 2008, URL: http://www.hls-dhs-dss.ch/textes/d/D11721.php

Stage K1: Konstanz to Märstetten

Marketing und Tourismus Konstanz GmbH, 2019, https://www.constance-lake-constance.com/experience-explore/attractions/cathedral/

Konzilstadt Konstanz, 2018, https://www.konstanzer-konzil.de/de/

Seelsorgeeinheit Konstanz-Altstadt, 2019, https://www.konstanz-kirche.de/html/st_stefan350.html

Marketing und Tourismus Konstanz GmbH, 2019, https://www.konstanz-tourismus.de/erleben-entdecken/sehenswertes/schnetztor.html

Katholisches Pfarramt St. Stefan Kreuzlingen, 2019, http://www.kath-kreuzlingen.ch/documents/Stefanskirche.pdf

Katholisches Pfarramt St. Stefan Kreuzlingen, 2019, http://www.kath-kreuzlingen.ch/xml_1/internet/de/application/d2/d69/f70.cfm

Spuhler, Gregor. Bernrain, in: Historisches Lexikon der Schweiz (HLS) 2002, URL: http://www.hls-dhs-dss.ch/textes/d/D8163.php

Katholisches Pfarramt St. Stefan Kreuzlingen, 2019, http://www.kath-kreuzlingen.ch/xml_1/internet/de/application/d2/d69/f73.cfm

Burgenwelt.org, 2019, http://www.burgenwelt.org/schweiz/schleifenrain/object.php

Amt für Archäologie Thurgau, 2019, https://archaeologie.tg.ch/fundstellen/fundstellen-mit-tafeln-im-gelaende/kemmental-ruine-schleifenrain.html/5921

Amt für Archäologie Thurgau, 2019, Information table at the Schleifenrain Castle ruins

Trösch, Erich. Märstetten, in: Historisches Lexikon der Schweiz (HLS) 2009, URL: http://www.hls-dhs-dss.ch/textes/d/D2024.php

Evangelische Kirchgemeinde Märstetten, 2019, https://www.evang-maerstetten.ch/

Gesellschaft für Schweizerische Kunstgeschichte GSK, 2005, Reformierte Kirche St. Jakob, https://data.geo.admin.ch/ch.babs.kulturgueter/PDF/kgs_05104_gsk-d.pdf

Burgenwelt.org, 2019, http://burgenwelt.org/schweiz/altenburg_tg/object.php

Stage K2: Märstetten to Fischingen

Salathé, André. Zezikon, in: Historisches Lexikon der Schweiz (HLS) 2014, URL: http://www.hls-dhs-dss.ch/textes/d/D1948.php

Informationsblatt in der St. Jakobskapelle Kaltenbrunnen, 2018

Evangelische Kirchgemeinde Affeltrangen, 2019, https://www.evang-affeltrangen.ch/kirche-affeltrangen

Salathé, André. Affeltrangen, in: Historisches Lexikon der Schweiz (HLS) 2001, URL: http://www.hls-dhs-dss.ch/textes/d/D1945.php

Stiftung Komturei Tobel, 2012, http://www.komturei.ch/fileadmin/customer/assets/grp/Bilder/Archiv/DOWNLOAD/Geschichte_Komturei_01072012.pdf

Sovereign Military Hospitaller Order of St John of Jerusalem of Rhodes and of Malta, 2019, https://www.orderofmalta.int/history/

Sovereign Order of Malta Switzerland, 2019, https://ordredemaltesuisse.org/en/swiss-association/history/

Rothenbühler, Verena. Tobel, in: Historisches Lexikon der Schweiz (HLS) 2012, URL: http://www.hls-dhs-dss.ch/textes/d/D1969.php

Wiesli, Josef, und Robert Borer. 300 Jahre Pfarrkirche Sankt Johannes Tobel 1707-2007. Tobel: Katholische Kirchgemeinde Tobel, 2008

Spuhler, Gregor. Sankt Margarethen, in: Historisches Lexikon der Schweiz (HLS) 2012, URL: http://www.hls-dhs-dss.ch/textes/d/D3192.php

Pastoralraum Hinterthurgau, 2019, https://www.pastoralraum-hinterthurgau.ch/de/kapellen/kapelle-st-margarethen

Pastoralraum Hinterthurgau, 2019, https://www.pastoralraum-hinterthurgau.ch/de/portraet-10/unsere-kirchen/st-antonius-kirche-muenchwilen

Spuhler, Gregor. Münchwilen, in: Historisches Lexikon der Schweiz (HLS) 2009, URL: http://www.hls-dhs-dss.ch/textes/d/D1957.php

Evangelische Kirchgemeinde Münchwilen-Eschlikon, 2019, https://www.evang-muenchwilen-eschlikon.ch/geschichte

Trösch, Erich. Sirnach, in: Historisches Lexikon der Schweiz (HLS) 2012, URL: http://www.hls-dhs-dss.ch/textes/d/D1964.php

Pastoralraum Hinterthurgau, 2019,https://www.pastoralraum-hinterthurgau.ch/de/portraet-10/unsere-kirchen/st-remigius-kirche-sirnach

Evangelisch-reformierte Kirchgemeinde Sirnach, 2019, http://www.evang-ref-sirnach.ch/index.php?id=60

Trösch, Erich. Oberwangen, in: Historisches Lexikon der Schweiz (HLS) 2009, URL: http://www.hls-dhs-dss.ch/textes/d/D3189.php

Gemeinde Fischingen, 2019, https://www.fischingen.ch/leben/kirchen/martinskapelle-oberwangen.html/276

Meile, Felicitas. Pastoralraum Tannzapfenland, 2019, https://www.pastoralraum-tannzapfenland.ch/de/unsere-kirchen-4/st-martin-kapelle-oberwangen
Gemeinde Fischingen, 2019, https://www.fischingen.ch/leben/kirchen/evangelische-kirchgemeinde-dussnang.html/186
Meile, Felicitas. Pastoralraum Tannzapfenland, 2019, https://www.pastoralraum-tannzapfenland.ch/de/unsere-kirchen-4/maria-lourdes-dussnang
Schildknecht, Benno. Fischingen (Kloster), in: Historisches Lexikon der Schweiz (HLS) 2005, URL: http://www.hls-dhs-dss.ch/textes/d/D301.php
Gemeinde Fischingen, 2019, https://www.fischingen.ch/leben/kirchen/benediktinerkloster-fischingen.html/187
Verein Kloster Fischingen, 2015, https://www.benediktiner-fischingen.ch/unsere-geschichte/
Meile, Felicitas. Pastoralraum Tannzapfenland, 2019, https://www.pastoralraum-tannzapfenland.ch/de/unsere-kirchen-4/st-johannes-der-taeufer-st-johannes-der-evangelist

Stage K3: Fischingen to Rapperswil

Meile, Felicitas. Pastoralraum Tannzapfenland, 2019, https://www.pastoralraum-tannzapfenland.ch/de/unsere-kirchen-4/st-anna-au
Spuhler, Gregor. Au, in: Historisches Lexikon der Schweiz (HLS) 2001, URL: http://www.hls-dhs-dss.ch/textes/d/D3163.php
Müller, Ueli. Fischenthal, in: Historisches Lexikon der Schweiz (HLS) 2012, URL: http://www.hls-dhs-dss.ch/textes/d/D86.php
Katholische Kirchgemeinde Bauma, 2019, http://www.kath-bauma.ch/fischenthal/geschichte/
Information sign at the Mühlebach Chapel, 2018
Reformierte Kirche Fischenthal, 2019, https://www.refkirchefischenthal.ch/1_Geschichte.php?navi=04.1
Stadler, Alois. Rapperswil (SG), in: Historisches Lexikon der Schweiz (HLS) 2017, URL: http://www.hls-dhs-dss.ch/textes/d/D1371.php
Katholische Kirche Rapperswil-Jona, 2019, https://krj.ch/rapperswil/
Stadt Rapperswil-Jona, 2019, http://www.rapperswil-jona.ch/de/tourismus/sehenswuerdigkeiten/welcome.php?action=showobject&object_id=6512
Gemeinde Rapperswil-Jona, Kulturbaukasten nr. 6: Stadtpfarrkirche St. Johann, Information table at the church, 2018
Kapuzinerkloster Rapperswil, 2019, https://www.klosterrapperswil.ch/leitbild-der-schweizer-kapuziner/
Burgenwelt.org, 2019, http://www.burgenwelt.org/schweiz/oberes_baliken/object.php
Stadt Rapperswil-Jona, 2019, http://www.rapperswil-jona.ch/de/tourismus/sehenswuerdigkeiten/welcome.php?action=showobject&object_id=6509
Burgenwelt.org, 2019, http://www.burgenwelt.org/schweiz/neu_rapperswil/object.php
Gemeinde Rapperswil-Jona, Kulturbaukasten nr. 5: Schloss Rapperswil, Information table at the castle, 2018
Niederhäuser, Peter und Basil Vollenweider. Schloss Rapperswil: Eckpunkte einer Geschichte ergänzt, March 2016, https://ogrj.ch/images/Kultur-Freizeit/Kultur/Schlossgeschichte.pdf

Stage 4: Rapperswil to Einsiedeln

Swiss Coordination Group UNESCO Palafittes, 2019, https://palafittes.org/, CH-SG-01, Rapperswil-Jona/Hombrechtikon–Feldbach
NZZ, 20.01.2001, Die Brücke auf dem Grund des Zürichsees
Zurich Tourism, 2018, https://www.rapperswil-zuerichsee.ch/de/besuchen/sehenswuerdigkeiten/bruecke-rapperswil-hurden
Stadt Rapperswil-Jona, 2019, http://www.rapperswil-jona.ch/de/vereine/naherholungimfreien/?action=showobject&object_id=6552
Stadt Rapperswil-Jona, 2019, http://www.rapperswil-jona.ch/de/tourismus/sehenswuerdigkeiten/welcome.php?action=showobject&object_id=6514
Ortsgemeinde Rapperswil-Jona, 2019, https://ogrj.ch/kultur-freizeit/kultur
NZZ, 20.04.2011, Madonna und Pilger für Heilig Hüsli
Information table at the Heilig Hüsli, 2018
Information table at the Our Lady Chapel, Hurden, 2018
Kirchgemeinde Freienbach, 2019, https://www.kirchgemeindefreienbach.ch/pfarrei-pfaeffikon/kirchen-kapellen/
Wyrsch, Paul. Hurden, in: Historisches Lexikon der Schweiz (HLS) 2008, URL: http://www.hls-dhs-dss.ch/textes/d/D7441.php
Ziegler, Peter. 2019, http://www.ufnau.ch/insel_geschichte.html
Zeitschrift Mitteilungen des historisches Vereins des Kantons Schwyz, 1933, https://www.e-periodica.ch/cntmng?var=true&pid=mhv-001:1933:39::33

Gemeinde Freienbach, 2019, https://www.freienbach.ch/freienbach/lebenarbeiten/leben/religion
Wyrsch-Ineichen, Paul. Ufenau, in: Historisches Lexikon der Schweiz (HLS) 2013, URL: http://www.hls-dhs-dss.ch/textes/d/D7423.php
Arnet, Helene. Tagesanzeiger 16.07.2015, Artikel: Wallfahrer und Wunderheiler
Arnet, Helene. Tagesanzeiger 20.04.2016, Artikel: Himmelreich und Höllenschlund
Wyrsch, Paul. Pfäffikon (SZ), in: Historisches Lexikon der Schweiz (HLS) 2010, URL: http://www.hls-dhs-dss.ch/textes/d/D7437.php
Burgenwelt.org, 2019, http://www.burgenwelt.org/schweiz/pfaeffikon/object.php
Gemeinde Freienbach, Information table at the Pfäffikon Castle Chapel, 2018
Schlossturm Pfäffikon SZ, 2019, http://www.schlossturm.ch/geschichte.html
Die Schweizer Schlösser, 2019, http://www.swisscastles.ch/Schwytz/pfaffikon_d.html
Klosterarchiv Einsiedeln, 2019, Statthalterei Pfäffikonhttp://www.klosterarchiv.ch/earchiv_detail.php?parent=19&start=0
Orgelmusikpfaeffikon.org, 2019, https://www.orgelmusikpfaeffikon.org/st-meinradskirche-pfäffikon/50-jahre-pfarrei-pfäffikon-1965-2015/st-anna-kapelle/
Jäggi, Gregor. Meinrad, in: Historisches Lexikon der Schweiz (HLS) 2008, URL: http://www.hls-dhs-dss.ch/textes/d/D10195.php
Kloster Einsiedeln, 2019, https://www.kloster-einsiedeln.ch/?id=48
Kloster Einsiedeln Wallfahrt, 2019, https://www.wallfahrt-einsiedeln.ch/?id=19
Information table at the Tüfelsbrugg am Etzel, 2018
Schönbächler, Patrick. Das Galgenchappeli in Einsiedeln, 2015/17
Information table at the Galgenchappeli in Einsiedeln, 2018
Bezirk Einsiedeln, 2019, http://www.einsiedeln.ch/bezirk/wo-ist-was/kirchen-kapellen-und-friedhoefe
Hug, Albert. Einsiedeln (Benediktinerabtei), in: Historisches Lexikon der Schweiz (HLS) 2008, URL: http://www.hls-dhs-dss.ch/textes/d/D11491.php
Einsiedeln Tourismus. info guide Einsiedeln, Februar 2018. https://www.eyz.swiss/fileadmin/user_upload/Einsiedeln-Ybrig-Zuerichsee/Bilder/Footer/Infoguide_Einsieden_de_en.pdf
Kloster Einsiedeln, 2019, https://www.wallfahrt-einsiedeln.ch
Kloster Einsiedeln, 2019, https://www.kloster-einsiedeln.ch
Museum Diorama Bethlehem Einsiedeln, 2019, https://www.diorama.ch/pages/de/museum.php
Panorama Gesellschaft Einsiedeln, 2019, http://www.panorama-einsiedeln.ch

Stage R1a: Rorschach to St. Gallen
Baumann, Max. Sankt Gallen (Kanton), in: Historisches Lexikon der Schweiz (HLS), 2017, URL: http://www.hls-dhs-dss.ch/textes/d/D7390.php
Katholische Kirche Region Rorschach, 2019, https://www.kkrr.ch/jakobsbrunnen.html
Huber, Johannes. Schweizerische Kunstführer GSK, Pfarrkirche St. Kolumban und Konstantius in Rorschach, 1995, text auf Katholische Kirche Region Rorschach, 2019, https://www.kkrr.ch/kolumbanskirche-geschichte.html
Katholische Kirche Region Rorschach, 2019, https://www.kkrr.ch/seelenkapelle.html
Evangelisch-reformierte Kirchgemeinde Rorschach, 2019, https://www.ref-rorschach.ch/geschichte
Meier, Stefan. Katholische Kirche Region Rorschach, 2019, https://www.kkrr.ch/herz-jesu-kirche.html
Anderes, Bernard. Rorschach, Ehemaliges Kloster Mariaberg, 1982, http://www.mariaberg.ch/Bau/Bau.htm
The Swiss Castles, 2019, http://www.swisscastles.ch/StGallen/sulzberg_d.html
Reck, Josef, and Wieland Frei. Katholische Kirche Region Rorschach, 2019, https://www.kkrr.ch/magdalena-geschichte.html
Bäschlin, Franz. Eine Wanderung über den Rorschachger Berg, im Monatszeitschrift Am häuslichen Herd, Band 54 (1950-51), Heft 21, S. 409-410, https://www.e-periodica.ch/cntmng?pid=ahh-001:1950:54::1254
20 Minuten, 12. März 2007, Stadt saniert Ruine Rappenstein, https://www.20min.ch/schweiz/ostschweiz/story/Stadt-saniert-Ruine-Rappenstein-13854158
Oekomenische Gemeinde Halden, 2019, https://www.haldenstgallen.ch/DE/71/Gemeindeportrait.htm
Hufenus, Maria. Daten zur Baugeschichte der Stadt St. Gallen von den Anfängen bis 2000, Stadtarchiv St. Gallen, 2004, https://stadtarchiv.ch/inhalt/Hufenus_Daten_zur_Baugeschichte.pdf
Evangelisch-reformierte Kirchgemeinde St. Gallen C, 2019, https://www.ref-sgc.ch/laurenzen-kirche-history
Vogler, Katharina. Das Dominikanerinnen-Kloster St. Katharina in St. Gallen zur Zeit der Reformation, Artikel in Zeitschrift für schweizerische Kirchengeschichte, 1934, https://www.e-periodica.ch/cntmng?pid=zfk-001:1934:28::332
Beck, Ulrich. Gelungene Symbiose von Denkmalpflege und Ökonomie – das Katharinen-Kloster in St. Gallen, 05.12.2013, in Denkmalpflege-Schweiz.ch, https://denkmalpflege-

schweiz.ch/2013/12/05/gelungene-symbiose-von-denkmalpflege-und-oekonomie-das-katharinen-kloster-in-st-gallen/

Evangelisch-reformierte Kirchgemeinde St. Gallen C, 2019, https://www.ref-sgc.ch/stmangen-kirche-history

Tremp, Ernst und Lorenz Hollenstein. Sankt Gallen (Fürstabtei), in: Historisches Lexikon der Schweiz (HLS), 2017, URL: http://www.hls-dhs-dss.ch/textes/d/D8394.php

Weltkulturerbe Stiftsbezirk St. Gallen, 2019, https://www.stiftsbezirk.ch/en/container/cathedral/cathedral-information/

Stiftsbibliothek St. Gallen, 2019, https://www.stiftsbezirk.ch/de/stiftsbibliothek/

Schweiz Tourismus, 2018, https://www.myswitzerland.com/en-ch/textile-crafts.html

Ortsbürgergemeinde St. Gallen, 2016, https://www.ortsbuerger.ch/files/content/Dokumente/OBG_Praesentation_EN_2016.pdf

Stage R1b: St. Gallen to Herisau

Weishaupt, Achilles. Appenzell (Kanton), in: Historisches Lexikon der Schweiz (HLS), 2011, URL: http://www.hls-dhs-dss.ch/textes/d/D7389.php

Weder, Christina. Tagblatt, 21.09.2017, 'Umnutzungen: St. Leonhardskirche ist ein unrühmliches Beispiel', https://www.tagblatt.ch/ostschweiz/stgallen-gossau-rorschach/umnutzungen-stleonhardskirche-ist-ein-unruehmliches-beispiel-ld.1014079

Grögli, Beat. Katholische Kirchgemeinde St. Gallen, Pfarrei St. Otmar, Die Kirche St. Otmar in St. Gallen, Kirchenführer für Erwachsene, 2003, https://www.stotmar.kathsg.ch/pdf/1462867785_kirchenfuehrer-fuer-erwachsene.pdf

The Swiss Castles, 2019, http://www.swisscastles.ch/StGallen/waldegg.html

Pilgern.ch, 2019, https://www.pilgern.ch/wp-content/uploads/2015/09/kapelle_maria_einsiedeln.pdf

Evangelisch-reformierte Kirchgemeinde Straubenzell St. Gallen West, 2019, https://straubenzell.ch/kirche-bruggen/

Katholische Kirchgemeinde St. Gallen, 2019, https://www.bruggen.kathsg.ch/DE/71/Pfarreiportrait.htm

Information Blatt bei der Vitrine von St. Fidelis in der St. Martin Kirche, Bruggen, 2019

Huber. Johannes. Kunst- und Kulturführer Kirche St. Martin Bruggen, Beschreibung der Engelbilder und Rosette, 1998

Kaiser, Markus. Sitter, in: Historisches Lexikon der Schweiz (HLS), 2011, URL: http://www.hls-dhs-dss.ch/textes/d/D8777.php

Evang.-ref. Kirchgemeinde Herisau, 2019, https://www.ref-herisau.ch/de/ueber-uns/portraet/unsere-kirche.html

Evang.-ref. Kirchgemeinde Herisau, Broschüre 'Die Reformierte Kirche in Herisau – Ein Kulturdenkmal', 06/2015

Katholische Pfarrei Herisau, 2019, http://www.kath-herisau.ch/geschichte.html

Fuchs, Thomas. Herisau, in: Historisches Lexikon der Schweiz (HLS), 2008, URL: http://www.hls-dhs-dss.ch/textes/d/D1293.php

Stage R2: Herisau to Wattwil

Evangelisch-reformierte Kirchgemeinde Oberer Necker, 2019, https://www.ref-oberernecker.ch/on-portraet

Neckertal Tourismus, Information Schild Evangelische Kirche bei der Kirche, 2018

Katholische Pfarrei Neutoggenburg, 2019, https://neutoggenburg.ch/peterzell/

Verein Ereignisse Propstei St. Peterzell, 2019, http://ereignisse-propstei.ch/propstei.php

Büchler, Hans. Sankt Peterzell, in: Historisches Lexikon der Schweiz (HLS), 2011, URL: http://www.hls-dhs-dss.ch/textes/d/D1386.php

Steigmeier, Andreas. Falck, in: Historisches Lexikon der Schweiz (HLS), 2003, URL: http://www.hls-dhs-dss.ch/textes/d/D20440.php

Büchler, Hans. Wattwil, in: Historisches Lexikon der Schweiz (HLS), 2016, URL: http://www.hls-dhs-dss.ch/textes/d/D1387.php

Evangelisch-reformierte Kirchgemeinde Mittleres Toggenburg, Im Wandel der Zeit, Kirchgemeinde Wattwil 1848-1998, 2019, https://www.ref-mtg.ch/wp-content/uploads/sites/2/2018/01/GeschichteWattwil.pdf

Katholische Pfarrei Neutoggenburg, 2019, https://neutoggenburg.ch/wattwil/

Fazenda da Esperanca, 2019, http://www.fazenda.ch/geschichte/

Gemeinde Wattwil, 2019, http://www.wattwil.ch/de/wirtschaftfreizeit/sehenswuerdigkeiten/welcome.php?action=showobject&object_id=9279

Gemeinde Wattwil, 2019, http://www.wattwil.ch/de/wirtschaftfreizeit/sehenswuerdigkeiten/welcome.php?action=showobject&object_id=8822

Steinhauser-Zimmermann, Regula Anna. Iberg (SG), in: Historisches Lexikon der Schweiz (HLS), 2008, URL: http://www.hls-dhs-dss.ch/textes/d/D10955.php

Burgenwelt.org, 2019, http://www.burgenwelt.org/schweiz/iberg_ch/object.php
Wiprächtiger, Hanspeter. https://www.kloster-wattwil.ch/geschichte, 2018
Schweizer, Christian. Pfanneregg, in: Historisches Lexikon der Schweiz (HLS), 2009, URL: http://www.hls-dhs-dss.ch/textes/d/D11996.php

Stage R3: Wattwil to Jona
Seelesorgeeinheit Eschenbach, Pfarrei Walde, 2019, https://se-eschenbach.ch/pfarrei-walde/gebaeude/kirchen-kapellen
Gähwiler, Ital, John Martin, Gottfried Kuster, Werner Kuster. Pfarrkirche, Kapellen und weitere Zeugen barocker Frömmigkeit. Eschenbacher Neujahrsblatt. Eschenbach: Gemeinde Eschenbach Kulturkommission, 2019
Seelesorgeeinheit Eschenbach, Pfarrei St. Gallenkappel, 2019, https://se-eschenbach.ch/pfarrei-st-gallenkappel/gebaeude/kirchen-kapellen
Stadler, Alois. Sankt Gallenkappel, in: Historisches Lexikon der Schweiz (HLS), 2017, URL: http://www.hls-dhs-dss.ch/textes/d/D1372.php
Schubiger, Benno. Schweizerische Kunstführer: St. Gallenkappel SG – Pfarrkirche St. Laurentius und St. Gallus, Basel: Gesellschaft für Schweizerische Kunstgeschichte, 1980. S. 14
Seelesorgeeinheit Eschenbach, Pfarrei St. Eschenbach, 2019, https://se-eschenbach.ch/pfarrei-eschenbach/gebaeude-m/kirchen-kapellen
Stadler, Alois. Eschenbach, in: Historisches Lexikon der Schweiz (HLS), 2017, URL: http://www.hls-dhs-dss.ch/textes/d/D1367.php
Katholische Kirchengemeinde Rapperswil-Jona, 2011, Broschüre Pfarrkirche und Pfarrei Maria Himmelfahrt Jona, https://krj.ch/wp-content/uploads/maria-himmelfahrt-jona.pdf

Stage S1: Neuhaus to Siebnen
Meyer, Helmut. Kappelerkriege, in: Historisches Lexikon der Schweiz (HLS), 2009, URL: http://www.hls-dhs-dss.ch/textes/d/D8903.php
Seelsorgeeinheit Obersee, Pfarrei St. Jodokus, 2019, http://www.seelsorgeeinheit-obersee.ch/index.php/historisches/pfarrkirche-damals
Kilger, Laurenz. Geschichte des Dorfes Schmerikon, Verkehrsverein Schmerikon, 1953, S. 159-160
Michel, Kaspar. Grinau, in: Historisches Lexikon der Schweiz (HLS), 2013, URL: http://www.hls-dhs-dss.ch/textes/d/D7417.php
Burgenwelt.org, 2019, http://www.burgenwelt.org/schweiz/grynau/object.php
Röm.-katholische Kirchgemeinde Tuggen, 2019, http://www.pfarrei-tuggen.ch/index.php/kirchen-und-kapellen-tuggen
Jacober, Ralf. Tuggen, in: Historisches Lexikon der Schweiz (HLS), 2014, URL: http://www.hls-dhs-dss.ch/textes/d/D722.php
PfA Altendorf Urk. Nr. 11 und Stückelberger E. A.: Geschichte der Reliquien in der Schweiz in: Schriften der Schweiz. Zürich: Gesellschaft für Volkskunde, 1902. p. 76
Röm.-kath. Pfarramt Siebnen, 2019, http://pfarrei-siebnen.ch/pfarrkirche/
Jacober, Ralf. Siebnen, in: Historisches Lexikon der Schweiz (HLS), 2011, URL: http://www.hls-dhs-dss.ch/textes/d/D7439.php
Genossame Siebnen, 2019, http://www.genossame-siebnen.ch/de/st-nikolaus-kapelle.html
Evangelisch-reformierte Kirchgemeinde der March, 2019, http://www.ref-kirche-march.ch/de/portrait/geschichtefs/

Stage S2: Siebnen to Etzel Pass
Meyerhans, Andreas. Galgenen, in: Historisches Lexikon der Schweiz (HLS), 2005, URL: http://www.hls-dhs-dss.ch/textes/d/D717.php
Pfarrei Galgenen, 2019, https://kg-galgenen.ch/de/Ueber-uns/Kapelle-St-Jost
Mächler, Josef. Altendorf, in: Historisches Lexikon der Schweiz (HLS), 2009, URL: http://www.hls-dhs-dss.ch/textes/d/D716.php
Katholische Pfarrei St. Michael Altendorf, https://pfarrei-altendorf.ch/index.php/kappelle_st._johann.html
Jörger, Albert. Schweizerische Kunstführer Altendorf SZ, Pfarrkirche und Kapellen, Bern: Gesellschaft für Schweizerische Kunstgeschichte, 1983. P. 14-21
Burgenwelt.org, 2019, http://www.burgenwelt.org/schweiz/alt_rapperswil/object.php

www.ingramcontent.com/pod-product-compliance
Lightning Source LLC
LaVergne TN
LVHW091019080826
845145LV00002B/299

* 9 7 8 3 9 0 6 8 6 1 3 2 6 *